Autonomy and the Challenges to Liberalism
New Essays

In recent years, the concepts of individual autonomy and political liberalism have been the subject of intense debate, but these discussions have occurred largely within separate academic disciplines. *Autonomy and the Challenges to Liberalism* contains for the first time new essays devoted to foundational questions concerning both the notion of the autonomous self and the nature and justification of liberalism.

Written by leading figures in moral, legal, and political theory, this volume covers, among other things, the following topics: the nature of the self and its relation to autonomy, the social dimensions of autonomy and the political dynamics of respect and recognition, and the concept of autonomy underlying the principles of liberalism.

John Christman is Associate Professor of Philosophy and Political Science at Pennsylvania State University.

Joel Anderson is Research Lecturer in the Department of Philosophy at the University of Utrecht, The Netherlands.

Autonomy and the Challenges to Liberalism

New Essays

Edited by

JOHN CHRISTMAN
Pennsylvania State University

JOEL ANDERSON
University of Utrecht

CAMBRIDGE UNIVERSITY PRESS

CAMBRIDGE UNIVERSITY PRESS
Cambridge, New York, Melbourne, Madrid, Cape Town, Singapore, São Paulo, Delhi

Cambridge University Press
The Edinburgh Building, Cambridge CB2 8RU, UK

Published in the United States of America by Cambridge University Press, New York

www.cambridge.org
Information on this title: www.cambridge.org/9780521120319

© John Christman and Joel Anderson 2005

This publication is in copyright. Subject to statutory exception
and to the provisions of relevant collective licensing agreements,
no reproduction of any part may take place without the written
permission of Cambridge University Press.

First published 2005
This digitally printed version 2009

A catalogue record for this publication is available from the British Library

Library of Congress Cataloguing in Publication data
Christman, John Philip.
Autonomy and the challenges to liberalism : new essays / edited by John Christman,
Joel Anderson.
p. cm.
Includes bibliographical references and index.
ISBN 0-521-83951-3
1. Liberalism. 2. Autonomy (Philosophy) I. Christman, John Philip.
II. Anderson, Joel, 1965– III. Title.
JC574.C487   2005
128–dc22   2004050307

ISBN 978-0-521-83951-8 hardback
ISBN 978-0-521-12031-9 paperback

Contents

Contributors		*page* vii
Preface		xi
1	Introduction *John Christman and Joel Anderson*	1

PART I THE SELF: CONCEPTIONS OF THE AUTONOMOUS SELF

2	Decentralizing Autonomy: Five Faces of Selfhood *Diana Tietjens Meyers*	27
3	The Self as Narrator *J. David Velleman*	56
4	Autonomy and Self-Identity *Marina A. L. Oshana*	77

PART II THE INTERPERSONAL: PERSONAL AUTHORITY AND INTERPERSONAL RECOGNITION

5	Taking Ownership: Authority and Voice in Autonomous Agency *Paul Benson*	101
6	Autonomy, Vulnerability, Recognition, and Justice *Joel Anderson and Axel Honneth*	127
7	Autonomy and Male Dominance *Marilyn Friedman*	150

PART III THE SOCIAL: PUBLIC POLICY AND LIBERAL
PRINCIPLES

8 Autonomy, Domination, and the Republican Challenge to
Liberalism 177
Richard Dagger

9 Liberal Autonomy and Consumer Sovereignty 204
Joseph Heath

10 Political Liberty: Integrating Five Conceptions of
Autonomy 226
Rainer Forst

PART IV THE POLITICAL: LIBERALISM, LEGITIMACY,
AND PUBLIC REASON

11 Liberalism without Agreement: Political Autonomy and
Agonistic Citizenship 245
Bert van den Brink

12 The Place of Autonomy within Liberalism 272
Gerald F. Gaus

13 Moral Autonomy and Personal Autonomy 307
Jeremy Waldron

14 Autonomy, Self-Knowledge, and Liberal Legitimacy 330
John Christman

Bibliography 359
Index 377

Contributors

Joel Anderson is Research Lecturer in Philosophy at Utrecht University (The Netherlands). He works on issues of personal autonomy, practical reasoning, neuro-ethics, mutual recognition, and moral psychology. He has published articles in various journals, including *Philosophical Explorations, Constellations, Deutsche Zeitschrift für Philosophie*, and *Philosophy, Psychiatry, and Psychology*.

Paul Benson is Professor and Chair of the Philosophy Department at the University of Dayton. He works in the areas of ethics, action theory, and social philosophy. He has published articles on autonomy, oppressive socialization, and self-worth. He is completing a book tentatively entitled *The Place of Self-Worth in Free Agency*.

Bert van den Brink is Research Lecturer in Philosophy at Utrecht University (The Netherlands), specializing in contemporary social and political philosophy. He is the author of *The Tragedy of Liberalism: An Alternative Defense of a Political Tradition* (SUNY Press, 2000) and co-editor, with Maureen Sie and Marc Slors, of *Reasons of One's Own* (Ashgate, 2004).

John Christman is Associate Professor of Philosophy at Pennsylvania State University. He has written on property rights, individual autonomy, and liberal political philosophy. He is the author of *The Myth of Property: Toward an Egalitarian Theory of Ownership* (Oxford University Press, 1994) and *Social and Political Philosophy: A Contemporary Introduction* (Routledge, 2002) and is the editor of *The Inner Citadel: Essays on Individual Autonomy* (Oxford University Press, 1989).

Richard Dagger is Professor of Political Science and Philosophy at Arizona State University, where he directs the Philosophy, Politics, and Law Program for Barrett Honors College. He works in the areas of rights, political obligation, punishment, and other topics in political and legal philosophy. His books include *Civic Virtues: Rights, Citizenship, and Republican Liberalism* (Oxford University Press, 1997) and, with Terence Ball, *Political Ideologies and the Democratic Ideal* (Longmans, 2004).

Rainer Forst is Professor of Political Theory in the Departments of Social Sciences and of Philosophy, J. W. Goethe University (Frankfurt, Germany). His areas of specialization are political philosophy and ethical theory. He is the author of *Contexts of Justice: Political Philosophy Beyond Liberalism and Communitarianism* (University of California Press, 2002) and *Toleranz im Konflikt: Geschichte, Gehalt und Gegenwart eines umstrittenen Begriffs* (Suhrkamp, 2003).

Marilyn Friedman is Professor of Philosophy at Washington University in St. Louis and works in the areas of ethics, feminist theory, and political philosophy. Her books include *Autonomy, Gender, Politics* (Oxford University Press, 2002) and *What Are Friends For?: Feminist Perspectives on Personal Relationships and Moral Theory* (Cornell University Press, 1993).

Gerald F. Gaus is Professor of Philosophy at Tulane University, New Orleans. He is a faculty member of the Murphy Institute of Political Economy. His research interests are in political philosophy, social philosophy, and ethics. His books include *Justificatory Liberalism* (Oxford University Press, 1996), *Value and Justification: The Foundations of Liberal Theory* (Cambridge University Press, 1990), and *Contemporary Theories of Liberalism: Public Reason as a Post-Enlightenment Project* (Sage, 2003). He is a founding co-editor of the journal *Politics, Philosophy, and Economics*.

Joseph Heath is Associate Professor of Philosophy at the University of Toronto. He writes on political theory, moral philosophy, and rational choice theory. He is the author of *Communicative Action and Rational Choice* (MIT Press, 2001), *The Efficient Society* (Penguin, 2001), and, with Andrew Potter, *The Rebel Sell* (Harper Collins, 2004).

Axel Honneth is Professor of Social Philosophy at J. W. Goethe University in Frankfurt, Germany, and Director of the Institute for Social Research there. He has published on issues of political philosophy, ethics, moral psychology, and social theory. His books in English include *Critique of Power* (MIT Press, 1991), *The Struggle for Recognition: The Moral Grammar* *of Social Conflicts* (Polity Press, 1995), *The Fragmented-World of the Social* (SUNY Press, 1995), *The Morality of Recognition* (Polity Press, 2004), and, with Nancy Fraser, *Recognition or Redistribution?: A Political-Philosophical Exchange* (Verso, 2003).

Diana Tietjens Meyers is Professor of Philosophy at the University of Connecticut, Storrs. In the spring of 2003, she was awarded the Blanche, Edith, and Irving Laurie New Jersey Chair in the Women's and Gender Studies Department at Rutgers University. Her most recent monographs are *Subjection and Subjectivity: Psychoanalytic Feminism and Moral Philosophy* (1994) and *Gender in the Mirror: Cultural Imagery and Women's Agency* (2002). A collection of her (mostly) previously published articles, *Being Yourself: Essays on Identity, Action, and Social Life*, appeared in 2004. She is the editor of *Feminists Rethink the Self* and *Feminist Social Thought: A Reader*. She is the author of the forthcoming *Encyclopedia Britannica* article on philosophical feminism.

Marina A. L. Oshana is Associate Professor of Philosophy at the University of Florida. Her research focuses on issues in normative ethics and moral psychology. She has published articles in the area of autonomy and responsibility and is completing a book tentatively entitled *Personal Autonomy: Its Breadth and Limits*.

J. David Velleman is G. E. M. Anscombe Collegiate Professor of Philosophy at the University of Michigan, specializing in philosophy of action, ethics, and philosophy of mind. He is the author of *Practical Reflection* (Princeton University Press, 1989), *The Possibility of Practical Reason* (Oxford University Press, 2000), and *Self to Self* (Cambridge University Press, forthcoming). He is a founding co-editor of the journal *Philosophers' Imprint*.

Jeremy Waldron is the Maurice and Hilda Friedman Professor of Law at Columbia University, where he also is Director of the Center for Law and Philosophy. He has published widely in legal and political theory. He is the author of *God, Locke and Equality* (Cambridge University Press, 2002); *The Dignity of Legislation* (Cambridge University Press, 1999); *Law and Disagreement* (Oxford University Press, 1999); and *Liberal Rights* (Cambridge University Press, 1993).

Preface

The initial idea for this volume was to prepare an update of *The Inner Citadel*, the collection of essays on the concept of autonomy that John Christman had put together in 1989. Given the spate of terrific work since then, a new anthology seemed in order. But we also saw that discussions of the concept of autonomy needed to engage more fully with the growing body of literature on political liberalism, where there were strikingly similar lines of critique and rebuttal. Thus arose the idea for a collection of essays that would both update discussions of autonomy and connect them to debates over the foundations of liberalism.

The decision to solicit new essays allowed us to tailor our invitations to authors in a way that framed these issues from the outset, and we are particularly pleased with the way the authors took up and further developed those issues. The chapters were all written independently, but during the process of revising their contributions, the authors had access to drafts of each other's chapters, which allowed for interesting cross-pollination and a more cohesive overall volume. In addition, several of the authors had an earlier opportunity to exchange their views at symposia on autonomy in St. Louis in 1997 and 1999.

We would like to acknowledge Sigurður Kristinsson for his part in organizing these symposia with Joel Anderson, and Washington University in St. Louis and the University of Missouri, St. Louis, for supporting the events.

As with any complex, collaborative project, putting together this volume has required hard work and patience by many people – most importantly, our contributors. We are very appreciative of their commitment to the project. At Cambridge University Press, Terence Moore's faith in the project allowed it to get off the ground in the first place. Ronald Cohen handled the manuscript editing in an efficient and thorough manner and gave valuable stylistic advice. And Daniel Brunson helped greatly with the index and the final preparation of the manuscript. We thank all these individuals for their efforts.

We would also like to thank our respective academic departments for support for research connected with this project: for John Christman, the Departments of Philosophy and Political Science at Penn State, and for Joel Anderson, the departments of Philosophy at Washington University in St. Louis and, subsequently, at Utrecht University.

Finally, two personal notes. John would like to express his love and gratitude to Mary Beth Oliver for her insights, patience, and support throughout the process. And Joel would like to thank Pauline Kleingeld for helping to make it all not only possible but also so much better.

Autonomy and the Challenges to Liberalism
New Essays

1

Introduction

John Christman and Joel Anderson

Recent theoretical debates over political liberalism address a wide variety of issues, from citizenship and minority rights to the role of constitutional foundations and democratic deliberation. At stake in virtually all of these discussions, however, is the nature of the autonomous agent, whose perspective and interests are fundamental for the derivation of liberal principles. The autonomous citizen acts as a model for the basic interests protected by liberal principles of justice as well as the representative rational agent whose hypothetical or actual choices serve to legitimize those principles. Whether implicitly or explicitly, then, crucial questions raised about the acceptability of the liberal project hinge on questions about the meaning and representative authority of the autonomous agent. Similarly, in the extensive recent philosophical literature on the nature of autonomy, debates over the content-neutrality of autonomy or the social conditions necessary for its exercise ultimately turn on issues of the scope of privacy, the nature of rights, the scope of our obligation to others, claims to welfare, and so on – the very issues that are at the heart of discussions of liberalism regarding the legitimate political, social, and legal order.

Despite the conceptual and practical interdependence of liberalism and autonomy, however, the recent literature on liberalism has developed without much engagement with the parallel boom in philosophical work on autonomy, and vice versa. This book serves as a point of intersection for these parallel paths. The chapters connect the lines of inquiry centering on the concept of autonomy and the self found in relatively less "political" areas of thought with the debates over the plausibility of liberalism that have dominated political philosophy in the Euro-American tradition for some time. While the main focus of the collection is to explore the intersection we are describing, the chapters also represent efforts to make free-standing contributions to debates about autonomy as well as to the foundations and operations of liberal justice itself.

In what follows, we begin by outlining the recent debates over autonomy, before noting some of the challenges to liberalism that have motivated current rethinking within political theory. We then discuss four key themes at issue in both the debates over autonomy and the debates over liberalism: value neutrality, justificatory regresses, the role of integration and agreement, and the value of individualism. This is followed, by a summary of each of the chapters, with a brief discussion of how the individual essays create a dialogue among themselves concerning these broad and fundamental issues of political philosophy.

I   An Initial Characterization of Autonomy

As we map the terrain of these controversies, it will be helpful to spell out the central features of the conception of autonomy, and some key distinctions relating to it, that predominate in discussions of autonomy and autonomy-based liberalism.

Three terminological distinctions are central here. First is that between moral and personal autonomy. "Moral autonomy" refers to the capacity to subject oneself to (objective) moral principles. Following Kant, "giving the law to oneself" in this way represents the fundamental organizing principle of all morality.[1] "Personal autonomy," by contrast, is meant as a morally neutral (or allegedly neutral) trait that individuals can exhibit relative to any aspects of their lives, not limited to questions of moral obligation.[2] Under some understandings of the term, for example, one can exhibit personal autonomy but reject or ignore various of one's moral obligations. The chapters by Forst (10), Gaus (12), and Waldron (13) specifically address this distinction.[3] Second, the autonomy of *persons* can, in principle, be separated from *local* autonomy – autonomy relative to particular aspects of the person, say, her desires. Though the question of whether these ideas can and should be separated is an issue that theorists have directly debated in the literature.[4] Finally, we can distinguish between "basic" autonomy – a certain level of self-government necessary to secure one's status as a moral agent or political subject – and "ideal" autonomy – the level or kind of self-direction that serves as a regulative idea but not (or not necessarily) a set of requirements we must meet to secure our rights, be held morally responsible, and enjoy other status designators that basic autonomy mobilizes.

These distinctions are important, but the notion of autonomy still finds its core meaning in the idea of being one's own person, directed by considerations, desires, conditions, and characteristics that are not simply imposed externally on one, but are part of what can somehow be considered one's authentic self.[5] There is disagreement about whether the concept should rest on reference to a "true" self (see, for example, the chapters in Part I), but in general the focus is on the person's competent self-direction free of manipulative and "external" forces – in a word, "self-government."

To govern oneself, one must be in a position to act competently and from desires (values, conditions, and so on) that are in some sense one's own.[6] This delineates the two families of conditions that have played central roles in recent debates over autonomy: *authenticity* conditions and *competency* conditions. Authenticity conditions are typically built on the capacity to reflect on and endorse (or identify with) one's desires, values, and so on. The most influential model – that developed by Gerald Dworkin and Harry Frankfurt[7] – views autonomy as requiring second-order identification with first-order desires. Competency conditions specify that agents must have various capacities for rational thought, self-control, self-understanding, and so on – and that they must be free to exercise those capacities, without internal or external coercion.[8] Dworkin sums up this hierarchical account by saying that autonomy involves second-order identification with first-order desires under conditions of "procedural independence" – that is, conditions under which the higher-order identification was not influenced by processes that subvert reflective and critical capacities.[9]

This standard conception of autonomy fits well with standard accounts of political liberalism – and not by accident. In particular, the notion of "procedural independence" is meant to specify in a non-substantive way the conditions under which individual choice would count as authoritative – that is, in a way that makes no reference to constraints on the *content* of a person's choices or the reasons he or she has for them. In a thoroughly liberal manner, this shift to formal, procedural conditions allows this model to accommodate a diversity of desires and ways of life as autonomous.

II Challenges to Liberalism's Reliance on the Autonomous Individual

Within recent discussions of liberalism, debates over the nature of autonomy have emerged from a slightly different viewpoint. Liberalism can be characterized in a number of ways, a point addressed in several of the chapters here, but it generally involves the approach to the justification of political power emerging from the social contract tradition of the European Enlightenment, where the authority of the state is seen to rest exclusively on the will of a free and independent citizenry.[10] Justice, defined with reference to basic freedoms and rights, is thought to be realized in constitutional structures that constrain the individual and collective pursuit of the good. Central to the specification of justice in this tradition are the interests and choices of the independent, self-governing citizen, whose voice lends legitimacy to the power structures that enact and constitute justice in this sense.[11]

The multivocal contestation of this tradition has often centered on the conception of the person that functions as both sovereign and subject of principles of justice. In particular, the conception of the person as an autonomous, self-determining and independent agent has come under fire from various sources. Communitarians and defenders of identity politics point to the hyper-individualism of such a view – the manner in which the autonomous person is seen as existing prior to the formulation of ends and identities that constitute her value orientation and identity. Feminists point up the gender bias implicit in the valorization of the independent "man" devoid of family ties and caring relations; communitarians note the inability of such a view to make full sense of the social embeddedness of persons; and various postmodernists decry assumptions of a stable and transparent "self" whose rational choices, guided by objective principles of morality, define autonomous agency. From these various directions, the model of the autonomous person has drawn powerful calls for reconsideration.

What has emerged from recent discussions of both liberalism and the nature of the autonomous self is a set of controversies that mirror each other in provocative and constructive ways. Amidst the wide range of such controversies, four stand out as particularly relevant for our purposes: the question of value-neutrality, the problem of foundations, the questionable emphasis placed on unity and agreement, and the allegedly hyper-individualism of both autonomy-based liberalism and standard accounts of the autonomous self.

IIa Value Neutrality

One of the major disagreements in the philosophical literature is over whether autonomy should be understood in a "procedural" – and hence "value-neutral" – manner, or whether it is better understood in a "substantive" way. The latter view is defended for example, by Marina Oshana and Paul Benson in their chapters (4 and 5). On this view, autonomy must include conditions that refer to substantive value commitments, both by the autonomous person herself and by those around her – conditions concerning her own self-worth, the constraints others set, and the like. A driving force behind the call for substantive conceptions is, among other things, the claim that autonomy should not be seen as compatible with certain constrained life situations – such as positions of social domination and self-abnegation – no matter how "voluntarily" the person came to choose or accept that situation.[12]

Correspondingly, critics of liberalism have claimed that "procedural" liberalism fails to take account of the way in which fundamental value commitments constitute the identities and motivational structures of those citizens expected to accept and endorse principles of justice.[13] Like the defenders of substantive accounts of autonomy, "perfectionist" critics of liberalism claim that mechanisms of liberal legitimacy cannot demand of citizens that they bracket from deliberation of political principles those commitments that constitute their very identities.[14] These critics charge that "neutralist" liberalism removes from the political process the motivational anchor of these deep commitments, without which it is difficult to stave off political apathy and maintain civic engagement.[15] And strict value-neutrality requirements even threaten to "gag" citizens from expressing their most heartfelt concerns within the political process. With regard to both autonomy and liberalism, then, critics have raised the question of how one can ground political legitimacy in a conception of autonomous choice without allowing substantive values (communitarian or perfectionist) to play some role in the conception of autonomy utilized.

IIb The Regress Problem and the Foundations of Liberal Legitimacy
In another complex discussion concerning the conceptual conditions of autonomy, the issue has been raised as to whether reflective endorsement of first-order desires (or other aspects of the personality) is necessary or sufficient for the authenticity required of autonomy. Commentators have pointed out that such a condition invites a regress, since the question is left open as to whether any *given* act of endorsement (and the desires and values it rests on) merits the authenticity that it itself bestows on first-order aspects of the self. If so, and if authenticity is established through

critical reflection, then a *third-order* desire must be postulated to ground an endorsement of the second-order desire in order to retain the first. But this merely raises the same question once again concerning that third-order desire, and so on. Yet, if even the second-order appraisal is not tested for its authenticity, the question is left open as to whether a person thoroughly manipulated in her desires and values (hypnotized, brain-washed, etc.) would be called autonomous if those second-order attitudes were themselves manipulated by her captors.[16]

Critics of "hierarchicalist" conceptions of autonomy have also raised the question of why intrasubjective endorsement confers normative authority on first-order wants and values in the first place. What is special about the higher-order voices that render other aspects of the self so (metaphysically) special? We can certainly imagine cases where a person's first-order drives and motives are better reflections of their independent and self-governing natures (their "true selves," if you wish) than second-order reflections, which may themselves simply mirror relentless conditioning and inauthentic responses to social pressures. This point is touched on in the chapters by Meyers (2), Benson (5), and Christman (14). Meyers and Benson both express skepticism, for example, that higher-order reflective endorsement is the core element of autonomy in all its important guises, while Christman claims that in the context of liberal political theory, seeing autonomy as including self-reflection of this sort is crucial, despite difficulties with that process.[17]

In the political realm, a similar issue arises with regard to the traditional liberal assumption that citizens' choice is sufficient to legitimize political principles and policies. Critics have long been skeptical of the claim that mere public acclamation of some issue, even if such approval has been reflected on and consciously endorsed with reasons, reflects unmanipulated and independent voices when there exists pervasive ideological and other social pressures working to undermine such independent reflection.[18] These discussions parallel questions about a regress of conditions for autonomy in asking whether political legitimacy requires something more than the collective endorsement of political preferences. Similarly, it can be asked of procedural liberalism why plebescitary endorsement by legislative bodies (the element of government corresponding to "higher-order" reflection) should automatically render the judgments they produce legitimate. One of the challenges that democratic liberalism has always faced stems from cases in which formally valid procedures lead to abhorrent results, results that may even threaten the very foundations of liberalism. Is democracy its own justification, or must there be "extra-legislative" constitutional checks to ensure free, independent debate in the public sphere and ground legitimacy?[19]

IIc The Problematic Emphasis on Integration, Unity, and Agreement
Whereas the previous two challenges to standard approaches to autonomy and liberalism suggest the need for a more substantive approach, two other lines of critique accuse such approaches of *unduly* substantive (and contestable) value commitments. These critics charge that standard accounts of autonomy and liberalism are less value-neutral and pluralist than they claim, for they actually presuppose, for example, values of personal integration, or egoistic individualism. And the problems this raises concern not only theoretical coherence but also the inclusiveness of social and political application of principles centering on autonomy so conceived.

Various writers focusing on the standard conception of the autonomous person have raised trenchant questions about the degree to which such conceptions problematically assume a unified, self-transparent consciousness lurking in all of us and representing our most settled selves. These commentators point to the ways in which conflict and irresolvable ambivalence characterize the modern personality. They emphasize that our motivational lives must be understood as containing various elements that are hidden from reflective view and disguised or distorted in consciousness (as Meyers, and Anderson and Honneth, discuss in their chapters, 2 and 6). The idea of unified, transparent selves being a mark of autonomy has thus come to be seen as suspect.

In a parallel manner, critical analyses of political liberalism have centered on the desirability and coherence of demanding full collective endorsement by the governed in order to establish legitimacy. As van den Brink (11) suggests in his chapter, liberalism *without* agreement may well suit the deep and abiding conflicts (as well as multiple identities) characteristic of modern societies. Additionally, there has been much discussion among (especially) Marxist and other radical writers of the way in which liberalism's pretensions of deliberative transparency ignore or suppress what truly drives the social and political movements in a society – the dynamics of economic and social power and its often hierarchical distribution and exercise.[20]

IId Individualism

Also prominent in recent literature on both autonomy and liberalism are discussions of the alleged hyper-individualism of the liberal conception of the autonomous person. Feminists have developed extensive critiques of the overly masculine emphasis on separated, atomistic decisions operating in this conception. Communitarians have famously claimed that the liberal emphasis on autonomy has obscured the socially embedded nature of identity and value.[21] Motivated by these and related critiques, calls have been made to reconfigure the idea of autonomy in ways that take more direct account of the social nature of the self and the relational dynamics that define the value structure of most people. "Relational" and "social" accounts of autonomy have been developed to respond to such calls, defining the autonomous person in ways that make direct reference to the social components of our identities and value commitments.[22] The chapters by Meyers (2), Benson (5), Oshana (4), and Anderson and Honneth (6) all touch on this issue.

Communitarians, feminists, defenders of identity politics, and others have long claimed that liberal political philosophy rests on an unacceptably individualist understanding of human value and choice.[23] Some liberal theorists have insisted that the charge of hyper-individualism is overdrawn.[24] Others, famously, have followed Rawls's "political" turn in claiming that models of personhood at work in political principles serve merely a representative function for the purposes of consensus and compromise, rather than claiming universalistic applicability or metaphysical truth.[25] But other theorists have taken a second look at the idea of personhood at the center of liberalism, and adopted more socially embedded conceptions meant to be sensitive to charges of exclusionary individualism of this sort.[26] However, in the chapters by Dagger (8), Forst (10), Heath (9), and Anderson and Honneth (6), the issue of the split between traditional liberal individualism and more social conceptions of the self (as, for example, in "republican" traditions) is examined in a manner that sheds new light on these conflicts.

As can be seen from this review of these four broad challenges, there are parallel implications for discussions of the conceptual structure of autonomy and for debates over the problems and promise of liberal political philosophy. There is thus much to be gained by bringing these discussions together. The chapters collected here represent just this kind of cross-pollination. Although the discussions of liberalism and autonomy are interwoven throughout, we have arranged them thematically in a progression of sorts, tracing a spiral that moves from conceptions of the self and the individual (where autonomy has been conceptualized in seemingly less "political" ways) to the confrontation between self and other, to the role of autonomy in evaluative interpretations of social life and social policies, and then finally to the overt consideration of the political-theoretical importance of autonomy in the foundations of liberalism.

III   The Self: Conceptions of the Autonomous Self (Part I)

Since liberalism is centrally a view about the extent of legitimate interference with the wishes of the individual, it is not surprising that debates over liberalism have centered on the nature of the self. The respect that individuals claim for their preferences, commitments, goals, projects, desires, aspirations, and so on is ultimately to be grounded in their being the person's *own*. It is because those preferences, commitments, and so on are a person's own that disregarding them amounts to disregarding him or her *qua* that distinctive individual. By contrast, disregarding preferences, commitments, and so on that are the product of coercion or deception does not seem to involve a violation in the same sense, raising the vexing issue of what makes some preferences, commitments, and so on "one's own," and others not. Given the recent pressure on concepts of the true self, authenticity, or reflectively endorsed higher-order desires, further work is needed in order to clarify the grounds for treating individuals as the autonomous agents of their lives or the sovereign source of political authority. Central to this work are the questions – regarding the nature of the self – taken up in Part I by Diana Tietjens Meyers, David Velleman, and Marina Oshana.

In her chapter (2), "Decentralizing Autonomy: Five Faces of Selfhood," Meyers challenges the standard liberal assumption that autonomy is exclusively a matter of reflective self-definition and rational integration. She develops an account of autonomous agency as a matter of navigating a complex plurality of demands. Most fundamentally, she argues for the need to redress many theorists' overemphasis on self-definition to the neglect of *self-discovery*. Whereas self-definition is a matter of the self-analysis and inner endorsement so prominent in hierarchical accounts, self-discovery is more diffuse, and more a matter of sensitivity and openness. In order to clarify the skills needed for self-discovery – and to underscore their importance – Meyers develops a "five-dimensional account of the self": the self as unitary, social, relational, divided, and embodied. Corresponding to each of these dimensions of the self, she suggests, are agentic skills that are crucial to autonomy. Capacities for critical reflection and ego-integration are among them, but they belong to only one of the registers in which we come to discover who we are or even exercise self-direction. For, as Meyers points out, autonomy often emerges in unexpected places: the unexpected smashing of dishes in the sink, the body's refusal to relinquish its hold on life, or even a revealing slip of the tongue. Meyers concludes that unless we have the skills to stay in touch with the non-unitary and non-individual components of the self, we lack what is needed for full autonomy, however good we might be at critical reflection.

Like Meyers, Velleman (Chapter 3) is concerned with the issue of how to understand autonomous agency once one has given up the idea that there is a "true self" to be discovered. If the self turns out not to be a fixed star to guide one's deliberations but rather a shifting, inchoate, plural, and perhaps even illusory point of reference, it becomes much harder to say what it is that makes some desires truly one's own and others not. Unlike Meyers, Velleman *does* see unification of the self as a central component of autonomous agency. Taking as his point of departure Daniel Dennett's idea that the self is no more *real* than a person's center of gravity – that the self is simply one's "narrative center of gravity" – Velleman argues that although our selves are indeed our narrative inventions, they are nonetheless real, because "we really are the characters whom we invent." Velleman is not, however, defending the view that anything goes, that there are no constraints on that narrative. But neither are these constraints *external* to the self. His ingenious move here is to point out that we not only identify narrative patterns in our actions, we also choose actions so as to ensure that there is a pattern into which they will fit. Otherwise, we cannot make sense of ourselves. The idea of the self as narrator is thus not a fantasy of arbitrary control; we cannot make ourselves up simply by wishing. Instead, when we are living the life we are narrating, it is built into the task that we have to ensure both that the narrative fits the life and that the life continues to fit the narrative. This does not require that autonomous agents always continue a past trajectory, but any departures from past patterns must then cohere with a larger narrative identity and self-conception.[27]

But however much we may write our own narratives, we do so under conditions that are not of our own choosing. This is a central theme in Oshana's chapter (4). She takes up the thorny issue of whether – and, if so, under what conditions – one can act autonomously on the basis of inescapable components of one's identity. Classical liberal conceptions of autonomy typically focus on voluntary consent as the sole basis for legitimate choice, whether in the domain of personal autonomy or political deliberation. This suggests that one acts autonomously only if one acts from values, desires, traits, and so on that one could give up if one wanted to. In the 1980s, this assumption of detachment came under fire from such theorists as Harry Frankfurt and Michael Sandel, who argued that such a requirement would eliminate far too many of our best reasons for acting. In particular, if "sheddability" were a necessary condition for a component of one's identity to count as a grounds for autonomous action, then it would be non-autonomous to act out of love for family members or, in general, from many of our deepest commitments (commitments, incidentally, that liberalism was designed to protect).[28] But if autonomy involves acting from reasons that are most fully one's own, then it would seem that conceptions of autonomy must not rule out attachments and commitments, for it is often precisely those that it is *unthinkable* for us to give up that are most centrally constitutive of who we are.[29] As Oshana points out, however, some defining and inescapable components of one's identity may be unwanted. She insightfully analyzes her own case of having ascribed to her the racial identity of an African-American. This racial attribution is inescapable and clearly determinative of who she is, despite the fact that, as a biracial woman, she is alienated from it. This seems to generate an unwelcome implication for authenticity-based accounts of autonomy. For if autonomy requires wholehearted endorsement of one's self-conception, then one cannot allow into one's self-conception any components about which one is ambivalent. But in some cases, Oshana argues, this creates an indefensible disjunction between either being autonomous or viewing oneself clearly – for example, acknowledging the social reality of being African-American. One response, for which Oshana has a great deal of sympathy, is to say that this is a further cost of living in a racist society, and that promoting autonomy is a matter of promoting justice, racial and otherwise. Her core theoretical response, however, is to call for a rethinking of the requirement that one not be alienated from components of one's identity. It may be, she suggests, that full authenticity is not actually necessary for autonomy.

IV   The Interpersonal: Personal Authority and Interpersonal Recognition (Part II)

Oshana's point about the ambivalent character of having one's identity tied to the attitudes of others provides a bridge to the chapters in Part II, which situate the exercise of autonomy within the interpersonal domain.

The chapters by Paul Benson (5) Joel Anderson and Axel Honneth (6), and Marilyn Friedman (7), represent distinct approaches to the idea of the "social," "relational," or "intersubjective" self that emerged especially in feminist work of the late-1980s, and has continued since.[30] A central challenge faced by defenders of "social" conceptions of autonomy is how to acknowledge the ways in which individuals' most authentic desires are not merely generated within but even *authorized* by their social context, while at the same time keeping in mind the ways in which interpersonal relations can distort and dominate individuals' desires. There is widespread agreement on rejecting the idea that authenticity and autonomy come exclusively through retreating into an "inner citadel" of detached, higher-order reflection. What is less clear, however, is what should replace this notion, if one is to avoid eviscerating the idea that exercising autonomy – and demanding the respect for individual autonomy that is central to liberalism – is a matter of opposing others' demands for conformity or submission.

Benson's approach to autonomy focuses on the dual aspects of being *accountable to others* for one's self-authorization. In light of various difficulties with accounts of autonomy that focus on identifying with one's motivational states, Benson argues that we should rethink the active, reflexive character of autonomy in terms of the agent's assertion of her authority to speak for her actions, and the desires, values, and so on that provide the warrant for those actions. As autonomous agents, we invest ourselves in our actions by vouching for ourselves as authorized to speak for them. This emphasis on autonomous agents' reflexive attitudes is in line with standard views of autonomy. But Benson's approach departs from such views in analyzing autonomous actions as the actions of agents who vouch for their authority to give reasons for their behavior, should they be called on to do so. This shift to a social and discursive perspective on self-authorization raises anew the issue so central to liberalism – how to understand the authority of those whose accounts of their actions are dismissed in the larger social context. The stakes are high here, for as Benson points out, "internalized invisibility can defeat agents' capacities to take ownership of what they do." One central difficulty with approaches that conceptualize autonomy as requiring that one be able to *actually satisfy* others' demands for an account of oneself is that it can end up denying marginalized voices the authority (as autonomous agents) to assert their concerns. Benson's strategy for avoiding this difficulty is to tie autonomy not to a stronger requirement of full discursive competence but rather to the act of taking responsibility for responding to "potential challenges which, from [*a person's*] *own* point of view, others might appropriately bring to his view." In this way, Benson's account situates the idea of personal autonomy within a social and discursive context, but still leaves the focus on the claim that individuals stake to being heard.

Like Benson, Anderson and Honneth situate autonomy within the interpersonal context of answering for one's actions, and they too are concerned with the ways in which a lack of social recognition can impair an individual's autonomy. But their view of recognition differs from that of Benson. For Anderson and Honneth, autonomy emerges only within – and is largely constituted by – relations of mutual recognition.[31] Building on that central idea, they focus on the vulnerabilities of individuals regarding the development and maintenance of their autonomy and, in particular, on the question of what it would mean for a society to take seriously the obligation to minimize individuals' autonomy-related vulnerabilities. According to their dialogical model of autonomy, individuals are much more deeply dependent on their social environment for the acquisition, maintenance, and exercise of their autonomy than liberals usually acknowledge. Therefore, questions of social justice need to be reframed to focus on equality of access to participation in the relations of recognition through which individuals acquire the autonomy needed for true freedom.

Friedman is also deeply concerned about the ways in which relationships of inequality, injustice, and domination undermine personal autonomy, and especially the autonomy of women in interpersonal relationships. But her approach is quite different from Anderson and Honneth's. Although she would no doubt agree that more just and egalitarian social relations would greatly enhance the opportunities for developing personal autonomy, instead she reframes the question of the nature and value of autonomy in terms of the question of what autonomy women need in the face of apparently intransigent patterns of male domination. Given the evidence that male domination is likely to be a long-term feature of the social world, she argues, the type of autonomy particularly valuable to women is the capacity to resist subordination, by "acting for the sake of wants or desires that were not adapted to mimic the wants or needs of their dominators." Thus, although Friedman is well aware of the importance of social relationships for the formation of autonomous selfhood,[32] her research into the dynamics of domestic violence in particular has lead her to sound a clear note of caution regarding attempts to rethink autonomy in ways that make it indistinguishable from oppressive forms of accommodation and submission. As her chapter here makes clear, however "social" or "relational" autonomy may be, what lends such urgency to its value is its role in shielding individuals within relational and political contexts from oppression and subordination.

V The Social: Public Policy and Liberal Principles (Part III)

One traditional way of drawing the line between liberal and "republican" approaches to political principles is in terms of the level of public participation and active citizenship required by one's status as a free person. Traditionally, the liberal emphasis on the "liberty of the moderns" has placed protection *from* social and political pressures to engage in public activity at the center of conceptions of justice, whereas republican politics have linked the obligations of public life and participation in the collective self-government that defines social freedom with the status of a free citizen. Richard Dagger, in his chapter (8), argues that when autonomy is seen as occupying a central place in (the best version of) republican politics, this contrast blurs significantly. He makes this point by examining two influential recent attempts to revitalize republican theory (by Philip Pettit and Quentin Skinner), attempts that seek to highlight the contrast with liberalism. Dagger shows how close attention to the concept of autonomy relied on in both traditions dilutes the supposed clash between these traditions.

Many of the alleged tensions between liberalism and traditional republican conceptions of justice also turn on the contested meaning of political *freedom* or *liberty* and its relationship to an understanding of citizen autonomy, especially insofar as that understanding assumes a division (and potential opposition) between autonomy as individualized self-government and autonomy as collective, socially instituted self-legislation. The complex relationship between individual liberty and autonomy (in both its individualized as well as more social manifestations) has been the subject of numerous discussions.[33]

Rainer Forst (Chapter 10) investigates the meaning of political liberty in a way that rests on, and insists on the protection of, five conceptions of autonomy, each of them salient in different contexts but all related to the overall protection of citizen sovereignty (in both the individual and collective senses). To enjoy political liberty, for Forst, is to enjoy the status of the citizen of a political community and thereby to be positioned to engage in procedures of reciprocal justification of guiding principles. This "intersubjective" conception of liberty depends on the protection of individual autonomy in various respects, including: (1) *moral* autonomy (the ability to act on reasons that take others into account, and thereby contribute to the justification of coercive practices); (2) *ethical* autonomy (the formation of a distinct identity and conception of the good, including second-order abilities to reflect on and alter such conceptions); (3) *legal* autonomy (the protection from being forced to live according to others' value conceptions); (4) *political* autonomy (maintaining one's status as a participant in public justification); and (5) *social* autonomy (having access to the internal and external means of securing one's status as a member of the political community). Forst concludes that "citizens are politically free to the extent to which they, as freedom-givers and freedom-users, are morally, ethically, legally, politically, and socially autonomous members of a political community."

The challenges to classical liberalism coming from republican political theory highlight the precariousness of assumptions about citizens' ability to choose independently of social pressures.[34] The lively debate around such issues of *political* sovereignty contrasts sharply with discussions of "consumer sovereignty," which tends to be either quietistic and uncritical or naive and paternalistic. The familiar challenge is how to accommodate strong intuitions about the way in which "consumerist" pressures (say, from advertising) lead to *substantively* bad choices without slipping into paternalism or elitism about people's choices. In his chapter (9), Joseph Heath argues that such a critique is possible, but that theorists must proceed with caution. After identifying the failures in typical critiques of consumer sovereignty, Heath argues that two such lines of critique – those focusing on failures of collective action – can indeed be defended, but these critical strategies should be understood as resting on a richer understanding and appreciation of consumer autonomy rather than on a call for its limitation. In the process, Heath highlights the need for a more nuanced conception of individual autonomy. For example, he mentions that critiques of consumer sovereignty based on the pervasive nature of advertising often naively consign all socially influenced desires to the category of non-autonomy, critiques that display an over-zealous skepticism about preference change, thereby masking a surreptitious perfectionism of political values. However, a fully worked out model of autonomy that is meant to apply to contexts of this sort should aid us in differentiating socially *manipulated* desires changes from merely socially *influenced* ones, and of doing so in a way that does not end up violating principles of value-neutrality. In this way, critical appraisals of the role of advertising in undermining autonomous consumer choice would rest on firmer ground.

VI The Political: Liberalism, Legitimacy, and Public Reason (Part IV)

As mentioned earlier, autonomy figures in the structure of liberalism as the feature of the subject whose endorsement of principles of justice provide the fundamental legitimacy of those principles. However, assuming full consensus – such as a Rawlsian overlapping consensus by agents who consider themselves free and equal autonomous persons but who are motivated by mutually incompatible moral viewpoints – is not universally accepted as either a necessary or a sufficient condition for the justification of principles of justice. Bert van den Brink argues in his chapter (11), in fact, that liberalism *without* agreement must be accepted as the working model of justification in light of the deep and abiding multiplicity of value frameworks in the modern world. Establishing legitimacy without agreement demands a collective understanding of a constitutional structure that is itself evolving and subject to review. The autonomous citizen under such a model is more than merely the bearer of rights; she is a person with the capacity both to accept and to contest conceptions of citizenship on which such constitutional structures rest. Public reason, then, demands that citizens be secured not only capacities for deliberation and public discourse, but also the social *virtues* of "civic endurance" and "civic responsiveness." The former must be exercised by those victims of social inequality who contest dominant principles but who must accept the evolving nature of social institutions. The latter is required of those (alleged) beneficiaries of social injustice who must be open to challenges from victims and sensitive to the systematic ways in which such challenges can be suppressed and misunderstood. The result, van den Brink argues, is the establishment of "agonistic" autonomy, as a component of reasonable pluralism.

Liberalism is often characterized as based on the commitment of the priority of the right over the good. However, an alternative view of liberalism sees its foundations as more substantive – namely, that the particular principle of "right" that must be secured prior to the promotion of the good of citizens is the protection of individual *liberty*.[35] On this view, liberalism is a political morality that requires that any interference with the freedom of action of any person is unjust unless that interference can be justified, and it must be justified in terms that the victim of the interference can somehow accept as a reason. This ties the structure of liberalism inherently to the giving of reasons and the justification of actions. Gerald Gaus, in his chapter (12), explores this structure and its implications for the conception of autonomy that functions at its center.

Gaus points out how liberalism is traditionally understood to rest on the value of *personal* autonomy, autonomy conceived in a morally neutral manner without specific reference to substantive values. *Moral* autonomy, on the other hand, takes up the Kantian mantle of defining the self-governing person as having the capacity to grasp certain objective moral norms. Gaus argues, however, that insofar as liberalism requires that interferences be justified on the basis of reasons that all accept – and the standard for acceptance displays a modest internalism by claiming that such reasons must appeal to considerations operative in or accessible by the motivational system of the person accepting the reason – then liberalism cannot rest simply on the protection of personal autonomy. For unless we understand the autonomy of citizens as containing commitments to shared moral norms, then no such general justifications can be successful, and the overall legitimacy of coercive political principles (all of which involve interferences with freedom of action) would be lost. This, then, is Gaus's way of addressing the issues of value-neutrality and justificatory regress raised earlier.

The line between personal and moral autonomy, and that distinction's relevance to liberal political theory, is the central target of Jeremy Waldron's chapter (13). Waldron examines Kant's positions on the importance of protecting individual freedom and, in particular, Kant's claim that pursuing one's own happiness is morally praiseworthy, even though it involves the heteronomous pursuit of one's own desires, whereas being coerced by another is categorically wrong, even though it equally involves being moved by external desires – that is, desires that are not fully one's own (in Kant's strict sense). Indeed, one can wonder, Waldron suggests, whether Kantian theory makes room for valuing personal autonomy as such. There is some basis for interpreting Kant as seeing reason as playing a key role in the choice of non-moral ends, and hence securing a basis for respect of others' pursuit of happiness (despite its involvement in pathological desire). But the question remains as to what extent moral autonomy (the value-laden, substantive conception of self-government) is implicated in the traditional liberal respect for (only) personal autonomy?

The central liberal principle that citizens should be allowed to pursue their own conception of the good involves recognition of personal autonomy insofar as that pursuit is understood to proceed autonomously – that is, as the pursuit of ends endorsed by second-order (or some such) reflection and evaluation. Moreover, in a political conception of liberalism, such as Rawls's, there must also be general consensus on such principles achieved in a way consistent with each seeing herself and her co-citizens as free and equal persons autonomously pursuing a plan of life. (This "seeing" of herself and others need not involve believing it to be true of them, merely that they can be represented as such for the purposes of consensus building.) For the overlapping consensus to be generated, however, people must be willing to circumscribe their conception of the good by the conditions necessary for a similar pursuit on the part of others. And given the deep plurality of such conceptions, the value of personal autonomy must be kept clearly separate from the value of moral autonomy, since the latter defines autonomy with reference to a single comprehensive set of moral values. But personally autonomous citizens do not merely endorse their first-order preferences out of some passing desire; rather they see their individual commitments as an act of *conscience* – a morally obligatory commitment to self-imposed principles (manifesting, that is, moral autonomy). So the problem is that if personal autonomy and moral autonomy are seen as too separate, it is unclear why personally autonomous citizens following their conscience would be willing to circumscribe their pursuits by the requirements of consensus. But if the autonomy respected in the liberal state is moral autonomy, then respect for a deep and abiding plurality of moral viewpoints is thereby threatened. Waldron leaves us with that ponderous and trenchant dilemma.

In the final chapter (14), John Christman takes up the role of autonomy in public reason and liberal legitimacy. He confronts, in particular, those critics who argue that autonomy-based liberalism is problematic because it makes unreasonable assumptions about a person's ability to know herself. Christman begins by clarifying and supplementing the claim that persons are systematically opaque to themselves regarding their motivations, deepest commitments, and psychological dynamics. Despite this, however, respecting people's autonomy in ways that ask them to represent themselves, so to speak, is required by the dynamics of collective choice and public reason that political legitimacy depends on. Public reason is necessary for the establishment or even merely the aim of legitimating principles of justice, and the dynamics of public reason demand that participants engage with each other as sincere representatives of points of view who are willing to give reasons to others as a way of justifying (potentially) shared principles, and to do this in a way that does not revert simply to a Hobbesean clash of desires. Seeing the process of public legitimation this way provides a principled argument for recognizing and respecting people's abilities to reflectively endorse their own commitments (their autonomy) despite the admission that in doing so we will often systematically misunderstand our own deepest motives. But holding people responsible for what they reflectively accept about themselves is essential in the dynamic of democratic interchange that political legitimacy demands.

VII   Conclusion

This attention to the relationship between different conceptions of autonomy and the requirements of public deliberation brings to the fore a set of themes that weave through virtually all of the papers in this volume. In what ways can autonomy be defined so as to take seriously the broad multiplicity of value orientations, modes of reasoning and reflection, conceptions of identity, and approaches to politics and social life that mark the modern condition? And how can respect for autonomy take seriously the way that identities as well as abilities to pursue values and relationships are fundamentally structured by the social dynamics one finds oneself within, social dynamics whose very structure ought to be the subject of politics? The key tensions in debates over the meaning of autonomy – substantive versus procedural notions, the contested requirement of reflective self-endorsement, the complex relationship between internal authenticity and social definitions of identity, and so on – are replicated in political debates over the possibility of legitimate principles of justice in a complex, pluralistic world. What these chapters at least show is the irresponsibility, if not impossibility, of separating these lines of inquiry: the conceptual, the moral, and the political are all mutually implicated in reflections on these issues.

Notes

1. Thomas Hill, "The Kantian Conception of Autonomy," in John Christman, ed., *The Inner Citadel: Essays on Individual Autonomy* (New York: Oxford University Press, 1989), 91–105.
2. Gerald Dworkin, *The Theory and Practice of Autonomy* (New York: Cambridge University Press, 1988), 34–47.

3. According to Waldron, for example, the standard Kantian distinction between the pursuit of mere desire – what personal autonomy refers to – and willful adoption of the moral law – moral autonomy – breaks down once one considers the role these notions play in the protection of individual liberty that is central to liberal politics.
4. See, for example, Marina Oshana, "Personal Autonomy and Society," *The Journal of Social Philosophy* 29 (1998): 81–102.
5. For a general discussion of the concept of autonomy, see Bernard Berofsky, *Liberation from Self*. New York: Cambridge University Press, 1995; John Christman, entry on "Autonomy in Moral and Political Philosophy" in Edward Zalta, ed., *The Stanford Encyclopedia of Philosophy*, http://plato.stanford.edu/contents.html; Gerald Dworkin, *The Theory and Practice of Autonomy*. New York: Cambridge University Press, 1988; Lawrence Haworth, *Autonomy: An Essay in Philosophical Psychology and Ethics*. New Haven: Yale University Press, 1986; Richard Lindley, *Autonomy*. Atlantic Highlands, NJ: Humanities Press International, 1986; Catriona Mackenzie and Natalie Stoljar, "Introduction: Autonomy Refigured," in *Relational Autonomy: Feminist Perspectives on Autonomy, Agency, and the Social Self*. New York: Oxford University Press, 2000; Alfred Mele, *Autonomous Agents: From Self-Control to Autonomy*. New York: Oxford University Press, 1995; and Diana T. Meyers, *Self, Society, and Personal Choice*. New York: Columbia University Press, 1989.
6. As has regularly been pointed out, conceptions of autonomy that see only *desires* as the focal point will be too narrow, as people can exhibit autonomy relative to a wide variety of personal characteristics, such as values, physical traits, relations to others, and so on; any element of body, personality, or circumstance that figures centrally in reflection and action should be open to appraisal in terms of autonomy (see Richard Double, "Two Types of Autonomy Accounts," *Canadian Journal of Philosophy* 22 (1992): 65–80, p. 66).
7. Frankfurt's view is not explicitly an account of autonomy, but rather of freedom of the will. See Harry Frankfurt, "Freedom of the Will and the Concept of a Person," in *The Importance of What We Care About* (Cambridge: Cambridge University Press, 1987), 80–94. Nevertheless, the account has been absorbed into the literature on autonomy as a model of that notion.
8. On the variety of competency conditions, see for example, Bernard Berofsky, *Liberation from Self*, Chapter 8; Robert Young, *Autonomy: Beyond Negative and Positive Liberty* (New York: St. Martin's Press, 1986); Lawrence Haworth, *Autonomy*, 83–122; and Diana T. Meyers, *Self, Society, and Personal Choice*, 76–97.
9. See Gerald Dworkin, "The Concept of Autonomy," in John Christman, ed., *The Inner Citadel: Essays on Individual Autonomy* (New York: Oxford University Press, 1989), 54–62, p. 61. Partially in response to objections of the sort discussed, Dworkin has revised his view to exclude an explicit requirement of identification. For Dworkin, autonomy involves (among other things) the *capacity to raise the question* of whether one identifies with the desires in question (*The Theory and Practice of Autonomy*, p. 15).
10. Of course, this model of popular sovereignty has been known to exhibit serious exclusionary tendencies, specifically concerning the makeup of this "citizenry." For a discussion, see Carol Pateman *The Sexual Contract* (Stanford,

CA: Stanford University Press, 1988) and Charles Mills, *The Racial Contract* (Ithaca, NY: Cornell University Press, 1997).
11. As noted, this characterization is the subject of much debate. For overview discussions, see Will Kymlicka, *Liberalism, Community and Culture* (Oxford: Clarendon, 1989), chapters 2–3, and John Christman, *Social and Political Philosophy: A Contemporary Introduction* (London: Routledge, 2002), Part I.
12. See, for example, Natalie Stoljar, "Autonomy and the Feminist Intuition," in *Relational Autonomy*; Paul Benson, "Freedom and Value" *Journal of Philosophy* 84 (1987): 465–86; Sigurdur Kristinsson, "The Limits of Neutrality: Toward a Weakly Substantive Account of Autonomy," *Canadian Journal of Philosophy* 30 (2000): 257–86; Diana T. Meyers, "Feminism and Women's Autonomy: The Challenge of Female Genital Cutting," *Metaphilosophy* Vol. 31 no. 5 (October, 2000): 469–91; and Robert Paul Wolff, *In Defense of Anarchism* (New York: Harper & Row, 1970).
13. See Michael Sandel, *Liberalism and the Limits of Justice*, 2nd ed. (Cambridge: Cambridge University Press, 1999).
14. See Joseph Raz, *The Morality of Freedom* (Oxford: Clarendon, 1986); George Sher, *Beyond Neutrality: Perfectionism and Politics* (Cambridge: Cambridge University Press, 1997); Thomas Hurka, *Perfectionism* (New York: Oxford University Press, 1993); Bert van den Brink, *The Tragedy of Liberalism: An Alternative Defense of a Political Tradition* (Albany, NY: SUNY Press, 2000); Richard Dagger, *Civic Virtues: Rights, Citizenship, and Republican Liberalism* (Oxford: Oxford University Press, 1997); and Steven Wall, *Liberalism, Perfectionism and Restraint* (New York: Cambridge University Press, 1998).
15. See Charles Taylor, "What's Wrong with Negative Liberty?" in *Philosophy and the Human Sciences*, vol. 2 of *Philosophical Papers* (Cambridge: Cambridge University Press, 1985), 211–29.
16. For discussion of this difficulty, see Christman, "Introduction" to *The Inner Citadel* (New York: Oxford University Press, 1989), 11.
17. Earlier discussion of this issue can be found in Marilyn Friedman, "Autonomy and the Split-Level Self," *Southern Journal of Philosophy*, vol. 24, no. 1 (1986) 19–35, and Irving Thalberg, "Hierarchical Analyses of Unfree Action," in *The Inner Citadel*, 123–36. In fact, Frankfurt himself acknowledges that "The mere fact that one desire occupies a higher level than another in the hierarchy seems plainly insufficient to endow it with greater authority or with any constitutive legitimacy" (Frankfurt, "Identification and Wholeheartedness," in *The Importance of What We Care About*, 166f.). Indeed, this is already clear in the 1976 essay, "Identification and Externality," reprinted in *The Importance of What We Care About*; see esp., 65f.
18. This charge takes many forms, from focusing on how advertising subverts supposedly free-market behavior to the manner in which public interchange has become subverted by the dominance of corporate and ideological structuring. See, for example, Jürgen Habermas, *The Structural Transformation of the Public Sphere* (Cambridge, MA: M.I.T. Press, 1991).
19. This is a complex issue about which much has been written. See, for example, Jürgen Habermas, *Between Facts and Norms*, William Rehg, trans. (Cambridge, MA: MIT Press, 1996); and Jeremy Waldron, *The Dignity of Legislation*

(Cambridge: Cambridge University Press, 1999), for discussion of some aspects of it.

20. See, for example, Michel Foucault *Discipline and Punish: The Birth of the Prison*, Alan Sheridan, trans. (New York: Vintage Books, 1995); David Harvey, *The Condition of Postmodernity* (Oxford: Basil Blackwell, 1989); William Connolly, *Identity/Difference* (Ithaca, NY: Cornell University Press, 1991); and Wendy Brown, *States of Injury: Power and Freedom in Late Modernity* (Princeton, NJ: Princeton University Press, 1995). Liberal writers who show sensitivity to these challenges (in some form) include Donald Moon, *Constructing Community: Moral Pluralism and Tragic Conflicts* (Princeton, NJ: Princeton University Press, 1993) and Bert van den Brink, *The Tragedy of Liberalism*. For an overview discussion, see John Christman, *Social and Political Philosophy: A Contemporary Introduction*, chapter 7.

21. See, for example, Carol Gilligan, *In a Different Voice: Psychological Theory and Women's Development* (Cambridge, MA: Harvard University Press), 1982; Nell Noddings, *Caring: A Feminist Approach to Ethics and Moral Education* (Berkeley, CA: University of California Press, 1984); Michael Sandel, *Liberalism and the Limits of Justice*; and Alasdair MacIntyre, *After Virtue* (Notre Dame, IN: Notre Dame University Press, 1984).

22. See, for example, Catriona Mackenzie and Natalie Stoljar, "Autonomy Reconfigured" and John Christman "Feminism and Autonomy," in Dana Bushnell, ed., *Nagging Questions* (Lauham, MD: Rowman & Littlefield, 1994), 17–39.

23. See, for example, the essays in Mackenzie and Stoljar, eds., *Relational Autonomy* and Young, *Justice and the Politics of Difference*, chapter 4).

24. See Will Kymlicka, *Liberalism, Community and Culture*, 47–99; see also Forst, *Contexts of Justice: Political Philosophy Beyond Liberalism and Communitarianism*, John M. M. Farrell, trans. (Berkeley, CA: University of California Press, 2002).

25. Rawls, *Political Liberalism* (New York: Columbia University Press, 1993); John Gray, *Post-Liberalism: Studies in Political Thought* (New York: Routledge, 1993).

26. See, for example, Jack Crittenden, *Beyond Individualism* (New York: Oxford University Press, 1992).

27. For a discussion that raises questions about the use of narrativity as a condition of personhood, see John Christman, "Narrative Unity as a Condition of Personhood," *Metaphilosophy* (Oct. 2004).

28. For a discussion of this issue, see Alfred Mele, *Autonomous Agents*, Chapter. 4; John Christman, "Liberalism, Autonomy, and Self-Transformation" *Social Theory and Practice* Vol. 27, no. 2 (2001), 185–206; and Joel Anderson, "Autonomy and the Authority of Personal Commitments: From Internal Coherence to Social Normativity," *Philosophical Explorations: An International Journal for the Philosophy of Mind and Action* 6 (2003): 90–108.

29. See Harry Frankfurt, *The Importance of What We Care About*: Chapter 13; *Necessity, Volition, and Love* (Cambridge: Cambridge University Press, 1987): Chapters 9, 11, 14, and Sandel, *Liberalism and the Limits of Justice*.

30. See Diana T. Meyers, *Self, Society, and Personal Choice*; Seyla Benhabib, *Situating the Self: Gender, Community and Postmodernism in Contemporary Ethics* (New

York: Routledge 1992); Marilyn Friedman, *What are Friends For? Feminist Perspectives on Personal Relationships and Moral Theory* (Ithaca, NY: Cornell University Press, 1993); and "Autonomy and Social Relationships: Rethinking the Feminist Critique" in D. Meyers, ed., *Feminists Rethink the Self* (Boulder, CO: Westview Pres, 1997), 40–61; Paul Benson, "Feminist Second Thoughts About Free Agency" *Hypatia* (1990): 47–64; John Christman, "Feminism and Autonomy"; Eva F. Kittay, *Love's Labor: Essays on Women, Equality and Dependency* (New York: Routledge, 1999); Loraine Code, "Second Persons," in *What Can She Know? Feminist Theory and the Construction of Knowledge* (Lanham, MD: Rowman and Littlefield, 1991). See also Jürgen Habermas, "Individuation through Socialization: On George Herbert Mead's Theory of Subjectivity," in *Postmetaphysical Thinking*, William Hohengarten, trans. (Cambridge, Mass.: MIT Press, 1992), 149–204; and Joel Anderson, "Wünsche zweiter Ordnung, starke Wertungen und intersubjektive Kritik: Zum Begriff ethische Autonomie." *Deutsche Zeitschrift für Philosophie* 42 (1994): 97–119.

31. See Honneth, *The Struggle for Recognition: The Moral Grammar of Social Conflicts*, Joel Anderson, trans. (Cambridge: Polity Press, 1995).
32. See Friedman, *What Are Friends For?* (Cornell University Press, 1993) and *Autonomy, Gender and Politics* (Oxford: Oxford University Press, 2003).
33. Most notably, perhaps, Isaiah Berlin, "Two Concepts of Liberty," in *Four Essays on Liberty* (London: Oxford University Press, 1969), 118–72.
34. This is particularly clear in Philip Pettit's "republican" account of freedom as non-domination in *A Theory of Freedom*.
35. See, for example, Raymond Geuss, "Liberalism and Its Discontents" *Political Theory*, Vol. 30, no. 3 (2001): 320–39.

PART I

THE SELF

Conceptions of the Autonomous Self

2

Decentralizing Autonomy

Five Faces of Selfhood

Diana Tietjens Meyers

People are cast into highly variable and unpredictable circumstances. Sometimes they face appalling situations. Sometimes they face predicaments of mind-boggling complexity or paralyzing opacity. Even the most familiar, seemingly routine situations are nuanced in unforeseen ways, and ignoring these subtleties can only lead to missteps, misunderstandings, or worse. I take it that an account of autonomy should capture the agentic resourcefulness people need to cope with life's vicissitudes, ordeals, and upheavals.[1] To do this, an account of autonomy must explain how one can encounter unexpected constraints, discern novel opportunities, and improvise on the spot without parting company from one's authentic traits, affects, values, and desires. More specifically, a tenable account of self-discovery and self-definition must be premised on a view of authenticity that countenances sufficient adaptability to make sense of these agentic capacities. In this chapter, I seek to extend the range of autonomous agency while preserving a rich enough view of autonomous reflection and choice to draw the vital distinction between enacting authentic attributes and enacting inauthentic ones.[2]

There are all sorts of good reasons to classify conduct as nonautonomous, but I suspect that philosophers misclassify some conduct because it stems from agentic capacities that have wrongly fallen into disrepute among autonomy theorists. Autonomy theorists for whom Kant's moral philosophy is the *locus classicus* tend to gravitate to a mentalistic, individualistic conception of the autonomous subject and to a rationalistic account of autonomous deliberation and volition. In this view, forms of agency that evidently are not anchored in rational powers are deemed autonomous only if they can somehow be assimilated to reason.

Consequently, much of the philosophical literature is devoted to designing rational certification procedures to draw conduct into the orbit of autonomy.

Two considerations have led me to question autonomy theory's focus on critical reason and rationally mandated volition. First, there are several creditable conceptions of the self in widespread use both in scholarly contexts and in everyday discourse, and it strikes me as troubling that the idea of autonomy has become so entwined with one of them that the others seem altogether problematic from the standpoint of autonomy. To flesh out this concern, I set out five conceptions of the self – the unitary self, the social self, the relational self, the divided self, and the embodied self (Section I). For each conception, I sketch how it represents the constitution of individual identity, and I explain how that view of identity sets up friction with autonomy. Second, thinking freshly about my own experience has led me to suspect the privileging of one of these conceptions – the unitary self – over the others. Bringing two recent experiences (recounted in Section II) to bear on this issue prompted me to reconsider the role of the relational self and the embodied self in autonomy. The kinds of experiences I describe present puzzles for autonomy theory because, although it is hard to believe that my conduct did not comport with authentic traits, affects, values, and desires, it is far from clear that I rationally reviewed and endorsed these attributes, and it is all too clear that my will was not under rational control.

In my view, the best way to meet the challenge posed by these experiences is to recognize the social self, the relational self, the divided self, and the embodied self as potential sites of autonomous self-discovery, self-definition, and self-direction. I begin to make my case for this claim by describing forms of practical intelligence associated with each of these conceptions of the self (Section III). But since agreeing that there are agentic skills linked to each conception of the self does not rule out denying that these skills secure autonomy, I consider how a theory of retrospective autonomy or a "personal style" theory of autonomy might explain the autonomy of the sorts of experience I sketch in Section II without adverting to any of these skills (Section IV). I argue, however, that neither type of theory provides a convincing analysis of the forms of agency that interest me, although they do point up the need to rethink self-discovery and self-definition. Thus, my strategy is to focus on self-discovery and self-definition and to argue that a plausible account of these processes would accommodate the agentic skills of the social self, the relational self, the divided self, and the embodied self, as well as the unitary self (Section V).

But an obvious objection to this decentralized approach is that I have fractured autonomous subjectivity beyond repair – that five-dimensional subjectivity is an unwieldy, disjointed monstrosity. In reply, I explain how easily and cogently autobiographical narratives reconcile these seemingly disparate motifs (Section VI). Since this self-descriptive form is available, there is no need to reduce autonomy to its rationalistic dimension, and autonomy theory can make sense of otherwise unintelligible autonomy phenomenology.

I Five Conceptions of the Self and Five-Dimensional Subjectivity

In this section, I lay out what I take to be the five principal conceptions of the self that are commonly invoked in vernacular discourses and that are currently prominent in philosophical thinking, as well. They are the unitary self, the social self, the relational self, the divided self, and the embodied self. Associated with each of these conceptions is a distinctive endowment of desirable attributes and capacities. Likewise, each conception provides a particular kind of answer to the question of what an individual is like – that is, each sees individual identity as derived from a different source and as invested in a different dimension of human existence. As a corollary, each pinpoints a different set of contributions to autonomy as well as a different set of threats to autonomy (apart from coercive threats).

The *unitary self* is the independent, self-monitoring, self-controlling self that has been pivotal to autonomy theory. As the seat of rationality and thus rational deliberation and choice, the self-as-unitary is often viewed as the ground for free will and responsibility. Indeed, the self-as-unitary and the autonomous self are so closely identified that they almost seem indistinguishable.[3] To be rationally reflective and free to carry out one's rationally reached decisions is to be autonomous, on many accounts. I submit, though, that intelligence and good sense should not be equated with reason, and that if reason is kept distinct from these broader desiderata, rationalism is not without its perils for autonomy. A zealous commitment to reasoned decision-making can leave the individual inhibited, rigid, unspontaneous, and shallow – in a word, inhuman.

The *social self* is the socialized or enculturated self. This conception of the self underscores people's assimilation of social norms and mastery of appropriate ways to act and interact, as well as their assimilation of culturally transmitted values, attitudes, and interpretive frameworks through which they perceive and negotiate social relations. Internalized, this material contributes to the individual's identity, and thus the identity of the self-as-social is invested in a community and its cultural heritage. While it is obvious that individuals cannot create their own value systems and styles of conduct *ex nihilo* and that individuality is parasitic on socialization and enculturation, it is also clear that these normalizing processes pose a danger to autonomy. When individuals have little opportunity to explore alternative value systems and social practices, and when dominant values and practices are rigorously enforced, socialization and enculturation function as indoctrination, which precludes critical reflection on the values and desires that shape one's choices.

The *relational self* is the interpersonally bonded self. As relational selves with lasting emotional attachments to others, people share in one another's joys and sorrows, give and receive care, and generally profit from the many rewards and cope with the many aggravations of friendship and family membership. These relationships are sources of identity, for people become committed to their psychocorporeal and to others whom they care about, and these commitments become integral to their psychocorporeal economies. Thus, the self-as-relational is invested in a circle of family and friends, and the lives of individuals are incalculably enriched by these ties. Yet, these ties also threaten autonomy, for responding to others' needs and fulfilling one's responsibilities to them can become so consuming that the individual is deprived of any opportunity to pursue personal goals and projects.

The *divided self* is the psychodynamic self. Split between consciousness and self-awareness, on the one hand, and elusive unconscious affect and desire, on the other, the self-as-divided is characterized by inner depth, complexity, and enigma. The fluid but distinctive psychocorporeal economy of the self-as-divided is manifest in a unique – indeed, a vibrantly individualized – personality. In an important respect, the value we place on autonomy pays tribute to this conception of the self, for autonomy enables people to express their individuality in the way they choose to live. Yet the self as divided alerts us to another peril for autonomy – namely, unconscious drive and repressed desire. In pathologies such as obsessive compulsive disorder, these forces take over the individual's agency. But the peril is not limited to this extreme. To the extent that individuals are oblivious to unconscious materials, their self-knowledge is incomplete and possibly distorted, and to the extent that their choices and actions are shaped by these obscure forces, individuals lack control over their lives.

Outside of legal theory, the *embodied self* is often overlooked in discussions of autonomy. This is rather surprising since embodiment is necessary for taking action or partaking in sensuous pleasure. Moreover, people are deeply invested in their body image – their sense of what they look like and what their physical capabilities are. Consequently, attacks on their bodily integrity can be traumatic. Because the attributes of the embodied self are central to individual identity and agency, U.S. law generally treats the embodied self as sacrosanct.[4] Still, the self-as-embodied deserves sustained attention from autonomy theorists, for health, physical proficiencies, and vitality expand the scope of autonomy, whereas illness, frailty, and disability put autonomy in jeopardy.[5]

Laid out this way, it seems obvious that each of these conceptions captures a significant dimension of selfhood – of what it's like and what it means to be a human subject. Before proceeding, though, I would like to comment briefly on the terminology I have introduced here. I have referred to the self-as-unitary, as-social, as-relational, as-divided, and as-embodied. In what follows, I shall use these expressions interchangeably with the more idiomatic expressions – "the unitary self," "the social self," "the relational self," "the divided self," and "the embodied self." However, I wish to stress that the latter expressions, though familiar, are also misleading, for they seem to reify these different selves. They make it seem that each person is somehow an aggregate of five selves. The implausibility of this claim then leads to the supposition that one must decide which kind of self one really is and somehow subsume the other four phenomenal selves within that conception. I think that this move is wrongheaded, and I like the "self-as" terminology because it deflects this reductionist proclivity.[6] What I mean to convey by the "self-as" terminology is that each of these conceptions represents a focus of attention, a dimension of subjective life, and a way of framing a self-understanding or a project. Accordingly, these expressions should not be viewed as mirroring ontology, but rather as labeling phenomenological and epistemological perspectives.

It is important to note as well that in the social-scientific and philosophical literature, these five conceptions of the self are not as discrete as I have made them seem for the purposes of my argument in this chapter. In psychoanalytic object relations theory, for example, the relational self is also divided and social. Likewise, philosophical accounts of the autonomous self often recognize that the self is divided while positing the unitary self as a regulative ideal, and feminist ethics of care often focus on the relational self while presuming its enculturation and rationality.

In my concluding remarks, I shall revisit the issue of the interconnections between these conceptions of the self.

II Authentic Attributes and Decentralized Self-Direction

My aim in this section is to discredit the assumption that autonomous agency is inseparable from the reasoning skills of the self-as-unitary. To that end, I shall sketch two predicaments, one pertinent to the self-as-relational and another pertinent to the self-as-embodied. In both, I would maintain, I enacted authentic attributes, but it is doubtful that I acted autonomously. In these two cases, what raises doubts about my autonomy is the fact that I did not decide to act as I did because I would be enacting my authentic attributes. Indeed, I experienced no introspectable decision-making process at all. Nevertheless, instead of concluding that my autonomy was compromised, I shall suggest that the self-as-relational and the self-as-embodied sometimes function as agents of autonomous self-discovery, self-definition, and self-direction. In the interest of concision, I shall leave it to readers to imagine examples of how the self-as-social and the self-as-divided might also enact authentic attributes, but in later sections I shall develop reasons to think that these dimensions of the self can function in ways parallel to those of the self-as-relational and the self-as-embodied.[7]

My first case focuses on the self-as-relational. A few years ago, I learned that I had developed a metabolic condition that requires me to restrict my diet. Alas, I love good food. There are almost no foods I don't enjoy, and I've always enjoyed the conviviality of eating with friends. Consequently, adhering to this diet is not easy for me, but by and large I've managed to. I've come to realize, though, that doing so has been a complex relational achievement. My husband and some of my close friends have patiently listened to my gripes, and they've even abstained from ordering or serving forbidden dishes when I'm around. Not only does their compassion and sympathetic self-restraint reduce my exposure to temptation, but also their willingness to adapt helps me overcome my resistance to adapting. This sort of support, valuable as it is, has received considerable attention from autonomy theorists.[8]

Instead, I would like to spotlight a quite different relational mechanism of control. I have discovered that when I am with people who know of my condition but who don't refrain from indulging in pleasures I must forego, I seldom succumb to temptation. The mere knowledge that there would be witnesses to my delinquency curbs my appetite. I don't ask people to encourage me to stick to my diet, and no one ever has. Yet their knowing presence prevents me from violating my diet.

In informing associates about my situation, do I delegate responsibility? Do I make these individuals into enforcers of my values? It might seem that I exercise self-control because I created a social network of knowledge that suppresses self-destructive behavior. But in an important respect this construal is inaccurate, for it exaggerates the role of my rational will. When I first told people about my condition, my intentions were different. I informed good friends because one tells good friends important news, and I informed people who invited me to dinner parties because I wanted to avoid awkward situations. In time, however, as I encountered these confidants in other contexts, I realized that these individuals were preempting my occasional renegade impulses.[9] Without realizing what I was doing, and unbeknownst to these individuals, I had transferred some of my agentic powers to our relationships. Now that I know this trick, I can deliberately recruit acquaintances into this scheme, and to do so would seem a straightforward case of making them unwitting extensions of my autonomous will. But I submit that before I anticipated the full consequences of my telling people about my predicament, a relational conative capacity simply materialized as an unintended consequence of my disclosures, and this conative capacity enabled my self-as-relational to autonomously refuse harmful delectables.

My other case concerns the self-as-embodied. Several years ago, I was hiking by myself on Mt. Rainier. While descending a vast, steep, hard-packed snowfield quite high on the mountain, I slipped and fell twice, and I broke a wrist each time. There was no one else around. After picking myself up from the first fall, I thought for a moment about whether I should go back up to Camp Muir, a base camp used for summiting where I had encountered a few people and that was much closer than the ranger station at Paradise, thousands of vertical feet below. I quickly decided that returning made no sense, and continued down the mountain. At that point, my body took over in two respects. Without ever pausing to figure anything out, I took measures to protect myself from further injury, for example, sitting and using my legs to propel myself down especially steep places. Also the wonder-drug adrenaline kept me energized, pain-free, and fear-free throughout the ordeal. My body improvised quite ingeniously, and proceeded with extraordinary determination and alacrity in the face of considerable danger. So I consider myself lucky to have had a clever, courageous self-as-embodied.

Here I must ask for your indulgence and beg you not to dismiss this seeming category mistake out of hand. Apart from reflexes, we don't have good ways of talking about situations in which one's body assumes control and acts on one's behalf, as it were.[10] Ordinarily, we think of adrenaline's psychoactive properties as analogous to those of Prozac – the former functions as an anti-cowardice drug, just as the latter functions as an anti-depressant. It seems natural, then, to say that this hormone temporarily made me – the agentic consciousness – courageous. Yet putting things this way seems false in my case, for at the time I did not feel infused with courage. In fact, it was not until later when friends asked me if I had been afraid that it occurred to me that I could have been afraid or that anyone might consider what I'd done courageous. Nevertheless, my body was certainly doing exactly what a courageous body would do.

It would not be odd either to say that it was lucky that my body was strong and vigorous enough for me to be able to extricate myself from the mess I had gotten myself into. Although true, this observation fails to capture my body's expeditiousness in managing my descent. Of course it does not strain credulity to say that one's body has acquired certain skills – for example, the ability to swim – and that these ingrained capabilities can take over and ensure survival – for example, in a boating accident. I would stress, though, that learned mountaineering skills contributed very little to my actions. Thus, the idea of a trained, adept body isn't quite to the point. Nevertheless, I would like you to entertain the possibility, peculiar though it may seem, that my self-as-embodied bravely and resourcefully orchestrated an autonomous descent for me.

It might be objected that the fact that someone does not definitely want to act otherwise, puts up no resistance to acting as the self-as-relational or the self-as-embodied ordains, and does not come to regret going along this way is necessary but not sufficient for autonomy. In addition, the agent must *really* want to act as she does, and, as the following hypothetical case shows, it cannot be a mere coincidence that her conduct meshes with her authentic attributes.

Here is an example of such a coincidence. I often send donations to an organization called City Harvest, which collects leftover food from restaurants and grocery stores and uses it to feed destitute people. There are quite a few charitable organizations in New York City that seek to reduce hunger. But since I particularly approve of City Harvest's methods and its effectiveness, I see my donations as autonomous gestures, and I intend to continue giving. Suppose, though, that late one night as I am walking home, a City Harvest Robin Hood threatens me with a knife and demands my wallet. Preferring safety over the meager contents of my wallet, I relinquish my money. Although my action conforms with my values and past practices, I don't regard it as autonomous, for, however worthy the cause, I was forced to hand over my cash. In the aftermath, I might console myself by reflecting that I would have sent them at least that much anyway. Still, since my control over this donation was severely diminished, it was not autonomous.[11] Rephrasing Isaiah Berlin's famous remark, people cannot be forced to be autonomous.

The autonomy of conduct elicited by interpersonal relations or issuing from bodily processes may seem like "forced autonomy," too. The same objection, I would note, applies to conduct prompted by enculturation or fueled by the workings of the unconscious. In each case, something other than reason gives rise to action, and canonical mentalist, individualist presuppositions about autonomous volition raise doubts about the autonomy of such action. From that point of view, it seems that in these cases, internal or internalized forces impel one to act. Yet there are some striking ways in which the two personal experiences I have described diverge from the Robin Hood mugging scenario.

Most striking is the fact that the nature of the compulsion, if compulsion is not a misnomer in the cases I set out, is entirely different. There is no violence or threat of violence in my friends' inadvertent aid controlling over my unruly appetite or my body's carrying me to safety despite the treacherous mountain terrain. Also significant is the fact that people who are unwittingly keeping me within my dietary regimen are not intentionally manipulating me, nor are they imposing a choice I would eschew. Indeed, it might be a smart move to deliberately enlist some more of these innocent accomplices. Nor is my clever, courageous body acting against my interests or wishes – there's nothing about the post-accident descent that I would have done differently if I had wasted time thinking over the advantages and disadvantages of functional arms and hands or plotting each step. In contrast, I would never choose to be terrorized into fulfilling my charitable obligations. Finally, the City Harvest Robin Hood is a stranger, and this mugger could not have known whether I needed that money for some other compelling purpose. But the self-as-relational and the self-as-embodied are not strangers. Indeed, they are more than acquaintances. They are aspects of me, aspects of my identity, aspects of who I am.[12] The same goes for the self-as-social and the self-as-divided. All in all, then, the gulf between me and effective agentic power seems far wider in the City Harvest Robin Hood scenario than it does in my real-life experiences.

For these reasons, I think it would be unwise to short-circuit inquiry by declaring my experiences heteronomous. Still, it is not clear how autonomy-defeating, alien motivations differ from autonomy-preserving, authentic ones. The succeeding sections of this chapter propose a way to distinguish the autonomous agency of the self-as-relational, as-embodied, as-divided, and as-social from nonautonomous behavior arising from these dimensions of the self.

III The Agentic Skills of the Five-dimensional Subject

Mere doings are not autonomous. Nor is aimless, self-defeating, or subservient behaving.[13] As a first step toward persuading you that conduct stemming from the self-as-social, the self-as-relational, the self-as-divided, or the self-as-embodied can be autonomous, I urge that attending to these dimensions of selfhood brings to light some neglected agentic skills. Moreover, I urge that these skills endow people with forms of practical intelligence that can be seen to facilitate self-discovery, self-definition, and self-direction. If this is so, it seems to me that we cannot dismiss the possibility that the self-as-unitary is not the preeminent arbiter of autonomy.

Skills are forms of know-how. There are standards of performance – in deep water there's a big difference between a non-swimmer and a swimmer, and in any pool there's a big difference between an average recreational swimmer and an Olympic contender. Skills can be taught, and they can be practiced, cultivated, and improved. Even a rudimentary skill like walking, which babies seem to pick up with minimal adult assistance, is sometimes painstakingly taught – for example, in the aftermath of a severe spinal injury, the victim might need a physical therapist's "tutoring" to regain the ability to walk. Skills can be exercised thoughtfully, but they need not be. You can just swim without thinking about it, or you can concentrate on perfecting your butterfly stroke. Proficiency enables people who possess a skill to correct their own mistakes – for example, a pianist senses her lagging tempo and picks up the pace. Likewise, proficiency enables people to adapt to varying circumstances – for example, a dietician customizes menus to suit particular nutritional needs. So, skills are learnable, improvable, flexible, standard-governed abilities to engage in different types of activity, and autonomy skills are skills that contribute to self-discovery, self-definition, and self-direction.

Turning to the social self and our experience of enculturation, it is necessary to recall the role of cultures in people's lives. A culture encodes a collective intelligence – the accumulated wisdom of a social group coupled with its share of folly and falsity. Cultures prescribe ways to meet ineluctable needs, they disseminate models of lives well lived, and they furnish a worldview that enables people to experience life as meaningful. The self-as-social is imbued with this collective intelligence. Of course, it is often pointed out that from the standpoint of autonomy that is precisely the trouble. The social self is too imbued with this collective intelligence to be autonomous. In my view, however, this objection rests on an impoverished conception of culture, on a misunderstanding of enculturation, and perhaps on a misunderstanding of autonomy as well.

To be autonomous, one needn't be outlandish. For many people, living autonomously means living a fairly conventional life.[14] In these cases, it is obvious how cultures help to secure conative resolve. Insofar as one's values and projects coincide with a culturally entrenched way of life, one's social context powerfully reinforces one's resolve to live up to those values and carry out those projects. Still, it is important to notice that lending its imprimatur to certain ways of life is only a small part of a culture's involvement in volition. Cultures do not merely impart doctrines. They also impart skills, including skills that enable people to seek and obtain social approval and, if not approval, tolerance. Thus, a cultural environment integrates the self-as-social in practices of self-revelation and self-justification that afford opportunities to test one's values and aspirations and that solidify one's resolve, whether or not social endorsement is ultimately forthcoming.[15]

That cultures contribute to the capacity for social dissent may come as a surprise if one pictures cultures as exquisitely coherent systems of beliefs and practices embalmed in amber. But since a static culture is a dead culture, thriving cultures have built-in mechanisms of change.[16] To be a cultural initiate, then, is to know how to use these mechanisms – that is, to know how to resist uncongenial cultural norms and defective cultural values. Thus, cultures endow the self-as-social with resistance skills as well as resolve skills, both of which are integral to autonomy.

Interpersonal relationships are also implicated in people's capacity for autonomy. Feminist consciousness-raising is a paradigm of self-discovery, self-definition, and self-direction. Through the synergy of pooled memories, dreams sparking off each other, and energizing solidarity, the relational selves participating in these groups became preternaturally smart, visionary, and willful.[17] In other words, the interpersonal skills of the self-as-relational transformed women's seemingly personal complaints into political critique and oppositional activism. We find the same skills in play on a smaller scale. A friend may discern an intimate's distress before she consciously registers it herself, and sometimes the friend understands the distress and grasps what needs to be done about it far better than the sufferer does. Listening to a friend can jump-start autonomy or prevent autonomy from flagging. Indeed, I doubt that autonomy can survive in an interpersonal vacuum. If the tabloid press has any use at all, it is to record an endless stream of evidence that opting for extremely attenuated social relations is not especially conducive to autonomy – people's autonomy skills get rusty and languish for want of interaction with others, and crazy or vicious ideas take root more easily.

People frequently depend on friends to bolster their resolve to undertake a daunting, but needed change of direction or to persevere despite discouragement with a project. But receptivity to explicit suasion is by no means the whole of the volitional structure of the self-as-relational. As we have seen, constellations of companionship can in themselves constitute individual resolve, and they need not be set up deliberately. As with the collaborative insights of consciousness-raising groups, volitional structures can arise through the dynamic of interaction.

Now, it might seem that I am describing a passive subject rather than an autonomous subject – someone who absorbs and yields to other people's ideas, not someone who is living by her own lights. But few, if any, real people are relational sponges. Discriminating receptivity to others' criticism, reassurance, and advice is a skill that can be deficient in either of two respects – one can have too little facility in distinguishing helpful from unhelpful input or too little facility in assimilating the benefits of others' perceptions. Here, it is worth remembering that relationships are (or should be) cooperative endeavors. Individuals exercise interpersonal skills that shape their relationships, and thus they have some control over the trustworthiness of their associates as partners in autonomy. If people express their values, needs, interests, and so forth in fashioning their relationships, they not only act autonomously in maintaining these ties, but they also minimize the risk of the relational self's receptivity.[18] Under these circumstances, exercising discriminating receptivity to others is less dangerous and more likely to augment autonomy.

Intelligence is not exclusively a property of the conscious mind. Unconscious thought processes work on abstract or personal problems while we sleep; unconscious memory processes post reminders and revives lost meanings; unconscious imaginative processes generate fantasies that can open liberating possibilities; unconscious self-evaluative processes issue warnings manifested in pangs of guilt and in outbreaks of anxiety, frustration, boredom, agitation, confusion, and the like. Moreover, when a person's values, goals, and commitments become embedded in subconscious desire and affect, that individual's determination to stay the course is less liable to falter.

The unconscious mind is plainly a resource for self-knowledge, self-definition, and self-direction. But it might be objected that none of the phenomena I have singled out involve skills. They are merely psychocorporeal incidents that require interpretation and psychocorporeal structures that happen to back up authentic values, goals, or commitments. Although the actual operation of these processes is mysterious and largely beyond our control, some of them – notably memory, imagination, and self-evaluation – are subject to deliberate cultivation. Also the operation of these processes, though not always predictable, is patterned, and can be judged more or less availing.[19] These features of unconscious processes bring them into the ambit of skills. But the case for the contribution of the self-as-divided to autonomy need not depend on the admittedly debatable claim that the unconscious mind is by itself a repository of skills, for consciousness is as much a part of the self-as-divided as the unconscious. Thus, it is this whole system – the self-as-divided – that is skilled in selectively appropriating unconscious materials, and it seems clear that the interpretive, reflective, and intention-forming skills of this system are needed for autonomy. Now, it goes without saying that the self-as-divided is not an unalloyed blessing from the standpoint of autonomy. Unconscious processes can defeat autonomous plans, as well as support them. But since there are numerous accounts in the psychological literature of how autonomy is possible for a divided self, I shall not pause to rehearse them here or to argue that a divided self can gain autonomy.[20]

Foucauldians will find nothing to quarrel with in the claim that the body is a site of skills that perpetuate the social order but that also generate resistance to it. For Foucault, disciplinary regimes inscribe social identities on the body by instilling styles of comportment and bodily routines that enforce these identities. Yet, deviations from these disciplines – and deviations are inevitable, in Foucault's view – constitute opposition to the status quo.

I mention Foucault because I agree that characteristic deportment and demeanor express what one is like and because I agree that ingrained bodily configurations and habitual bodily practices help to preserve one's sense of self. It is well known how profoundly disorienting alienation from the body brought on by physical pain, illness, or injury can be.[21] It is also worth underscoring the fact that somatic discontent and damage can be excellent barometers of injustice and potent catalysts for resistance.[22] Feminists have called for an end to women's sexual deprivations and vulnerabilities, and advocates of workers' rights have organized against backbreaking and repetitive labor. In a related vein, I also agree with Foucault that strategic refusals to replicate normalizing bodily conventions can pose a sharp challenge to an oppressive social order. Nevertheless, I do not propose to rely on Foucault to make my case for the embodied self's contribution to autonomy, for the theory in which he couches his insights about the self-as-embodied makes it hard to see how individuals could assert control over their deviations from entrenched disciplines and thus hard to see how they could autonomously redefine themselves or overcome oppression.

What is missing from Foucault's account, as I understand it, is an appreciation of the practical intelligence of the skilled embodied self. Think of how subtle messages delivered through body language can be, and remember that body language is a skill that people seldom exercise self-consciously. Also, consider why self-defense training helps traumatized sexual assault victims recover.[23] It gives them reason to believe that they are safer because they feel confident that their bodies would assuredly and forcefully react if they should ever be attacked again. Notice, however, that if these individuals had reason to fear that the self-as-embodied would be prone to lose control and misuse its fighting techniques, say, by aggressing against loving partners or children in their care, this new capability would not be much of a comfort. It is both because the self-as-embodied has acquired a crucial form of practical intelligence – not just a batch of hand-to-hand combat moves – and because self-defense training increases the likelihood that the individual will act on her desire to protect herself that this physical skill seems constitutive of victims' autonomous agency.[24] If the skills of body language and self-defense are typical of the skills of the self-as-embodied, there is no reason to exclude the self-as-embodied from autonomous volition.

In highlighting the agentic skills of the self-as-social, as-relational, as-divided, and as-embodied, I am not denying that autonomous people need the rational skills of the self-as-unitary. Autonomous people often call upon instrumental reason to figure out how to achieve their goals, and they use abstract reasoning skills to notice, to assess, and sometimes to resolve conflicts within their value systems. What I am questioning is that these skills suffice to account for autonomy and that exercising these skills is always necessary to achieve autonomy.

IV Reckoning with Anomalous Autonomy Phenomenology

At this point, it might be acknowledged that, like the self-as-unitary, the self-as-social, as-relational, as-divided, and as-embodied are sites of agency-enabling skills, yet it might be doubted that the skills I have inventoried are autonomy skills. Since autonomy may seem to require deliberate self-direction, and since so many of these skills operate with little or no conscious supervision, they may seem like poor candidates for inclusion. In this section, I consider two ways to account for the autonomy of my dietary control and my mountain descent without invoking these skills. Specifically, I ask whether the idea of retrospective autonomy or the idea of personal style can circumnavigate the problem posed by the subconscious, unmonitored functioning of these skills.

It seems undeniable that people sometimes spontaneously act in atypical ways, and that in retrospect they realize that this devil-may-care moment revealed a previously submerged, yet highly desirable, potentiality, one that the individual regrets not actualizing in the past and very much wants to actualize more fully in the future. Limiting autonomy to pre-authorized action would deny that such spontaneous departures from critically examined and certified patterns of behavior could be autonomous. Serendipity and surprise would be expelled from autonomous life. Only after such anomalous behavior had been scrutinized and judged to be expressive of authentic traits, affects, values, and desires could similar future behavior count as autonomous. Since this exiguous view is vulnerable to the familiar objections that autonomy valorizes bourgeois planning and stability and masculinist rationalism,[25] an account of retrospective autonomy – that is, critically reflecting on past conduct and validating it after the fact – is indispensable.

John Christman proposes a promising theory of retrospective validation. For Christman, an agent is autonomous with respect to a desire "if the influences and conditions that gave rise to the desire were factors that the agent... would not have resisted had she attended to them," and the agent making the judgment about these influences and conditions is minimally rational and not self-deceived.[26] In other words, authentic past desires are desires that were formed by processes one now freely accepts.

I am not at all sure that Christman's theory of retrospective autonomy would certify my mountain descent and my gustatory inhibition as autonomous. Of course, I'm glad I somehow got to be the sort of person who could make her way down the snowfield, and I am not sorry that I somehow became the sort of person who is sensitive to others' opinions of me. I have to confess, though, that I don't have a very clear idea of what caused me to turn out this way. Moreover, when I speculate about the influences and conditions that may have given rise to my capacities and character, I find much to criticize, for I grew up in a fairly typical 1950s Euro-American, middle class, patriarchal nuclear family. Within the household precincts, my father's authority was unquestioned and unshared. He modeled decisiveness and competence, and he strictly suppressed displays of weakness in his children. He set high standards, and he bestowed approval sparingly. No doubt, these aspects of my upbringing greatly influenced the way I've turned out, and they seem especially relevant to the examples of embodied autonomy and relational autonomy I've proposed. Since I would not choose to raise children in a similarly inegalitarian and censorious environment, however, it seems to follow that neither of my cases qualifies for autonomy.

Now, Christman might ask whether overall I disapprove of the way I was raised, and I would readily acknowledge that I do not. In innumerable respects, I was extremely fortunate to have had the parents I had and the upbringing they gave me. But does that mean that everything I do now is autonomous since my upbringing was not unequivocally bad? Or does it mean that nothing I do now is autonomous since it is impossible to distinguish those of my present actions that are caused primarily by deplorable influences or conditions that I now wish I had resisted from those of my actions that are not so tainted. Evidently, our understanding of desire and capability formation is far too crude to draw the distinctions Christman's account of retrospective autonomy requires.

But what if our social-psychological knowledge was less fragmentary and conjectural? I would remain skeptical that a subtle and reliable theory of desire and capability formation would settle whether the episodes I have sketched were instances of autonomy. If this high-powered theory revealed that the worst features of my childhood experience were the principal factors responsible for my mountain descent and my avoidance of unhealthy foods, I would wonder whether I should have resisted those noxious influences and opprobrious conditions. After all, had I resisted, I might be maimed today, or my health might be rapidly deteriorating. Perhaps I would be better advised to reject Christman's account of retrospective autonomy, which could omit some actions that further my core values and that further these values in ways that I have no reason to repudiate.

What I would like to suggest here (and what I shall argue in Section V) is that a model of autonomy that centralizes competency and authority in the rational oversight functions of the self-as-unitary underestimates the role of self-discovery and overestimates the role of self-definition in autonomy.[27] Theories of this sort assign self-discovery an exclusively instrumental role. Self-examination is a necessary preliminary to critically evaluating one's past social background or one's present attributes. Also, one must recognize one's temptations and weaknesses if one is to take steps to counteract them and keep them from thwarting enactment of authentic traits, affects, values, and desires. But why should self-discovery be relegated to these ancillary roles in autonomy?

I suspect that the impulse to subsume self-discovery under self-definition is symptomatic of a misguided conflation of socialization with indoctrination and the correlative conflation of self-determination with self-creation. If I cannot actually cleanse myself of social input and create myself from scratch, at least I can approximate this ideal by rationally defining myself – that is, by exposing and evaluating my attributes and by figuring out how to accent my strengths and improve what I find lacking. Now, I do not deny that there is a place for such "self-management" in the autonomous life. That is why I have included the self-as-unitary among the dimensions of the autonomous subject. In my view, however, it would be a mistake to assume that self-definition must always take precedence over self-discovery in autonomous living and that self-definition must always take this cerebral form.

Perhaps it is not always necessary to authenticate traits, affects, values, and desires in rational self-definitional reflection. Perhaps people have authentic traits, affects, values, and desires that they discover in acting. Perhaps people autonomously define themselves in part by enacting these discovered traits, affects, values, and desires.

It seems to me that a key virtue of "personal style" theories of autonomy is that they do not over-emphasize self-definition through critical reflection. For example, Richard Double's "individual management style" theory requires only that choices be in keeping with a person's characteristic decision-making method to count as autonomous. Different people have different "individual management styles" – some like to chart their course in advance and work steadily toward their goals; others like to play the odds and see where life takes them; some like to rely on personal precepts and ideals to figure out what to do; others like to turn to religion or some other authority for guidance; and so forth.[28] In Double's view, to make choices in one's characteristic way, whatever that is, is to be autonomous.[29]

Double's latitudinarian account neutralizes the charge that autonomy is the province of dull plodders and hyper-rationalists by minimizing the role of reflective self-definition in autonomy. Moreover, it honors individual uniqueness. But can this go-with-the-flow theory pick out actions stemming from authentic traits, affects, values, and desires?

Consider the experiences I described in Section II. In one sense, both of them were, for me, altogether extraordinary. I had never before been obliged to deprive myself of any culinary pleasures to speak of. I had never been alone and seriously injured in a hazardous environment before. Thus, it is difficult to say what my "individual management style" is in such predicaments. Since Double acknowledges that one might have different characteristic ways of making different sorts of decisions – one might scrupulously calculate investment decisions, but see whatever movie happens to be playing at a convenient theater and time – the indeterminacy of one's characteristic decision-making style in unprecedented situations is not a trivial objection to his theory.[30] Just when it seems autonomy matters most of all – that is, in an emergency or other exceptional situation in which what you do really counts – Double's theory falls silent.

But maybe I'm being unfair. Perhaps there was more continuity between my everyday individual management style and my responses to these unprecedented situations than I have admitted. I do tend to trust my body. I generally assume that I have enough strength, agility, and coordination to carry me through, although you will be forgiven if you are thinking that in light of my multiple hiking injuries this must be a case of delusional overconfidence. So it seems that there was no manifest conflict between my reliance on my physical competence on Mt. Rainier and my usual decision-making practices. My dispersal of appetite control, however, is rather aberrant for me. I'm generally pretty good at self-discipline and pretty self-reliant about staying on course and living up to commitments. Indeed, it bothers me a bit that I could not muster the willpower to resist tempting foods entirely on my own. Thus, it seems that if Double's theory has anything to say about my experiences, it would pronounce my mountain descent autonomous and my refusing forbidden foods heteronomous.

I am not convinced that this conclusion would be right, however. I suspect that insofar as it seems right, it is because the locus of control in the Mt. Rainier case is within my individual unit – my body is ontologically part of me – whereas in the dietary restriction case, the locus of control extends beyond my individual unit – other people are not ontologically part of me. If it is possible, however, that, in the sense of identity that is germane to the issue of autonomy, I am just as much a relational self as I am an embodied self, this metaphysical truism is irrelevant.

On Double's view, then, whether my relationally assisted compliance with my diet is autonomous must turn on whether relying on others' opinion of me to motivate myself is altogether alien to my quotidian individual management style, and of course it is not. Like most people, I care what others think, and that influences what I do. But notice that Double's theory now seems to be conferring autonomy a little too promiscuously. Since people's individual management styles are typically quite dense and flexible, it is hard to imagine a realistic case that Double's theory would decisively pronounce heteronomous. Only a person who is living an out-and-out caricature of a particular individual management style could act in ways that would be disqualified as autonomous. For normal people, the distinction between the authentic and the inauthentic collapses.

The trope of the self-made man limns conceptions of self-definition, and its contrary, the trope of finding yourself, limns conceptions of self-discovery. What I have sought to show in my discussion of Christman's and Double's views is that tipping the balance toward either of these images yields an untenable account of autonomy. Of course, no serious student of autonomy takes either of these tropes literally, and common sense tells us that self-discovery and self-definition are intertwined. Still, the problems I have pointed to in Christman's and Double's views suggest how very difficult it is to keep self-discovery and self-definition in balance. Overemphasizing critical self-analysis and self-definition disqualifies conduct that enacts traits, affects, values, and desires that could only be disavowed at one's peril. Overemphasizing self-discovery and uncritical self-acceptance leaves us without resources to identify conditions of self-alienation and acts of self-betrayal.

V Balancing Self-Discovery and Self-Definition

What makes us think that we *ever* enact authentic traits, affects, values, and desires? How does one ever know what one really cares about? Which commitments are one's own? Whether one's life accords with one's true self?

People who are innocent of postmodernism, and many clinical psychologists, associate autonomy with feelings of wholeness – in colloquial terms, feeling in touch with oneself, feeling at one with oneself, and feeling right in one's skin.[31] From a phenomenological perspective, then, what is distinctive about enacting authentic traits, affects, values, and desires, is that doing so, whether in a particular situation or throughout one's life, gives people the sense of wholeness that is characteristic of autonomy. Of course, individuals are supplied with an almost constant stream of visceral and affective feedback referencing their conduct. For autonomous people, the predominant tenor of this feedback runs the gamut from steady equanimity and low-key satisfaction to occasional incandescence and zingy exhilaration. In the aggregate, these positive feelings anchor a confident sense of who one is, of one's worthiness, and of one's ability to translate one's traits, affects, values, and desires into acceptable conduct – in short, a sense of wholeness.[32]

In contrast, for people who find some of their traits less than admirable, who are not sure what matters to them, who are uneasy about their relationships, or who feel overpowered by desires, much of this feedback is far from reassuring. Emotional disquiet – anxiety, confusion, anger, humiliation, frustration, discouragement, exasperation, embarrassment, guilt, shame, and so on – impugns autonomy. And so does bodily distress – restlessness, tensed muscles, headache, fatigue, tearfulness, palpitations, and the like. Nor should we overlook the fact that complacency signals inveterate inattentiveness, if not obtuseness that bespeaks questionable autonomy, too. Dissonant cues such as these, together with affirming cues on the satisfaction-exhilaration spectrum, comprise the expressive vocabulary of the self-as-social, as-relational, as-divided, and as-embodied. This visceral and affective vocabulary is a trenchant vehicle for communicating avowal and disavowal and for advocating either persisting in or altering one's course. Autonomous people are attuned to and responsive to these messages. Reports of self-alienation or poor fit between self and action prompt self-monitoring, possibly leading to change.

Sometimes negative affective or visceral cues initiate an arduous process of analysis and self-questioning that may ultimately persuade the individual to craft a program of self-*re*definition. Philosophers typically focus on this enterprising sort of self-transformation. As often as not, however, the import of these cues is assimilated and integrated into the individual's agentic infrastructure without conscious mediation, and the individual's subsequent conduct reflects this adjustment. In addition, it is necessary to bear in mind that positive cues are as important as negative ones. They let us know what we are doing right.

Now, someone might object that turning autonomy over to the social self, the relational self, the divided self, and the embodied self blunts autonomy's critical edge. Many conformists feel ashamed when they abrogate pointless customary practices. Aren't their social selves defending the status quo? Many U.S. mothers feel anxious and guilty when they work outside the home. Aren't their relational selves telling them to confine themselves to domesticity? Many sexists feel confused or angry when women bring charges of sexual harassment. Aren't their divided selves arguing for women's subordination? Many bigots' bodies knot up when they find themselves among African Americans. Aren't their embodied selves opposing racial integration? In short, doesn't autonomy mandate rationally probing these affective and visceral responses?

I hasten to point out that mobilizing critical reason by no means guarantees that these people will change their minds and adopt less reactionary views. Critical reason does not confer sensitivity to affective and visceral cues, nor does it ensure insight into their import. Still, it is undeniable that rationally examining these psychocorporeal responses would at least provide an opportunity to grasp the harmfulness of the views with which they are linked. So, let me reiterate that I have not excluded the reasoning skills of the self-as-unitary from my conception of the autonomous subject, and I have no doubt that rational reflection can be salutary. Still, I would deny that rational reflection is always essential to autonomy.

The objection under consideration and the suggestion that autonomy cannot be salvaged without critical reason are premised on a mistaken view of the relation between social doctrines and subjective responses as well as an oversimplified view of subjectivity.[33] There is no one-to-one correspondence between social norms and practices, on the one hand, and affective or visceral responses, on the other. An anxious, guilty working mother need not read her feelings as an argument for 1950s style homemaking. She could just as well read her feelings as an argument for on-site daycare. Moreover, subjectivity is far from homogeneous. No one's affective and visceral responses are altogether harmonious. Even the diehard bigot has probably had pleasant encounters with African Americans now and again. Thus, autonomous individuals cannot escape the need to negotiate the conflicts among their affective and visceral responses and to separate authentic traits, affects, values, and desires from inauthentic ones.

Still, it must be admitted that many people have a prodigious capacity to suppress disconcerting feelings, to rationalize misjudgments, and to excuse blunders. That is why a sense of wholeness is not sufficient for autonomy. That is why agentic skillfulness is necessary as well. There is no reason, however, to limit our conception of this skillfulness to critical reason, for to do so would be to ignore the complexity and scope of the skills of the self-as-social, as-relational, as-divided, and as-embodied.

Exercising the latter skills is an ongoing process of self-reading and self-configuring. The skilled self-as-social registers convergences and clashes with cultural norms, accounts for convictions and conduct when appropriate, and revises these accounts as necessary. The skilled self-as-relational elicits, internalizes, and deploys candid reactions and sympathetic counsel from associates. The skilled self-as-divided retrieves, symbolizes, and interprets subjective material. The skilled self-as-embodied senses inclinations as well as needs, micro-manages itself to meet performance standards, and maneuvers to achieve goals.

My suggestion is that autonomous people have a diverse, well-developed, well-coordinated repertoire of agentic skills that they exercise routinely and adeptly. Moreover, I am suggesting that in being repeatedly enacted under the auspices of these agentic skills, a trait, affect, value, or desire is reviewed and re-reviewed, and its authenticity is validated. If I am right, it follows that the presumption that people's cultural, relational, intrapsychic, and bodily endowment is alien and must be overcome or rationally mastered to attain autonomy is mistaken. Provided that people have developed reasonable facility in exercising agentic skills, their everyday choice-making and action authenticate or disown elements of this endowment.

It is characteristic of skills that the greater one's proficiency, the more rapidly and successfully one contends with variable conditions, recovers from lapses, and corrects one's mistakes. Like the agentic skills of the self-as-unitary, the agentic skills of the self-as-social, as-relational, as-divided, and as-embodied keep familiar traits, affects, values, and desires in full view, disclose unrecognized attributes, notice problematic self-enactments, and devise and carry out corrective measures. Self-discovery is not exclusively an analytical introspective and interpretive project. We discover much about who we are in doing what we do. Self-definition is not exclusively a project of critical reflection and reconfiguration. We define ouselves as we act, and we cannot redefine ourselves without altering our patterns of action. Self-discovery and self-definition can, but need not be, intentional undertakings. Thanks to the agentic skills of the self-as-social, as-relational, as-divided, and as-embodied, one may find out who one is, and one may reaffirm, renew, revamp, recondition, or repair oneself as one acts and interacts.

Neither living skillfully nor feeling whole suffices for autonomy. The requirement of agentic skillfulness counters the objection that one may feel good about one's life and yet remain utterly oblivious to the damage one causes and deluded about the esteem one's efforts and attainments deserve. In virtue of agentic proficiency, one's self is being constituted and reconstituted in an ongoing and intelligent way. Thus, there is no reason to distrust positive affective and visceral feedback and no reason to suspect that one's sense of wholeness attests to rampant self-deception. The requirement of feeling whole counters the objection that one can act skillfully and live a lie. People who are estranged from themselves – whether by choice, negligence, or ineptitude or because they are forced to capitulate to an inimical social context – lack this sense of wholeness. Their lives fail to mesh with their authentic self, and they feel the loss. Turning this point around, since exercising agentic skills well typically confers a lively awareness of oneself and others together with a robust sense of engagement with others while fully inhabiting oneself, it is no wonder that someone who uses these skills adeptly would develop a sense of wholeness.

Elsewhere, I have urged that autonomous people exercise a repertoire of skills to engage in self-discovery, self-definition, and self-direction, and that the authentic self is the evolving collocation of attributes that emerges in this ongoing process of reflection, deliberation, and action.[34] Here, I have argued that the agentic skills of the self-as-social, as-relational, as-divided, and as-embodied, along with those of the self-as-unitary, belong among the reflective, deliberative, and volitional skills that comprise autonomy competency, for these agentic skills give rise to choices and actions that tap authentic attributes. In exercising these skills, one constitutes and enacts one's authentic self.[35]

I readily concede, though, that none of the skills I identified in Section III infallibly taps into authentic traits, affects, values, and desires, and that no one can completely avoid waywardness and self-betrayal. But privileging the reasoning skills of the self-as-unitary would not solve this problem and would leave us with an account of autonomy that is inapplicable to a vast array of circumstances in which autonomy is badly needed. Proficiency with respect to agentic skills is a matter of degree. Most people have a pretty good idea of how proficient they are in various respects, and they can work on improving weak skills if they want to. Thus, one's autonomy is a function both of one's overall level of facility with respect to autonomy competency and of how successfully one uses these skills on any given occasion – success being gauged by affective and visceral commentary.

All sorts of things can interfere with exercising autonomy competency, or block it altogether. Some of these obstacles are peculiar to a particular occasion or a particular person, but some of them are embedded in cultures and social structures. In the latter case, the value of autonomy, together with the widespread desire to lead an autonomous life, provides a prima facie reason to change those norms, practices, and institutions that impede individual autonomy. It is at this juncture that autonomy theory provides a platform for social critique. Although it is indisputable that we must be satisfied with partially autonomous lives, we should not reconcile ourselves to pervasively, intractably nonautonomous lives.

VI Decentralizing Autonomous Subjectivity and Agency

To avoid misunderstanding, it is necessary to call attention to a certain artificiality in my discussion. Because I have sought to link autonomy skills to the self-as-social, as-relational, as-divided, and as-embodied, my exposition might leave the false impression that these "selves" are compartmentalized agents of autonomy. But, on the contrary, an autonomous *person* has a smoothly functioning repertoire of complementary autonomy skills, and adroitly calls on one or more of these skills as needed. The unitary self, the social self, the relational self, the divided self, and the embodied self are not ontologically distinct selves with no direct access to each other.[36] They merely – and, I fear, cumbersomely – signal different sources of identity, different threats to autonomy, and different autonomy-skill specialties.

Still, we should not be tempted to seek a reductionist account of the autonomous subject or to pare down our view of autonomous agency just because we have no theory that synthesizes the five conceptions of the self that I have invoked. In fact, individuals have at their disposal a means to accommodate the self-as-unitary, as-social, as-relational, as-divided, and as-embodied in a single self-conception – namely, the autobiographical narrative. Unfolding life-stories weave together all of these disparate motifs with amazing ease.[37] In fact, I am inclined to think that one reason narrative accounts of selfhood have attracted so many exponents is that they finesse the incongruity of positing a five-dimensional self-as-unitary, as-social, as-relational, as-divided, and as-embodied.[38] However, I also believe that to find such narrative accounts attractive is implicitly to acknowledge the urgency of retaining all of these conceptions of the self in some form.[39] Thus, I see theories of the narrative self both as furnishing a convenient way for five-dimensional subjects to articulate their autonomy and as confirmation that autonomy theory must reckon with five-dimensionality.[40]

Notes

1. Autonomy theorists do not agree, however, about what a theory of autonomy should accomplish. David Velleman's account, for example, seeks to distinguish "action from mere behavior and...from mere activity" (*The Possibility of Practical Reason.* New York: Oxford University Press, 2000), p. 6.
2. This distinction is indispensable to feminist theory as well as to theories concerned with other types of systematic social domination and subordination. In this work, it is not enough for an account of autonomy to analyze the bases for ascribing actions to individuals or for holding individuals responsible for their actions. To account for both subordination and resistance to it, these theories also need to be able to distinguish colonized consciousness and collaboration in one's own subordination from emancipated consciousness and autonomous choice and action.
3. Unity enters into accounts of autonomy in two different ways. In the Kantian approach that John Rawls endorses, autonomy is traced to reasoning, the hallmark of which is consistency – that is, unity. In the Humean approach that Harry Frankfurt endorses, autonomy depends on an integrated – that is, unified – personality that need not be achieved through reason. In this chapter, I use the term *self-as-unitary* to refer to the Kantian conception.
4. For discussion of this august legal tradition and the disturbing exception to it that the courts have recently carved out for pregnant women and the protection of the fetuses they are carrying, see Susan Bordo, "Are Mothers Persons? Reproductive Rights and the Politics of Subjectivity." In *Unbearable Weight* (Berkeley, CA: University of California Press, 1993).
5. I want to emphasize, however, that illness, frailty, and disability by no means preclude autonomy.
6. I defend this claim in "Narrative and Moral Life," in Cheshire Calhoun, ed., *Setting the Moral Compass* (New York: Oxford University Press, 2003).
7. Here are a couple hints for thinking about how the self-as-social and the self-as-divided might contribute to autonomy. As many social psychologists have pointed out, enculturation commonly combines with social situations to assume control over people's conduct. Ingrained conventions of politeness, for example, keep an assortment of sensitive topics out of many people's conversation at dinner parties. Often enough, the agent does not really want to do anything different from what is customary. Also, many of you have probably noticed, too, that the self-as-divided sometimes exhibits wonderful powers of divination. I have often awakened from a deep sleep knowing exactly how to deal with a vexing interpersonal or intellectual problem. Thankfully, my unconscious mind has solved the problem for me, and I go ahead and do its bidding.
8. For a related discussion of interpersonal support in relation to agency, see Susan J. Brison, "Outliving Oneself: Trauma, Memory, and Personal Autonomy." In Diana Tietjens Meyers, ed. *Feminists Rethink the Self* (Boulder CO: Westview Press, 1996).
9. As autobiographical narratives are wont to do, this story has spawned subplots since I originally drafted this chapter. However, I shall not go into

these complications, for they do not bear on the philosophical point implicit in my earlier narrative.

10. For these observations about agency and the body, I am indebted to a conversation with Elise Springer in which she remarked that she thinks of some practices of evaluation as being "in the body." Her comment made a strong impression on me and prompted me to think about the body as a locus of control.

11. George Sher argues that such actions are autonomous provided that the agent is responsive to reasons, such as safety is more important than property ("Liberal Neutrality and the Value of Autonomy," *Social Philosophy and Policy* 12 (1995): 136–159). Whatever the merits of his arguments, however, it would be question-begging in the context of the issues I am raising to agree that coercion and autonomy are compatible.

12. This point also distinguishes my mountain descent as it actually happened from the following scenario. Suppose that my accidents cause me to become paralyzed with fear. Luckily, a Saint Bernard (recruited and trained to patrol Mt. Rainier National Park in order to "downsize" the ranger force and save money) finds me. Toting a brandy cask and pulling a sled, the Saint Bernard anesthetizes me with drink, nudges me onto the sled, and takes me to the ranger station. Awakening later, I would undoubtedly thank the Saint Bernard for hauling me to safety and medical treatment. But for the same reasons that my Robin Hood-induced donations are not autonomous, and for additional reasons that I develop later in this chapter, my descent would not be autonomous.

13. But for a contrary view, see Paul Benson's chapter (5), in which he argues that "trivial" behavior can be autonomous. For Benson, one is autonomous when one "takes ownership" of one's actions. In contrast, my account accents self-governance.

14. For a critique of the idea that autonomy requires eccentricity or rebellion and defense of autonomous conventionality, see Diana Tietjens Meyers, *Self, Society, and Personal Choice* (New York: Columbia University Press, 1989), p. 75.

15. I think this line of thought adds weight to Paul Benson's suggestion that "normative competence" is necessary for autonomy ("Free Agency and Self-worth," *Journal of Philosophy* (1994): 650–668 at 660–663).

16. It goes without saying that cultures also have built-in mechanisms of self-perpetuation. I discuss the tension between cultural stability and cultural transformation as well as the tension between cultural stability and individual autonomy in "Feminism and Women's Autonomy: The Challenge of Female Genital Cutting," *Metaphilosophy* 31 (2000):469–491.

17. See Naomi Scheman, "Anger and the Politics of Naming," in *Engenderings* (New York: Routledge, 1993).

18. Notice that whereas the City Harvest Robin Hood neither knows nor cares about his victims' needs and values, philanthropically gung-ho individuals will/should temper their expressions of enthusiasm for charitable giving when interacting with friends who need their money for other purposes. If they persist in extolling the virtues of giving, and if their thoughtless zeal

is making their less affluent friends feel like guilty outsiders, the latter are justified in asking them to turn down the volume. Nevertheless, they may turn their friends' seeming insensitivity into an opportunity to explore whether they have struck the right balance between personal need and helping needy others. Unlike the City Harvest Robin Hood, whose solicitation methods thwart interpersonal skills and preclude interpersonal exchange, friendship, even when it goes awry, can foster the autonomy of the self-as-relational.

19. There is more similarity between unconscious thought processes and reasoning than philosophers usually acknowledge. If rationality, much less practical rationality, is not reducible to formal logical deduction, the outcome of reasoning processes is not predictable either. Likewise, reasoning may or may not turn out to have been availing.

20. Nancy Chodorow provides a helpful discussion of some of these theories in "Toward a Relational Individualism: The Mediation of Self through Psychoanalysis," in *Feminism and Psychoanalytic Theory* (New Haven: Yale University Press, 1989).

21. This phenomenon is familiar in medical settings. But it is worth noting that Jon Krakauer's account of summiting Mt. Everest features the prolonged and relentless physical disruption and discomfort the climbers endured and links it to the moral dislocation and curtailment of personal agency that contributed to the fatalities on the mountain during his expedition (*Into Thin Air* (New York: Villard, 1997). It would be interesting to learn whether studies of famines and similar calamities bear out this line of thought.

22. Susan Babbitt discusses how non-propositional knowledge of oppression can be lodged in and expressed by the body ("Feminism and Objective Interests: The Role of Transformation Experiences in Rational Deliberation," in Linda Alcoff and Elizabeth Potter, eds., *Feminist Epistemologies* (New York: Routledge, 1993), pp. 257–259.

23. Susan Brison discusses the role of self-defense skills in restoring the autonomy of sexual assault victims in "Outliving Oneself," p. 31.

24. Another case I find illuminating is one that medical ethicists and physicians address. Hospitals strongly encourage patients to make out living wills, and many patients declare that they do not want extraordinary measures taken to prolong their life if there is no realistic hope of recovery. However, when the need for some extraordinary measure arises and the patient is able to consent to it or not, it is standard practice to ask again whether the patient wants to be treated. Many patients reverse themselves at this moment of crisis, and medical practitioners defer to their decisions in order to respect their autonomy. It seems to me highly dubious that these patients have rationally reviewed their values and priorities and figured out what was wrong with their earlier decisions. On the contrary, it seems to me that for many people, the authentic supremacy of the value of continued life is embedded in their bodies, their self-as-embodied revolts against the dry rationalism of their earlier judgment, and their request for treatment is the autonomous self-as-embodied speaking.

25. See Kathryn Addelson. *Moral Passages: Toward a Collectivist Moral Theory* (New York: Routledge, 1994), Chapter 5; Margaret Walker, "Getting Out of

Line: Alternatives to Life as a Career," in *Mother Time* (New York: Rowman and Littlefield), 1999, pp. 97–106.
26. John Christman, "Autonomy and Personal History," *Canadian Journal of Philosophy* 21 (1991): 1–24 at 22. I am pleased to see that in his chapter for this volume and elsewhere, Christman revises his position. He now holds that "what matters is the person's relation to the attitude or characteristic *given* its etiology rather than her attitude *toward* that etiology (simpliciter)." Thus, a person might not feel alienated from a character trait despite feeling alienated from the process through which the trait was formed, and enactments of the trait would be autonomous. I do not have space to discuss Christman's current view in the detail it deserves. But I would like to point out that the concerns I set forth about our inability to isolate the etiologies of our traits seem to apply both to Christman's earlier view and to the view he develops here.
27. Christman now stresses (1) that alienation and nonalienation are affective states, and therefore that his account of autonomy does not rely solely on the rationality of the self-as-unitary, and (2) that the rational reflection required for autonomy is undertaken on a need-to-know basis, and therefore that his account of autonomy does not stipulate that the autonomous self must be unified (see his chapter in this volume).
28. Richard Double, "Two Types of Autonomy Accounts," *Canadian Journal of Philosophy* 22 (1992): 65–80 at 68–69.
29. Ibid., p. 69.
30. Ibid., p. 69.
31. For example, see Chodorow, op. cit., p. 159.
32. Some accounts of autonomy call attention to affective states, such as *feeling powerful* (Jennifer Nedelsky, "Reconceiving Autonomy: Sources, Thoughts, and Possibilities," *Yale Journal of Law and Feminism* 1 (1989): 7–36 at 23–26); *Self-Worth* (Paul Benson, "Feeling Crazy: Self-Worth and the Social Character of Responsibility," in Catriona Mackenzie and Natalie Stoljar, eds., *Relational Autonomy* (New York: Oxford University Press, 2000), pp. 72–80); and *self-trust* (Trudy Govier, "Self-Trust, Autonomy, and Self-Esteem," *Hypatia* 8 (1993): 99–120 at 104–109). They claim that these states of mind empower people to choose and act autonomously. But since feeling powerful can be overblown, and since self-worth and self-trust can be unwarranted, I am convinced that feeling this way is not a good index of autonomy unless these reflexive attitudes stem from exercising autonomy skills well. Without this backing, such attitudes may be a better index of social advantage or of effective defenses against severe disadvantage. Thus, I would examine the sources of these feelings before I attributed autonomy to an individual.
33. I suspect that this objection is also fueled by a failure to honor individuality. If autonomous individuals enact unique authentic selves, we should not expect uniformity in autonomous lives. To be sure, some autonomous individuals join with like-minded associates and rebel against social ills. Many others subvert the system and enact dissident values in less public and dramatic ways. But some autonomous individuals find ways to express their sense of self within existing social constraints. A theory of autonomy cannot dictate

the traits, affects, values, and desires of the authentic self, nor can it anticipate the trajectory of individual autonomous lives.

34. Meyers, "Narrative and Moral Life," pp. 53 and 76; also see my "Intersectional Identity and the Authentic Self? Opposites Attract!" in *Relational Autonomy*, 172–173 and my *Gender in the Mirror: Cultural Imagery and Women's Agency* (New York: Oxford University Press, 2002), Chapter 1.

35. It may seem that this view locks us into a vicious circle. If the authentic self has no existence apart from a person's exercising autonomy skills, how can we tell which skills are autonomy skills? How can we tell which skills enable one to discover and shape one's authentic self and to enact authentic values and desires? It seems to me that the requirement of feeling whole provides the leverage we need to resist this objection. Agentic skills that promote this positive sense of self count as autonomy skills.

36. For a complementary treatment of identity through time, see Susan James, "Feminism in Philosophy of Mind: The Question of Personal Identity," in Miranda Fricker and Jennifer Hornsby, eds., *The Cambridge Companion to Feminism in Philosophy* (Cambridge: Cambridge University Press, 2000).

37. For a discussion of autobiographical narrative and autonomous subject, see J. David Velleman's Chapter 3 in this volume.

38. For a example, Richard Rorty, "Freud and Moral Reflection," in Joseph Smith and William Kerrigan, eds., *Pragmatism's Freud* (Baltimore: Johns Hopkins University Press, 1986), p. 18; Marya Schechtman, *The Constitution of Selves* (Ithaca NY: Cornell University Press, 1996), pp. 93–135; Margaret Walker, *Moral Understandings* (New York: Routledge, 1998), pp. 106–129; Seyla Benhabib, "Sexual Difference and Collective Identities: The New Global Constellation," *Signs* 24 (1999): 335–361 at 341–350; Hilde Nelson, *Damaged Identities, Narrative Repair* (Ithaca, NY: Cornell University Press, 2001) p. 15.

39. My concern about narrative accounts of the self is that they tend to obscure autonomy competency – that is, the extensive repertory skills needed to achieve and renew autonomy – or, in other words, the repertory of skills one must exercise in order to be in a position to tell the story of an autonomous protagonist. Autonomy competency is not reducible to story-telling facility. One can be a beguiling raconteur without being autonomous. I develop this line of thought in "Narrative and the Moral Life," op. cit.

40. I am grateful to Susan Brison, John Christman, Hilde Lindemann Nelson, Margaret Urban Walker, and an anonymous reviewer for Cambridge University Press for their helpful suggestions about earlier drafts of this chapter. I presented it at the conference on Reasonably Autonomous Persons: Rationality, Neutrality, and the Self, which was sponsored by Washington University and the University of Missouri, St. Louis, as the Irving Thalberg Memorial Lecture at University of Illinois, Chicago, and at a colloquium of the Dalhousie University Philosophy Department, and I am indebted to these audiences for their comments.

3

The Self as Narrator

J. David Velleman

Many philosophers have thought that human autonomy includes, or perhaps even consists in, a capacity for self-constitution – a capacity, that is, to define or invent or create oneself.[1] Unfortunately, self-constitution sounds not just magical but paradoxical, as if the rabbit could go solo and pull himself out of the hat. Suspicions about the very idea of this trick have sometimes been allayed by appeal to the political analogy implicit in the term "self-constitution": a person is claimed to constitute himself in the same way as a polity does, by writing, ratifying, and revising articles of constitution.[2] But a polity is constituted, in the first instance, by its constituent persons, who are constituted antecedently to it; and suspicions therefore remain about the idea of self-constitution at the level of the individual person.

One philosopher has tried to save personal self-constitution from suspicions of paradox by freely admitting that it is a trick. A real rabbit can't pull himself out of a hat, according to this philosopher, but an illusory rabbit can appear to do so: the secret of the trick is that the rabbit isn't real. We ask, "But if the rabbit isn't real – and there's no magician, either – then who is performing the trick?" He replies, "Why, of course: the hat." A rabbit can't pull himself out of a hat, but a hat can make it appear that a rabbit is pulling himself out of it.

Notwithstanding my frivolous analogy, I think that there is much to be learned from this view of self-constitution, and so I propose to examine it in detail and to offer my own variation on it. The author in question is Daniel Dennett, and his view is that the autonomous person (the rabbit) is an illusion conjured up by the human organism (the hat).[3] In the end, I will adopt most of Dennett's view, except for the part about the rabbit's being unreal. In my view, the rabbit really does pull himself out of the hat, after all.

Dennett's metaphor for this process is not sleight-of-hand but fiction. In Dennett's metaphor, the self is the non-existent author of a merely fictional autobiography composed by the human organism, which neither is nor embodies a real self.[4] So understood, the self has the status of an *abstractum*, a fictional object that we "use as part of a theoretical apparatus to understand, and predict, and make sense of, the behavior of some very complicated things"[5] – namely, human beings, including ourselves.

Dennett compares the human's autobiography to the spider's web or the beaver's dam:

> Our fundamental tactic of self-protection, self-control, and self-definition is not spinning webs or building dams, but telling stories, and more particularly concocting and controlling the story we tell others – and ourselves – about who we are. [. . .] These strings or streams of narrative issue forth *as if* from a single source – not just in the obvious physical sense of flowing from just one mouth, or one pencil or pen, but in a more subtle sense: their effect on any audience is to encourage them to (try to) posit a unified agent whose words they are, about whom they are: in short, to posit a *center of narrative gravity*. [RS, 418]

The point of this last phrase is that an object's physical center of gravity can figure in legitimate scientific explanations but mustn't be identified with any physical part of the object:

> That would be a category mistake. A center of gravity is *just* an abstractum. It is just a fictional object. But when I say it is a fictional object, I do not mean to disparage it; it is a wonderful fictional object, and it has a perfectly legitimate place within serious, sober, *echt* physical science. [CNG, 104]

Similarly, the "unified agent" conjured up by our narrative is a theoretical abstraction, but it too has a legitimate place in a serious theory. Dennett concludes the analogy as follows:

> [W]e are virtuoso novelists, who find ourselves engaged in all sorts of behavior, more or less unified, but sometimes disunified, and we always put the best "faces" on it we can. We try to make all of our material cohere into a single good story. And that story is our autobiography. The chief fictional character at the center of that autobiography is one's *self*. And if you still want to know what the self *really* is, you are making a category mistake. [CNG, 114]

What exactly is the category mistake that we make about the self, according to Dennett? I shall first attempt to identify the mistake, and then I'll consider whether it really is a mistake. Specifically, I'll ask whether

Dennett himself can afford to call it a mistake, given the philosophical commitments he undertakes in the course of diagnosing it. I shall argue that in at least some respects, the conception of the self that Dennett calls mistaken is in fact likely to be correct.

In arguing against Dennett's diagnosis of this mistake, I shall not be arguing against his positive conception of the self as the fictive protagonist of a person's autobiography.[6] On the contrary, I'll argue that Dennett's positive conception of the self is largely right. My only disagreement with Dennett will be that, whereas he regards an autobiography as fictive and consequently false in characterizing its protagonist, I regard it as both fictive and true. We invent ourselves, I shall argue, but we really are the characters whom we invent.

Dennett describes our mistaken conception as "the myth of selves as brain-pearls, particular concrete, countable things rather than abstractions."[7] Sometimes he suggests that this myth mistakenly credits the self with physical existence, as "a proper physical part of an organism or a brain."[8] But he also considers a version of the myth in which the self resides in software rather than hardware, as "a supervisory brain program, a central controller, or whatever."[9] Mostly, Dennett relies on metaphors that can be read as alluding either to hardware or software: the "Oval Office in the brain, housing a Highest Authority"[10] or "the Cartesian Theater with its Witness or Central Meaner"[11] or "the central headquarters responsible for organizing and directing all the subsidiary bureaucracies that keep life and limb together."[12]

Dennett cannot be faulted for describing the self in metaphorical terms. His thesis, after all, is that the self is like one of those mythical beasts that incorporate parts from different creatures and straddle boundaries between different realms, in a way that defies literal description. Yet unless we understand what Dennett thinks is wrong with our conception of the self, we cannot understand what he thinks is right about his own, alternative conception. So we must look behind Dennett's metaphors for the error that they purport to reveal.

In Dennett's view, our error about the self is to assume that the protagonist of a human being's autobiography is identical with the author. Dennett imagines that his own autobiography opens in the manner of *Moby Dick* – "Call me Dan" – and he claims that this opening sentence would prompt us to apply that name to "the theorists' fiction created by...well, not by me but by my brain [...]."[13] In Dennett's view, then, the author of his autobiography is his brain, whereas the "me" whom we call Dan is a purely fictional narrator, who is no more the real author of the story than Ishmael is the author of the story that begins "Call me Ishmael." Dennett concludes:

> Our tales are spun, but for the most part we don't spin them; they spin us. Our human consciousness, and our narrative selfhood, is their product, not their source. [RS, 418]

But in what respect does the real source of Dennett's autobiography differ from the fictional source that it conjures up for itself? Why should Dan be compared to Ishmael rather than the author of a veridical autobiography, who really is identical with the protagonist of his story?

This question is especially pressing in light of the sophistication with which Dennett is obliged to credit his real autobiographer. The brain that composes Dennett's autobiography has to be so clever as to approximate the powers of its supposedly fictional protagonist. We may therefore suspect that Dennett, now in his capacity as philosopher, has tacitly posited the existence of a real self to serve as the inventor of the supposedly fictional one. Dennett anticipates and counters this suspicion:

> Now, how can I make the claim that a self – your own real self, for instance – is rather like a fictional character? Aren't all *fictional* selves dependent for their very creation on the existence of *real* selves? It may seem so, but I will argue that this is an illusion. Let us go back to Ishmael. Ishmael is a fictional character [. . .]. But, one thinks, Ishmael was created by Melville, and Melville is a real character – was a real character – a real self. Doesn't this show that it takes a real self to create a fictional self? I think not, but if I am to convince you, I must push you through an exercise of the imagination. [CNG, 107]

The exercise mentioned here is to imagine a robot that emits a running narration of its life, as the story of a character named Gilbert:

> "Call me Gilbert," it says. What follows is the apparent autobiography of this fictional Gilbert. Now Gilbert is a fictional, created self but its creator is no self. Of course there were human designers who designed the machine, but they did not design Gilbert. Gilbert is the product of a process in which there are no selves at all. [*Ibid.*]

Dennett insists that he is not committed to crediting the robot with selfhood:

> That is, I am *stipulating* that this is not a conscious machine, not a "thinker." It is a dumb machine, but it does have the power to write a passable novel. [*Ibid.*]
> . . .

[T]he robot's *brain*, the robot's computer, really knows nothing about the world; *it* is not a self. It's just a clanky computer. It doesn't know what it's doing. It doesn't even know that it's creating this fictional character. (The same is just as true of your brain: *it* doesn't know what it's doing either.) [CNG, 108]

One might challenge this stipulation as self-contradictory. Stipulating a "dumb machine" that writes a "passable novel," one might think, is like stipulating a blind man who sees. If someone sees, then he isn't really blind; and if something writes a passable novel, then it can't be all that dumb, no matter how loudly it may clank.[14] How, then, can Dennett claim that the computer generating Gilbert's story doesn't know what it's doing?

Part of the answer is that, according to Dennett, the computer isn't conscious; but I want to set aside the concept of consciousness, which is only one aspect of selfhood. To be sure, Gilbert's autobiographer portrays him as conscious, while Dennett denies that he really is. But the robot's claim to be conscious is not quite the same as his claim to be a self. For as we have seen, claiming to be a self entails claiming not only the status of "Witness," who is the subject of experience, but also that of "Central Meaner," "central controller," or "Highest Authority."[15] Indeed, Dennett defines a center of narrative gravity as a fictional "unified agent."[16] Leaving aside the question whether Gilbert's autobiographer is conscious, then, we can ask whether he really is a unified agent in the sense that would satisfy the terms of this fiction.

Here again, one might think that Dennett's stipulation is incoherent, on the grounds that describing something as the author of a novel already entails describing it as a unified agent. Yet I am willing to grant, for the sake of argument, that a passable novel could be authored by a machine endowed with no "Highest Authority," "Central Meaner," or other ironically capitalized locus of agency. What I suggest, however, is that Dennett has equipped Gilbert's and Dan's autobiographers with more than the mere capacity to produce passable novels, and that in doing so, he has implicitly equipped them with enough of a self to be agents.

Dennett denies agency to the inventors of Gilbert and Dan primarily by denying them agential unity. He defends this denial by citing the example of a termite colony:

The revisionist case is that there really is no proper-self: none of the fictive-selves – including one's own firsthand version – corresponds to anything that actually exists in one's head

At first sight this might not seem reasonable. Granted that whatever *is* inside the head might be difficult to observe, and granted that it might also be a mistake to talk about a "ghostly supervisor," nonetheless there surely has to be some kind of a supervisor in there: a supervisory brain program, a central controller, or whatever. How else could anybody function – as most people clearly do function – as a purposeful and relatively well-integrated agent?

The answer that is emerging from both biology and Artificial Intelligence is that complex systems can in fact function in what seems to be a thoroughly "purposeful and integrated" way simply by having *lots of subsystems doing their own thing* without any central supervision. Indeed most systems on earth that appear to have central controllers (and are usefully described as having them) do not. The behavior of a termite colony provides a wonderful example of it. The colony as a whole builds elaborate mounds, gets to know its territory, organizes foraging expeditions, sends out raiding parties against other colonies, and so on. [...] Yet, in fact, all this group wisdom results from nothing other than myriads of individual termites, specialized as several different castes, going about their individual business – influenced by each other, but quite uninfluenced by any master-plan. [SO, 39–40][17]

Dennett illustrates the unreality of central supervision in humans with the phenomenon of Multiple Personality Disorder (MPD). Writing with a collaborator, Nicholas Humphrey, he hypothesizes that a child subjected to severe abuse may be forced to invent more than one fictional self, whereupon the child is obliged to elect one of these fictional characters as "Head of Mind," who can then be occasionally deposed by competitors.[18] The currently active personality purports to be in control, but we who observe the succession of pretended controllers know that, in reality, nobody is home.

There is no doubt but that Dennett's fictionalism about the self provides an attractive explanation for the phenomenon diagnosed as MPD. According to Dennett, the self is like an imaginary friend from our childhood – an especially close imaginary friend who became not merely our *alter* ego but, so to speak, our *auto* ego. Just as some of us may have developed more than one imaginary friend, if we had unusual emotional needs, so others may have developed more than one self, in response to unusual circumstances, such as sexual abuse. What could be easier for a child already engaged in populating an imaginary world? And just as our imaginary playmates vied for the status of being our "best friend," so our imaginary selves may vie for the status of being our "true self." If so, then we suffer from MPD. Different selves take control at different times, but only in the same way as different imaginary friends succeed one another as favorite.

At this point, however, there is a gap in Dennett and Humphrey's account. When one imaginary friend supplants another as favorite, nothing much changes in the real world. But when one self supplants another in a patient diagnosed with MPD, the patient's behavior changes dramatically: he walks a different walk, talks a different talk, and expresses different states of mind. Surely, something has changed in the processes controlling his behavior.

Here is how Dennett and Humphrey explain changes of personality:

> The language-producing systems of the brain have to get their instructions from somewhere, and the very demands of pragmatics and grammar would conspire to confer something like Head of Mind authority on whatever subsystem currently controls their input. [...] Suppose, at different times, different subsystems within the brain produce "clusters" of speech that simply cannot easily be interpreted as the output of a single self. Then – as a Bible scholar may discover when working on the authorship of what is putatively a single-authored text – it may turn out that the cluster makes *best sense* when attributed to different selves. [SO, 42–43]

According to this explanation, different modules in the brain take control of the language-producing systems, yielding output whose interpretation calls for postulation of different Heads of Mind. Different selves thus correspond to different actual centers of control, but the selves are still fictional personifications of those centers, different *abstracta* postulated for the sake of interpreting a narrative containing severe discontinuities.

The problem with this explanation is that it accounts only for changes in the patient's verbal behavior, whereas multiples are reported to change their posture, gait, handwriting, and their projects and pursuits as well. Why should discontinuities in the patient's autobiography be accompanied by corresponding changes in the patient's course and manner of action? If a human being just contains "lots of subsystems doing their own thing," then why can't one of them do its thing with his feet even as another does its thing with his mouth, so that he walks the walk of one personality while telling the story of the other?

An answer to this question is implicit in some of Dennett's descriptions of self-narration, but it attributes more sophistication to the self-inventor than Dennett acknowledges. The answer is that an autobiography and the behavior that it narrates are mutually determining.

In the case of the self-narrating robot, Dennett imagines a strict order of determination in one direction. He observes that "[t]he adventures of Gilbert, the fictional character, [...] bear a striking and presumably noncoincidental relationship to the adventures of this robot rolling around in the world."[19] And he explains this relationship between story and life by suggesting that the one is determined by the other: "If you hit the robot with a baseball bat, very shortly thereafter the story of Gilbert includes being hit by a baseball bat by somebody who looks like you." Presumably, the robot is designed to tell a story that corresponds to the life of that very robot.

What Dennett doesn't seem to imagine, in the case of this robot, is that he might also be designed to make his life correspond to his story. As Dennett tells it, the robot gets locked in a closet, calls out "Help me," and later sends us a thank-you note for letting him out. But surely a robot smart enough to thank us for letting him out of the closet would also be smart enough to tell us before he went back in. "I'm going into the closet," he would say, "Don't lock the door." And then he'd go into the closet, just as he had said he would. (If he didn't do what he had said, he might get stuck somewhere else and have to wait for help while we went looking for him in the closet.) A robot that can maintain correspondence in one direction, by saying that he's locked in the closet when he is, should be able to maintain correspondence in the other direction, by going into the closet when he has said that he will. Thus, whereas the robot will sometimes update his story to reflect recent events in his career, at other times he will narrate ahead of himself and then follow a career that reflects his story.

Although Dennett doesn't attribute this sort of sophistication to the robot, he does implicitly attribute it to a patient with MPD:

Consider the putatively true case histories recorded in *The Three Faces of Eve* (Thigpen & Cleckley, 1957) and *Sybil* (Schreiber, 1973). Eve's three faces were the faces of three distinct personalities, it seems, and the woman portrayed in Sybil had many different selves, or so it seems. How can we make sense of this? Here is one way, a solemn, skeptical way favored by the psychotherapists with whom I have talked about the case: When Sybil went in to see her therapist for the first time, she was not several different people rolled into one body. Sybil was a novel-writing machine that fell in with a very ingenious questioner, a very eager reader. And together they collaborated to write many, many chapters of a new novel. And, of course, since Sybil was a sort of living novel, she went out and engaged the world with these new selves, more or less created on demand, under the eager suggestion of a therapist. [CNG, 111]

What does Dennett mean when he says that Sybil "engaged the world with these new selves"? Surely, he means that Sybil *acted out* the stories that she and her therapist had composed. She was a "living novel" in the sense that she not only narrated the roles she played but also played the roles that she narrated.

That's why Sybil's behavior always manifested the personality whose story she was telling at the moment. Her life shaped her story, and her story shaped her life, all because she was designed to maintain correspondence between the two. Hence the control of her speech and the control of her movements were not entirely independent. They were in fact *inter*dependent, since the controller of her speech must have been responsive to her movements, and the controller of her movements must have been responsive to her speech.

Yet if a self-narrator works in both directions, then the self he invents is not just an idle fiction, a useful abstraction for interpreting his behavior. It – or, more precisely, his representation of it – is a determinant of the very behavior that it's useful for interpreting.[20] Indeed, the reason why the narrator's representation of a centrally controlling self is so useful for interpreting his behavior is that it, the representation, really does control his behavior to some extent.

Of course, the central controller he has may not be much like the one he represents himself as having. After all, a self-narrator doesn't represent himself as being centrally controlled by his own story.

Or does he?

In order to answer this question, we must consider some prior questions that Dennett overlooks. First, consider whether the behaviors attributed to Gilbert by the robot's novel-writing computer include the behavior of writing the novel. When the robot gets locked in a closet, he tells about Gilbert's being locked in a closet; but when he tells the story of Gilbert, does he also tell about Gilbert's telling that story? He says "Call me Gilbert"; but does he ever say, "I'm Gilbert and this is my story"? He writes a note that says "Thank you," but can he also write a note that says "I'm writing to say thanks"? I can't imagine why not.

Nor can I imagine how the robot would tell the story of Gilbert without including information about the causes and effects of the events therein. When he calls for help, he might well elaborate, "I've gotten myself locked in the closet," thus attributing his current predicament to what he did a moment ago. And when he writes his thank-you note, he might well begin, "I'm writing because you let me out of the closet," thereby attributing his present behavior to an earlier cause. A story that merely described one event after another, without mentioning any causal connections, would hardly qualify as a narrative.

Thus, the features of himself that the robot can ascribe to Gilbert ought to include this very activity of self-description; and he should also be able to describe the causes and effects of his activities, including this one. Hence in ascribing his activities to Gilbert, the robot should be able to describe the causes and effects of his doing so.

Now, what causal role might the robot attribute to his own remark "I'm going into the closet"? He might say, "I'm telling you this because I'm on my way into the closet," thereby casting his speech as an effect of his movements. But this remark would be strictly accurate only if the robot was going into the closet anyway and was merely reporting on his current trajectory. What I have imagined, however, is that the robot goes into the closet partly because of having said so, in order to maintain correspondence between his story and his life. Insofar as the robot can report on the causes and effects of his behavior, then, he ought to say, "I'm going into the closet partly because I've just said so" – or, perhaps, "I'm hereby heading for the closet," a remark that implicitly ascribes this causal role to itself.

I think that human self-narrators make such remarks frequently, whenever they make promises or other verbal commitments, which may be as trivial as "I'm heading for the closet." As you putter around the office at the end of the day, you finally say, "I'm going home," not because you were already about to leave, but because saying so will prompt you to leave. As your hand hovers indecisively over the candy dish, you say, "No, I won't," not because you weren't about to take a candy, but because saying so may stop you from taking one.[21] These utterances are issued *as* commitments, in the understanding that they will feed back into your behavior. Hence you do understand that your running autobiography not only reflects but is also reflected in what you do.

These observations suggest that the "central controller" of a person may indeed be a fiction, not in the sense that it is a fictional character in the person's autobiography, but in the sense that it *is* the person's autobiography – the reflective representation that feeds back into the person's behavior.[22] This central controller is in fact what social psychologists call the self. In the social-psychology literature, the word "self" denotes a person's self-conception rather than the entity, real or imagined, that this conception represents. And the same literature reports evidence for the feedback loop I have posited.

Researchers have found, for example, that subjects tend to predict that they will vote in the next election at a far higher rate than the average turnout; but that the turnout among those who have predicted that they will vote is also higher than the average.[23] Many who wouldn't otherwise have voted, it seems, end up voting because of having predicted that they would, thus conforming their lives to their stories.[24] Like Sybil, who "lived out" the novels that she composed with her therapist, these subjects lived out the predictions that they were prompted to make by the experimenters.

Similar research has documented a slightly different phenomenon, known as the attribution effect. Subjects can be led to act annoyed or euphoric depending on whether they are led to believe, of artificially induced feelings of arousal, that they are symptoms of annoyance or euphoria.[25] Subjects can be prevented from acting shyly in unfamiliar company by being led to attribute their feelings of anxiety to something other than shyness.[26] And researchers can modify the degree of retaliation that a subject carries out against putative aggressors by modifying the degree of anger that he believes himself to be feeling toward them.[27] All of these experiments suggest that people tend to manifest not just what they're feeling but also what they represent themselves as feeling. Whether they behave angrily depends, not just on whether they are angry, but on whether they interpret their feelings by updating their autobiographies with the attribution "I'm angry." Whether they behave shyly depends on whether the current episode of their autobiography says "I'm feeling shy."

Here the subjects are "living out" their self-conceptions in a more holistic sense. Unlike the self-predicting voters, they aren't doing things that they have described themselves as doing. Rather, they are doing things that would accord with what they have described themselves as feeling. But this process, too, is implicit in Dennett's account of self-narration. For as we have seen, Dennett says that "[w]e try to make all of our material cohere into a single good story."[28] And acting in accordance with our self-ascribed emotions is a way of ensuring that our story-material will cohere.

Consider how this process might be implemented in the robot who calls himself Gilbert. If the robot is locked in the closet, his internal state may include the initiation of a subroutine that searches for avenues of escape from danger and quickly selects the one most readily available. This subroutine will have a name – say, "fear" – and so the robot will report "I'm locked in the closet and I'm starting to get frightened." And now two different modules in the robot will dispose him to take action. One is the fear module, which may recommend breaking down the door as one of several preferred alternative avenues of escape; the other is the narrative module, which will recommend "I'm breaking down the door" as one of several preferred continuations the story. If after he said "I'm getting frightened," the robot continued his story with "I think I'll back up my hard disk," then he would no longer be writing a passable novel, since his "material" wouldn't cohere. His narrative module will therefore favor "I'm breaking down the door" as a more coherent way to continue the story. And the narrative module can go ahead with this continuation of the story, confident of being borne out by the robot's behavior, since the robot is sure to break down the door once his preexisting fear is reinforced, in motivating that behavior, by his disposition to maintain correspondence between his story and his life.

Thus, having attributed an internal state to himself ("I'm getting frightened"), the robot is influenced to act in accordance with that attribution. Like a human being, he tends to manifest fear not only because he's "feeling" it but also because he "thinks" it's what he's feeling.

I have now introduced the idea of the robot's having a "narrative module" that produces Gilbert's autobiography. This module must incorporate, first, the function of ensuring that the robot's story corresponds to its life and, second, the function of maintaining the internal coherence of the story itself. The module must be designed to produce a text that is both consonant with the facts and sufficiently consonant with itself to qualify as a story.

Moreover, I have suggested that the robot can maintain correspondence between its story and its life in either direction, by narrating its actions or by acting out its narrative. Hence in pursuit of narrative coherence, the module can sometimes choose, among possible turns in its story, the one that would best fit the story thus far, precisely because it can then influence the robot's life to take the corresponding turn. The narrative module needn't always depend on the robot's career to provide material for a coherent story; it can sometimes tell a coherent story and induce the robot's career to follow.

In previous work, I have argued that a creature equipped with such a module would amount to an autonomous agent.[29] I won't repeat those arguments here, but let me briefly illustrate some of them with the help of Dennett's self-narrating robot.

As Gilbert rolls down the hall, he may autobiographically announce where he is going. But he needn't just report where he is already programmed to go, since his disposition to maintain correspondence between story and life will dispose him go wherever he says he's going. Suppose that he is in the middle of his Fetch New Batteries subroutine, which sends him to the supply closet (where he sometimes get locked in). The fact remains that if he said "I'm on my way to the library," his disposition to maintain correspondence would dispose him to head for the library instead. So if another, concurrently running subroutine can get Gilbert's speech-producing module to emit "I'm on my way to the library," then it may be able bring about a change of course.

Now, Gilbert's disposition to maintain correspondence wouldn't be sufficient to make him head for the library if no other subroutines inclined him in that direction. Even if he said "I'm on my way to the library," his Fetch New Batteries routine would still favor heading for the supply closet, and his disposition to bear out his story would be unlikely to override a routine for obtaining essential resources. But I imagine his inner workings to be in the following, rather complicated state. Various task-specific subroutines are running concurrently, and some of them are making bids for control of his locomotive unit, to propel him toward one destination or another. His Fetch New Batteries subroutine is bidding for a trip to the supply closet, while his Departmental Service subroutine may be bidding for a trip to the library, in order to fill a faculty member's request for a book. Meanwhile, the narrative-composing module is busy updating the story of Gilbert's most recent adventures and the ongoing evolution of his inner states, including which task-specific subroutines are running and where they are bidding him to go. And the disposition of this module to maintain correspondence between his story and his life, though not sufficient by itself to override other demands for locomotion, is sufficient to tip the balance in favor of one or another of those demands. So if Gilbert says "I'm heading for the supply closet," his disposition to bear out his story will reinforce the battery-fetching demands, and he'll head for the supply closet; whereas if he says "I'm heading for the library," his disposition to bear out his story will reinforce the demands of departmental service, and he'll head for the library instead. As long as the competition among those subroutines is not too lopsided, the narrative module is in a position to decide where Gilbert goes.

When I say that the narrative module can "decide" where Gilbert goes, I mean it can literally *decide*. For as we have seen, this module is in a position to have Gilbert speak the truth in naming any one of several destinations, each of which he would thereby head for, if he said so. The novelist in Gilbert can therefore *make up* where Gilbert is headed, choosing among different available turns in his story, none of which is privileged as the turn that the story must take in order to be true. As a self-narrator, then,

Gilbert faces an epistemically open future – which gives him, in my view, as much free will as a human being.[30]

On what basis will the narrative-composing module make its decision? It can declare a winner in the contest among demands for locomotion, but on what basis will it adjudicate among those demands? The answer, already implicit in Dennett's theory, is that it will adjudicate on the basis of how best to continue the story – how to "make [its] material cohere."[31]

In many cases, acting on one demand will already make more narrative sense than acting on another, and the narrative-composing module will therefore declare a winner simply by telling the more coherent continuation of the story. But if neither continuation would make more narrative sense at this point, then the module can fill in more detail about its current situation, by recording which demand is stronger than the other or by recording more of the circumstances – which may arouse more internal states, which can in turn be recorded. At some point, the story will *become* more amenable to one continuation or other, and the narrative module can go ahead with the better continuation, thereby making its decision.

In this way, I believe, the module will decide on the basis of considerations that serve as reasons for acting. In canvassing Gilbert's outer circumstances and inner states, it will weigh them as considerations in light of which various possible actions would make sense. It will thus weigh Gilbert's circumstances and states as providing a potential *rationale* for his next action – that is, an account that would make the action intelligible, a coherent development in his story. When the novelist in Gilbert writes in the action with the best rationale, he will in effect be deciding for reasons.

Note that this claim places significant constraints on the conception of narrative coherence on which I can rely. One might have thought that whether an action would make for a coherent continuation of Gilbert's story ultimately depends on whether he has reason for taking it. My claim, however, is that whether Gilbert has reason for taking an action ultimately depends on whether it would make for a coherent continuation of his story. Because I make the latter claim, I cannot adopt the former in order to explicate narrative coherence, since my account would then become viciously circular: narrative coherence cannot ultimately depend on rational justification if rational justification ultimately depends on narrative coherence.

Of course, *we* can tell a story about Gilbert that makes sense because it portrays him as taking actions for which he has reasons; for we can portray him as taking actions because they cohere with *his* story. Indeed, I have already claimed that self-narration takes account of its own effect on the subject's behavior, by portraying him as *hereby* heading for the supply closet or the library. To this extent, self-narration already relies for some of its coherence on the fact that the subject is doing what coheres with this very story – hence on the fact that he is doing something for which he has reasons, as I conceive them. But this fact cannot be the sole basis for the narrative coherence involved. There must be some prior basis on which the subject's action makes sense in light of his story before it can also make sense in light of his tendency to do what makes sense.

The nature of narrative coherence is a topic that lies beyond the scope of this chapter.[32] But I have already indicated one basis on which Gilbert can regard actions as cohering with his story independently of his having reasons for taking them. I have supposed that Gilbert understands his own inner workings, in the form of the various subroutines that are vying to control his behavior. Gilbert understands that whatever he does will be controlled by one of these subroutines and will consequently make sense by virtue of having a causal explanation, which cites the relevant subroutine as the controlling cause. In considering which action would make for a coherent continuation of his story, Gilbert can look for an action that would have the most satisfying causal explanation in light of the subroutines vying for control.

Of course, where Gilbert has subroutines vying for control, human beings have conflicting motives, which serve as controlling causes of their behavior. Where Gilbert looks for an action that would best be explained by his subroutines, humans look for an action that would best be explained by their motives. That's why humans look to their motives – that is, to their desires and beliefs – as reasons for acting.

In deciding for reasons, the inner novelist plays the role that is ordinarily attributed to the self. A third conception of the self has therefore emerged. According to Dennett's conception of the self, with which I began, the self is the merely fictional protagonist of a self-narrator's autobiography. According to the second conception, the self is the autobiographer's reflective representation, which guides his actions as well as his speech. What has now emerged, however, is that control rests with the narrative module – the inner novelist, recording the subject's last step and declaring his next step, in a way that amounts to deciding for reasons. According to the third conception, then, the self is the narrator.

This third conception of the self no longer supports the skepticism of Dennett's initial conception. The protagonist of Gilbert's autobiography is no longer, as Dennett believes, a merely fictional character whose shoes cannot be filled by the actual author. Now that the robot has a central controller that makes decisions for reasons, he has a self, and so his story has come true.

Note that what fills the shoes of the protagonist in the story of Gilbert is the robot, not the robot's self. "Gilbert" is not the name of a self; it's the name of a unified agent who *has* a self, in the form of an inner locus of agential control. My current claim is that the self-narrating robot really is endowed with a self in this sense and can therefore live up to the portrait of the protagonist in his autobiography. He is endowed with a self because his inner narrator is a locus of control that unifies him as an agent by making decisions on the basis of reasons.

The self-narrating agent is a bit like an improvisational actor, enacting a role that he invents as he goes. The difference is that an improvisational actor usually invents and enacts a role that he is not playing in fact. His actions represent what they are not – actions other than themselves, performed out of motives other than his. By contrast, the self-narrator is an ingenuous improviser, inventing a role that expresses his actual motives in response to real events. He can improvise his actual role in these events because his motives take shape and produce behavior under the influence of his self-descriptions, which are therefore underdetermined by antecedent facts, so that he partly invents what he enacts.

Yet how can an agent act out invented self-descriptions without somehow falsifying them, by being or doing something other than is therein described? How can enacting a role fail to involve fakery or bad faith?

The answer is that when the agent invents descriptions to be enacted, he describes himself as the inventor-enactor of those descriptions. He describes himself as *hereby* heading for the supply closet or the library, thus describing his actions as flowing from these descriptions, as realizations thereof. The protagonist in his autobiography is therefore both fictive and factual – fictive, because his role is invented by the one who enacts it; factual, because it is the role of one inventing and enacting that role.

To be sure, a self-narrator can go beyond what is factual, if he applies self-descriptions whose autobiographical application won't make them true. Although he can sometimes tip the balance of his antecedent motives in favor of leaving the office by saying "I'm leaving," at other times he can't, and then a declaration of departure would be ineffectual – an instance of weakness of will. Alternatively, his motives for going home may already be sufficient to make him go home no matter what he says – in which case, "I'm leaving" is the only true thing for him to say. Within these constraints, however, the self-narrator retains considerable latitude for invention. Even if he is already determined to leave the office, he is probably capable of going home or going out for a drink, or perhaps just taking a walk, depending on what he writes into his story.

To this extent, I can endorse Dennett's claim that the self is a fictive character. Where I disagree with Dennett is over the claim that, being fictive, this character doesn't exist in fact. Dennett thinks the real-life author of an autobiography is significantly different from the character portrayed as the protagonist. I think that the author of an autobiography is just like the protagonist, since the protagonist is portrayed as a self-improvising character, the inventor-enactor of his own story – or, as I prefer to say, an autonomous agent.

My disagreement with Dennett over the truth-value of a human being's autobiography results from two subsidiary disagreements. On the one hand, Dennett believes that a human being has no central controller, whereas I believe that Dennett himself is committed to crediting a human being with a central controller, in the form of a narrative intelligence. On the other hand, Dennett believes that a human being's autobiography portrays his central controller as a "brain pearl" or Cartesian ego, whereas I believe that this autobiography portrays the central controller as the narrative intelligence that it is. We live up to our aspirations with respect to selfhood, then, partly because we have more of a self than Dennett expressly allows, and partly because we aspire to less than he thinks.

I have overlooked another disagreement with Dennett, which I should mention before closing. Although Dennett tries to deny the unity of the self-narrating agent, he commits himself expressly to the unity of the narrative – to the proposition that "We try to make all of our material cohere into a *single* good story."[33] Indeed, the unity of this narrative seems to account for the temporal unity of the purely fictional self in which Dennett believes. This fictional character remains one and the same self because he is the protagonist in one and the same continuing story.[34]

In my view, however, we tell many small, disconnected stories about ourselves – short episodes that do not get incorporated into our life-stories. The process of self-narration shapes our day-to-day lives in units as small as the eating of a meal, the answering of a phone, or even the scratching of an itch; but our life stories do not record every meal eaten, every phone answered, or every itch scratched. Because the narratives of these minor episodes are never unified into a single story, their protagonist cannot derive his unity from theirs. The agent who types this letter 'a' is the same person who cut his forefinger with that pocketknife in the summer of 1959, but not because there is any single narrative in which he figures as the protagonist of both episodes.

So when I describe the inner narrator as a unified self, I am not speaking of the temporal unity that joins a person to his past and future selves; I am speaking of agential unity, in virtue of which a person is self-governed, or autonomous. In my view, autonomy is not related to personal identity in such a way that a single entity plays the role of self in both phenomena: that which makes us self-governed is not that which makes us self-same through time.[35]

Notes

The material in this chapter was first presented to a seminar on the self, taught in the fall of 1999 at the University of Michigan. Versions of the chapter have been presented to the Philosophy Departments of the University of Pittsburgh, the University of Maryland, the University of Chicago, and the University of Göttingen; to a conference on Morality and the Arts at the University of California, Riverside, with John Martin Fischer serving as commentator; and as one of the Jerome Simon Lectures at the University of Toronto. I have received helpful comments from the audiences on these occasions as well as from Linda Brakel and Dan Dennett.

1. A list of philosophers who have held this view would include Charles Taylor (*Sources of the Self: The Making of the Modern Identity* [Cambridge, MA: Harvard University Press, 1989]; *Human Agency and Language* [Cambridge: Cambridge University Press, 1985]); Harry Frankfurt (*The Importance of What We Care About* [Cambridge: Cambridge University Press, 1987]); Christine Korsgaard (*The Sources of Normativity* [Cambridge: Cambridge University Press, 1996]; "Self-Constitution in the Ethics of Plato and Kant," *Journal of Ethics* 3 [1999]: 1–29); Tamar Schapiro ("What is a Child?" *Ethics* 109 [1999]: 715–38); and Michael Bratman ("Reflection, Planning, and Temporally Extended Agency," *Philosophical Review* 109 [2000]: 35–61).
2. See, especially, Schapiro.
3. See Daniel Dennett: "The Origins of Selves," *Cogito* 3 (1989): 163–73 [hereinafter OS]; "The Reality of Selves," in *Consciousness Explained* (Boston: Little, Brown and Company, 1991), Chapter 13 [RS]; "The Self as a Center of Narrative Gravity," in *Self and Consciousness: Multiple Perspectives*, eds., Frank S. Kessel, Pamela M. Cole, and Dale L. Johnson (Hillsdale, NJ: Erlbaum Associates,

1992), 103–115 [CNG]; with Nicholas Humphrey, "Speaking for Ourselves," reprinted in *Brainchildren: Essays on Designing Minds* (Cambridge, MA: MIT Press, 1998), 31–58 [SO].
4. Dennett describes his view as a "middle-ground position" on the question "whether there really are selves" (RS, 413).
5. CNG, 114–15.
6. I use the term "fictive" because, to my ear, it shares with "fictional" the sense of "invented" or "made up", but not the sense of "untrue." Those who do not already share these linguistic intuitions should take them as stipulated hereby.
7. RS, 424. See p. 423: "independently existing soul-pearls."
8. RS, 420.
9. RS, 420.
10. RS, 428.
11. RS, 422.
12. OS, 163.
13. RS, 429.
14. If the objection here is merely that writing a passable novel is an activity that is most perspicuously interpreted as the product of a conscious thinker, then Dennett can of course agree, since he believes that positing a conscious thinker, Gilbert, is the most perspicuous way of interpreting the novel-writing robot. What he denies is that writing a novel requires a real, conscious thinker of the sort that would be postulated by such an interpretation.
15. Quoted at notes 9–11.
16. RS, 418, quoted after n. 13.
17. See also OS, 167–68, and RS, 416, where Dennett remarks, "There is [. . .] no Oval Office in the anthill," just as he subsequently remarks that "there is no Oval Office in the brain" [RS, 429].
18. SO, 41. For another narrative-based analysis of MPD, see Valerie Gray Hardcastle and Owen Flanagan, "Mupltiplex vs. Multiple Selves: Distinguishing Dissociative Disorders," *The Monist* 82 (1999) 645–57.
19. CNG, 108. Note, then, that Dennett does not conceive of autobiographies as "entirely confabulated" narratives in which "anything goes" (Hardcastle and Flanagan, 650, 653).
20. Flanagan says, "[T]he self as represented has motivational bearing and behavioral effects. Often this motivational bearing is congruent with motivational tendencies that the entire system already has. In such cases, placing one's conception of the self into the motivational circuits enables certain gains in ongoing conscious control and in the fine-tuning of action" ("Multiple Identity," p. 140).
21. I discuss cases like these in "How to Share an Intention," *Philosophy and Phenomenological Research* 57 (1997): 29–50; and in *The Possibility of Practical Reason* (New York: Oxford University Press, 2000a).
22. Dennett almost strays into this second conception of the self. For example:

> A self, according to my theory, is not any old mathematical point, but an abstraction defined by the myriads of attributions and interpretations (including self-attributions

and self-interpretations) that have composed the biography of the living body whose Center of Narrative Gravity it is. As such, it plays a singularly important role in the ongoing cognitive economy of that living body, because, of all the things in the environment an active body must make mental models of, none is more crucial than the model the agent has of itself. [RS 426–27]

Dennett begins this passage by speaking of the self as an abstract object posited by the host's autobiography. But then he speaks of the self as playing "a singularly important role in the ongoing cognitive economy" of the host, and finally he describes it as "the model that the agent has of itself." At this point, it is unclear whether he is speaking of an abstract object or of the host's representation of it, which is a real element in the host's psychology, positioned to play a causal role in his mental economy.

23. Greenwald, A. G., Carnot, C. G., Beach, R., and Young, B., "Increasing Voting Behavior by Asking People if They Expect to Vote," *Journal of Applied Psychology*, 72 (1987): 315–18.
24. I explore this literature in "From Self-Psychology to Moral Philosophy," in *Action Theory and Freedom, Philosophical Perspectives* 14 (2000), 349–77. For a more recent philosophical discussion of this phenomenon, see Richard Moran, *Authority and Estrangement: An Essay on Self-Knowledge* (Princeton: Princeton University Press, 2001), 38 ff.
25. Schachter, S., and Singer, J. E., "Cognitive, Social and Physiological Determinants of Emotional States," *Psychological Review* 69 (1962): 379–99.
26. Brodt, S. E., and Zimbardo, P., "Modifying Shyness-Related Social Behavior Through Symptom Misattribution," *Journal of Personality and Social Psychology* 41 (1981): 437–49.
27. Berkowitz, L., and Turner, C., "Perceived Anger Level, Instigating Agent, and Aggression," in *Cognitive Alteration of Feeling States*, eds. H. London and R. E. Nisbett (Chicago: Aldine, 1972), 174–89; Zillman, E., Johnson. R. C., and Day, K. D., "Attribution of apparent arousal and proficiency of recovery for sympathetic activation affecting excitation transfer to aggressive behavior," *Journal of Experimental Social Psychology* 10 (1974): 503–15; Zillman, D., "Attribution and Misattribution of Excitatory Reactions," *New Directions in Attribution Research*, vol. 2, eds. John H. Harvey, William Ickes, and Robert F. Kidd (Hillsdale, NJ: Erlbaum, 1978), 335–68.
28. CNG, 114, quoted on p. 57.
29. See *Practical Reflection* (Princeton: Princeton University Press, 1989); http://www-personal.umich.edu~velleman/Practical_Reflection; and *The Possibility of Practical Reason* (Oxford: Oxford University Press, 2001).
30. For a detailed defense of this claim, see my "Epistemic Freedom," *Pacific Philosophical Quarterly* 70 (1989): 73–97; reprinted in *The Possibility of Practical Reason*.
31. CNG, 114.
32. But see my "Narrative Explanation," *The Philosophical Review* 112 (2003): 1–25.
33. CNG, 114 (quoted on p. 57), emphasis added.
34. This view is endorsed by Flanagan, "Multiple Identity," p. 136: "Augustine's *Confessions* is an autobiography. It is the story of a single self. This is established

in part because Augustine is able to produce an account that narratively links up the multifarious episodes of his life from the first-person point of view."

35. I argue for this view in "Identification and Identity," in *Contours of Agency*, a Festschrift for Harry Frankfurt, edited by Sarah Buss and Lee Overton (Cambridge, MA: MIT Press, 2002), 91–123.

4

Autonomy and Self-Identity

Marina A. L. Oshana

Introduction

In discussions of autonomous agency, much attention is paid to the psychological, social, and historical conditions the autonomous person must satisfy, and to the various epistemic and metaphysical phenomena that might jeopardize these conditions. Discussants assume, in ascribing autonomy to individuals, a "self" that is capable of acting, that this self has a coherent and sustained identity over time, and that the actor is "truly" or "deeply" herself in acting. A capacity for unimpaired critical self-reflection is included in standard accounts of autonomy as well. The task of self-reflection is to appraise aspects of a person's self, such as cognitive, affective, valuational, and dispositional states, as well as personal commitments, social roles, and ideals, to determine if these are components of the person's life with which the person "wholeheartedly identifies" or embraces without reservation so as to render them "authentic" to her.[1]

Accounts of autonomous agency vary in the details. For example, defenders of a liberal conception of autonomy might disagree about the nature of authenticity. Other philosophers repudiate all such depictions of the autonomous self on the grounds that they falsify the nature of the self, and the conditions of its identity and authenticity. Among postmodernists, for example, the charge arises that the assumption of a coherent self misrepresents persons in presupposing a permanency of identity, where in fact the identity of persons is pliant.[2] Communitarians charge that the ideal of authenticity, "of being true to myself and my particular way of being"[3] by an "inwardly generated" set of criteria is inaccurate because it overlooks the fundamentally dialogical character of human development. We become who we are through our interaction and conversations with others; "we define our identity always in dialogue with, sometimes in struggle against, the things our significant others want to see in us."[4]

In what follows, I am going to overlook concerns about whether traditional accounts of autonomy portray persons in an accurate fashion. My interest here is not in the question of whether a coherent and sustained identity is metaphysically or socially plausible, or even desirable. (I believe it is all three, but that is beside the point.) Rather, the task of this chapter is to assess carefully the role played by an agent's conception of herself, or her "self-identity," in accounts of autonomy, her conception being rooted in a pliant or stable identity notwithstanding.

I will explore four questions: One, what constitutes self-identity or an agent's conception of herself? Two, in what fashion is autonomous agency dependent upon and characterized in terms of the person's conception of herself? Three, insofar as a person's conception of herself is a component of her autonomy, must the agent endorse, or at least fail to repudiate, the elements constitutive of her self-conception? Four, when do the elements constitutive of a person's conception of herself impair autonomy? My objective in answering these questions is to show that having a self-conception is an essential component of being autonomous and, moreover, that an agent's self-conception need not be authentic in the manner traditional accounts describe if the agent is to be autonomous.

I The Concept of Self-Identity

Who am I and how do I conceive of myself? Since a person's self-conception may fail to reflect who she in fact is, these are different questions. The first question addresses the person's identity, while the second cites her self-identity or self-conception. An answer to the first question is found in what Amelie Rorty and David Wong call one's "central identity traits" – the characteristics and relationships that are integral to a person's nature, motives, and life-plans. Identity traits may consist of beliefs, preferences, values, articles of faith, dispositions of temperament, habits, commitments and ideals, as well as relationships, social roles, and biology. Those integral to a person's identity can be demarcated in several ways. Rorty and Wong note, first, that these tend to be characteristics upon which other aspects of oneself, such as one's predilection to certain beliefs, desires, attitudes, relationships, social roles, and actions depend. Second, inasmuch as one's identity encompasses a set of general ends and values, one's central identity traits guide practical deliberation, affecting a person's motives for action as well as the acts she performs and the manner of performance. Third, central traits such as gender and ethnicity animate social interaction by influencing the way a person is categorized and dealt with by others. Fourth, central traits include those dispositional and affective characteristics that dominate in situations that require coping with stress or conflict, characteristics that are, importantly, "the focus of self-evaluation and self-esteem."[5]

While these traits are not exhaustive of identity, certain of them provide the raw material out of which a conception of self emerges. One becomes aware of oneself – one's self-conception is thrown into relief – in the course of an intellectually, emotionally, and experientially oriented investigation of oneself.[6] This sort of inquiry "tend[s] to arise when there are problems of action and policy, when an "identity crisis" triggers an attempt to articulate an individual ... identity, particularly when there is disagreement about [its] characterization and importance."[7] Not every stage of this process occurs at a level of deliberative and conscious investigation; self-awareness can confront one uninvited. And some aspects central to one's self-conception or self-identity may be hidden from scrutiny. But I will use the phenomenon of deliberate investigation as an illustration of the manner in which one's conception of self emerges most explicitly and lucidly.

For example, one investigates the beliefs that could move one to act. Or one notices the sensations or emotions certain activities, relationships, and states of affairs elicit in oneself. One takes stock of the set of one's experiences, and appraises their value. Thus the task of becoming aware of oneself has a cognitive and a non-cognitive dimension. What emerges from this process of exploration is a picture of how one identifies oneself – that is, a self-conception.

Not every aspect of a person's self-conception draws from, or is constituted out of, one's central identity traits. One's self-conception may be inaccurate or confused, even if one's identity cannot be inaccurate. For example, my self-conception might include the belief that I am the present King of France. What unites some of the principal identity traits and provides them with their centrality to self-identity, as opposed to identity of a self more generally, is that each holds us in a peculiarly tenacious way. Their centrality to a person's self-conception is established by the fact that a person will regard herself as radically changed if the trait is lost or strongly modified. At root, how we conceive of ourselves is typified most readily in what we consider to be the ineliminable and intractable aspects of ourselves.

Ia Volitional Necessity

The concepts of the ineliminable, the intractable, and the unthinkable have been developed by Harry Frankfurt in a series of thoughtful and innovative essays. Frankfurt argues that a person's essential nature or identity as an agent is constituted by his necessary *personal* characteristics – certain ineliminable beliefs, desires, values, articles of faith, personal relationships, and so forth without which the person cannot be what he is – and these are characteristics of a person's will. Frankfurt states:

> To the extent that a person is controlled by his volitional necessities, there are certain things that he cannot help willing or cannot bring himself to do. These necessities substantially affect the actual course and character of his life. But they affect not only what he does: they limit the possibilities that are open to his will, that is, they determine what he cannot will and what he cannot help willing. Now the character of a person's will constitutes what he most centrally is. Accordingly, the volitional necessities that bind a person identify what he cannot help being... Just as the essence of a triangle consists in what it must be, so the essential nature of a person consists in what he must will. The boundaries of his will define his shape as a person.[8]

Frankfurt's discussion speaks to what I have called a person's self-conception or self-identity. He locates the core of self-identity in the will – that is, in the desires, preferences, and attachments a person wants to be motivated by. Specifically, self-identity is fashioned out of, and delineated by, certain types of higher-order desires – namely, those that we make ineliminable because of our evaluative commitment to them.[9] Frankfurt's idea is that we cannot help but will certain states of affairs because we care deeply – inextricably – about them. To do or to be otherwise is simply "unthinkable."

Assuming this is right, we each have a distinct volitional character by virtue of which we can make choices. Three questions arise. One, how is this volitional character disclosed to us? Two, what distinguishes the volitionally necessary aspects that constitute a person's self-conception, and not just her identity? Three, what is the nature of this necessitation?

A person's volitional character can be identified by employing the following thought experiment. The person asks herself: "What would I do if confronted with circumstances that tested my values, or required me to adjust my values? Which of those characteristics and attachments seemingly vital to my identity would I be willing to abandon even were I deeply conflicted about doing so? Finally, what would I not repudiate insofar as I remain the person I want to be?" By this test, one selects from the motivations that constrain her will, and thus her identity, those motives for action that constrain her because she cares about them. One arrives at a point where it is impossible, given one's self-conception, to be even weakly responsive to subjective reasons to alter those aspects central to who one considers oneself to be. Such aspects become subjectively ineliminable. To paraphrase Gerald Dworkin, it is by first raising the question of whether one will accept or reject certain characteristics of one's identity that a person's self-conception or self-identity is revealed; in discovering what she cannot help but accept or reject, a person defines her nature and takes responsibility for the kind of person she is.[10]

The variety of necessitation here is specified counterfactually. Volitional necessity is contextualized against the circumstances in which a person finds her will tested. The volitionally necessary aspects of identity typically become aspects of *self*-identity because they are authenticated, or embraced, or cared about. One's self-conception is conspicuous in those characteristics and attachments a person could not bring himself to part with even were he able to do so, in those actions he finds "inconceivable" to perform, and in those choices he considers "unthinkable," *insofar as he remains the person he is*. But it is a genuine form of necessitation nonetheless, given that the characteristics a person finds himself left with are ones without which he cannot be true to himself.

As a case in point, I know I could never abandon my mother to a life of great poverty, which would surely be her fate were I not to provide for her in a modest financial way. The locution "I could not live with myself" is apt, as is "I would not recognize myself." Suppose it was apparent that my mother was squandering her income on frivolous and impulsive purchases. This might constitute good reason to stop providing for her financially, since it would be obvious that her income was not being used in a way that alleviated her impoverishment. In this case, however, I would be more likely to seek the reason behind her conduct, and attempt to address it. If the behavior were out of character, I might insist that my mother seek counseling or medical assistance to determine whether the behavior resulted from a psychological or physiological impairment. Or if boredom and loneliness were factors, I might encourage her to seek the diversion of companionship and of pastimes I know her to enjoy.

One might object that while frivolous spending does not count as a strong enough reason to motivate me to stop providing for my mother, other reasons might do so. If I were presented with irrefutable evidence that my mother was using the income I sent her to supply her grandchild with dangerous and illicit drugs, I would surely be moved not only to deny her further assistance but to threaten to report her to the authorities as well. But my self-conception might well require – make volitionally necessary – that I act on the youngster's behalf in this case. No doubt I would feel some measure of guilt – I might even feel conflicted – and my decision would only come after I had exhausted all conceivable alternative avenues for altering my mother's behavior. The very fact that I experience this struggle signals the depth of commitment I feel toward the welfare of my mother and the depth of my concern that her needs are met. But I could not live with myself were I to continue to support her financially. The circumstances have changed, and mandate a change in response, but this change reflects who I am in a deep way.

Of course, should the situation remain as I originally described it, I could not remain true to myself – I would not recognize myself as the person I am – were I to withhold assistance from my mother. That action simply is not among my options in the original situation, even though I may have the motive, the occasion, and the ability to perform it: "Here I stand; I can do no other."[11]

I value the attachment to my parent in a way that contributes meaning to my life, and my valuing the attachment plays a role in the realization and sustenance of the conception of myself I embrace. Not providing financial assistance to my mother is an action to which I am averse, and happily so; this aversion is something I would not want to lose.[12] What is noteworthy for my autonomy is that in a manner of speaking, the aversion is irresistible: there are very few circumstances where I could overcome the aversion consistently with my self-conception. The responsiveness-to-reasons test establishes that where I do overcome the aversion, it is only because I cannot remain true to my self-conception by continuing to act in a beneficent way. To do so would signal a greater loss or a marked revision of my self-conception. But given the circumstances that typically obtain, the test establishes that *I* cannot gather the will to perform this action; *I* am volitionally limited by the things I care about in this special way – people, beliefs, values, affective states – and these limitations define, in part, who I consider myself to be.

More deeply, it may be impossible, given my self-conception, that I should form an intention to become the kind of person who could abandon her parent to poverty. Even if it were possible for me to consider acting in this way, I could not want *myself* to do so. Here I both "resist the effort to do what I remain deeply averse to doing" and resist the idea of being defined in any other way.[13] As Thomas Nagel claims in *The Possibility of Altruism*:

> There is nothing regrettable about finding oneself, in the last analysis, left with something which one cannot choose to accept or reject. What one is left with is probably just oneself, a core without which there could be no choice belonging to a person at all. Some unchosen restrictions on choice are among the conditions of its possibility.[14]

Ib Circumstantial Necessity

Certain components central to a person's nature may be inescapable, not because she cares about them and cannot imagine this being otherwise consistently with her self-conception, but because they are factors over whose presence in the person's life and effect on her life she has no say. Such factors may be described as ones acquired as the result of constitutive and circumstantial luck. These include certain idiosyncratic physical and mental abilities (strengths as well as afflictions), and the talents, temperament, gender, sex, ethnicity, and familial relationships that distinguish a person. For example, the attachment I have to my mother is one that depends on my biography. These aspects are doubly inescapable since one does not cultivate them – they are acquired by birth, biology, gender, and the like – and they invariably shape a person's identity.

The elements of identity that are inescapable in this sense interest me especially for two reasons. First, they force the question of the extent to which a person's self-identity is wedded to whatever happens to be her identity. For example, to what extent is a person's self-conception bound up with the inescapable fact that she is of mixed ethnicity yet demonstrably "African-American"? To what extent is a person's self-conception bound up with the inescapable fact that she is a woman? These aspects announce to the world who a person is whether or not she accepts these factors as fixing her self-identity. The phenomenon here is not that of volitional necessity. Most people cannot "forget themselves" with respect to the racial and gender classifications that bind them, but this is not because race and gender *do* constrain a person's will (though they *can* constrain a person's will).

Second, one may feel alienated from these traits, just as one may feel empowered by virtue of them. If a person would prefer that some of these factors did not contribute to her identity in the ways they do, the problem of alienation with respect to aspects of her self-conception arises. The question of interest, then, is this: If a person does not want her identity to include any number of the inescapable aspects of herself, is her self-identity undermined and in a way that vitiates her autonomy? This question brings into focus a point of disagreement between the views of self-identity and autonomy to which I subscribe, and the requirements of autonomy defended by mainstream theorists. It also points to a possible asymmetry between endorsement as an element of the *unthinkable*, or the volitionally necessary, and endorsement as an element of the *inescapable*, at the heart of which are the concepts of authenticity and its antithesis, alienation. I will address this issue shortly.

The point of this section has been to show that the unthinkable and the inescapable coalesce into something constitutive of a person's self-identity or self-conception. Some of these properties form a person's definite volitional character; they provide the limits that anchor her judgment and specify the requirements of her integrity.[15] Together, they form the basis for the self-conception she seeks to express. Some ineliminable factors are so essential to a person's self-conception that at a certain level, authenticity with respect to them ceases to be an issue.

II Why Autonomous Agency Depends Upon Having a Self-Conception

The concept of autonomy requires a ground, parameters that give the notion of self-directed choice and action plausibility and coherence. The practice of autonomy also calls for a ground, something that enables persons to guide their actions and choices. A person cannot embark upon a life of autonomy, and autonomous choice and action cannot commence nor be sustained, where she lacks a definite, if not fully articulate, set of objectives, preferences, or principles that enable her life-plans to be unequivocally his own. Without an antecedent moral, cognitive, and conative structure, we are "vacant of identifiable tendencies and constraint... unable to deliberate or to make conscientious decisions"[16]

Being autonomous requires first and foremost that a person have the capacity and the disposition to know her will and know which of her beliefs, desires, affective states, relationships, and so on are distinctive of and essential to her self-conception. Most importantly, the autonomous agent knows the aspects of her self-identity on which she can rely, or which she is confident will manifest and be effective, for better or for worse, as the circumstances mandate. The autonomous agent must recognize that these characteristics and attachments are central to who she is, and to how she perceives herself, and she must be familiar with the role they occupy in her world.

I am not claiming that an individual need carry her self-identity in stark relief at every moment, or even most of the time. Indeed, persons who are constantly attentive to themselves are not thought to possess a healthy consciousness of themselves but rather are self-conscious, or in a state that tends to disable self-motivated action. I *am* claiming that an absence of self-reflection, and an indifference to one's self-conception, eclipse autonomous agency. Agent autonomy consists in taking control of – or, better, ownership of – one's life.[17] Someone who does not, as a rule, acknowledge some cognitive, affective, attitudinal, and behavioral characteristics and attachments as part of her self-conception, nor concede the absence of others, and who lacks a desire for self-understanding, if not a capacity for self-evaluation, is not in a position to assume an active and authoritative voice in the direction of her life. This is because guiding one's life calls not just for a self, or an identifiable entity, but for an agent alive to herself as someone with a particular vision, with plans and expectations, concerns, values, and commitments that merit and invite a range of treatment on the part of others and that can be more or less successfully realized.[18] Having a self-conception provides some assurance – certainly not complete, but essential – that a person's governance over her life is her own.

It would appear, then, that a ground of autonomy would be one's self-conception – the goals, preferences, or principles of choice – aspects of the will – it would be unthinkable to abandon or to repudiate, as well as those constitutive and circumstantial elements it is impossible to escape. Without an antecedent self-conception, even one that is a work-in-progress, one cannot be autonomous. This is not because the characteristics constitutive of a person's self-conception mandate that her life-choices assume a certain shape or take a particular direction. It is because these supply a compass for finding the direction of action that best comports with what is emotionally, imaginatively, and cognitively meaningful to the agent.

III Autonomy and Alienation

The prototypical account of autonomy requires that a person conceive of herself as someone who can affect the world in light of a perspective and

n for life that is of her making. A corollary is that an autonomous
 nt takes responsibility for her self-identity. But what does taking
responsibility involve, and how does this occur? Specifically, must the
elements constitutive of a person's self-conception be authentic if she is
to take responsibility for her self-identity and thus for her autonomy?

"Authenticity" is a term employed widely among discussants of agent autonomy (and responsibility) to refer to a property of the constituents of personal autonomy. Authenticity is standardly taken to be a function of the structure of a person's cognitive states, conative states, or values, and, more recently, of the attitude of acceptance a person adopts toward the genesis of these cognitive states, conative states, or values. The idea is that a person is autonomous if she is moved by values, desires, beliefs, and attitudes that would withstand unimpaired self-scrutiny. Presumably, the legitimacy of a person's attachments, partnerships, ethnic and cultural identity, and social roles can also be authenticated for autonomy by similar tests. One simply asks how the person regards these phenomena when they are examined in an unblemished, critical light, or how the person would regard them were she to reflect upon their development and their effect upon her. Are they seen as aspects of herself to which she feels an affinity, or as roles she wants to occupy? Or does she feel disaffected and estranged from them, to the extent that she repudiates them? If the former, the story goes, the criterion of authenticity is met, and we can be secure in the thought that the elements that influence the direction of an agent's choices and actions are definitively the agent's own. The key for autonomy, thus, is whether or not the person feels alienated from those aspects of herself that affect her choices and actions.[19]

Making authenticity the hallmark of autonomy forces us to examine the status of those factors that contribute to our identity and to our self-conception in ways we cannot escape but that we wish fervently would play a less essential and focal role. Must a person endorse, be satisfied with, or at least fail to feel alienated from what is volitionally necessary and what is inescapable if these are to be included within her self-conception? Must a person endorse, be satisfied with, or at least fail to feel alienated from what is volitionally necessary and what is inescapable if the person is to be autonomous?

If, as I have suggested, volitional constraints upon a person's will reflect her self-conception because they survive a counterfactual thought-experiment test, then some version of authenticity would appear to be entailed. But in fact it is misleading to claim that the volitionally necessary aspects of identity typically become aspects of *self*-identity when and only when they are authenticated by a process of intentional, critical introspection and self-scrutiny. Frankfurt is vague on this point, but at times indicates that what provides volitional necessity with the anchoring or terminating stature it has (one is no longer free to raise the question "is this what I most want to do?") is precisely that volitional necessity does not presuppose the agent's scrutiny and active endorsement. (Indeed, a person might even find herself at odds with some of her deepest volitional commitments. I might wish, for example, that I were less constrained by my attachment to my mother. I do not think, however, that the knowledge that one is dissatisfied with the centrality certain volitional constraints occupy in one's self-concept need challenge autonomy. I will return to this point momentarily.)

Additionally, it may be preferable for the view of autonomy I defend that I make no use of authenticity in grounding volitional necessity and self-identity, given that I want ultimately to deny authenticity as a condition of autonomy. Thus John Santiago has questioned the necessity (not to mention the advisability) of relying on *any* aspect of Frankfurt's model of psychological autonomy in delineating the conditions for agent autonomy, preferring a more thoroughly social or "narrative" anchor for self-awareness than endorsement or authenticity provide. But I see no need to throw out the baby with the bath water – Frankfurtian accounts contribute a fruitful explanatory analysis of the psychological element of agent autonomy. The question to ask is not why allow volitional necessity a central role in self-identity and agential autonomy, but whether that role, as detailed here, relies on endorsement (explicitly or otherwise). I deny authenticity *qua* critically reflective endorsement or satisfaction.

Others might worry whether authenticity is ever a requirement of the inescapable circumstantial aspects of a person's self-conception. It is with respect to my views on this matter that Jennifer Hawkins has questioned whether the view of the self that I attribute to Frankfurt is correct.[20] Hawkins contends that Frankfurt only includes among the components of self-identity evaluative commitments and other motivational states. Mine is a wider notion of self-identity in that I include important descriptive items such as cultural aspects of the self, satisfaction with which or wholehearted commitment to which are irrelevant for autonomy, and so not, Hawkins contends, required by Frankfurt. If Hawkins is correct, then the target view of autonomy and authenticity I am criticizing is not Frankfurt's (and not Frankfurtian). But I believe Hawkins is incorrect: In the first place, Frankfurt includes among the elements of a person's self the non-optional characteristics and commitments that a person simply finds himself with, or discovers about himself; these are *foundational* to his higher-order evaluations rather than the product of such evaluations. An individual's more general evaluative commitments are invariably premised on aspects of the self such as race, gender, and sexual orientation.[21] Second, such aspects of the self are not merely descriptive, since the individual so described cannot avoid evaluating himself under these very descriptions. In both respects, descriptive elements such as race and gender are things a person must embrace, repudiate, or take some adjudicative stance toward. If the authenticity condition of autonomy is central to and exhaustive of Frankfurt's (and others') view of autonomy, and authenticity is not needed for autonomy, then the view must be revised.

In short, what is at issue here is whether the standard picture of authenticity can be of use for autonomy in cases where a person's self-identity is bound up with facts both inescapable and unwanted. Is a person's autonomy circumscribed, and her self-identity inauthentic, to the degree that the boundaries that define her (to herself and to the world) include factors she would prefer not fix her self-conception? In such cases, the person cannot help but identify herself via factors that she wishes did not occupy so central and essential a role in her self-conception. As Rorty and Wong rightly note, a person can acknowledge the centrality of characteristics and relations to her self-identity, and the tremendous social and psychological force of these, while valuing neither the characteristics and relations nor their centrality.[22]

Consider the phenomenon of race-consciousness, or awareness of the societal significance of one's race. For all the talk of color-blindness, and despite the fact that race is at best only a quasi-scientific concept, one's race is tremendously significant in so racially stratified a society as the United States. For persons who are not white, racial identity is so ingrained that one cannot, some have said, "forget oneself" or fail to be appreciative of one's racialized identity.[23] Forgetting one's race involves a lapse of self-awareness.

It would seem paradoxical, then, that a person could be capable of such lapses. An African-American woman such as myself might even be chronically guilty of such breaches if she were not alive to many of the norms of the African-American female sub-culture, though others were, and although she were reminded of these norms in the expectations of others. Arguably, being alive to one's racialized identity means accepting certain norms as appropriate standards for choice and action. But a person might appreciate her heritage and take pride in it (just as she might experience shame or embarrassment when members of the sub-culture behave badly), even while failing to be fully part of it. Suppose that being *culturally* black is not an aspect of a person's self-identity, although being African-American remains an inescapable part of that person's self-conception. In my own life, for example, race does not just anchor my identity – who I am. Race also anchors my self-conception, and how I regard myself at the same time it interferes with my self-conception. It anchors what I stand for, and what I stand behind, at the same time as it presents obstacles to my realization of these.

It may be impossible for an African-American woman who pursues a career in (say) philosophy to avoid seeing herself as an anomaly in a predominantly white (and male) profession. She will, like it or not, be confronted with the suspicion that she fails to adhere to certain norms of conduct that are expected of her. And her "failure" to appropriate the expected accoutrements of her racialized identity may come at substantial cost – suspicion or hostility from some members of the black community, curiosity or patronization from some members of the liberal white community, anger from those threatened by "uppity" behavior, by the fact that as a Black woman, she has apparently forgotten what she is supposed to be like. The Black female academic might feel pressed to explain herself, and she might experience a conflicted sense of self. But none of this necessarily comes at a cost of her autonomy, as we shall see.

A member of a racial minority whose professional and personal relationships are "out of place" will often assume a stance *vis-à-vis* her racialized identity that is marked by restlessness, if not by outright resistance. Following Frankfurt, the racial minority might not be *satisfied* with the central place this ineliminable and unchangeable aspect of herself occupies in her self-identity. For example, I would prefer that race did not so essentially inform my self-conception. If I am not actively alienated from this central identity trait, at least I fail to be wholehearted with respect to its being part of my self-conception. Persons like myself might not wish to be identified by some of the norms of the African-American female sub-culture, nor wish their self-conception to be bound up with these norms because of how they bind a person. Such norms bind *vis-à-vis* the false belief that African American women behave in an identifiable way. They bind by what K. Anthony Appiah calls the "scripted" or non-optional components of collective identity, the point of which is to supply a person's life with a certain "narrative unity."[24] These components consist of, I assume, certain values, behavioral norms, practices, and social expectations.[25]

One might resist this script, but not because the script is inescapable. Rather, one might resist it if one does not "choose to make *these* collective identities central to individual identities."[26] While such identity casting is socially attributed, it is not an identity every individual subjectively accepts.[27] I can say that while my racialized identity may be of impersonal value, any personal meaning I invest in it is not that of the collective identity. In terms suggested by Joseph Raz, my racialized identity is frequently a tie I find myself burdened with against my will, and which I would rather be without but from which I cannot shake myself free.[28] That I do not value this scripted identity does not mean that it is of a type that lacks value, since the value of a type of attachment "does not depend exclusively on the fact that those whose attachments they are embrace them willingly or with approval."[29] But that I do not choose to accept this scripted identity reveals an important component of my self-conception. It is unthinkable of me to embrace any script that would call upon me to define myself against a standard I disavow and wish to divest of personal value.[30]

I have claimed that a person's autonomy is grounded in her self-identity or self-conception, in those components of her identity she cannot repudiate without doing violence to the person she is. And race is very much an inescapable component in this sense. We cannot escape the racialized norms that define us, and that inform our self-concept, even where we regard these norms as alien. Consciously or not, welcome or not, one's racialized identity contravenes upon most aspects of one's self-conception. The concern is whether one can reconcile the person one takes herself to be with social expectations of who one is (and who one ought to be). Can a person, for example, be autonomous despite the fact that she does not endorse, or wholeheartedly identify with, an aspect of her character that is essential to her self-identity? Does the person who forgets her race, or gender, lack a "healthy, authentic psychology"?[31] Is such a person condemned to a diminished state of autonomy as a result of this forgetfulness?

IV How One's Self-Conception of the Ineliminable Might Impair Autonomy.

IVa Threats to Autonomy

I am not convinced that every instance of forgetting oneself, even where the object of one's lapse is as integral to a person's self-conception as is race, robs a person of a "healthy, authentic psychology." Suppose that I regarded neither my African-American heritage nor any accompanying norms as subjectively ineliminable aspects of my self-conception. This is perhaps an uncommon phenomenon, one that is difficult to maintain for precisely the reason that factors such as race are so entrenched in our society. But there are cases of persons for whom this is true, and one would be foolish to claim that this alone yields diminished autonomy. What would yield diminished autonomy would be to *deny* my African-American heritage and any associated norms their centrality in my public life and within the relational positions I occupy. By denying an essential identity-forming aspect, I would not only fail to attend to the manner in which racial narratives play out in social interaction but would falsify myself. This would signal a kind of self-betrayal or self-deception, an attempt to defeat my identity.[32] And the effect would be a kind of practical disability, making self-management a more complicated endeavor. But while self-betrayal and self-deception are disabling, they are very different phenomena from that of acknowledging, with eyes wide open, the experience of disaffectedness from certain aspects of one's self-conception.[33] The former injures autonomy, whereas the latter does not.

Acknowledgment of race aside, the fact that a person might wish to escape the grip of these scripted identities does not of itself gainsay autonomy any more than the fact that they are inescapable does so. Insofar as ineliminable and scripted characteristics of a person's self-conception such as racial identity and race consciousness impugn autonomy, they do so for reasons quite different from threats to psychological authenticity.

To understand this, we need to note that certain traits of character that are intractable aspects of one's self-conception – either because their absence is unthinkable, or because they are inescapable – are only part of what grounds our autonomy. For a person's self-conception might fail to represent accurately her social and psychological circumstances. And it is these circumstances and the type of life they permit that are germane to autonomy, not the fact that aspects such as racial identity and race consciousness are scripted, ineliminable, or unwanted.

To be autonomous is to stand in a certain position of authority over one's life with respect to others. Thus, if a person is to be autonomous, the circumstances to which he authentically assents must grant him the latitude to choose and to live in a self-directed fashion. Racial identity doesn't always allow this, as we all know. K. Anthony Appiah charges that in the context of a racist society, "it will not even be enough to require being treated with equal dignity despite being Black for that will require a concession that being Black counts naturally or to some degree against one's dignity. And so one will end up asking to be respected *as a Black*."[34] No matter how successful a person might be in liberating herself from the psychological appurtenances of race, or in maintaining race-consciousness free of racial self-consciousness, or in appropriating her racially scripted identity so as to give it the stamp of authenticity, race can encumber a person in a fashion antithetical to autonomy. Being Black in a racist society situates one in a position that narrows the range of one's autonomy even if being Black is not in itself antithetical to autonomy.

Autonomy requires that equilibrium of power be effected by the agent between herself and society. The possibility of effecting such equilibrium and the ease with which this is achieved depends largely on the energy that social navigation requires. The invasive quality of racial scripting to self-management stems from the fact that racial scripting more often than not is disabling in practice. It is not enough for autonomy that a person authentically embrace the social constraints mandated by the inescapable aspects of her life, for the fact that she finds these constraints acceptable does not mean they are acceptable or adequate for self-governance. One's self-conception as a member of a marginalized group, and the very grounds that nurture this self-conception, can frustrate autonomy, in part because autonomy calls for social recognition and respect of a sort "scripting" often impedes, even where one's self-conception is authentically her own as mainstream accounts require.

Accordingly, navigating the defined contours of one's racial identity may require that a person forget herself in order to be herself – in order to keep to the self-conception that affirms and sustains her autonomy. The African-American academic, for example, might be obliged to break away from the decorum expected of a black woman, if this decorum includes, say, eshewing scholarship on the work of colonial and pre-colonial European men, or forgoing intimate associations with white people. Forgetting oneself may be the way the African-American female academic must live if her autonomy is to flourish. Autonomy requires a person having the freedom to distance herself, or to step back, from the socially given roles and practices that contribute to her identity.

The lesson is not that the self-conception of the autonomous agent must be free of the effect of ineliminable forces upon identity such as race. Rather, the lesson is that because being autonomous requires, in typical cases, that a person be in a certain kind of social network, what can decide autonomy is the effect factors such as social roles and characteristics such as allegiance to members of one's racial group and a commitment to notions of correct racial behavior have on one's life. Being subject to racial profiling, for example, both by those in one's own race and by those in a dominant race, frustrates autonomy, even for the person who subjectively identifies with and values the centrality of race and of racialized norms in her self-conception.

IVb Why Authenticity Is Not Needed for Autonomy
I noted earlier that I part company with recent accounts of autonomy over the question of how the phenomena of authenticity and alienation affect self-identity, and thus agent autonomy. If autonomy calls for an absence of alienation, as mainstream accounts charge, then a person cannot be autonomous if she feels estranged from an aspect of her character that is essential to her self-conception. It is imperative that the force of this conclusion be appreciated. The point is not simply that a person will not be autonomous *vis-à-vis* some characteristic she happens to have. The point is that she will not be autonomous *simpliciter* because the characteristics from which she feels alienated and that she wishes to repudiate, but cannot, are essential to her self-conception and therefore, according to the views with which I am disagreeing, to her status as a self-directed individual.

I suspect this is not the conclusion defenders of the standard conception of autonomy want to adopt. Fortunately, it need not be our conclusion. The concept of autonomy need not militate against viewing a person as autonomous even if she is alienated from an aspect of her self-conception. I need not be satisfied with, or feel an affinity with, every aspect of my self-conception if I am to be autonomous. I may even be resigned to certain aspects of my self-conception. For example, I might be resigned to the fact that some choices – such as the choice not to help my mother – are unthinkable for me, and I may not endorse the fact that my will is inhibited in these ways. But this does not make me nonautonomous with respect to my self-identity. And a sensible account of autonomy can explain this. A sensible account of autonomy can explain both the essentiality of something like race to self-identity in a racist society and explain why something like race might be resisted as central to self-identity. It is central because it grounds choice and self-description; it is rejected because of the constraints upon self-navigation it creates. But since the standard account of autonomy as authenticity *qua* endorsement or absence of estrangement cannot adequately explain either, the standard account must be revised.

Authenticity demands more than is necessary for a plausible account of local autonomy – that is, of autonomy *vis-à-vis* one's choices – and one's propositional, affective, and relational states. Certainly there is a sense in which autonomy requires that a person not be disaffected from the entire corpus of those aspects of her life that are central to her self-identity. For if a person were disaffected to the point of denying these aspects as central to herself, we would be hard pressed to locate a core self-conception that grounds self-government. But as the phenomena of racial forgetting and rebellion against one's socially instituted racial identity show, a person can be autonomous despite the fact that she feels actively alienated from aspects of her character that are essential to who she is and how she conceives of herself. For this reason, I reject the idea that reflective endorsement of the inescapable aspects of one's identity or an absence of estrangement subsequent to critical scrutiny is a requirement of autonomy. What is required instead is the far weaker stipulation that a person be disposed to acknowledge the factors that configure her self-conception.[35]

Notes

This chapter is dedicated to the memory of my mother, Julie Oshana.

1. The concept of wholeheartedness is developed by Harry Frankfurt in "Identification and Wholeheartedness," *The Importance of What We Care About*, (Cambridge: Cambridge University Press, 1988). A discussion of the authenticity condition is found in Gerald Dworkin, *The Theory and Practice of Autonomy* (Cambridge: Cambridge University Press, 1988).
2. See Seyla Benhabib, *Situating the Self: Gender, Community and Postmodernism in Contemporary Ethics* (New York: Routledge, 1992).
3. Charles Taylor, "The Politics of Recognition," in Amy Gutmann, ed., *Multiculturalism* (Princeton, NJ: Princeton University Press, 1994), p. 28.
4. Taylor, ibid., p. 33. Diana Meyers draws a similar point in turning attention to the relational aspect of the self as autonomous in her chapter (2) "Decentralizing Autonomy: Five Faces of Selfhood" in the present volume.
5. Amelie O. Rorty and David Wong, "Aspects of Identity and Agency," in *Identity, Character, and Morality: Essays in Moral Psychology*, (Cambridge, MA: MIT Press, 1990), p. 20. Central identity traits "affect what is (perceptually, imaginatively, emotionally, and cognitively) salient to an agent... They affect the formation of habits, systems of beliefs and desires" (p. 26). The first criterion denotes the degree to which a trait has objective ramifications. I have appropriated the four criteria from among the classifications Rorty and Wong offer.
6. Charles Taylor contends that "identity is defined by our fundamental evaluations," which form "the indispensable foundation or horizon out of which we reflect and evaluate as persons." The quotation is from Taylor, "What is

Human Agency?" in T. Mischel, ed., The Self: Psychological and Philosophical Issues (Oxford: Blackwell, 1977). Rorty and Wong cite Taylor, as quoted at p. 30, *Identity, Character, and Morality: Essays in Moral Psychology.*
7. Rorty and Wong, "Aspects of Identity and Agency," p. 30, op.cit.
8. Harry Frankfurt, "On the Necessity of Ideals," in *Necessity, Volition, and Love* (Cambridge: Cambridge University Press, 1999), p. 113. Of course, one's self-conception is not settled only by volitionally necessary aspects of one's character. Certain cognitive and affective states that act as temporal signposts in our psychic and physical development (adolescence, questioning one's faith, coming to know oneself as suited or not suited for parenthood) also settle one's self-conception, though it is characteristic of these that they are stages, to disappear as our self-conception assumes a new form. Frankfurt does not employ the concept of the unthinkable to explicate an idea of one's self-identity, as I do here. But insofar as one's self-identity is (in part) predicated on one's essential nature, Frankfurt's discussion is instructive.
9. In my view, this commitment is one we discover as much as it is one we choose. One's self-identity is revealed as one comes to recognize what is unthinkable. Self-awareness, as Diana Meyers suggests, is as much a process of self-discovery as it is of self-definition. See her chapter (2) "Decentralizing Autonomy: Five Faces of Selfhood" in the present volume.
10. Gerald Dworkin, *The Theory and Practice of Autonomy*, p. 20, op. cit. As I have noted, one's self-conception might be unveiled by less deliberative mechanisms.
11. Martin Luther, *Speech at the Diet of Worms*, April 18, 1521.
12. Frankfurt states that "In cases of volitional necessity, the aversion [to perform an action] is not only irresistible; it is also in some sense endorsed by the person." See his "On the Necessity of Ideals," p. 111–12, and his "Autonomy, Necessity, and Love," pp. 129–41, also in *Necessity, Volition, and Love*, op. cit.
13. Frankfurt, "On the Necessity of Ideals", p. 112, op. cit.
14. Nagel, *The Possibility of Altruism* (Oxford, Clarendon Press, 1970), p. 23.
15. Following Frankfurt, "Rationality and the Unthinkable," in *The Importance of What We Care About* (Cambridge: Cambridge University Press, 1988), p. 179.
16. Frankfurt, "Rationality and the Unthinkable," p. 178, and "On the Necessity of Ideals," op. cit., p. 110.
17. The language of ownership is borrowed from Paul Benson, who claims that autonomy requires the agent to recognize herself as one who takes ownership, or as one who has the authority to answer for herself. See his chapter (5) "Taking Ownership: Authority and Voice in Autonomous Agency" in the present volume.
18. In correspondence, John Santiago questioned this, noting that one can lack an organizing principle for life and still be autonomous. (Meyers raises a similar point in her Chapter 2 in the present volume.) Santiago is correct, but I think a person's autonomy is likely to be more vulnerable if he is inattentive to his place in the world and the "map" he, rather than others, have authorized for that place.

19. In "The Faintest Passion," Frankfurt introduces the idea that authenticity requires that a person feel satisfied with the desires that move her to act. This represents a modification of (or, at least, an attempt to clarify) his earlier view that authenticity calls for wholehearted or decisive identification, but I shall ignore the nuances here. The point is that some manner of identification, and some absence of alienation, must be in place if authenticity and autonomy are to be secured. Wholeheartedness "consists in being fully satisfied that some attitude or psychic elements rather than others that inherently (non-contingently) conflict with them, should be among the causes and considerations that determine [his] cognitive, affective, attitudinal, and behavioral processes" (op. cit., p. 103). To be satisfied is to experience an absence of restlessness or resistance to one's condition, where this "derives from a person's understanding or evaluation of how things are with him" (ibid., 105). One is satisfied with the condition of the self when one "has no interest in bringing about a change in one's condition (even if a change would be willingly accepted) even if a change would make him better off" (ibid., 102).
20. Hawkins commented on an abridged version of this chapter for a session on "Autonomy" at the Pacific Division Meetings of the American Philosophical Association held in San Francisco in March, 2003.
21. In a sense, a person's self-conception antedates and informs the process of critical self-reflection. Perhaps one's self-conception is unveiled in the course of a critically self-reflective process, and what the person identifies with or fails to experience as alienating might offer an indication of how she regards herself. And a person might find that her self-conception is solidified in the course of critical self-reflection. But this unveiling subsequent to critical self-reflection does not establish or constitute a person's self-identity. What a person identifies with or repudiates is determined by who she already is. The effect of wholehearted identification or authenticity one experiences relative to one's cognitive and conative states, to one's physicality and to one's social attachments, depends largely on the self-conception brought to the process of reflective appraisal.
22. Rorty and Wong, "Aspects of Identity and Agency," p. 23, op. cit.
23. Anita A. Allen, "Forgetting Oneself," in Diana Tietjens Meyers, ed., *Feminists Rethink the Self* (Boulder, CO: Westview Press, 1996), pp. 104–123. My ideas on the phenomenon of forgetting oneself owe much to Allen's provocative essay. Forgetting oneself, as Allen tells it, "entails simultaneously remembering and not remembering your own identity as a person who accepts and adheres to" certain moral and non-moral norms and behavioral requirements. It is to fail to conform "our emotions, actions, and habits to certain socially instilled general prescriptive principles" that we have internalized and that are "constitutive of individuals situated in communal forms of life."(pp. 105 and 106, op. cit.) And what Charles Taylor calls "collective social identities" engender a certain consciousness of oneself, exemplified in one's attitude toward oneself and beliefs about oneself. See Taylor, pp. 32–3, in *Multiculturalism*, op. cit.

24. The idea of narrativity as a constitutive feature of agential identity is discussed by J. David Velleman in "The Self as Narrator," Chapter 3 in the present volume. Diana Meyers and Paul Benson offer different but correlated models of agential autonomy premised in part on an autobiographical narrative account of the agent. See their chapters (2 and 5, respectively) in the present volume.
25. As Anita Allen writes, "We are not so much born with race as born into race as a feature of our social worlds. Yet our racialized social worlds exert such an influence that we seldom entirely escape the pull of constitutive norms." Allen, "Forgetting Oneself", p. 120, op. cit. And K. Anthony Appiah remarks, "We make up selves from a tool kit of options made available by our culture and society." See his "Identity, Authenticity, Survival: Multicultural Societies and Social Reproduction," in *Multiculturalism*, op. cit., p. 155.
26. Appiah, "Identity, Authenticity, Survival: Multicultural Societies and Social Reproduction," p. 159, op. cit., my emphasis.
27. Rorty and Wong, "Aspects of Agency and Identity," p. 23, op. cit.
28. Joseph Raz, *Value, Respect, and Attachment* (Cambridge: Cambridge University Press, 2001), p. 17.
29. Raz, *Value*, ibid., p. 16.
30. One might charge that my *rejection* of a racialized identity grounded in certain norms is authentic, and that this is necessary for greater autonomy.
31. Allen, "Forgetting Oneself," p. 120, op. cit.
32. Frankfurt discusses the phenomenon of self-betrayal in "The Faintest Passion," especially section 3, pp. 97–98, op. cit. Raz raises a similar point: He remarks that identity-forming attachments "are the sources of meaning in one's life, and sources of responsibilities . . . They are normative because they engage our integrity. We must be true to who we are, true to it even as we try to change. Thus, identity-forming attachments are the organizing principles of our life . . . They give it shape as well as meaning. In all that, they are among the determinants of our individuality. And they are partly past dependent. To deny our past is to be false to ourselves." Raz, *Value, Respect, and Attachment*, p. 34, op. cit.
33. A certain measure of reconciliation between the agent and the aspects of her identity integral to her autonomy is thus necessary. But integration is not a sign of authenticity.
34. Appiah, "Identity, Authenticity, Survival: Multicultural Societies and Social Reproduction," p. 161, op. cit.
35. Earlier versions of this chapter were presented to the Philosophy Departments at Washington University in St. Louis and at the University of Florida. I am grateful to the audiences for their helpful remarks. I also thank David Copp, Jennifer Hawkins, John Santiago, and Sara Worley for their comments on ancestors of this chapter.

PART II

THE INTERPERSONAL

Personal Authority and Interpersonal Recognition

5

Taking Ownership

Authority and Voice in Autonomous Agency

Paul Benson

How can any of my actions genuinely be my own? How can they be more than just intentional performances, with whatever investment of my will that involves, but also belong to me in the special way that makes me autonomous in performing them? How, in other words, can any of my actions be my own in such a way that they arise from or manifest my capacities for self-governance?

The literature on (locally) autonomous agency[1] employs a number of metaphors to characterize the difference between merely intentional action and action that is, in the fullest sense,[2] the agent's own. Harry Frankfurt's metaphors are among the most vivid and compelling. A person who acts autonomously genuinely "participates" in the operation of her will, as opposed to being "estranged" from herself or being "a helpless or passive bystander to the forces that move" her.[3] Agents who act intentionally but without autonomy do not do what they "really want" to do; their effective volitions are "external to" or "outside" them.[4] The pervasive notion in this literature that persons who are autonomous in acting act upon wills that are fully their own or that really belong to them suggests an initial answer to the questions with which the chapter opened. I am autonomous in acting just when I *take ownership* of my actions, or at least have the unimpeded capability to take ownership of what I do and regularly exercise that capability.[5] But considerable mystery clings to this concept of taking ownership as applied to intentional agency. None of the best-known contemporary accounts of personal autonomy succeeds in dispelling this mystery satisfactorily. The aim of the chapter is to make a start at understanding better what it is to take ownership of one's actions.

Other theories of autonomy tend to conceive of taking ownership as a matter of establishing some special relationship between one's self and one's actions. To be autonomous in acting, according to these views, is to act on the basis of who one is, practically speaking, or what one stands for. At a minimum, autonomous agency is thought to consist in acting with a will from which one is not alienated or has not dissociated oneself. In the first section of the chapter, I explore some general problems with these identity-based theories. I then develop, in the second section, an alternative model for understanding agential ownership by examining the sort of authority and social position implicated in taking ownership of what one does. The distinctive authority involved in taking ownership does not depend on the authorization of agents' wills in relation to their reflective identities. Rather, this authority concerns agents' position to speak for their actions in the face of potential criticisms. In this model, autonomous agency turns out to bear normative, social, and discursive content. Personal autonomy is neither content-neutral nor individualistic in the ways many theories have supposed. Agents act for reasons; autonomous agents, who fully own their wills, act for reasons for which they possess a special authority to speak or answer.

The chapter's third section appeals to the concept of *self-authorization* in order to explain how the proposed model captures both the active and reflexive features of taking ownership. Agents take ownership of their actions and wills by claiming authority to speak for their intentions and conduct. The final section of the chapter briefly discusses the relation between attitudinal and objective elements of autonomy, and points toward the potential significance of the self-authorization account for liberal political theory. With respect to the latter, the chapter suggests that interpreting autonomous agency as a kind of socially situated self-authorization could support helpful responses to familiar complaints that liberalism is excessively individualistic or rationalistic or adopts an unduly narrow view of the social constitution of people's practical identities.

I Ownership and Practical Identity

The idea that agents can take ownership of their intentions and actions in virtue of the relation their acts have to their reflective practical concerns or values carries considerable intuitive appeal. According to this idea, I can bring my will and conduct within the compass of my agential ownership when my actions arise from or are incorporated within the sphere of what I really care about. Such actions are genuinely my *own* because they are appropriately related to my *identity* as a caring, reflectively willing creature. These relations to my practical identity constitute what I do as acts that *I* really perform.

Many types of identity-based theories of taking ownership have been proposed.[6] For our present purposes, it suffices to note four roughly delineated types. First, *identification theories*, such as those developed by Harry Frankfurt and more recently by Michael Bratman, hold that persons take ownership of what they do when they identify with the motives that lead them to act. Identification, according to Frankfurt, consists in structurally-defined reflective endorsement that is decisive or wholehearted, or in volitional necessities that the agent cannot help but reflectively endorse.[7]

Second, some theories concentrate on *evaluative self-disclosure*. For example, Gary Watson proposes that agents genuinely own their actions when those actions arise from their systematic evaluative commitments. Watson writes,

... if what I do flows from my values and ends, there is a ... sense in which my activities are inescapably my own: I am committed to them. As declarations of my adopted ends, they express what I'm about, my identity as an agent. They can be evaluated in distinctive ways (not just as welcome or unwelcome) because they themselves are exercises of my evaluative capacities.[8]

According to self-disclosure views, agents can express in their actions who they really are, practically speaking, without forming reflective states of identification with the particular volitions on which they act.

Nomy Arpaly and Timothy Schroeder set out a third type of identity-based theory.[9] They argue that identification and self-disclosure theories both wrongly presume that some privileged dimension of the self – whether it be capacities for decisive, wholehearted endorsement of volitions, or capacities to embrace and disclose systems of value – constitutes the "real self" for purposes of understanding agential ownership. Arpaly and Schroeder propose instead that agents genuinely own their actions just when those acts are produced by beliefs and desires that are well integrated within agents' whole personalities, where integration is a function of the psychological depth of these states.[10] This is a *whole-self* conception of ownership.[11]

Finally, a fourth kind of identity-based theory claims that *reflective non-alienation* accounts for the ownership that autonomous agents are capable of. This type of position holds that both identification and evaluative self-disclosure theories are too restrictive. Persons can be autonomous in acting without actually subjecting their motives to reflective scrutiny and without expressing any systemically embedded value judgments. But whole-self theories are too weak, the argument runs, because they ignore the historical development of well-integrated motives, which could include autonomy-undermining manipulation. This fourth kind of view, as developed by John Christman,[12] maintains that persons own their actions when they act on motives whose processes of development they would not resist, upon reflection, where such reflection would satisfy certain constraints of competence, minimal rationality, and the like. In such a theory, agents take ownership of their wills and actions just in case they do not, or (counterfactually) would not, *disown* them after suitable reflection upon their history. Since this fourth type of account, unlike the other three types of theory, does not locate agents' ownership of their actions in any actual type of relationship between agents' practical commitments and wills, reflective non-alienation accounts might be considered minimalist versions of identity-based interpretations of taking ownership.

It has often been noted that identity-based theories fail to supply sufficient conditions for autonomy. The processes or states of identification, evaluation, psychological integration, or (hypothetical) reflective scrutiny that are supposed to cement the connection between persons' wills and their practical identities can themselves come about through histories of brainwashing, trauma, pervasive social control, psychosis, and so on that intuitively undermine autonomy. Even reflective non-alienation theories that explicitly address autonomy-inhibiting histories of motivational development characteristically fail to suffice for autonomy. For, like the other types of theory, they presume at bottom that unimpeded reflection can underwrite autonomy no matter how undeveloped (due to immaturity or extreme apathy, say) or how malformed (due to mental illness or psychological abuse) the agent's practical self might be.[13]

Rarely has it been recognized that identity-based theories set forth conditions that are also too strong to be necessary for autonomy.[14] I can take ownership of my actions even when they do not align with who I am or what I stand for. Consider, for instance, trivial acts such as picking at a callus on my hand, swivelling my office chair, or snaring a distracting piece of lint off my desk, where these activities rise above the level of sub-intentional behaviors. These acts aren't worthy of reflective identification, don't express what really matters to me, and may well not arise from psychologically deep sources.[15] Trivial acts may come about through processes that would withstand reflective scrutiny, but the results of hypothetical reflection upon those processes hardly seem germane to my autonomy. In fact, upon reflection, I would (and do) feel quite alienated from the ways in which I am moved to do so many trivial, utterly insignificant things, especially as they fill up so much of my life. Yet, for all that, I am autonomous in performing them.

This argument about the problem that trivial, but autonomous, action poses for identity-based accounts is not merely a variation on the more familiar objection that those accounts cannot explain perversely-willed, autonomous agency. Perversity involves deciding to do what contravenes one's firmly endorsed value judgments, but without weak will. Perverse action can be autonomous. Some would find perversity to be an especially clear demonstration of the capability to take ownership of one's intentions. Identification theories and evaluative self-disclosure theories will have difficulty explaining this.[16] Whole-self and reflective non-alienation theories will have less trouble. Trivial action, however, presents a stumbling block to all of these theories because it directly challenges the connection they presume between what agents really care about and which actions they genuinely own.

A different problem for identity-based theories stems from the fact that they presume various ideals of integrated practical identity. Autonomous agents can take ownership of what they do even when their commitments and concerns conflict so deeply that they cannot be wholehearted, so long as the sources of their conflicts are so dear to them that they would not want, all things considered, to resolve them. Such persons are not ambivalent in the sense of being vacillating, muddle-headed, or indecisive. They are ambivalent *authentically*, for their internal practical divisions are fixed firmly in their mature, reflective self-understandings. María Lugones presents a compelling illustration of such authentic ambivalence in her discussion of the reasons why, as a Latina and a lesbian, she cannot adopt a coherent, unified practical identity.[17] Lugones is firmly committed, as a Latina, to struggling against racism. She is also strongly committed, as a lesbian, to participating in lesbian communities that offer alternatives to heterosexism. Yet neither of these commitments can be integrated satisfactorily with the other in present social circumstances. Cheshire Calhoun explains Lugones's dilemma: "Within Hispanic culture, lesbianism is an abomination. Within the lesbian community, Hispanic values and ways of living do not have central value. As a result, 'Latina lesbian' is not a coherent identity...."[18] The cultural situation Lugones faces leaves her no alternative but to maintain a divided identity,[19] not because of thoughtlessness, self-deception, or lack of self-control, but precisely because of her reflectiveness, integrity, and steadfast care. Lugones can nonetheless act reasonably and own what she does. Lugones has undoubtedly worked out strategies for living wisely with her evaluative disharmony, just as she has worked out ways to survive the multiple oppressions that bear down upon her.[20]

Identification theories cannot explain Lugones's autonomy, because she cannot be wholehearted in or resolutely satisfied with her reflective endorsements. Self-disclosure theories do no better, since they suppose that without a coherent evaluational standpoint, a person has no self to express. For instance, Lugones cannot display who she is, within the penumbra of her conflict, without also displaying who she is not. Arpaly and Schroeder's whole-self account maintains that well-integrated motives cannot be opposed to other psychologically deep beliefs and desires. By this standard, some of an authentically ambivalent person's core concerns cannot be sufficiently integrated within her personality to prompt autonomous action. This is counterintuitive. Finally, Christman's formulation of a reflective non-alienation theory likewise fails to make room for autonomy within authentic ambivalence. His position requires that agents "experience no manifest conflicts of desires or beliefs which significantly affect [their] behavior."[21] Nor are authentically ambivalent agents like reforming smokers who, Christman argues, can accept manifest conflict autonomously if they have a rational plan to overcome it.[22]

There is much more I could say here to develop these criticisms of theories that seek to root agential ownership in some special alignment between will and practical identity.[23] I hope these abbreviated remarks adequately convey the need for a different way of conceiving of autonomous agents' distinctive ownership of their conduct.

II Ownership and Authority

Notice that identity-based approaches interpret agential ownership as a matter of persons' having a certain authority over their will and conduct. Identification, evaluative self-disclosure, psychological integration, and critical reflection are purported to be constitutive means by which agents *authorize* their intentions as their own and thereby acquire genuine ownership of them. For instance, Frankfurt speaks of making particular motives "authoritative for the self" by endorsing or identifying with them.[24] Identifying with a motive, he says, should "endow it with greater authority or ... constitutive legitimacy."[25] It is plausible that agential ownership should consist in a sort of authorization, since ownership, in its ordinary senses, normally means having authority over the use or disposition of something. Like ordinary ownership, the authority involved in agential ownership is a normative affair. Much as owners' authority over their property need not coincide with their possessing *de facto* control over it, autonomous agents' authority as owners of their conduct does not consist simply in their having the power to perform it or not. Non-autonomous agents can have that power, too.

Although taking ownership plausibly consists in some kind of normative authorization, identity-based accounts go astray when they conceive of this authorization as directed toward particular motivational states (or their histories). For, as we have seen, the motives upon which autonomous agents act need not be authorized as belonging to or expressing what they really care about. Rather, these motives are their own, I propose, because autonomous agents have a certain authority in acting upon them. In other words, the authorization that constitutes autonomy is an authorization of *agents* with respect to their wills, not, in the first instance, authorization of their motives or courses of action. Identity-based theories are wrong not only in focusing so intently on persons' practical commitments, values, or personality integration; they are also mistaken to focus on the authenticity of particular motives, as opposed to the authority that agents claim in taking ownership of them.

This proposal finds confirmation in the fact that identity-based theories do much better at detecting impairments in particular volitions that inhibit autonomy than in locating wider features of agents and their social locations that diminish autonomy. For instance, identity-based accounts often detect successfully the effects on autonomy of recalcitrant, unendorsed motives that intrude upon the will. These theories are not well equipped, however, to explain why pervasive social conditioning of an Orwellian sort interferes with autonomy, or why histories of extreme abuse or mental illness or even the normal conditions of young childhood diminish autonomy (when they do not undermine reflective, intentional agency altogether).[26] I suggest that these latter cases affect autonomy because they modify agents' proper authorization as owners of their intentions, not because they give rise to particular motives that can be determined on independent grounds to be inauthentic.[27]

In addition to carrying some, as yet unexplained, normative content, the authorization of agential owners also has a social, or relational, dimension. Consider again the analogy with property ownership. The authority of property owners is relational on at least two levels.[28] First, owners' authority sets limits on what others can reasonably claim from the property. But rights of ownership are neither absolute nor inviolable. Owners' prerogatives can be qualified by others' needs and interests when they are serious and urgent enough. At the deeper level of justification, the authority, as well as the responsibilities, of ownership are carved out within a system of social institutions and relations in order to adjudicate, in a fair and reasonable manner, among people's competing claims to and interests in the material resources of the natural and artificial worlds. Practices of ownership are justified theoretically by the functions they serve within a fair system of social cooperation.

Similarly, agents' ownership of their conduct is embedded within a network of social relations and potential interpersonal claims. To have the authority of owning one's acts is to stand in a certain position with respect to others' potential expectations for one's conduct. Intuitively, this position is captured in the idea that those who take ownership of their intentions and actions are appropriately positioned to own up to them, or to speak for them. Even when autonomous agents lack the moral (or legal, and so on) understanding to be properly accountable or responsible for what they do, their ownership of their actions means that they have the authority to face potential criticism for what they do autonomously, to stand by their acts in the face of potential normative expectations.[29] This is so even when, as in cases of trivial action or authentic ambivalence, agent-owners do not stand wholeheartedly *for* what they do.

Identity-based accounts fail to discern this intrinsic social dimension of autonomy. In those accounts, social relations may influence causally the connections between identity and will that determine autonomy. Those accounts can also allow that the content of persons' practical concerns encompasses interpersonal relations. But they do not recognize any inherent, constitutive connection between agential ownership and persons' social relations. They entail the notion that persons can own their motives independently of their socially structured authority to stand by what they do. In this regard, my proposal contrasts with the constitutive individualism of other theories.[30]

The social dimension of agential ownership also exhibits the discursive significance of autonomous agents' distinctive authority. Autonomous agents specially own what they do in that they are properly positioned to give voice to their reasons for acting – to speak or answer for their acts, or to give account of them – should others call for their reasons. Their position does not depend upon their having privileged access to the conditions that best explain their behavior. Nor must autonomous agents be more proficient than others at constructing reasons that could justify their acts.[31] Rather, the special authority conveyed in local autonomy concerns who is properly situated to face and answer potential criticism. Autonomous agents are authorized to stand at the nodal point defined by the targeting of potential criticisms and the voicing of reasons in response.[32] Once more, autonomy does not guarantee that persons have the specific moral or legal competence to be fully accountable for what they do.[33]

The discursive dimension of agent-ownership loosely parallels the discursive import of property ownership. Other things being equal, the owner is the one who ultimately has the authority to speak for the disposition of her property or its consequences in the face of potential criticisms.[34] Furthermore, this discursive feature of autonomy reverses and clarifies the common intuition that autonomous acts have distinctive self-expressive powers. The common intuition, exemplified well in Watson's position, holds that autonomous acts reveal what agents really care about, as those acts (purportedly) have been (or would be) certified by those agents as what they really wanted to do. In line with my earlier criticism that identity-based theories focus too narrowly on particular motives and acts at the expense of agents, I would urge that the self-expression necessarily involved in autonomy consists in the self's displaying her regard for her own authority to speak for her actions, not the acts' being specially fit for displaying the person's practical self. My autonomous acts fully belong to me because, whether or not they manifest my values – and they well might not – I am the one duly positioned to serve as the voice for those acts. I possess this authority regardless of whether I really most wanted to perform them or would have refrained from rejecting them upon informed reflection. The next section examines how I come by this authority.

To review: I have identified three dimensions along which the framework I propose for interpreting agential ownership contrasts with identity-based theories. The proposed framework highlights autonomous agents' authority with respect to their will, rather than the authorization of particular motives as authentically their own; and my framework conceives of this authority as having both intrinsic social content and discursive import. At the same time, however, the idea that agents take ownership of what they do by gaining authority to speak, or answer, for their acts in the face of potential criticism can explain the notable intuitive plausibility of identity-based theories. The various considerations those theories attend to are normally also considerations that directly affect persons' fitness to give voice to their reasons for acting in response to potential challenges. Actions driven by motives that the agent reflectively rejects (or would reject) or by motives that conflict deeply with the agent's settled personality or with what she cares about are typically actions for which she lacks the authority to speak. Nevertheless, as I have maintained that identity-based theories fail to capture either necessary or sufficient conditions of autonomy, I freely concede that there can be marked discrepancies between persons' abilities to act on the basis of their reflective practical concerns and persons' authorization to speak or answer for what they do.

III Taking Ownership by Claiming Authority

The next task is to explain how the authorization of agents as potential answerers for their acts can incorporate two prominent features of taking ownership – namely, its active character and its reflexive character. If the expressions "making one's own" or "taking ownership" are apt, then autonomous agents' authority is not something they acquire passively. Autonomous agents must gain ownership with regard to their conduct because, in some sense, they actively claim or seize it.[35] Moreover, we need to explain autonomy's reflexivity. If the capacity to take ownership of what one does is to suffice for one's self-governance as an agent, then we should inquire how gaining authority to speak for one's actions also comprises self-rule, the self's governance of itself. I propose in this section that both the active and reflexive characters of agential ownership can be understood if agents' authority arises through their *self*-authorization.

As I begin to develop this proposal, it will be helpful to consider a case of heteronomy that illustrates some of the ways in which my account makes stronger demands than identity-based theories impose. This will clarify the significance of conceiving autonomous agents' authority in social and discursive terms. It will also bring to light my proposal's emphasis upon attitudinal elements of autonomous agency. I have already implied that my account sets more permissive conditions than identity-based theories in some respects, since it should tolerate the autonomy of agents who perform trivial acts or who act out of authentic ambivalence. Neither the triviality of an action nor authentically ambivalent commitments, in themselves, necessarily threaten the agent's authority to speak for her will and conduct. But my account also sets more restrictive standards for autonomy in other respects.

Persons who satisfy standard identity-based conditions of autonomy can nevertheless fail to take ownership of what they do because of their attitudes toward their social competence or worth. Occupying a position of authority to speak for one's intentions and acts seems to depend not only on one's objective fitness to play the social role of potential answerer, but also on one's regard for one's abilities and social position. I will sketch briefly an example that makes this point intuitively plausible before presenting a general argument for this idea by appealing to the role of self-authorization in autonomy.

Consider someone who, on the basis of race,[36] has systematically been treated as socially invisible, as lacking the dignity of a person and eligibility to participate in distinctively personal forms of relationship, such as citizenship, friendship, or familial love. For example, imagine someone brought up within racialized practices that embody many of the attitudes that sustained chattel slavery and, later, Jim Crow in the United States. If this person has been depersonalized consistently enough, and if the personal attachments that might have given her a sense of her own dignity have continually been shattered or degraded, then she might come to internalize her social invisibility. She might regard herself as unfit for the kinds of relationship for which only persons are eligible,[37] at least across many of the spheres of her social existence.[38]

Ralph Ellison constructs a voice for such internalized invisibility in *Invisible Man*.[39] In the novel's prologue, Ellison's unnamed protagonist remarks that others refuse to see him as anything but a figure in their nightmares, a phantom-like projection of their contradictory desires and fears. He observes that his invisibility to others has often made him doubt whether he really exists: "It's when you feel like this that, out of resentment, you begin to bump people back. And, let me confess, you feel that way most of the time. You ache with the need to convince yourself that you do exist in the real world."[40] This vivid, but anonymous, character struggles throughout the novel to secure some social basis that could support a confident sense of his own personal dignity, only to be driven into despair and "hibernation" in the forgotten cellar of a whites-only apartment building. He is keenly aware of the effects his internalized invisibility has had upon his ability to make his actions his own.

> I can hear you say, 'What a horrible, irresponsible bastard!' And you're right. I leap to agree with you. I am one of the most irresponsible beings that ever lived. Irresponsibility is part of my invisibility; any way you face it, it is a denial. But to whom can I be responsible, and why should I be, when you refuse to see me?[41]

The character's point is not simply that his prolonged social invisibility as a person has confounded his moral capacities, although he does concede this.[42] His concern is also that he cannot speak or answer for his actions since, having incorporated his invisibility to others in his own attitudes toward himself, he cannot take up the social position of answerer for his conduct. "Responsibility rests upon recognition,"[43] the character proclaims, signaling not only that the absence of social recognition he has had to endure as an object of racial contempt has infected his moral capacities from without, but also that his internalization of his invisibility – his failure to treat himself as having the full standing of a person – has corroded his autonomy from within.

Ellison's protagonist probably fails to meet the conditions of most identity-based accounts of autonomy. His mind is too divided for wholehearted identification or the like ("I became too snarled in the incompatible notions that buzzed within my brain"[44]). Setting aside his profound ambivalence, however, his invisibility to himself would not have to obstruct his ability to take ownership of his intentions by the standards of those accounts. His internalized social death *might* impede reflective endorsement of his will, the integration of his motives within his personality, or his ability to confront reflectively the actual history of his motives without deep alienation; but it *need* not carry those consequences. This is one reason why my account of autonomous agents' authority fares better than identity-based theories: it addresses directly the social and discursive dimensions of taking ownership that explain how internalized invisibility can defeat agents' capacities to take ownership of what they do.

Note that persons like Ellison's protagonist could suffer damaged autonomy stemming from their failure to treat themselves as having full personal worth, apart from whether others actually recognize them as persons. If persons gravely doubt or distrust their own capability or worthiness to face and respond to criticism, then they cannot take ownership for their actions, even if others treat them as fit to speak for their own reasons and decisions. Agents who feel dissociated from their actions, as Ellison's character does, are usually also victims of social invisibility (if they are not mentally ill). It is conceptually possible, however, to undergo invisibility-to-self without suffering non-recognition by others. The damaged autonomy of Ellison's protagonist is as much a function of his way of regarding himself as it is a function of others' treatment of him.[45]

Some ambiguities in the case of internalized invisibility call for clarification of the sense of authority which, I claim, is implicated in taking ownership.[46] First, autonomous agents' sense of their authority to speak for their will and action is not bound to the conventional social norms in relation to which (actual) others would be most likely to appraise them. The problem that internalized social death poses for the autonomy of

Ellison's protagonist is not that he feels unequipped to appreciate the normative domains in relation to which others would be likely to formulate evaluative responses to his actions. That would be a problem for his normative competence, and thus for his full accountability in the relevant normative domains, but not for his autonomy. What matters for his ability to take ownership of his conduct is that he be able to take up the authority to speak for his actions in response to potential challenges which, from *his own* evaluative standpoint, others might appropriately bring to his conduct.[47] The "invisible man's" autonomy has been damaged because, suffering serious doubt about his own personhood, he does not regard himself as worthy to answer for what he does by the normative standards that he accepts.

Furthermore, this means that agents' sense of their position as prospective voices for their actions can reasonably vary across normative domains. An agent may be debilitated by self-doubt in one normative context, yet take up a position to speak for her reasons within another normative sphere. This underscores the significance of acknowledging the social and discursive dimensions of agential ownership. A full specification of the constituents of a person's autonomy in some concrete situation would require specifying the normative domains with respect to which she properly claims the necessary authority to answer for her acts.

The example of internalized social invisibility supplies some intuitive ground for thinking that persons' attitudes toward their fitness and worthiness to be potential answerers for their acts can stand in the way of their having the authority to speak for what they do, and so can prevent them from being able to take ownership of their will and conduct. That persons' self-regard should figure in their autonomy is hardly surprising. We need a more general basis, however, for understanding why this particular sort of socially and normatively informed self-regard should matter for agents' authority as answerers. It might seem, after all, that having such authority does not depend on persons' attitudes toward whether or not they have it. The key to comprehending the significance of reflexive, first-person attitudes for autonomy lies in the active quality of agential ownership. Persons cannot acquire ownership of what they do, in the sense that pertains to autonomy, simply by finding themselves passively in the position of owners. This sort of ownership is necessarily active; we can have it only by *taking* it.[48] Most identity-based theories of agential ownership have also sought to elucidate its active character. Frankfurt, for instance, commonly speaks of "taking responsibility" for motives in order to underscore the active nature of decisive commitment or identification.[49]

In order to grant a duly active role for agents in possessing the authority to speak for their acts, we should conceive of this authority as depending, in part, upon an active process of authorization that autonomous agents enact upon themselves. Persons can occupy the position of potential answerers only if they *claim* authority as answerers. In other words, agents do not acquire the authority to speak for what they do solely by virtue of satisfying requirements external to their self-regard. They must also treat themselves as warranting that position of authority, and the complex of attitudes this involves must contribute actively to their actually having authority as answerers.[50]

The notion of self-authorization naturally arouses suspicion. It is reasonable to wonder whether actively treating oneself as having authority really differs from passively acknowledging that one meets independent, objective criteria of agential authority. It is sensible to question whether the psychological content of self-authorization will be too thick to be attributed plausibly to all free agents, especially in their trivial callus-picking or lint-snaring modes. Self-authorization might also seem to be too active, akin to the excessively voluntaristic existentialist maxim, "choose choice."[51] If the self-authorization that is to be necessary for the autonomy of deliberate actions must itself be a deliberate action, then a vicious regress might not be far off if self-authorizations are themselves actions to be performed autonomously.

These suspicions can be allayed, in part, by recognizing that treating oneself as being in an authoritative position to speak for one's actions, where this treatment is also a claiming of authority, is not altogether different from cases of third-person authorization. We sometimes invest authority in others explicitly and self-consciously by deliberately performing actions that, in the context at hand, we properly understand as investing authority. We often invest institutional authority in this way, for example; we assign, hire, appoint, delegate, promote. Other investments of authority are neither self-conscious and explicit nor formal. These commonly occur within interpersonal relationships, although they also take place within more formally structured, institutional settings. For instance, I can authorize my partner to speak for both of us on various matters without explicitly granting her this right. I might do so, in some contexts, just by choosing not to speak for myself, where both she and I understand that her authority to speak for me would not have obtained (other things being equal) had I not treated her as having that authority. In some contexts, I might authorize her without doing anything deliberately or self-consciously. I can invest her with authority to speak for me by virtue of my attitudes about her authority, given our shared understanding that my regard for her authority properly contributes to her actually having it. Thus, authorization (whether reflexive or not) may itself be a fully deliberate action; it may involve the performance of other actions without itself being a full-fledged action; or it may be a wholly attitudinal activity.[52]

These observations reveal how one's authorization of oneself as an answerer could be something other than merely a recognition of some independent, pre-existing authority one has to speak for one's conduct. One claims authority for oneself as a potential answerer only if one understands that one would not have this authority without treating oneself as having it. Moreover, it is not psychologically unrealistic to attribute self-authorization to all autonomous agents, even in their least reflective moments, because self-authorization can be entirely attitudinal, implicit, and un-self-conscious in most contexts. As I swivel in my office chair, I claim the authority to give account of my swivelling, or in effect have done so through broader claims to authority I have made in the past,[53] partly because I implicitly treat myself as having that authority, and understand that I would not possess it otherwise. (After all, why wouldn't I be in a position to answer for this?) Similarly, a worrisome regress of self-authorizations cannot get underway if self-authorization need not itself be a full-blown action and therefore need not be an action that autonomous agents perform autonomously.

There will, of course, be situations in which autonomous agents' claiming authority as potential answerers will be likely to take the form of explicit, deliberate actions. For instance, where people struggle to reconstitute their autonomy in the face of socially entrenched demoralization like that displayed in the earlier example of internalized invisibility, they may have to enact their claim to authority deliberately and perhaps in some public way in order to secure in their own minds their regard for their competence and worthiness to speak for themselves.[54] Self-authorization might also have to be enacted self-consciously in therapeutic contexts in order to overcome psychological barriers to patients' acquiring the requisite self-regard and understanding its importance. Some practice in deliberate self-authorization is also a common part of the social training whereby children come to develop the attitudes and capabilities necessary for full autonomy. Parents urge their children to treat themselves as fit and worthy to speak for what they do, and help them to grasp the often weighty practical implications of their dawning authority.[55] These cases of deliberate self-authorization do not, however, yield any general argument that self-authorization launches a vicious regress.

If the self-authorization that contributes to autonomy is not normally a full-blown action, and often does not involve performing other actions, then one might wonder how it can be active enough to explain taking ownership. First, to state what I have already implied, the active character of taking ownership that concerns me here is not a matter of deliberate action. Phenomena can be active in the sense of comprising motivated activities, for example, without being actions.[56] Recall that claiming authority for ourselves as ones who are in a position to speak for our conduct involves understanding that treating ourselves in this way is a necessary condition of our having such authority. Adopting the requisite attitudes toward ourselves plays an indispensable part in effecting our authorization as answerers, and we understand this. The conclusion of Ellison's *Invisible Man* can be read as making precisely this point, among others. The protagonist decides, notwithstanding his continuing invisibility, to end his hibernation, to "shake off the old skin," and to embrace the "possibility that even an invisible man has a socially responsible role to play."[57] The novel holds out the prospect that by taking a new stance toward his social position as an agent, the "invisible man" can take up the authority he formerly has lacked and so overcome, in some measure, "the true darkness [that] lies within [his] own mind."[58]

Second, the attitudes toward our own authority that contribute to our coming to possess it are potential objects of our reflection and decision making. While self-authorization typically transpires without reflection or decision, autonomous agents can reflectively scrutinize whether they should treat themselves as having the authority to speak for what they do, and they can decide to treat themselves as such (or not). Self-authorization is active, then, because it is an activity arising partly out of our self-regard, and it transpires within the reach of our capabilities to reflect, decide, and act.[59]

Third, self-authorization is active, because it normally involves taking responsibility for ourselves in a certain respect. When we invest someone with authority, we ordinarily hold that person accountable for how she exercises that authority (barring special circumstances that interfere with her capacity to be responsible). We expect her to answer for her use of her authority. Accordingly, when we claim authority to answer for our actions, we normally place ourselves under a demand that we answer for how we exercise that authority. Autonomous agents typically hold themselves accountable as answerers. This explains the widespread view that taking ownership of our actions is also a matter of taking responsibility, although this is not a conceptual necessity, according to my account.[60] Since taking responsibility for ourselves as answerers is something in which we are engaged actively even when we do not do it deliberately, this exhibits a further active dimension of self-authorization.

I have proposed that persons' authorization to speak for their actions can reflect both the active and the reflexive character of taking ownership because agents assume such authority for themselves when they act autonomously. The distinctive authority that autonomous agents possess in relation to their decisions and acts arises in part from the way they treat themselves. In this manner, my suggestion that we think of autonomy in light of normative, relational, and discursive authorization keeps faith with the fundamental conviction that autonomy is the self's governance of itself. The role of self-authorization in autonomy also explains our intuitive conviction that internalized invisibility can undermine autonomy. Agents can be prevented from taking ownership of what they do, independent of the conditions set out in identity-based theories, because their social circumstances lead them to withdraw their claim to authority as answerers or inhibit them from ever treating themselves in the first place as sufficiently competent and worthy to speak for their actions.

IV Objective Constraints and Political Significance

That the self-authorization account I propose must incorporate some objective constraints on autonomy becomes clear when we consider that agents' attitudinal regard for their own competence and worthiness to answer for their acts can be developed through histories that plainly disrupt autonomy. For instance, coming to trust our capabilities for reflection or for self-regulative adjustment of our intentions in an entirely unreasoned way – say, on the basis of unnoticed manipulation by others that bypasses our faculties of rational consideration (and that we have not deliberately arranged beforehand) – evidently does not sustain our ownership of what we do. In order to succeed in claiming authority for ourselves to speak for what we do, it is not enough simply that we treat ourselves as having this authority and understand that treating ourselves in this way is a precondition of our actually having it. It is also necessary that we *properly* treat ourselves as fit and worthy to possess such authority, where the objective elements of such propriety constrain the attitudinal aspects of autonomy I have been discussing.

One way to discern the conditions under which treating ourselves as having agential authority can actually succeed in conveying authority is to consider what kinds of revelation about the circumstances under which our attitudes were formed would, upon rational consideration, typically undermine our sense of our competence and worthiness as answerers. Applying this criterion leads to at least four sorts of objective constraints on autonomy: first, that agents' attitudes toward their own capabilities and worthiness to function as answerers be formed in a suitably rational way on the basis of their evidence;[61] second, that agents not be rendered incapable of acquiring otherwise socially available information that would be practically germane to their decisions (as in societies dominated by Orwellian propaganda); third, that agents' attitudes not be modified through processes that circumvent their capacities for rational consideration, broadly construed[62] (as in forcible mind control); and fourth, that the norms in relation to which agents regard themselves as capable of articulating their reasons for acting be publicly shareable, even if not actually publicly instantiated. Space does not permit discussion of these constraints here.[63]

The theoretical import of these constraints is, in part, that they hold out the promise of explaining more traditional components of autonomy having to do with the character of agents' capacities for reflection, their access to information, or their ability to regulate their intentions. Hence, I hope in future work to show that approaching the subject of autonomous agency by inquiring first into persons' authority to speak for their conduct will also provide a way to understand these more familiar features of autonomous agency.[64] Moreover, I suspect that attending to the normative, relational, and discursive dimensions of autonomy brought to light in the proposed self-authorization account will be instructive for efforts in political philosophy to combat some familiar complaints against liberalism. Liberalism has long been accused of being excessively individualistic in its politics, its accounts of value, and its presumed understandings of selfhood. These charges have only become more trenchant with the rising prominence of communitarianism over the past two decades. Much work has been done to address these objections, but too little of it has concentrated on the purportedly individualistic character of personal autonomy. The social and discursive dimensions of autonomy, as I have begun to describe them, promise to be revealing when considered in this light. The position of authority that autonomous agents claim for themselves is, I have argued, socially situated and relationally structured; both the capabilities and attitudes this position demands concern interpersonal exchange governed by publicly shareable norms. There is nothing unduly individualistic about the conception of selfhood this view might suggest. Nor does this understanding of autonomy promote some asocial, atomized view of human well-being or political life.

The self-authorization account does not merely enable us to recognize many respects in which interpersonal relationships and social practices contribute causally to the development of capacities for autonomy.[65] My account also shows that social and discursive elements belong intrinsically to autonomous agency. This suggests that liberalism might properly claim the resources not only to appreciate the causal reach of persons' social formation and dependence but also to respect the constitutive depth of human sociality.

The attitudinal aspects of autonomy might also give liberal theories more to say in response to charges that liberalism requires a universalizing, impartialist perspective from which to apprehend the rights and duties of citizenship, a perspective that cannot discern the political meanings of socially-defined differences among persons and that tends toward narrow, rationalist abstraction in its view of political agency.[66] By attending to agents' regard for their own authority to speak for their actions, the self-authorization account asks us to take seriously persons' specific, multifaceted perspectives on their agency. My earlier discussion of Ellison's *Invisible Man* reveals that this account can face head-on the complex, socially situated character of a person's agency, even in circumstances of oppression. By focusing on agents' attitudes toward their ability to speak for their decisions and actions, this view may also provide liberalism with richer resources for appreciating demands for political voice and recognition in relation to the value of personal autonomy. Moreover, we can escape the rationalistic connotations of much liberal theorizing by admitting the place of emotionally textured, reflexive attitudes in persons' capacity to take ownership of what they do. The self-authorization account also avoids excessive rationalism by permitting descriptions of autonomous agents' powers of reflection and self-regulation that do not revolve around rarefied intellectual skills of detachment and analysis.[67]

The self-authorization view of autonomy does not mandate liberal politics, of course. Nor does it specify an interpretation of political rights to individual or collective autonomy. But this view's recognition of the norm-laden, relationally and discursively structured features of taking ownership of our actions suits it well to the task of appreciating the character of personal agency within a liberal polity.

A final observation is in order. My case against identity-based theories of autonomy is not independent of the reasons why my alternative account of taking agential ownership might assist liberal theorists in responding to communitarian, contextualist, or post-modernist criticisms. The perception that liberalism depends upon unacceptable strains of individualism, universalism, impartialism, or rationalism tends to be bolstered by the representations of autonomous agency that emerge from identity-based theories. Those theories portray autonomous agents as being capable of various sorts of decisiveness, motivational or evaluative coherence, personality integration, or reflective self-acceptance that can readily be fashioned, fairly or unfairly, as targets for liberalism's critics. In presenting an alternative to these presumptions that admits trivial acts and profoundly divided agents into the realm of autonomy, the self-authorization account is rendered a less ready target for anti-liberal attacks.[68]

Notes

1. I am interested in local autonomy, the condition of being self-governing in the performance of particular actions and the formation of the particular intentions that motivate them. I am not concerned directly with the global notion of autonomy, which involves the ability to exercise authentic, reflective self-control over extended portions of one's life. Prominent theorists who construe autonomy in a global manner include Gerald Dworkin, *The Theory and Practice of Autonomy* (Cambridge: Cambridge University Press, 1988); Lawrence Haworth, *Autonomy: An Essay in Philosophical Psychology and Ethics* (New Haven, CT: Yale University Press, 1986); Diana T. Meyers, *Self, Society, and Personal Choice* (New York: Columbia University Press, 1989); Marina A. L. Oshana, "Personal Autonomy and Society," *Journal of Social Philosophy* 29 (1998): 81–102; and Robert Young, *Personal Autonomy: Beyond Negative and Positive Liberty* (New York: St. Martin's Press, 1986). For an argument that local autonomy is a more basic concept than global autonomy, see John Christman, "Autonomy and Personal History," *Canadian Journal of Philosophy* 21 (1991): 1–24, at 2–4.
2. Cf. Harry Frankfurt's distinction between one's having a desire and "the fact that the desire is in the fullest sense" one's own. "Identification and Wholeheartedness," reprinted in *The Importance of What We Care About* (Cambridge: Cambridge University Press, 1988), pp. 159–76, at 170.
3. "Freedom of the Will and the Concept of a Person," reprinted in *The Importance of What We Care About*, pp. 11–25, at 21, 22.
4. Frankfurt, "Identification and Wholeheartedness," p. 165, 166. Also see "Identification and Externality," reprinted in *The Importance of What We Care About*, pp. 58–68, esp. at 64–8.
5. Local autonomy might in this way depend upon some more global condition. For our present purposes, I am interested both in the actual condition of being autonomous in acting and the capabilities necessary for being self-ruling in action. Cf. Joel Feinberg's distinctions among four concepts of autonomy in *Harm to Self* (New York: Oxford University Press, 1986), pp. 27–51.

6. Many of these theories were developed as accounts of free agency, free will, or moral responsibility, not personal autonomy. Nevertheless, because these theories all endeavor to interpret agential ownership, they can fairly be presented as accounts of autonomous agency. As will become clear, I am less interested in the specific features of these theories than in their general approaches to the relation between ownership and practical identity. For further examination of the relation between autonomy and identity, see Marina Oshana's Chapter (4) in the present volume.
7. For the main variations of Frankfurt's understanding of identification, see especially Harry G. Frankfurt, "Freedom of the Will and the Concept of a Person"; "Identification and Wholeheartedness"; "The Faintest Passion," reprinted in *Necessity, Volition, and Love* (Cambridge: Cambridge University Press, 1999), pp. 95–107; and "On the Necessity of Ideals," reprinted in *Necessity, Volition, and Love*, pp. 108–16. Bratman attempts to understand identification by way of decisions to treat motives as reason-giving, where the agent is satisfied with such decisions. See Michael E. Bratman, "Identification, Decision, and Treating as a Reason," *Philosophical Topics* 24 (1996): 1–18.
8. "Two Faces of Responsibility," *Philosophical Topics* 24 (1996): 227–48, at 233. Also cf. Watson's "Free Agency," *Journal of Philosophy* 72 (1975): 205–20. Susan Wolf also seems to think that some kind of evaluative self-disclosure is necessary, though not sufficient, for autonomy. See her discussion of the relation between "real self views," such as Watson's, and her own "reason view" in *Freedom within Reason* (New York: Oxford University Press, 1990), pp. 74–5.
9. "Praise, Blame, and the Whole Self," *Philosophical Studies* 93 (1999): 161–88.
10. *Ibid.*, pp. 171–5.
11. Also see Robert Noggle's treatment of psychological integration and personal autonomy in "Kantian Respect and Particular Persons," *Canadian Journal of Philosophy* 29 (1999): 449–77.
12. In addition to Christman's chapter (14) in this volume, see "Autonomy and Personal History"; "Defending Historical Autonomy: A Reply to Professor Mele," *Canadian Journal of Philosophy* 23 (1993): 281–90; and "Liberalism, Autonomy, and Self-Transformation," *Social Theory and Practice* 27 (2001): 185–206, at 200–6.
13. For more thorough development of this criticism as applied to Christman's theory, see my "Autonomy and Oppressive Socialization," *Social Theory and Practice* 17 (1991): 385–408; and section 3.4 of my *Answering for Ourselves: The Place of Self-Worth in Free Agency* (in progress).
14. A prominent exception is Sarah Buss, "Autonomy Reconsidered," in *Midwest Studies in Philosophy*, vol. 19, eds. Peter A. French et al. (South Bend, IN: University of Notre Dame Press, 1994), pp. 95–121. See also Diana T. Meyers's chapter (2) in this volume, in which she criticizes autonomy theorists' preoccupation with "the self-as-unitary."
15. In calling such actions trivial, I do not mean to suggest that they fall altogether outside the reach of normative assessment. For a persuasive case that even

such actions fall within the scope of moral evaluation, see Samuel Scheffler, *Human Morality* (New York: Oxford University Press, 1992), chapter 2.
16. See Gary Watson's discussion of "perverse cases" in "Free Action and Free Will," *Mind* 96 (1987): 145–72, at 150.
17. See María Lugones, "Hispaneando y Lesbiando: On Sarah Hoagland's *Lesbian Ethics*," *Hypatia* 5 (1990): 138–46. Also see her "Playfulness, 'World'-travelling, and Loving Perception," *Hypatia* 2 (1987): 3–19; and "On the Logic of Pluralist Feminism," in *Feminist Ethics*, ed. Claudia Card (Lawrence, KS: University Press of Kansas, 1991), pp. 35–44. Diana Meyers's discussion of intersectional identity and authentic selfhood is also helpful. See "Intersectional Identity and the Authentic Self?: Opposites Attract!" in *Relational Autonomy: Feminist Perspectives on Autonomy, Agency, and the Social Self*, eds. C. Mackenzie and N. Stoljar (New York: Oxford University Press, 2000), pp. 151–80.
18. Cheshire Calhoun, "Standing for Something," *Journal of Philosophy* 92 (1995): 235–60, at 239.
19. Lugones prefers to characterize herself as having plural or multiple selves, not simply a divided self. However, she grants that these selves can establish connections with each other; they can communicate with and understand one another, as well as critically evaluate each other. See "Hispaneando y Lesbiando," pp. 144–5. Because both of these "selves" must contribute to Lugones's practical decision-making and to her action, I prefer to regard them as different evaluative sub-systems of a single self. For related discussion of the role of practical deliberation and agency in constituting personal identity over time, see Christine M. Korsgaard, "Personal Identity and the Unity of Agency: A Kantian Response to Parfit," *Philosophy and Public Affairs* 18 (1989): 101–32. Amy Mullin offers other criticisms of the tendency to represent divided identities as multiple selves in "Selves, Diverse and Divided: Can Feminists Have Diversity without Multiplicity?" *Hypatia* 10 (1995): 1–31.
20. Cf. Meyers's discussion of "the self-as-divided" in her chapter (2) in the present volume.
21. "Defending Historical Autonomy," p. 288.
22. *Ibid.*, pp. 287–8. Christman's chapter (14) in the present volume points toward a change in his interpretation of ambivalence.
23. See Benson, *Answering for Ourselves* (in progress), chapter 3.
24. "Identification and Wholeheartedness," p. 175.
25. *Ibid.*, p. 166.
26. Note that Wolf uses similar examples to illustrate the inadequacy of "real self views" of freedom and responsibility. *Freedom within Reason*, p. 37.
27. See the discussion of internalized social invisibility in Section III following.
28. Another level of relationality, which I do not discuss, involves the way in which social relations shape the emergence of specific rights from more fundamental ones. See Richard Dagger, *Civic Virtues: Rights, Citizenship, and Republican Liberalism* (New York: Oxford University Press, 1997), pp. 31–6.
29. This idea connects forward- and backward-looking aspects of agency in an interesting way. According to a more standard view, autonomous agents can be in a position retrospectively to stand by what they have done only because

they have prospectively defined or determined themselves in performing their actions. My proposal reverses this relationship. As agents autonomously decide to act, and so face forward into the futures they create, they do so by virtue of occupying a position of ownership that subsequently enables them to look back at what they have done and serve as potential answerers for it.

30. This is not to deny that identity-based views of ownership might incorporate social, or relational, theories of mind, intentional agency, or value. My point is only that these views do not suppose that autonomy *per se* has anything more than a contingent dependence on agents' social situation. For other treatments of autonomy's relationality see the chapters by Meyers (2), Oshana (4), Anderson and Honneth (6), and Friedman (7) in the present volume.

31. Of course, the fact that autonomy does not entail privileged epistemic or justificatory capabilities does not mean that autonomous agents might have little or no understanding of their reasons for acting.

32. The idea that autonomous agency consists in being properly positioned, or having the authority, to speak or answer for one's reasons may seem confusing. For we are used to thinking that a person's authority to speak for her action depends on some prior fact about her being autonomous in performing the action. Thus, my proposal may strike some as being circular. Another instance of circularity could also appear to be involved. For example, if agents' authority to speak for their conduct is thought to depend upon their owing others an account of their reasons, then my view could seem to presuppose autonomy in order to explain it, since having this obligation to account for their actions might presuppose that the agents acted autonomously. As should become clearer in the next section, my position is that it is agents appropriately claiming the authority to speak for their actions that renders them autonomous in performing those actions, and hence potentially subject to an obligation to answer for them. The conditions that explain what it is to take up this authority and to do so appropriately therefore constitute autonomy, rather than presupposing it.

33. Christman's chapter (14) in the present volume presents a related political argument for the significance of persons being placed in a position to speak for themselves.

34. Of course, this authority is transferable and subject to delegation in ways that personal autonomy is not.

35. I am grateful to Sigrun Svavarsdottir for suggesting the terminology of "claiming" or "seizing" authority.

36. Or the socially accepted attribution of a racial identity. Sally Haslanger offers a helpful analysis of what it means to belong to a racialized group in "Gender and Race: (What) Are They? (What) Do We Want Them To Be?" *Noûs* 34 (2000): 31–55. Also see K. Anthony Appiah's discussion of racial identity in "Race, Culture, Identity: Misunderstood Connections," in K. Anthony Appiah and Amy Gutmann, *Color Conscious: The Political Morality of Race* (Princeton: Princeton University Press, 1996), esp. pp. 74–105.

37. I do not address here the various forms that such self-regard might take. Robin Dillon has usefully argued that such instances of damaged self-respect

need not involve persons' failures to understand intellectually their merit or their status as persons. Rather, persons may suffer damaged "basal self-respect," which concerns their emotionally laden, non-propositional, prereflective grasp of their worth. See Dillon's "Self-Respect: Moral, Emotional, Political," *Ethics* 107 (1997): 226–49.

38. It may be psychologically impossible for a person to be entirely invisible to all others as a person. Accounts of slavery in the United States suggest, for instance, that even those slaves who internalized many of the conventional justifications for slavery never entirely internalized their slave-status. For one thing, many slaves lived or interacted with other slaves for whom their personhood was not in question. In his comparative analysis of slavery across many cultures, Orlando Patterson writes, "There is absolutely no evidence from the long and dismal annals of slavery to suggest that any group of slaves ever internalized the conception of degradation held by their masters. To be dishonored – and to sense, however acutely, such dishonor – is not to lose the quintessential human urge to participate and to want a place" (*Slavery and Social Death* [Cambridge, MA: Harvard University Press, 1982], p. 97). For further relevant discussion, see Laurence M. Thomas, *Vessels of Evil: American Slavery and the Holocaust* (Philadelphia: Temple University Press, 1993), chapter 6; and Joshua Cohen, "The Arc of the Moral Universe," *Philosophy and Public Affairs* 26 (1997): 91–134, esp. 107.

39. Ralph Ellison, *Invisible Man* (New York: Random House, 1952).
40. *Ibid.*, p. 4.
41. *Ibid.*, p. 14.
42. The protagonist says in the novel's epilogue, "Let me be honest with you – a feat which, by the way, I find of the utmost difficulty. When one is invisible he finds such problems as good and evil, honesty and dishonesty, of such shifting shapes that he confuses one with the other, depending upon who happens to be looking through him at the time" (*ibid.*, p. 572).
43. *Ibid.*, p. 14.
44. *Ibid.* In light of my claim that autonomy is compatible with authentic ambivalence, it is interesting to see that Ellison's character begins to regain a sense of his personal worth when he reconciles himself to the moral ambivalence that he previously found so disorienting. "Now I know men are different and that all life is divided and that only in division is there true health" (*ibid.*, p. 576). "... [T]oo much of your life will be lost, its meaning lost, unless you approach it as much through love as through hate. So I approach it through division" (*ibid.*, p. 580).
45. This is not to say that he has as much responsibility for his predicament as do others.
46. For further development of these clarifications, see my "Free Agency and Self-Worth," *Journal of Philosophy* 91 (1994): 650–68, esp. 661–3; and *Answering for Ourselves*, chapter 4, section 4.3.
47. Autonomous agents must be disposed to engage with external criticisms. The point of restricting their sense of authority as answerers to possible criticisms that might arise from evaluative standpoints they accept is simply to mark clearly the boundary between taking ownership, as autonomy requires, and taking up a position of full responsibility to others.

48. Cf. the requirements of Lockean theories of property that property can only be acquired by actively taking unowned things out of their natural condition, within certain constraints, or by the active transfer of ownership from one party to another. The notion of active assumption of authority belongs in common to many theories of property and many theories of autonomous agency, not to mention theories of political obligation.
49. "Three Concepts of Free Action," reprinted in *The Importance of What We Care About*, pp. 47–57, esp. at 53–4; and "Identification and Wholeheartedness," pp. 170–1. Similarly, Watson emphasizes free agents' active exercise of their evaluative capacities or their active commitment to a conception of value. See "Two Faces of Responsibility," pp. 233–4. Also note Bratman's attention to decision as a key feature of identification in "Identification, Decision, and Treating as a Reason."
50. Christman's chapter (14) in the present volume would situate this claim within a Kantian, as opposed to a Hobbesian, formulation of liberalism.
51. Cf. Sartre's statement, "Actually it is not enough to will; it is necessary to will to will" (*Being and Nothingness*, trans. Hazel Barnes [New York: Philosophical Library, 1956], p. 444). He continues, "... the for-itself can *be* only if it has chosen itself. Therefore the for-itself appears as the free foundation of its emotions as of its volitions" (*ibid.*, p. 445).
52. I use "activity" in David Velleman's sense. Activities are purposeful doings that fall short of being full-blooded actions but rise above mere happenings. See *The Possibility of Practical Reason* (Oxford: Oxford University Press, 2000), pp. 1–31.
53. Cf. John Martin Fischer and Mark Ravizza's proposal that we take responsibility for acting from a particular kind of action-mechanism. In their view, I am responsible for performing a particular action now by virtue of having taken responsibility in the past for acting from mechanisms of the type on which I am now acting. See *Moral Responsibility and Control* (Cambridge: Cambridge University Press, 1998), pp. 214–7.
54. Bernard Boxill makes a similar claim when arguing that the moral function of protest is often to secure the protesters' own knowledge that they respect themselves or to confirm their own faith in their personal worth. See "Self-Respect and Protest," *Philosophy and Public Affairs* 6 (1976): 58–69.
55. These examples of the importance, in certain contexts, of explicit acts of self-authorization indicate why autonomy requires self-authorization, not merely the absence of agents' withdrawal of authority from themselves.
56. Again, see Velleman, *The Possibility of Practical Reason*, pp. 1–31.
57. *Invisible Man*, pp. 580, 581.
58. *Ibid.*, p. 579.
59. A similar point is sometimes made about identification. For instance, Frankfurt maintains, most notably in "Freedom of the Will and the Concept of a Person" and in "The Faintest Passion," that higher-order volitions need not be formed deliberately. Bratman also recognizes "an extended sense" of identification that does not require an actual decision to treat desires as reason-giving ("Identification, Decision, and Treating as a Reason," p. 13).

60. See Frankfurt, "Three Concepts of Free Action," pp. 53–4; also "Identification and Wholeheartedness," pp. 170–1. Watson also adopts a related view of taking responsibility in "Two Faces of Responsibility," p. 234.
61. Cf. the similar condition that Fischer and Ravizza include in their account of taking responsibility in *Responsibility and Control*, pp. 213–4, 235–6.
62. I do not take rational consideration to be narrowly intellectual. It can encompass imagination, attention, and many varieties of emotional responsiveness.
63. For extended discussion of these conditions, see *Answering for Ourselves*, sections 5.2–5.4, 6.1. Space also does not permit an examination here of ways in which these constraints might handle two related difficulties. One difficulty concerns those who do not claim agential authority for themselves when it seems they should. The converse difficulty concerns those who take up such authority too readily, claiming the position of answerers when it seems they should not.
64. I accept, then, that sound assessments of agents' autonomy will, in particular cases, often turn more directly on these familiar features of autonomy than on the character of agents' self-regard. This does not detract from my contention that in some important and badly neglected cases, autonomy hinges directly on agents' stance toward their own status as potential answerers for their actions. Nor does it detract from the general thesis that agents' attitudes toward their authority as answerers lie at the center of an illuminating theory of autonomous agency.
65. Helpful discussions of the roles that social factors have in the development of autonomy include Richard Dagger, *Civic Virtues: Rights, Citizenship, and Republican Liberalism*; Lawrence Haworth, *Autonomy*; Diana T. Meyers, *Self, Society, and Personal Choice*; Marilyn Friedman, "Autonomy and Social Relationships," in *Feminists Rethink the Self*, ed. Diana Tietjens Meyers (Boulder, CO: Westview Press, 1997); John Christman, "Feminism and Autonomy," in *Nagging Questions: Feminist Ethics in Everyday Life*, ed. Dana Bushnell (Lanham, MD: Rowman & Littlefield, 1995); and Marina A. L. Oshana, "Personal Autonomy and Society."
66. Iris Marion Young advances an influential version of such charges in *Justice and the Politics of Difference* (Princeton: Princeton University Press, 1990), especially chapter 4.
67. I develop this point in *Answering for Ourselves*, chapter 5.
68. I am greatly indebted to comments offered on previous versions of this chapter by fellow members of the Ohio Reading Group in Ethics (ORGiE) and by an audience at Bowling Green State University. For their questions and suggestions, I would like to thank David Copp, Justin D'Arms, Janice Dowell, Dan Farrell, Don Hubin, Marina Oshana, Sigrun Svavarsdottir, David Sobel, and David Velleman.

6

Autonomy, Vulnerability, Recognition, and Justice

Joel Anderson and Axel Honneth

One of liberalism's core commitments is to safeguarding individuals' autonomy. And a central aspect of liberal social justice is the commitment to protecting the vulnerable. Taken together, and combined with an understanding of autonomy as an acquired set of capacities to lead one's own life, these commitments suggest that liberal societies should be especially concerned to address vulnerabilities of individuals regarding the development and maintenance of their autonomy. In this chapter, we develop an account of what it would mean for a society to take seriously the obligation to reduce individuals' autonomy-related vulnerabilities to an acceptable minimum. In particular, we argue that standard liberal accounts underestimate the scope of this obligation because they fail to appreciate various threats to autonomy.

The reason these vulnerabilities have been underestimated, we believe, is because autonomy has generally been understood in an essentially individualistic fashion. The alternative account of autonomy we sketch here highlights the ways in which individuals' autonomy can be diminished or impaired through damage to the social relations that support autonomy. By articulating a conception of autonomy in terms of, more specifically, a theory of mutual recognition, we aim to pinpoint the individualistic bias in liberal accounts and the concomitant underestimation of our dependence on relationships of respect, care, and esteem. We conclude by anticipating some broader implications of this for how proceduralist accounts of social justice ought to be revised.

I From Classic Individualism to Welfare-Rights Protections

Before challenging the individualism of traditional forms of liberalism (and their underlying accounts of autonomy), it is important to understand this commitment from a historical standpoint. Beginning in the early modern period, a conception of freedom and autonomy gained prevalence in Europe, both in philosophy and everyday life, that has decisively shaped our current understanding of social justice. As individuals increasingly pursued their own independent paths through life, there was an increasing tendency to draw the normative implication that personal freedom and autonomy were a matter of allowing individuals to develop their personally selected pursuits undisturbed. The guiding intuition emerged that the less others constrain one's actions, the greater one's ability to act in accordance with one's own preferences. From the outset, of course, liberal theorists recognized that this freedom was limited. Kant, for one, insisted that liberty and autonomy were to be restrained by the moral requirement that one's chosen pursuits be compatible with everyone else's autonomy.[1] But these caveats do nothing to alter the core idea that the autonomy of individuals increases with the reduction of restrictions.

This individualistic conception of autonomy not only has historical pedigree; it also has come to seem just *obvious* to many. Again, this development is understandable. It reflects the important historical process by which, within the social context of modernity, individuals have increasingly shed traditional social ties and role-ascriptions to engage in their own "pursuit of happiness." But this modern conception of autonomy actually sneaks in an additional component – namely, the idea that individuals realize their autonomy by gaining independence from their consociates. This is not to say that this conception *equates* autonomy with isolation. But within culture at large, the images that accompany the emergence of this conception of autonomy suggest that *any* constraints reduce an individual's autonomy. As part of this development, however, an individualistic conception of personal autonomy has crept into modern theories of social justice. The point of creating a just society comes to be seen as allowing people to be as little dependent on others as possible. The conceptual consequences of this individualist strain have been massive. They include not only the idea, for example, that autonomy increases with wealth but also the idea that unchosen membership in a community represents a threat to personal autonomy.

This characterization of liberalism as individualistic is familiar from communitarian political philosophy and some feminist theories of autonomy, and in many cases it has been acknowledged by liberal theorists themselves. Even conceptions of justice that focus on reducing interference do not actually assume that everyone really *is* a rugged individualist. But individualistic accounts certainly are best suited to those who have no need for the benefits of social cooperation or other forms of support. The drive to maximize negative liberty thus seems to rely on a misleading idealization of individuals as self-sufficient and self-reliant. This focus on eliminating interference thus misconstrues the demands of social justice by failing to adequately conceptualize the neediness, vulnerability, and interdependence of individuals. If, by contrast, we recognize that individuals – including *autonomous* individuals – are much more vulnerable and needy than the liberal model has traditionally represented them as being, a very different picture of the demands of social justice emerges.

The first step in this direction comes from theorists who highlight the extent to which personal autonomy requires the resources and circumstances necessary for actually being able to lead the life one determines to be worthwhile.[2] This typically shifts the notion of liberal rights to a more positive account, one that includes especially socio-economic rights. This "materialization" of the way in which liberal rights schemes support autonomy (and justice) takes us a long way from hard-edged rugged individualism. It adds significant content to the concept of autonomy by underscoring some of the social conditions for the possibility of autonomy, including the need for education, adequate food and shelter, real opportunities for participating in one's (minority) culture, and so on. Consider, for example, the autonomy of people with mobility-limiting disabilities. Unless physical accommodations are made for such persons – wheelchair ramps, accessible vehicles, and so on – their ability to exercise their basic capabilities will be restricted in a way that constitutes a loss of autonomy. In general, the argument here is that the commitment to fostering autonomy – especially of the vulnerable – leads to a commitment, as a matter of social justice, to guaranteeing what one might call the *material and institutional circumstances of autonomy*. We view this as an important step in the right direction, but it is not our focus here.

Instead, we propose to take up and further develop another expansion of the claims of social justice in line with a conception of autonomy that goes by various names – relational, social, intersubjective, situated, or recognitional – but can be summarized in the claim that "Autonomy is a capacity that exists only in the context of social relations that support it and only in conjunction with the internal sense of being autonomous."[3] Although such theories are developed in response to a variety of concerns, for our purposes here they serve to highlight vulnerabilities that are overlooked by even the conceptions of social justice and autonomy that accommodate the material and institutional circumstances of autonomy. In the next four sections, we outline our preferred version of such an account, a "recognitional" theory of autonomy.[4] In Sections VI and VII, we turn to the implications that this has for political theory and social justice.

II A Recognitional Account of Autonomy

The key initial insight of social or relational accounts of autonomy is that full autonomy – the real and effective capacity to develop and pursue one's own conception of a worthwhile life – is achievable only under socially supportive conditions. It is an impressive accomplishment that, on the path from helpless infancy to mature autonomy, we come to be able to trust our own feelings and intuitions, to stand up for what we believe in, and to consider our projects and accomplishments worthwhile. We cannot travel this path alone, and we are vulnerable at each step of the way to autonomy-undermining injustices – not only to interference or material deprivation, but also to the disruptions in the social nexus that is necessary for autonomy. In developing a more "social" approach, most theorists tend to focus on one of two points. Some theorists criticize approaches to liberalism or autonomy as "individualistic" for failing to adequately accommodate the centrality of relationships in the lives of autonomous agents, specifically for failing to recognize that meaningful lives can (and generally do) include forms of attachment that are authentic even though they cannot be easily be shed, such as parents' bonds to their children.[5] Alternatively, defenders of "social" approaches criticize individualistic accounts of autonomy for failing to appreciate the importance of dialogue within an adequate account of the critical reflection central to autonomy.[6]

These are important points to make. But they are not enough to support the core contention from which the shift to a more social account gets its normative point – namely, that one's autonomy is *vulnerable to disruptions in one's relationship to others*. If this idea is to be accommodated, there are thus reasons to look for a different approach.[7] One particularly promising approach, in our view, situates agents' social vulnerability in the ways in which being able to lead one's own life is dependent on one's being supported by relations of recognition.[8] In a nutshell, the central idea is that the agentic competencies that comprise autonomy require that one be able to sustain certain attitudes toward oneself (in particular, self-trust, self-respect, and self-esteem) and that these affectively laden self-conceptions – or, to use the Hegelian language, "practical relations-to-self" – are dependent, in turn, on the sustaining attitudes of others. In a tradition going back to Hegel and George Herbert Mead,[9] these three modes of "relating practically to oneself" can be viewed as being acquired and maintained only through being recognized by those whom one also recognizes. Self-trust, self-respect, and self-esteem are thus neither purely beliefs about oneself nor emotional states, but are emergent properties of a dynamic process in which individuals come to experience themselves as having a certain status, be it as an object of concern, a responsible agent, a valued contributor to shared projects, or what have you. One's relationship to oneself, then, is not a matter of a solitary ego reflecting on itself, but is the result of an ongoing *intersubjective* process, in which one's attitude toward oneself emerges in one's encounter with an other's attitude toward oneself.

The importance of mutual recognition is often clearest in the breach. Consider, for example, practices and institutions that express attitudes of denigration and humiliation. They threaten individuals' own self-esteem by making it much harder (and, in limit cases, even impossible) to think of oneself as worthwhile. The resulting feelings of shame and worthlessness threaten one's sense that there is a point to one's undertakings. And without that sense of one's aspirations being worth pursuing, one's agency is hampered. This claim is neither exclusively conceptual nor exclusively empirical. It is, of course, psychologically *possible* to sustain a sense of self-worth in the face of denigrating and humiliating attitudes, but it is harder to do so, and there are significant costs associated with having to shield oneself from these negative attitudes and having to find subcultures for support. And so even if one's effort to maintain self-esteem in the face of denigrating treatment is successful, the question of justice is whether the burden is fair.[10]

If this initial characterization of the autonomy-impairing effects of denigration is plausible, it becomes clear how important an individual's social environment is, since the conditions for autonomously leading one's own life turn out to be dependent on the establishment of relationships of mutual recognition. Prominent among these relationships are (1) legally institutionalized relations of universal respect for the autonomy and dignity of persons (central to self-respect); (2) close relations of love and friendship (central to self-trust); and (3) networks of solidarity and shared values within which the particular worth of members of a community can be acknowledged (central to self-esteem).[11] To illustrate and render plausible the outlines of what we are calling the "recognitional approach," it will be useful to examine each of these three relations-to-self, their significance for autonomy, and the social contexts that support them. In addition, however, in order to show that accommodating this shift requires a move away from standard liberal approaches, we need to show that the rights-based individualism of such approaches is inadequate for accommodating the autonomy-related vulnerabilities that the recognitional approach brings to light.

III Self-Respect

We begin with self-respect and with the familiar liberal idea that autonomy and self-respect go hand in hand. Rawls, for example, considers self-respect to be a basic condition for the pursuit of a good life. Sen argues for the inclusion of the capability to "stand up in public without shame" as a part of the basic capability set to which individuals have a fundamental claim. And Joel Feinberg suggests that "... what is called 'human dignity' may simply be the recognizable capacity to assert claims."[12] If one takes respect (including self-respect) to have, as its object, an agent's authority to raise and defend claims as a person with equal standing, then self-respect can be seen as the affectively laden self-conception that underwrites a view of oneself as the legitimate source of reasons for acting. If one cannot think of oneself as a competent deliberator and legitimate co-author of decisions, it is hard to see how one can take oneself seriously in one's own practical reasoning about what to do. Those with diminished self-respect – with less of a sense of their personal authority – thus are less in a position to see themselves as fully the authors of their own lives. Without self-respect, then, autonomy is impaired.

If we can identify factors that diminish self-respect, we will then have identified ways in which individuals' autonomy is vulnerable and in need of protection. Without getting into an exhaustive list of what diminishes self-respect, we can say that any such list would have to include subordination, marginalization, and exclusion. For these are ways in which individuals are denied the social standing of legitimate co-legislators. They are told, in effect, that they are not competent to shape decisions, and unless they have exceptionally strong inner resources for resisting this message, it will be hard for them to think of themselves as free and equal persons. In this sense, individuals' autonomy is vulnerable to being diminished by subordination, marginalization, and exclusion.[13]

It is this particular vulnerability that has made it a central task of social justice to guarantee individual rights.[14] In guaranteeing rights, a just legal framework protects individuals from these forms of disrespect. Indeed, within contemporary liberal culture, being a bearer of rights has almost come to be synonymous with having the self-respect of a full person. This close linkage is an excellent example of the central claim of the recognitional approach we are advocating: it is in virtue of patterns of recognition – in this case, legally institutionalized patterns – that the relevant practical relation-to-self is secured.

Clearly, liberalism's commitment to protecting individuals from threats to their autonomy entails a commitment to securing individual rights. But the recognitional approach gives a slightly different twist to this conclusion than do standard liberal approaches. For on the recognitional approach, guaranteeing rights does not ensure autonomy only directly (in the negative sense of blocking interference) but also supports autonomy *via* the support for self-respect.[15] As we shall argue later, this shift necessitates a rethinking of standard liberal approaches, even those as sophisticated as Rawls's.[16]

Before taking up that issue, we will first outline the other two practical relations-to-self that, according to the theory of recognition we are defending here, are vital for sustaining autonomy: self-trust and self-esteem. Both cases exhibit the same argumentative structure discussed in connection with self-respect: a practical relation-to-self is crucially important for a component of full autonomy; the development and maintenance of that practical relation-to-self is dependent, in turn, on patterns of recognition; and thus the autonomy of individuals is vulnerable to threats to those patterns. A society's commitment to protecting individuals' autonomy thus entails a commitment to protecting the related recognitional infrastructure: the more-or-less institutionalized relations of recognition that support not only self-respect, but also self-trust and self-esteem.

IV Self-Trust

In speaking of "self-trust" (or "basic self-confidence"), we have in mind the characteristic of an agent who has an open and trusting relationship to his or her own feelings, desires, impulses, emotions, and so on. Thus, whereas self-respect has to do with one's capacities for processing various considerations in deliberating about what to do, self-trust has to do with the affectively mediated perceptual capacities by which what is subjectively felt becomes material for deliberation in the first place. Again, think of what happens in the breach. There is strong clinical evidence that various forms of trauma – for example, that resulting from rape or torture – cause individuals to view their own feelings with suspicion, and to distrust their own desires.[17] The relevance of this for autonomy is clear: those who have lost this basic trust have lost the basis for leading their life in accordance with their most basic convictions, since they can no longer trust their desires to be authentically their own.[18]

However far most of us may be from the debilitating effects of such traumatic mistreatment, we all fall along a continuum regarding the particular capacity involved and the degree to which it is fostered by our social context. Self-trust is a vital component of anyone's autonomy because of the complexity of our access to our feelings, yearnings, fears, regrets, and so on. In part, the importance of self-trust stems from the difficulty of the interpretive work that must be done to understand oneself – and from the elusiveness of first-person authority reports.[19] But even these difficulties are radicalized by a further insight, associated with the "critique of the subject" – namely, the discovery of the unconscious. One of the enduring accomplishments of psychoanalytic theory lies in exposing the illusion both of complete transparency about our motives and of perfect harmony among our desires, even in the case of perfectly autonomous agents. This unavoidably inchoate, shadowy, and conflicted inner life suggests the need for a more *polyvocal* conception of how autonomous individuals relate to their desires, impulses, fantasies, and other dimensions of subjectivity.[20]

Of course, autonomy clearly requires that one be constituted in such a way that openness to both of these creative impulses does not mean that they simply take over the self. But the point of emphasizing polyvocality is to underscore that it is also crucial to avoid psychological rigidity. And to appreciate how much self-trust contributes to autonomy, it is important to see that it is not entailed by standard requirements of being rational or responsive to reasons, which is the way in which psychological rigidity is often handled in the philosophical literature.[21] In addition to being flexible enough to respond appropriately to life-changes, autonomous agents are also open to those sources of identity and choice that underlie practical reasons, in the primitive and inchoate urges, impulses, longings, and despairings that can come to be transformed into reasons. Thus, in this sense, the model of the autonomous agent that emerges from taking seriously the polyvocal character of the self is of a person who is not only freed from compulsive behavior patterns but is also open to new, as-yet undisclosed desires. This idea is reflected in the shift within the psychoanalytic conception of maturity, from a capacity for controlling one's inner urges (that is, "ego strength") to the potential for inner dialogue, for openness to both a multiplicity of internal voices and a variety of communicative relations to them.[22]

As with self-respect, however, self-trust is not a solo accomplishment. Its acquisition and maintenance are dependent on interpersonal relationships in which one acquires and sustains the capacity to relate to this dynamic inner life. And in the case of self-trust in particular, there is strong evidence from object-relations theory and intersubjectivist approaches to social psychology that self-trust emerges particularly within intimate relationships.[23] Especially given the ambivalent and conflicted nature of much of our inner life, the *genuine openness* characteristic of fully free and autonomous reflection and deliberation can be risky. The courage to engage with one's deepest feelings both openly and critically is facilitated by the sure love of others and the self-trust it supports. And insofar as being comfortable and confident doing this is essential to self-understanding, critical reflection, and thus autonomy, it becomes clear that there is an internal connection between the openness and freedom of one's inner life and the openness and freedom of one's social context.

The crucial implication of this discussion is that individuals' *autonomy* is also vulnerable, in principle, to anything that diminishes self-trust, either directly or indirectly. With regard to direct effects, we can note that because "intimate violations" such as rape and torture are so harmful to agents' self-trust and hence their autonomy, a society committed to protecting individuals has an additional reason to be committed to preventing such violations. With regard to indirect effects, the key result, for our purposes, is that a society's commitment to protecting the conditions for autonomy can also be seen to entail a commitment to protecting the kinds of relationships within which self-trust is developed and fostered. Thus, for example, work/family policies (such as parental leave) can be seen as part of a commitment to protecting and promoting one important component of the capacities constitutive of autonomy.[24]

V Self-Esteem: Semantic Vulnerability

Someone who was protected from the exclusions that undermine self-respect and the threats that undermine self-trust could, however, still have his or her autonomy jeopardized in another way (already mentioned in Section II): the conditions for developing a sense of self-worth and self-esteem can be impaired as a result of patterns of humiliation and denigration and can do so in a way that renders a person less able to be self-determining with regard to his or her projects. This potential threat to autonomy raises, in turn, further questions about social justice and the guaranteeing of autonomy.

To make clear the importance of self-esteem for autonomy, we can begin with an extension of the point from the previous section. For the self-interpretive activity central to autonomous reflection presupposes not only a certain degree of quasi-affective openness but also certain *semantic* resources. Again, this stems from one of the genuine insights of the twentieth-century critiques of modern – "Cartesian" – conceptions of the subject: individuals cannot decide for themselves what their (speech) acts mean. Rather, determining the worth and meaning of one's activities is fundamentally framed by the semantic and symbolic field in which that reflection occurs – what gets termed variously the "space of reasons" (McDowell), "horizon of significance" (Taylor), "regime of truth/knowledge" (Foucault), or socio-cultural means of need-interpretation (Fraser).[25] Thus, for example, the very possibility of being "openly lesbian" or "a stay-at-home dad" is framed by a whole constellation of evaluatively loaded ways of talking.

It is the unavoidably *evaluative* character of this symbolic-semantic field that has the crucial implications regarding autonomy. For if the semantic resources available for thinking about one's way of life are negatively loaded – if, for example, "stay-at-home dad" is taken to be a euphemism for "unemployed" – then it becomes hard to view it as worthwhile. Not impossible, perhaps. But without an especially high level of personal resilience, subcultural support, and persistent effort – that is, without other (often limited) sources of self-esteem – marginalized ways of life cease to be genuine options for individuals.

In itself, this restriction of options might not be seen as a threat to autonomy. But it has always been one of the strengths of the liberal tradition to highlight the degree to which such restrictions pose a threat to the individuality of persons. Think, for example, of J.S. Mill's *On Liberty*. But once we grant that those individual lifestyles provide the basis for a sense of being worthwhile as a consequence of their getting a certain confirming "uptake" within the social world, then the richness of the identity available to any individual can thus be restricted by limitations on the richness of the available semantic field. To the extent to which one's way of life not only fails to get uptake but is an active target of denigration and humiliation, the task of pursuing one's way of life as meaningful is even more fraught with difficulty.

In connection with autonomy, we can add a point about the effects that such denigration has on a person's sense of agency and personal effectiveness. This is a more formal consideration: to the extent to which one lacks a sense that what one does is meaningful and significant, it becomes hard to pursue it wholeheartedly. There is at least a tension between pursuing that way of life and thinking of oneself as doing something that makes sense. And, as David Velleman argues, being able to make sense of what it is we are doing is intimately tied up with actually doing it.[26] Thus, a socio-cultural environment that is hostile to considering what one does meaningful is *demoralizing*. Because of the way they can undermine self-esteem, systematic patterns of denigration thus pose a threat not merely to the happiness or identify but to the *agency* of those affected.

In short, for the exercise of autonomy, individuals are not only dependent on a semantic-symbolic environment that "meets them halfway" for enabling a rich self-interpretation; they are also vulnerable to hostile and denigrating semantic-symbolic environments that more directly assault or limit their autonomous agency. Accordingly, a conception of social justice that is seriously committed to protecting the autonomy of individuals must include a protection against threats of denigration.[27]

Pulling the strands of the last three sections together, we have the outlines of a recognitional model according to which autonomy represents an emergent property of individuals as the bearers of certain socially situated capabilities. This theoretical shift makes it much more straightforward to articulate and theorize the link between mutuality and individual enablement. Full autonomy – the real and effective capacity to develop and pursue one's own conception of a worthwhile life – is facilitated by relations-to-self (self-respect, self-trust, and self-esteem) that are themselves bound up with webs of social recognition. But self-trust, self-respect, and self-esteem remain more or less fragile achievements, and their vulnerability to various forms of injury, violation, and denigration makes it a central matter of justice that the social contexts within which they emerge be protected.

VI   Recognition and the Language of Rights

In returning to questions of social justice and political liberalism, we now take up the question of the extent to which this recognitional approach to autonomy raises challenges for liberalism. In particular, we shall consider two attempts to accommodate the vulnerabilities we have been discussing, attempts that we see as not entirely successful. First, we discuss, in a cursory fashion, the limitations of trying to articulate in the language of rights the imperatives generated by these vulnerabilities. Then, in the next section, we discuss, at somewhat greater length, the question of whether Rawls's theory of justice can accommodate these considerations adequately.

Initially, a rights-based approach might seem perfectly well suited to articulating the idea that a commitment to social justice requires that society protect individuals with regard to their autonomy-related vulnerabilities. As we noted earlier, rights-based approaches have tended to focus on the conditions for self-respect – such as rights to full participation – to the exclusion of self-trust and self-esteem. But it might be argued that we have not yet shown that the claims to conditions supportive of the acquisition and maintenance of self-esteem and self-trust could not be accommodated within the language of rights, at least as rights-claims vis-à-vis the circumstances of justice. This is what has been attempted, for example, in the politics of identity, where groups have sought to claim a right to be recognized, as individuals, for their cultural needs. But the idea of addressing these needs for recognition in the vernacular of rights has turned out to be a quagmire. The central problem is that it misses its target, for what one needs is to be loved or esteemed – and precisely not because one has a legal claim to it. Moreover, attempts to conceptualize human needs and vulnerability in the domains that support self-trust and self-esteem in terms of rights that can be *individually* possessed are strained beyond plausibility: it is particularly clear here that these are fundamentally relational circumstances. Knowing oneself to be the object of very personal concern or having the sense that one's undertakings are considered worthwhile – these are not matters that one person has in *independence* from a relationship. They are emergent properties of relationships of a certain sort.

Once this point is acknowledged, it becomes attractive to reconsider, more radically, the individualistic understanding of *rights* as well. For rights too have this general intersubjective structure. These rights – and the power and freedom they accord to individuals – are actually the result of members of a community recognizing each other as free and equal. To view them as free-standing is to confuse an emergent property for something independently existing. According to this non-individualistic conception of the way in which rights support personal autonomy, first developed by Hegel, gains in freedom and power come from having others see one's needs and aspirations as legitimate. These gains are welcome at the individual level, of course, and that is where they are subjectively experienced: I can do things I couldn't do before. But they remain, essentially, the product of social relationships with a decisive characteristic: individuals mutually recognize, acknowledge, and accept each other as consociates. It is in this sense that traditional rights language is problematically individualistic, in that it conceptualizes rights-guaranteeing relations as a matter of specific powers that can be distributed among individuals as if they were individual possessions.

Rights do, of course, have a central place in any plausible conception of how a just society protects and enables individual autonomy. The question is whether they can do it alone. Without denying their importance, we think it is clear that the medium of rights is inadequate to address the full vulnerability of humans. Legal relations are a clumsy medium for securing many aspects of an individuals' ability to develop and pursue their own conception of a worthwhile life. An adequate approach must start out from the broader range of social institutions and interpersonal contexts within which one finds the recognitional relations crucial for autonomy.

VII Rethinking Proceduralist Justice in Light of the Recognitional Model

Up to now, we have not yet considered how various protections from autonomy-related vulnerabilities ought to fit together or how to set priorities among these various vulnerabilities. Answering these questions involves developing a substantive normative theory. Here, however, our concern is with the prior question as to the procedure for justifying *any* such answers. This is the task of specifying the standpoint from which to determine the content of social justice.

Within political theory today, there is widespread agreement on the proceduralist assumption that normative justification is to be located in the deliberative contexts in which the potential members of the relevant society reach an understanding, under real or fictitious conditions of impartiality, about the principles that are to regulate their future cooperation. This underlying demand for impartiality is intended to both guarantee the general acceptability of the results and provide a principle of inclusivity vis-à-vis all members of society. The principles on which the participants in this deliberative social contract would agree serve to regulate the relations between persons, represented as interested in the most autonomous possible realization of their individual life-plans.

Rawls's theory of justice as fairness represents the most influential version of this proceduralism. The question we now wish to pose is whether a recognitional understanding of autonomy-relevant vulnerabilities necessitates a rethinking of Rawls's version of this proceduralism. We shall argue that to some extent it does. This leaves open the question of whether the best way to accommodate the recognitional insights into these vulnerabilities is through modifying proceduralism or adopting a non-proceduralist approach.[28]

Starting out from the idea that a fictional deliberative context is the best way to operationalize insights into universally acceptable principles of justice, the first task is to determine the normative presuppositions for an impartial standpoint, one that includes all participants. The idea is to ensure that none of the parties to the deliberations endorses a particular proposal only because he or she could benefit from it. This goal of generating an impartial standpoint through purely procedural means is what led Rawls to introduce the idea of a "veil of ignorance," as a way to ensure that those seeking to find agreement on principles governing their fair cooperation are not permitted to have any knowledge of their talents or social position.[29] That subtle move provides a way of ensuring that the parties in this thought experiment must be thought of as neutral legislators, since they cannot have any self-regarding interests. For the rest, Rawls (like almost all contract theorists before him) attributes to the parties merely instrumental capacities for practical reasoning, in order to avoid having to take up complex and controversial claims about the moral character of humans.

In the present context, we are not interested in discussing this part of Rawls's theory, although from the standpoint of Hegel and other intersubjectivistic thinkers, this is a highly problematic move, insofar as it makes it very difficult to explain why the parties should subsequently be motivated to abide by the agreed-upon principles.[30] Rather, we are interested in the extent to which the Rawlsian characterization of the veil of ignorance ends up allowing the fact of human intersubjectivity to disappear more than necessary from view. Don't the parties need to have some awareness – even within the procedural constraints that are to generate impartiality – of their intersubjective vulnerability if they are to qualify as human, as the sort of creatures for whom the institutions of justice are so essential?[31]

What makes this more than an artificial question is the way in which it reveals the impossibility of determining the justificatory procedures in complete independence from assumptions about the defining characteristics of human personhood. Rawls insists that the parties in the original position should not have knowledge of what people in the society are like, except the most basic features of their instrumental rationality.[32] Given what we have said thus far, this suggests that Rawls allows the veil of ignorance to fall a bit too low. For if liberal justice is centrally about protecting individuals in areas in which they are vulnerable – especially as it pertains to threats to their autonomy – then it would seem to be of vital importance that the parties in the original position have a clear understanding of the recognitional needs that must be met if individuals' autonomy is to be adequately protected and enabled. Unless the parties share this understanding, it is hard to see how the principles they develop could do justice to these vulnerabilities and needs.

There are several responses open to Rawls. He could insist that in the original position, parties should indeed be ignorant of empirical considerations regarding human vulnerabilities, but that these issues can be addressed at the "legislative" level. This is the move that he makes, for example, with issues of health care policy, where he argues that although considerations regarding the prevalence of various illnesses are excluded from deliberations within the original position, they can be taken up later, in the legislative stage.[33] Similarly, it might be that the specification of the primary goods, within the original position, ought not to admit considerations about the nature of our vulnerability to injury to our self-trust, self-respect, and self-esteem, but that those considerations could be taken up in the legislative stage, without their needing to be built into the fundamental principles of justice. The problem with this is not only that, if the recognitional approach is on the right track, the capacities at issue are more extensive than the faculty or "moral power" that Rawls discusses for having "a capacity for a conception of the good."[34] More straightforwardly, the autonomy-related capacities that are vulnerable to injustice are so widely and deeply implicated in central aspects of deliberation that it would be foolhardy to trust this to a subsequent legislative stage.

But perhaps the more fundamental issue at stake here has to do with the degree to which we should appeal to quasi-empirical aspects of human personhood in developing a conception of justice for liberal societies. Indeed, Rawls insists that the notion of a "person" that is essential to his conception of justice as fairness is "normative and political, not metaphysical or psychological."[35] Thus, the fact that we are vulnerable could be accommodated within justice as fairness by saying that the basic structure needs to protect persons from threats to their "moral power" to form a conception of a worthwhile life-plan, and thus needs to secure the primary goods necessary for that. And this is quite extensive, for what is at issue is a matter of the requisite powers of moral personality and the other capacities that enable persons to be normal and fully cooperating members of society over a complete life.[36] It is not implausible, for example, that it could include the same conditions for the development of autonomy that we have specified here – self-trust, self-respect, and self-esteem. The details would still need to be worked out, of course, but Rawls does have impressive resources for accommodating the sorts of points we have been making. Indeed, Rawls's discussion of self-respect already suggests that the parties in the original position must be aware of some of their needs for recognition. For it makes sense for parties to include the basic intersubjective good of self-respect in their deliberations over the basic structure of a just society only if they already understand that the conception and pursuit of their life-plans depend fundamentally on the esteem of others. Perhaps, then, the recognitional account of autonomy we have been developing identifies an area where important work needs to be done, but more as an elaboration of the basic Rawlsian approach than as a significant departure from it.

If this were all we accomplished here, it would already be a substantive contribution. We see, however, three grounds for thinking that Rawls's model still needs to be revised to accommodate the recognitionalist account of autonomy: (1) it needs to be more open to considerations based on what we know about human persons; (2) it needs to address more broadly the ways in which a society's recognitional infrastructure can leave the autonomy of individuals unacceptably vulnerable; and (3) it needs to acknowledge that the broad relevance of recognitional conditions necessitates a shift away from exclusively *distributive* issues. In the remainder of this chapter, we sketch out these three points and argue that they do, indeed, suggest the need for significant revisions to basic commitments of (Rawlsian) liberalism.

Consider, first, the issue of how relevant psychological considerations ought to be in deliberations about principles of justice. There are, of course, good reasons for not basing a conception of justice on a conception of human nature. The deeper theorists get into claims about what it is to be "truly human," the greater is the danger that the agenda for establishing justice will be set by (sub)culturally biased claims about what constitutes a proper form of life. But in his effort to accommodate the fact of reasonable pluralism, Rawls' makes a sharp split between political and "metaphysical" claims regarding the nature of human persons that is neither necessary nor, ultimately, defensible. It is not necessary because claims about human qualities need not be parochial: some basic needs are more or less universal, and as recent "capabilities approaches" have argued, an appeal to basic human needs and characteristics are not obviously incompatible with a commitment to inclusive, universalistic forms of liberalism.[37] We see no reason why a theory of justice ought to count as disrespecting pluralism simply as a result of incorporating empirical considerations about human vulnerabilities, such as the effect that certain forms of neglect have on the potential for forming rewarding personal relationships. The burden of proof is rather on those who would say that there are necessary illiberal effects resulting from allowing a given set of considerations to carry weight in deliberations within the original position. Moreover, the purportedly sharp split between "metaphysical" and "political" claims about personhood tends to break down upon closer examination. After all, everything we know about the conditions required for acquiring the two moral powers comes from experience with human persons. This knowledge is clearly relevant to issues of justice, but it is entirely unclear how this could be anything other than "psychological" knowledge about the nature of humans.

But even if we were to follow Rawls in limiting ourselves to a "normative/political" conception of the person (and to refrain from making claims about the nature of human persons), there is a second reason to think that the recognitional approach we have outlined here would require more a transformation than an extension of his approach: it improperly limits the scope of what goes into the notion of the "moral power" to conceive and pursue a way of life, or even what goes into the conditions for acquiring the positive disposition toward oneself that Rawls refers to as "self-respect (or self-esteem)."[38] In part, this is a matter of not giving much attention to the recognitional conditions for acquiring and maintaining self-trust (and thus of the associated openness to the creative impulses stemming from inner dynamics). Indeed, when Rawls says that the parties in the original position can be thought of as "heads of families,"[39] he is concerned with the idea of responsibility for the welfare of other family members and of descendents rather than with the importance of maintaining the intimate relations crucial for self-trust. Similarly, when Rawls discusses self-esteem, the social relations that he focuses on are limited to clubs and voluntary associations.[40] But this gives a far too restricted role to much more broad-reaching factors such as symbolic-semantic resources and the way those cultural patterns frame the range of available options. But most fundamentally, the point is that parties in the original position need much better understanding of these conditions for acquiring self-respect and self-esteem than Rawls equips them with. And including this knowledge – even when it is not centrally about human psychology – will unavoidably introduce into the discussion of the principles of justice issues about what qualities to promote, both as essential aspects of the autonomy-sustaining relations-to-self we have been discussing *and* as indirect conditions for the acquisitions of those capacities.[41]

Finally, and perhaps most speculatively, the intersubjectivism of the recognitional approach seems to require a reconceptualization of the nature of justice. As we have seen, the standard liberal combination of legally protected liberties and material resources does not exhaust the requisite conditions for fostering and protecting individuals' autonomy, given the additional dimensions of autonomy and the associated vulnerabilities. Once it is acknowledged, further, that even these preliminary conditions for autonomy are not a resource that can be distributed at will, then it becomes clear that we – like the parties in the original position – must undertake a rethinking of what the object of a theory of justice is. From the perspective of asking what the conditions are that equally guarantee the personal autonomy of all members of society, and equally protect them in their intersubjective vulnerability, the main focus of application for principles of justice becomes the structure and quality of social relations of recognition. As a result, this liberal conception of justice loses its character as a theory of *distribution*. It becomes instead – to put it somewhat provocatively – a normative theory of the *recognitional basic structure* of a society. What comes, then, to take the place of principles of just distribution are principles governing how the basic institutions of society secure the social conditions for mutual recognition. And that is a profoundly different – and largely unexplored – way of thinking about social justice.

VIII Conclusion

We have proposed here a *recognitional* model of autonomy that emphasizes the intersubjective conditions for being able to lead one's life as one's own, and sketched some implications that this may have for rethinking basic features of the liberal political order. Central to that model of autonomy is the idea that the acquisition, maintenance, and exercise of the array of competencies comprising autonomy depends on the establishment of particular ways of "relating to oneself practically," especially self-respect, self-trust, and self-esteem. Because these are, in turn, bound up with various social relations of recognition, autonomy turns out to presuppose, as a condition of its possibility, a supportive *recognitional infrastructure.* Because agents are largely dependent on this recognitional infrastructure for their autonomy, they are subject to autonomy-related vulnerabilities: harms to and neglect of these relations of recognition jeopardize individuals' autonomy.

This expanded conception of the ways in which individuals' autonomy can be undermined suggests an expanded scope for the core liberal obligation to guarantee individual autonomy. There are, to be sure, resources within liberalism for accommodating this expanded scope. If our argument here is sound, however, those resources are not entirely adequate. Liberalism faces a new challenge of doing justice to the profoundly intersubjective nature of autonomy.

Notes

We would like to thank Bert van den Brink, Pauline Kleingeld, and Chris Zurn for comments on a previous draft of this chapter.

1. Immanuel Kant, "Groundwork for a Metaphysics of Morals," in Mary J. Gregor (trans. and ed.), *Practical Philosophy* (Cambridge: Cambridge University Press, 1996), pp. 43–108.
2. A diverse sampling of such views might include Robert Young, *Autonomy: Beyond Negative and Positive Liberty* (New York: St. Martin's Press, 1986); Marina Oshana, "Personal Autonomy and Society," *The Journal of Social Philosophy* 29 (1998): 81–102; Amartya Sen, *Development as Freedom* (New York: Knopf, 1999); Joseph Raz, *The Morality of Freedom* (Oxford: Clarendon, 1986); John Rawls, *A Theory of Justice* (Cambridge, MA: Harvard University Press, 1971); Thomas W. Pogge, *Realizing Rawls* (Ithaca, NY: Cornell University Press, 1989); and Jürgen Habermas, *Between Facts and Norms,* trans. William Rehg (Cambridge, MA: MIT Press, 1996).
3. Jennifer Nedelsky, "Reconceiving Autonomy: Sources, Thoughts, and Possibilities," *Yale Journal of Law and Feminism* 1:1 (Spring 1989): 25. See also, for example, Catriona Mackenzie and Natalie Stoljar, "Autonomy Refigured," in Mackenzie and Stoljar (eds.), *Relational Autonomy: Feminist Perspectives on Autonomy, Agency, and the Social Self* (New York: Oxford University Press, 2000), 3–31; Marilyn Friedman, "Introduction: Autonomy in Social Context," in Creighton Peden and James P. Sterba (eds.), *Freedom, Equality, and Social Change* (Lewiston, NY: Edwin Mellen, 1989), pp. 158–69; John Christman, "Autonomy and Feminism"; Meyers, *Self, Society, and Personal Choice*; and Joel Anderson, "Autonomy and the Authority of Personal Commitments: From Internal Coherence to Social Normativity," *Philosophical Explorations* 6 (2003): 90–108.
4. We are using "recognitional" to denote attitudes, experiences, vulnerabilities, and so on that are related to claims to recognition. In some cases, it also serves to designate an approach based on recognition (as an equivalent for "*anerkennungtheoretisch*").

5. Regarding the importance of such "unsheddable" attachments, see John Christman, "Relational Autonomy, Liberal Individualism, and the Social Constitution of Selves," *Philosophical Studies* 117 (2004): 143–64; Harry Frankfurt, *Necessity, Volition, and Love* (New York: Cambridge University Press, 1999); Sarah Buss, "Autonomy Reconsidered," *Midwest Studies* 9 (1994): 95–121; Eva Feder Kittay, *Love's Labor: Essays on Women, Equality and Dependency* (New York: Routledge, 1999). See also, however, Marilyn Friedman's discussion of overlooked sensitivity to the relational within liberal accounts of autonomy in "Autonomy and Social Relationships: Rethinking the Feminist Critique," in *Autonomy, Gender, and Politics* (New York: Oxford University Press, 2003), 81–97.

6. See Diana T. Meyers, *Self, Society and Personal Choice* (New York: Columbia University Press, 1989); Seyla Benhabib, *Situating the Self: Gender, Community and Postmodernism in Contemporary Ethics* (New York: Routledge, 1992); Charles Taylor, "The Dialogical Self," in David R. Hiley, James F. Bohmann, and Richard Shusterman (eds.), *The Interpretive Turn: Philosophy, Science, Culture* (Ithaca, NY: Cornell University Press, 1991), 304–14; Joel Anderson, "A Social Conception of Personal Autonomy: Volitional Identity, Strong Evaluation, and Intersubjective Accountability" (Ph.D dissertation, Northwestern University, 1996); and Jürgen Habermas, "Individuation through Socialization: On George Herbert Mead's Theory of Subjectivity," in *Postmetaphysical Thinking*, trans. William Hohengarten (Cambridge, MA: MIT Press, 1992, 149–204).

7. Clearly, not everyone is interested in developing a social account, and many theorists may well find this to be a *mistaken* move. To show, against them, that the recognitional approach is the correct one would require a different argument than what we provide here. Our explicit aims, however, are more limited: first, to show that the recognitional approach has an initial appeal and plausibility; and second, to show that *if* one adopts this approach, then there are certain interesting implications that follow from this.

8. For further development of these ideas – as well as references to the empirical evidence in favor of them – see Axel Honneth, *The Struggle for Recognition: The Moral Grammar of Social Conflicts*, trans. Joel Anderson (Cambridge, MA: Polity Press, 1995); "Invisibility: The Moral Epistemology of 'Recognition'," *The Aristotelian Society*, supp. vol. LXXV (2001): 111–26; "Grounding Recognition: A Rejoinder to Critical Questions," trans. Joel Anderson, *Inquiry* 45 (2002): 499–519; *Suffering from Indeterminacy: An Attempt at a Reactualization of Hegel's Philosophy of Right* (Assen: Van Gorcum, 2000); and (with Nancy Fraser) *Redistribution or Recognition? A Political-Philosophical Exchange*, trans. J. Golb, J. Ingram, and C. Wilke (New York: Verso, 2003).

9. On the historical sources, see especially G. W. F. Hegel, "Jena Lectures on the Philosophy of Spirit," in Leo Rauch (ed. and trans.), *Hegel and the Human Spirit: A Translation of the Jena Lectures on the Philosophy of Spirit (1805–06) with Commentary* (Detroit: Wayne State University Press, 1983); George Herbert Mead, *Mind, Self, and Society* (Chicago: University of Chicago Press, 1955); and their discussion in Honneth, *The Struggle for Recognition*, chapters 1–4.

10. Note that our claim is merely that *part* of what makes practices of denigration, disrespect, and intimate violation unjust is that they impair autonomy or put that autonomy at significant risk. Obviously, these practices can also be criticized directly as subordinating or painful.
11. Two points need to be noted about this tripartite distinction of "spheres" of recognition relations, as it has been a source of controversy in discussions of the recognitional approach. (See, for example, Nancy Fraser's contributions to *Redistribution or Recognition?*) First, these three domains are not transhistorical "givens" but are rather established and expanded through social struggles that are fueled by feelings of outrage and indignation over recognition being denied or withheld. For our purposes here, we do not even need to presuppose that these are the only three relations of recognition, since all we are arguing here is that there are at least these three dimensions along which we are vulnerable. Second, since allowing for the historical contingency of these spheres (and the corresponding claims about self-trust, self-respect, and self-esteem being necessary for autonomy) opens up potential problems of normativity, it is important to note that the account we are presenting here needs to be supplemented by an account of how the historical emergence of normative claims for recognition can nonetheless have critical authority. Because of limited space, the reader will have to look elsewhere for that account – for example, in Honneth, *The Struggle for Recognition*, chapter 9; "Grounding Recognition," and "The Point of Recognition," in Fraser and Honneth, *Redistribution or Recognition?*, pp. 256–65.
12. John Rawls, *A Theory of Justice*, §67; Amartya Sen, "Social Exclusion: Concept, Application, and Scrutiny," *Social Development Papers* No. 1 (Asian Development Bank); and Joel Feinberg, "The Nature and Value of Rights," in *Rights, Justice, and the Bounds of Liberty* (Princeton: Princeton University Press, 1980), p. 143.
13. See also Avishai Margalit's development of the idea that "a decent society is one whose institutions do not humiliate people" in *The Decent Society*, trans. Naomi Goldblum (Cambridge, MA: Harvard University Press, 1996).
14. See, for example, Rainer Forst's discussion of "legal autonomy" in "Political Liberty" (Chapter 10 in the present volume).
15. Andreas Wildt, "Recht und Selbstachtung, im Anschluss an der Anerkennungslehren von Fichte und Hegel," in Michael Kahlo, Enst A. Wolf, and Rainer Zaczyk (eds.), *Fichtes Lehre von Rechtsverhältnis* (Frankfurt am Main: Klosterman, 1992), 127ff.
16. In speaking of "standard" liberal approaches, we intend to set to one side "perfectionist" approaches, many of which share our view that guaranteeing rights is a matter of guaranteeing access to valuable social practices, many of which presuppose, in turn, that one be able to act autonomously. See, for example, Raz, *The Morality of Freedom*; George Sher, *Beyond Neutrality: Perfectionism and Politics* (Cambridge: Cambridge University Press, 1997); and Steven Wall, *Liberalism, Perfectionism and Restraint* (New York: Cambridge University Press, 1998). For an excellent discussion, see Bert van den Brink, *The Tragedy of Liberalism: An Alternative Defense of a Political Tradition* (Albany: SUNY Press, 2000), chapter 4.

17. Elaine Scarry, *The Body in Pain: The Making and Unmaking of the World* (Oxford: Oxford University Press, 1985); Trudy Govier, "Self-Trust, Autonomy, and Self-Esteem," *Hypatia* 8 (1993): 99–120; Dorothy Brothers, *Falling Backwards: An Exploration of Trust and Self-Experience* (New York: Norton, 1995); and Susan J. Brison, *Aftermath: Violence and the Remaking of a Self* (Princeton: Princeton University Press, 2003).
18. Of course, the ability to *question* whether one's desires are "one's own" is an important component of autonomy more generally. But normally, when desires are questioned, they are questioned against a background of a web of convincing desires and values. The difficulty faced by those who have little self-trust is that so many of their most basic desires are being doubted that the process of reflection can get no foothold.
19. See, for example, Charles Taylor, *Sources of the Self: The Making of Modern Identity* (Cambridge, MA: Harvard University Press, 1989), part 1; Richard Moran, *Authority and Estrangement : An Essay on Self-Knowledge* (Princeton: Princeton University Press, 2001); Joel Anderson, "Competent Need-Interpretation and Discourse Ethics," in James Bohman and William Rehg (eds.), *Pluralism and the Pragmatic Turn: The Transformation of Critical Theory* (Cambridge, MA: MIT Press, 2001), 193–224; and John Christman, "Autonomy, Self-Knowledge, and Liberal Legitimacy" (Chapter 14 the present volume, Section II).
20. See Diana T. Meyer's discussion of "polyvocal" subjectivity in *Subjectivity and Subjection: Psychoanalytic Feminism and Moral Philosophy* (New York: Routledge, 1994), chapter 4–5; see also her discussion of skills of self-discovery in "Decentralizing Autonomy: Five Faces of Selfhood" (Chapter 2 in the present volume). The connection between this conception of autonomy and the "critique of the subject" is further elaborated in Axel Honneth, "Decentered Autonomy: The Subject After the Fall," in Charles Wright (ed.), *The Fragmented World of the Social: Essays in Social and Political Philosophy* (Albany, NY: SUNY Press, 1995), 261–72.
21. See, for example, Alfred Mele, *Autonomous Agents: From Self-Control to Autonomy* (New York: Oxford University Press, 1995), 131–43.
22. For a further development of this idea, see Honneth, "Postmodern Identity and Object-Relations Theory: On the Supposed Obsolescence of Psychoanalysis," *Philosophical Explorations* 3 (1999): 225–42.
23. See especially Donald Winnicott, *The Maturational Processes and the Facilitating Environment* (London: Hogarth Press, 1965); see also, Honneth, *The Struggle for Recognition*, pp. 95–107.
24. Along related lines, Christopher Beckett has recently argued that liberalism's commitment to promoting autonomy underwrites policies that encourage marriage-like relationships in "Autonomy, Liberalism, and Conjugal Love," *Res Publica* 9 [2003]: 285–301. Also crucially important for the protection of the contexts that nourish self-trust is a domain of privacy, which is not to be understood exclusively in terms of rights; see Beate Rössler, *Der Wert des Privaten* (Frankfurt am Main: Suhrkamp, 2001).
25. See, respectively, John McDowell, *Mind and World* (Cambridge, MA: Harvard University Press, 1994); Charles Taylor, *Sources of the Self*; Michel Foucault,

The Order of Things: An Archaeology of the Human Sciences, trans. A. M. Sheridan Smith (New York: Pantheon Books, 1970); and Nancy Fraser, "Struggle over Needs: Outline of a Socialist-Feminist Critical Theory of Late Capitalist Political Culture," in *Unruly Practices: Power, Discourse, and Gender in Contemporary Social Theory* (Minneapolis: University of Minnesota Press, 1989), pp. 161–87.
26. See, for example, J. David Velleman, *Practical Reflection* (Princeton: Princeton University Press, 1989).
27. See Margalit, *The Decent Society*; and Will Kymlicka, *Multicultural Citizenship: A Liberal Theory of Minority Rights* (Oxford: Oxford University Press, 1995).
28. For more historical development of the following argument, focused on Hegel, see Honneth, "Gerechtigkeit und kommunikative Freiheit. Überlegungen im Anschluss an Hegel," in B. Merker, G. Mohr, and M. Quante (eds.) *Subjektivität und Anerkennung: Festschrift Ludwig Siep* (Paderborn: Mentis Verlag, 2003).
29. See especially John Rawls, *Theory of Justice* and *Justice as Fairness: A Restatement* (Cambridge, MA: Harvard University Press, 2001).
30. See, for example, Bert van den Brink's Chapter 11 in the present volume.
31. Alasdair MacIntyre, *Dependent Rational Animals: Why Human Beings Need the Virtues* (Chicago: Open Court, 1999).
32. Rawls, *A Theory of Justice* §24.
33. Rawls, *Justice as Fairness*, pp. 171–3.
34. Rawls, *Justice as Fairness*, p. 19.
35. Rawls, *Justice as Fairness*, p. 19.
36. Rawls, *Justice as Fairness*, pp. 18; *A Theory of Justice* (Cambridge, MA: Harvard University Press, 1971).
37. See, for example, Martha Nussbaum, *Women and Human Development: A Capabilities Approach* (New York: Cambridge University Press, 2000).
38. Rawls, *A Theory of Justice*, p. 440.
39. Rawls, *A Theory of Justice*, p. 128.
40. Rawls, *A Theory of Justice*, §67.
41. A related point is made in the discussion of whether liberalism can justifiably insist that societies can do entirely without any (perfectionist) commitment to promoting various qualities and dispositions in their citizenry, such as "civic virtues." See, for example, Raz, *Morality as Freedom*, and Richard Dagger, *Civic Virtues: Rights, Citizenship, and Republican Liberalism* (Oxford: Oxford University Press, 1997) and his chapter (8) in the present volume.

7

Autonomy and Male Dominance

Marilyn Friedman

In recommending to would-be princes how best to consolidate their power, Machiavelli posed the rhetorical question as to whether it was better to rule by being loved or by being feared by a populace. Machiavelli answered that it was best to rule by promoting both attitudes, but that if a ruler had to choose, he should choose to rule through *fear*, "for love is held by a chain of obligation which, men being selfish, is broken whenever it serves their purpose; but fear is maintained by a dread of punishment which never fails."[1] Machiavelli was an astute observer of human motivation, missing only that love can sometimes be *grounded* on fear.

Fear of other persons can have a major impact on how we live our lives. When we have to cope on a chronic basis with people who threaten to harm us, we are less able to do what we want or value, or what really matters to us. Such fears can deeply affect our capacity to live and choose autonomously. In the face of threats from those we fear, we may have to devote ourselves to self-defense and, perhaps, even to simple self-preservation.[2] Not only do a person's particular choices and actions change as a result of her fear of others; her entire character may become distorted by the need for heightened vigilance and frequent self-defense.

There are many situations and relationships in the world that put certain people in chronic fear of certain other people. One state makes war on another state, one ethnic group oppresses another ethnic group, one religious group crusades against another religious group, one racial group enslaves another racial group. These sorts of conflicts sometimes involve ruthless atrocities – death and suffering on a massive scale. Personal autonomy for the oppressed is likely to be a lost cause, and its loss may be the least of their concerns under those conditions.

Domination is effective, at least in part, because dominant individuals use coercion or the threat of coercion to maintain their control. This chapter focuses in particular on male dominance. Male dominance is global. Evolutionary psychologist Felicia Pratto writes: "There are no human societies in which women dominate men. Instead, societies in which men dominate women are so common that male dominance has been considered a human universal."[3] Male dominance may be found in all, or nearly all, spheres of life. It appears in both "public" and "private" relationships between women and men. It involves men's greater control than women's of resources and power and men's control of women's sexuality and reproduction.[4] Wherever male dominance appears, women's autonomy is threatened.[5]

The analysis of how male dominance diminishes female autonomy may, of course, be generalized to other dominance relationships that bear the same features as male dominance. Care must be taken with this extension, however, since different kinds of dominance have distinct modes of operation and may not diminish autonomy in the same ways. One crucial context for the practice of male domination consists of intimate heterosexual relationships in which an individual woman (or several women) relate to an individual man who is the "head" of their household. Such asymmetrical relationships are usually legalized as marriage and regarded by many as the building blocks of society. Reproductive activity is the obvious reason for this social arrangement and, consequently, the explanation for the distinctive character of male dominance as contrasted with other forms of domination.[6] Unlike, for example, ethnic or racial groups, which can separate from each other and reproduce endogamously, women and men must mingle with each other intimately in order to reproduce themselves.[7]

Thus, rather than forming cohesive communities that might resist male dominance, women have been divided throughout nearly all human communities into small household units headed by men, who are usually socially authorized to rule their individual homes like "castles." Gender relationships involve individual women relating to, indeed often legally bound to, individual men in intimate settings. Few other forms of dominance are so individualized and leave the subordinated party so personally and directly under the authority or control of one or a few members of the group that holds sway.

Some philosophers have recently emphasized the social dimensions of autonomy.[8] Intimate and familial relationships are among the social relationships in which autonomy competency can be most readily nurtured. Subordination in these sorts of relationships, as occurs in male dominance, is therefore particularly detrimental to the development and exercise of women's autonomy competency.

Racial dominance has sometimes taken the form of the enslavement of members of one racial group by members of another racial group, and slavery is an obvious example of a dominance relationship that involves a similar sort of individualized servitude. In slavery, individual owners rule at least some of their individual slaves in the intimacy of household relationships. Yet slavery is not the only form that racial dominance can take. Racial dominance can take public forms such as political disenfranchisement and economic discrimination. Thus, racial dominance can leave members of the dominated group relatively free to forge their own "private" lives among themselves without the literal presence of dominant group members. Members of a dominated racial group may thus find, in their intimate lives, a refuge from racial domination and a locus for achieving some measure of personal autonomy. Male dominance is not like this; it has always affected domestic and intimate life. In addition, it has often involved the very confinement of women to domestic life with no other options. Where male dominance prevails, women have little or no refuge from its influence. It permeates both public and private spheres, thus proving inescapable in practice for most of the women who are affected by it.

Male dominance is bolstered by men's statistically greater degree of aggressiveness and fighting strength as compared to women. Women are thus, on average, denied the most useful traits by which people defend themselves against physical threats from other persons. These claims are mere statistical generalizations, obviously. Yet the statistical differences between women and men make it commonplace for the woman or women in any household to be less strong and less aggressive than the dominant man or men in the household. When men's aggressiveness and physical forcefulness is bolstered by social norms that legitimate their dominance, women are systematically subordinated, a consequence that cannot but have an affect on women's desires, fears, values, commitments – indeed their very characters.

Men are also dominant over women in the "public" spheres of most societies. Men typically hold the highest and most powerful offices of most societies and wield the greater share of social resources. Granted, some societies have committed themselves to sexual equality, and many members of those societies try to reduce the degree of male domination their societies permit. Several prominent countries have elected female heads of state, and some of these women have even led their countries in war.[9] In governments that rely heavily on military power, however, most top-ranked officials are male. On a global scale, male dominance remains pervasive and well entrenched. Also, any place in the world that is ruled by gangs or warlords, or in which the rule of law has broken down and anarchy prevails, is a place in which most or all of those with power are men.[10] It is no accident that there is no such word as "war-ladies."[11]

Thus, on a global level, there is little hope of eradicating male dominance any time soon even though the struggle to do so must continue. Meanwhile, this chapter is about how we should now rethink autonomy in light of the current global persistence of male dominance. Does the nature or value of autonomy change, given the ways in which the identities and life circumstances of women in many parts of the world lead them into positions of public and/or private subordination to men?[12]

I Traumatic Bonding

To grasp the features of male dominance "writ large," let's consider some extreme forms of general dominance relationships such as captivity and abuse. Captors who take hostages or political prisoners, as well as chronic women-batterers, try to exercise what Judith Herman calls "coercive control" over the lives of their victims while at the same time demanding from their victims expressions of "respect, gratitude, or even love." Herman writes, "In situations of captivity, the perpetrator becomes the most powerful person in the life of the victim, and the psychology of the victim is shaped by the beliefs and actions of the perpetrator."[13]

Accounts of how women are "seasoned" into prostitution by pimps or controlled by chronically abusive men, and of how hostages are terrorized into submission, show remarkable similarity in the techniques employed. The techniques depend mainly on forms of psychological control; captors use overt physical violence infrequently to attain their ends. They do rely, however, on the *threat* of physical violence. Thus, captors engage in "inconsistent and unpredictable outbursts of violence," the "capricious enforcement of petty rules," and "scrutiny and control of the victim's body and bodily functions" (77). As a result, the victim comes to regard the captor as all-powerful and to think that resistance will be futile. She comes to believe "that her life depends upon winning his indulgence through absolute compliance" (77). Victims may come to feel gratitude toward their captors for the smallest kindness or indulgence (77). Captors also try to isolate their victims from other social contacts from which they might derive support (79). Under these conditions, the victim will "come to see the world through the eyes of the perpetrator" (81). Victims become emotionally dependent on their captors and begin to seek a "common humanity" in their captors (82). Thus arises a kind of love, one that is grounded on fear.

Donald G. Dutton and Susan Painter have developed a theory of the "traumatic bonding" that occurs under conditions of captivity or abuse.[14] Traumatic bonding affects abused women, abused children, hostages, cult members, and even non-human animals under abusive conditions. It occurs when one party is more powerful than the other and dominates or subjugates the other, and when the abuse is intermittent in nature. The bonds are strongest when the abuse is "interspersed with permissive and friendly contact."[15] The pattern of "alternating aversive and pleasant conditions" is known in learning theory as "partial or intermittent reinforcement," and is very effective in "producing persistent patterns of behavior that are difficult to extinguish."[16]

What Herman and Dutton and Painter describe are reactions under extreme conditions, those of captivity and severe abuse. Many women do not regard the typical male dominance in their lives (if any) as literal captivity or as severe abuse (although we should not underestimate the amount of male dominance that is so). Our first response might be to think that traumatic bonding is irrelevant to an understanding of common forms of male dominance. Commonplace male dominance, however, may involve this effect after all, but at a reduced level, depending on the degree to which women are trapped and threatened in situations controlled by men. Oppression may be so subtle and concealed as to be, in J. Harvey's words, even "civilized."[17] In the micro-politics of daily life, women may indeed sometimes find themselves controlled by men in ways they cannot avoid. In some of those situations, women may feel cut off from social support and helpless to prevent what is happening. Even women who are secure from male aggression most of the time may find it intruding on occasion, suddenly and powerfully. As playwright David Mamet (certainly no friend of feminism) has revealingly remarked: "People can say what they will, we men think, but if I get pushed just one little step further, why I might, I just might – (FILL IN THE BLANKS) because she seems to have forgotten that I'M STRONGER THAN HER."[18] In other words, the phenomenon of traumatic bonding may well be "writ small" in the daily lives of many women worldwide.

II Male Dominance and Heteronomy

Personal autonomy has to do with behaving or living according to what is in some important sense "one's own." In brief, it involves an agent's acting from and according to wants or values that she has reflectively considered under conditions that were not unduly coercive or manipulative. Heteronomy, by contrast, involves behaving or living in accord with what is in some important sense *not*, or *other than*, one's own.

Heteronomy has two significant and familiar branches. First, one may live in accord with aspects of one's larger or whole self that are nevertheless not "one's own." Depending on one's theory of personhood or personal identity, these aspects might include one's desires, emotions, passions, inclinations, drives, addictions, or compulsions. Second, heteronomy may have to do with behaving or living in accord with what is in some important sense that of other persons. Such behavior may take the form of deference to other particular individuals or thoughtless conformity to group conventions or norms. Most contemporary discussions of autonomy in mainstream philosophy focus almost exclusively on sources of heteronomy that arise within the self, considered in abstract social isolation. They neglect the sorts of heteronomy that derive from interpersonal relations and the treatment of a self by others.[19] Male dominance is, in the first instance, a problem of this latter, or interpersonal, sort of heteronomy.

Elements of "internal" heteronomy, however, seem to be part of the whole story of male dominance. Aspects of someone's larger or whole self may make her especially vulnerable to interpersonal heteronomy. Someone may have character traits of (thoughtless) submissiveness that make her vulnerable to domination by others. Yet how do such traits arise? Surely one determinant of submissive character traits consists of a chronic lack of capacities for self-defense in the face of stronger, more aggressive others.

John Christman has observed that someone's bodily features form a background that shapes the choices she makes and, ultimately, her capacities for autonomy.[20] On Christman's view, bodily features do not arise as topics for a person's conscious reflection or reconsideration. Instead they "orient judgment and structure choice" (*ibid*). Christman forgets that people sometimes do focus conscious reflection on their bodily features, and make those features quite deliberate topics of choice and endeavor, for example, in health regimens, weight training, and cosmetic adornment. Christman is right, however, that the body is a background for choice.

One's embodiment is relevant to autonomy in at least two distinct but interrelated ways.[21] First, one's body plays a major role in one's capacity to do things. This idea is closest to Christman's concern. One's capacities to do specific things – one's talents and skills – open up options that might well otherwise be closed. The utter lack of capacity to do something can truncate one's desires and ambitions. A second aspect of embodiment that is important to this discussion, an aspect not mentioned by Christman, is the embodied vulnerability to harm. The harm that people can do to each other are of special relevance to autonomy. These two aspects of embodiment, capacity and vulnerability, are interrelated in that vulnerability to a particular harm diminishes as one's capacity to defend oneself against that type of harm increases. Women, for example, are particularly vulnerable to rape and domestic violence.

The notion of the embodied vulnerability to harm dovetails with the recent philosophical emphasis on the *social* nature and conditions of autonomy.[22] Many accounts of autonomy now take note of the social relationships required for persons to be autonomous and of the social nature of autonomous actions, characters, and lives. Embodied vulnerability to harm has crucial social dimensions. Someone's autonomy is especially threatened by her vulnerability to harms inflicted by other persons as forms of control. Dominating persons may use punishment, reprisals, and retaliation as means of influencing the behaviors of others. If someone refrains from doing what she really wants to do because she fears retaliatory violence from, say, her domestic partner, then she is behaving heteronomously. Thus, comparative bodily features (such as strength relative to that of others) help to determine how people interact with each other socially, and the social context of embodied *inter*relationships is a crucial background for both autonomy and heteronomy.

There is, of course, a psychological dimension as well as a physical dimension to someone's vulnerability to harm. Most human behavior occurs in social settings; it is not performed in isolation. People act in company with, and in affiliation with, others, often engaged with them in joint endeavors. Since much behavior, if not all of it, is socially situated, the capacities for autonomy must include some ability to shape the life one lives *with* others. Analogous to Aristotle's, Rousseau's, and Kant's ideal political citizens, an autonomous person is both "sovereign" and "subject" to the social order, participating in it but also helping to shape the interpersonal relationships that constitute it. Some people more than others have the capacity to behave in social settings in the way they want to or value. They may be able to exert more influence than others over joint endeavors. Or they may be better able than others to deflect opposition to what they themselves try to do. Those who are less capable than others of thus influencing social relationships are less able to act as they want or value in interpersonal contexts.[23]

Thus, interrelationships in all their dimensions, bodily or otherwise, provide the ground out of which emerge both autonomous and heteronomous behaviors. Yet the power that stems from physical strength and aggressiveness is particularly threatening because of its capacity to do immediate and severe damage. Chronic physical intimidation and battery can put a permanent mark on someone's character. It is important to remember, again, that women are far more vulnerable to sexual bullying and domestic violence than are men.[24]

There are various ways in which one can try to cope with domination and coercion. One may try to resist the domineering efforts of others, and perhaps even try to dominate them in return. This option, however, may lie beyond someone's capacities or may provoke retaliation, which only makes things worse. A safer way to cope with domination is to try to do what one wants to do in secret, furtively hiding what one does from the surveillance of dominating others. This alternative, however, imposes costs on one's life and character, such as having often to lie or dissimulate. One may also try to separate oneself from oppressive social relationships and to act apart from them. This measure, however, results in social isolation, something that many people find unbearable.

There is yet a fourth alternative. One can remain in a dominance relationship but try to placate the dominator by submissiveness, loyalty, and even affection. As I noted earlier, captives, when coping with extreme forms of coercive control, often come to identify with their captors and to take an interest in the well-being of their captors. Dominated persons may abandon wants and values that dominance relationships prevent them from realizing. A dominated person may try to convince herself that she never really wanted those things in the first place. From a third-person perspective, this behavior looks like a survival mechanism based on understandable fear. Yet to the submissive person, it may feel like genuine concern. As self-protective devices, loyalty and submissiveness are likely to be most effective when they are convincingly expressed, and this may require some measure of genuine sincerity. Somehow the dominated person may come to feel sincere concern for her abuser. Indeed, some former hostages continue to act with loyalty and affection to their former captors even when the danger is long past and the captors have been imprisoned for terrorism and kidnapping.[25]

Thus, being chronically dominated or controlled by others can alter the contours of someone's very personality. A captive or abused person's character may take on traits and dispositions aimed at pleasing her captor and protecting her against the captor's violence. Someone who is relatively socially powerless and therefore vulnerable to domination by a great many others may develop such traits as a matter of settled character, and may become thoroughly adaptively malformed as a result. She may become an unassertive, self-deprecating, servile, or obsequious person in general as a means of self-protection against the power of whoever can control her. And one common cause of such character traits seems to be the embodied experience of being chronically less powerful or aggressive compared with others when acting in interpersonal relationships. Most importantly, the resulting submissive character is more than a matter of simple preference deformation, since this alteration can constitute a *rational* strategy for self-protection in the face of interpersonal threats.

The psychological mechanism of submissiveness and even love in the face of threatening and unavoidable power seems to be a general human tendency, not confined to women. One reason for thinking this is the apparent presence of a kind of traumatic bonding even in some commonplace attitudes. One example of such attitudes is a familiar type of religious position that seems to be formally analogous to cases of pathological traumatic bonding. In most of the religions of the West, a supreme being is postulated and conceptualized as vastly more powerful than mere human mortals, often as omnipotent. There is good reason, from the theological perspectives of these religions, to fear the power of this being. That power, after all, may punish us through all eternity. It is rational for people to react to their god as they would to human captors they cannot escape who might also hold the power of life and death over them. After all, from a relationship with an omnipotent and omniscient god, there is never the option of exit. The "problem of evil," so much debated in Western philosophy and theology, deals with how to understand the inconsistent, unpredictable, and seemingly arbitrary harm and suffering that befalls innocent as well as guilty people in this world. "Evil," in this sense, is rather like the inconsistent and unpredictable harm, the "intermittent reinforcement," mentioned earlier, that captors inflict in order to secure their captives' submission.

Some religious attitudes thus seem remarkably like instantiations of the captive syndrome; they are conscious expressions of love and loyalty toward a fearsome, vastly powerful being one cannot overpower or escape. For Thomas Hobbes, one of the four "natural seeds" of religion is "devotion toward what men *fear*."[26] We try to placate the gods – or powerful persons – we can neither resist nor escape by obeying their commands or commandments, following their (divine) plans, loving them, and accepting the blame ourselves for the evils that occur (as do many abused women and some religious people).[27]

The occurrence in religious worship of something analogous to traumatic bonding suggests that deference and devotion toward what human beings fear is a common psychological tendency, not limited to women. Many men fear other men, and some men occasionally fear women. If male dominance, however, is partly based on men's statistically greater strength and aggressiveness compared with women, then women would tend to be the weaker parties in social relationships more often than would men, and particularly in one-on-one relationships between women and men. Women would therefore need to be submissive for self-protection in heterosocial relationships more often than men. And submissiveness, on the face of it, is in tension with autonomy.

III Adaptive Preferences

One of the more profound aspects of diminished autonomy that can result from domination by others occurs when dominated persons give up on wants and values that dominance relationships prevent them from realizing. In the case of male dominance, women may, for example, stop resisting sexual harassment or become complacent about wife-battering. In case this effect also involves the person trying to convince herself that she never really wanted to end those problems in the first place, the result would be a case of the familiar "sour grapes" phenomenon, or adaptive preference formation, famously analyzed by Jon Elster.[28] These sorts of adjustments seem to involve a clear loss of autonomy.

Henry Richardson, however, disagrees with that conclusion. He argues that adjusting our desires to fit what is attainable can *promote* autonomy. If we want what is genuinely valuable but we fail to achieve it, we risk losing self-esteem. Convincing ourselves that we did not really want the lost value is a way of regaining lost self-esteem, and regaining that lost self-esteem is necessary, Richardson argues, for being able to try to act autonomously again.[29]

Richardson illustrates this view using the literary character of Bully Stryver from Dickens's *A Tale of Two Cities*, a character who loves but ultimately loses the "beautiful and kind Lucie Manette." After Manette refuses to marry Stryver, he immediately gives up pursuing her, and denies to himself and others that he ever cared for her. Richardson argues that "some losses are so important" that we do not really lose autonomy by denying we ever cared about those lost aims. Instead, we actually promote our own autonomy by preserving the self-respect we need to "live to love another day."[30] Richardson's example evokes a famous line in an old song: "When I'm not near the girl I love, I love the girl I'm near."[31]

This strategy could be used by women who experience gender subordination. If women are less able to achieve what they seek when in the company of more dominant males, they may try, in order to maintain their self-respect, to convince themselves that what they were seeking is not genuinely valuable after all or that they never really wanted it. They may construe even their subordinated positions as values to be attained. As Simone de Beauvoir remarks generally of women in love, "She chooses to desire her enslavement so ardently that it will seem to her the expression of her liberty."[32]

Richardson recognizes that values differ, and indeed thinks that convincing oneself one did not really care about the lost end only promotes autonomy in case one was seeking something genuinely valuable. We disparage the phenomenon of "sour grapes" – that is, the process of adaptive preference formation, that leads us to view unattainable *grapes* as sour because, according to Richardson, possessing grapes is trivial as an aim, and no one should lose self-esteem over the failure to achieve it. We do lose self-esteem appropriately from the failure to attain something genuinely worthwhile, such as love, and in those cases, argues Richardson, the sour grapes preference adjustment does needed reparative work.

Richardson aptly characterizes the way in which many people do tend to behave after important failures but, unfortunately, he does not show that such preference adjustments have a reliable tendency to promote autonomy. Someone's gain in self-esteem in these cases may well be outweighed by other effects that tend to undermine autonomy. If I fail in my pursuit of *justice*, do I really promote my autonomy by denying I ever cared about justice? Am I likely to feel self-respect more from thinking I never cared about justice at all than from thinking I pursued it and lost? Perhaps there are some things we should feel good about having sought in vain, better, at any rate, than we should feel if we had never sought them at all – love, for example. In any case, it is not obvious that we do preserve our self-respect or promote our autonomy by coming to regard what we pursue in vain as valueless. Instead, we may merely debase our valuational efforts by making them too contingent on something's being attainable.

Perhaps Richardson means to limit his point to particulars: *this* love, *this* just cause. It is precisely in order not to give up on love or justice as such that I should try to distance myself from *this* lost love or *this* lost (just) cause. Even at this level, however, problems remain. Richardson seems to presuppose that self-esteem is better preserved by denying one ever cared about valuable *particulars* than by acknowledging that one failed in trying to attain them. This attitude is an instance of self-deception. Whether the goal is general or particular, self-deception about one's failures is fraught with difficulties. It may, for example, be unsuccessful. If the unattained end is self-consciously definitive of who someone is, and deeply intertwined with her other important ends, she may not be able to pretend readily that it is unimportant to her; repudiating the unattained end may undermine rather than promote her autonomy. In contrast to what Richardson maintains, the phenomenon of sour grapes may in fact bolster self-esteem precisely when the ends do not matter much to the respective agents. Thus, we have found no reason yet to think that women's adaptation to male dominance promotes women's autonomy.

IV Collateral Damage

Increasing the autonomy of women who are hampered by male dominance requires curbing or nullifying male dominance. If male dominance is based on greater biological sources of strength and aggression, then so long as human biological nature remains the same, curbing male dominance will require unending social constraints on male strength and aggressiveness. Even if male dominance is entirely a social construct, its evident persistence and pervasiveness at this time suggest that we will have to contend with it for the foreseeable future. We will have to socialize boys to be less aggressive than they are now, enforce legal prohibitions on male sexual coercion of women, and so on. Yet all social practices are subject to occasional breakdown. Whenever and wherever the practices that restrain male strength and aggressiveness break down, male dominance might well reassert itself as a major threat to women's autonomy. The global enhancement of women's autonomy thus seems to require practices and institutions that continuously and indefinitely curb male power advantages. Women thus depend profoundly on a properly functioning rule of law and other social institutions that reduce aggression and violence. This dependence, however, creates its own additional, collateral loss of women's autonomy. I shall explain.

In realizing autonomy, all people depend on social relationships and cultural resources. Women, however, seem to be more dependent in this regard than men. If women's autonomy is promoted by systems of social control by which men restrain themselves and each other from dominating women, then female autonomy would be more vulnerable than male autonomy to being undercut by social breakdown. Thus, in addition to requiring whatever support any person needs from social relationships in order to ensure commodious living, women would need extra social protection against male strength and aggression, since men are typically stronger and more aggressive than women. This need for extra protection against male power may reduce women's motivation to *criticize* the social institutions under which they live. Recall the familiar notion that women are more active churchgoers than men, despite the fact that religions are not usually leaders in gender equality. Women may be less critical of institutions of social control than they should be, given their heavy reliance on the security that social institutions can provide. If I, as a white woman in particular, believe that the police do protect me against violence, I might be disinclined to criticize the police for, say, racial bias in their methods, fearing implicitly that such criticism might weaken the capacity of law enforcement to protect me. My capacity for critical thinking would be constrained by my need for protection. This sort of outcome would involve an important and regrettable *collateral* loss of women's autonomy that results from male dominance.

V Rethinking Autonomy in Light of Male Dominance

Male dominance relies both on male power advantages over women and women's *human* tendencies to defer and devote themselves to those whose power they fear and cannot escape. Although women are making great strides in diminishing the power of male dominance in many societies, it will not be eliminated any time soon. Women's autonomy, in general, will therefore continue to be harder to realize than men's autonomy in the context of heterosocial interactions. Should this make a difference to a philosophical account of autonomy? Should we modify the philosophical account of autonomy? If so, how? I shall consider four possible modifications.

1. One sort of modification would be to rethink the nature or necessary conditions of autonomy in light of the pervasiveness of male dominance. Is personal autonomy as valuable as we have been led to think? Are powerful and seemingly more autonomous men really more autonomous than women after all? Perhaps people lack or lose personal autonomy to the extent that they do not respect the personal autonomy of others. That sort of view is not unfamiliar to us; it is, of course, Kant's view of moral autonomy. The Kantian moral law requires one to treat all persons as ends-in-themselves. Failing to respect the autonomy of others is failing to do one's moral duty, which, in turn, is the failure to be morally autonomous.

Can we say the same thing about personal autonomy? Is a failure to respect the personal autonomy of others at the same time a failure to be personally autonomous oneself? Contemporary, *content-neutral* accounts of personal autonomy, which I tend to favor,[33] reject that approach. On these accounts, autonomy involves governing oneself simply in accord with what is, in some important sense, "one's own." This bare idea, in and of itself, does not include the requirement of respecting the autonomy of others.

Henry Richardson seeks an intermediate position between content-neutral accounts of autonomy, which place no restriction on what one chooses, and morally substantive accounts of autonomy, such as the Kantian account, which do place restrictions on what one chooses. Richardson claims that it is indeed part of our normative requirements for considering someone to be autonomous that she respect the autonomy of others. That is, Richardson thinks we already tacitly regard someone as non-autonomous, no matter how self-determining she seems to be, if she does not respect the same self-determination in others.[34] Richardson's claim, however, is based largely on the intuitive force of a certain kind of example. In his example, a Lothario seduces women with no concern for what is right for them, and does so out of his own unreflective desires and inclinations. Richardson claims that Lothario's autonomy is reduced by his disregard of the autonomy of his female victims.

Unfortunately, Lothario's desires and inclinations confound Richardson's example. Influenced by the Kantian tradition, we may think that Lothario lacks autonomy, not because he disrespects the autonomy of his victims but rather because he acts from unreflective desires. Richardson's example would therefore not be conclusive, even if we were all to share his intuitions about it. Suppose, however, that Lothario is not driven by unreflective desire. Suppose instead that he seduces only upper-class women, and does so from a carefully calculated ambition to sleep his way up the corporate ladder, his predominant (and sincere) *reflective* value being career success. Would he still lack personal autonomy?

Richardson might insist that whenever someone disrespects the autonomy of others, she is acting from desire or inclination. Richardson claims that taking some account of others in the formation of one's own desires is "part of what we mean by not letting oneself be ruled by mere desire or inclination."[35] I question this claim. Avoiding rule by mere desire or inclination simply requires incorporating something other than mere desire or inclination into self-rule. This is all that is contained in the bare idea of not being "ruled by mere desire or inclination." The additional motivating factor need not be a consideration of the well-being or autonomy of others; it could simply consist, for example, in consideration of one's own long-range interests. On my view, someone can be personally autonomous without recognizing personal autonomy as a value or having any special respect for the autonomy of others – or even of oneself. Thus, the attempt to reconceptualize personal autonomy in order to show that dominant people do not have as much of it as they seem to have does not yet look very promising.

2. Alternatively, we could try to reconceptualize autonomy so as to show that submissive or subservient people have *more* autonomy than they might otherwise seem to have. Toward this end, it would be helpful to recall Joseph Raz's view that someone lacks autonomy if she lives under desperate or impoverished conditions that afford her no morally significant alternatives among which to choose.[36] A dominated person, according to Raz, has fewer morally significant alternatives than others because the need for self-protection makes it difficult or impossible to choose anything other than what will protect her. Raz seems to assume that someone who is forced to make choices that ensure merely her survival or self-protection is thereby denied autonomy. If the struggle to survive is a coercive force that ineluctably drives us to sacrifice what we otherwise want, care about, or value, then autonomy would be scarcely possible under conditions in which survival or basic material well-being are threatened.

Perhaps we should challenge Raz's view. It is a view with disturbing implications. On this view, autonomy would be significantly possible only when a person does not have to make great sacrifices to assure her survival or her minimal material well-being. The realization of autonomy would become something of a class-privilege, and people with meager resources would be largely out of luck. They would be simply deprived of conditions that would promote or elicit the development in them of the character-enhancing capacities for autonomy. This result prompts the concern that those who value autonomy might be doing so not because autonomy is intrinsically valuable but merely because it is a trait common among those who are comfortably enough situated so as to develop it and who happen to think well of them*selves*.

Consider women again. When women submit to male power with the aim of protecting themselves against harm, they are acting for reasons that are understandable and morally acceptable under the circumstances. Women's ultimate goal is not subordination; it is self-protection in the face of threats from other persons. Even if a woman's wants and values become adapted to and distorted by this aim, her adaptive attitudes are nevertheless the causal product of an understandable striving to survive under threat of force. Is there not perhaps a measure of autonomy after all in being a survivor?

We are also familiar with the idea that lives of obedience or submissiveness might nevertheless exhibit autonomy in some degree.[37] They do so when the person living the life has an overarching and self-defining commitment toward which the submissive life is a means. Lives of religious devotion are typical examples of this sort. As Sigurdur Kristinsson argues, if a submissive person retains, in addition, the tendency to change her behavior whenever she recognizes either that her submissiveness has become ineffective in attaining her goals or that her goals are worthless,[38] then she may well be realizing autonomy through submissiveness. This should be no less true when submissiveness is aimed at self-protection than when it is aimed at some "higher calling" such as a spiritual end.

There is something plausible about this strategy of construing mere survival and submissiveness as sometimes autonomous. However, the strategy is not fully satisfying on the issue of male dominance. In particular, it seems to diminish the wrongness of male dominance. If women can be as autonomous under male dominance as they can be apart from it, then we might have to conclude that male dominance is less of a hindrance to women's autonomy than it first appeared to be, and therefore less of a moral problem. Surely this is not the whole story. Part of what is wrong with male domination of women is precisely that it restricts women's options, impelling women to distort their priorities in order to protect themselves. Autonomy is a matter of degree. As a survivor under these conditions, a woman may have more autonomy than we first realized, but she still has less of it than she otherwise might have, and almost certainly less than her male counterpart whose options are not limited by a corresponding female domination.

I have considered two alternative ways of modifying our conception of the nature and necessary conditions of autonomy in light of male dominance, and have found each approach to be less than fully satisfying. I now turn to a different sort of strategy, that of reassessing the *value* of personal autonomy. Note that this is a separate issue from the nature and necessary conditions of autonomy. The mere conception of autonomy, of its nature and necessary conditions, does not dictate a particular assessment of autonomy's value. For that, we need a full-blown theory of personal autonomy. My remaining suggestions contribute to such an account.

3. One way in which to theorize the value of personal autonomy is simply to *devalue* it. Perhaps autonomy is overrated and not worth as much as we have been inclined to think. Perhaps some other behavioral tendencies, more typical of submissive or subordinated people, are worth *more* than we had previously realized. Heteronomy is often associated with dependency on other persons, and some feminists now emphasize the importance of dependency in human relationships.[39] Obvious forms of dependency are unavoidable for all of us at some stages of life, and hidden forms of dependency are probably unavoidable for all of us at all stages of life. Women's traditional gender roles, for example, are vitally important for children, the very elderly, and the infirm, who are attached to their (typically female) caregivers by reciprocal forms of dependence.[40] Dependence may seem to be the antithesis of autonomy, and the need for dependency in relationships that nurture us may seem to devalue autonomy by implication.

This line of thought, however, does not devalue autonomy after all. Granted, we are all interdependent. Dependency is necessary for human survival, and it promotes interrelationships of intimacy and love that ground some of our most profound values. This point does not show, however, that personal autonomy is not also valuable. Material and emotional dependencies are not incompatible with personal autonomy – that is, with persons behaving and living in accord with wants and values they have reflectively considered and come to hold without undue coercion and manipulation. No one can live a whole human life without dependencies of some sort at various, if not at all, times. One may be financially, physically, or psychologically dependent on the care and support of others, yet still choose autonomously how to live within those constraints. Thus, idealizing dependence does not necessitate devaluing autonomy. For that we would need a separate and direct case against autonomy or else showing that the two are mutually exclusive, a view I have argued against more fully elsewhere.[41]

4. A different way of reassessing the value of autonomy[42] is to reject a homogeneous account of its worth in favor of a heterogeneous account. That is, while personal autonomy is the same sort of trait or achievement for all persons, there is no one *evaluation* of autonomy that "fits all" who realize it. On this approach, the value of autonomy differs depending on whose autonomy is in question. In particular, autonomy is more valuable for dominated people than for dominators. After all, dominated people have more to overcome in realizing autonomy than do dominators, so their realization of it is more of an achievement. More importantly, the autonomy of the dominated promotes realization of the moral equality of persons, whereas the autonomy of dominators, insofar as they are dominating others, works against the realization of that ideal. This value differentiation is the major adjustment I recommend to our understanding of personal autonomy in light of the vexing persistence of male dominance, with its roots in male excesses of strength and aggressiveness.

Personal autonomy has intrinsic value, and in this respect its value is equal among all who realize it. Autonomy also, however, has instrumental value insofar as it serves other values. In particular, it serves the social realization of the moral equality of all persons. The notion of the moral equality of persons developed gradually in the West along with the idealization of *moral* autonomy. According to Jerome Schneewind, the ideal of autonomy arose as a reaction to earlier moralities of obedience, moralities according to which not all persons are equally capable of discerning what morality requires or motivating themselves to live accordingly. According to moralities of obedience, those persons who lack moral abilities (namely, most of us) can live moral lives only by obeying those who do have the requisite moral capacities. On this view, women, who lack moral capacities, need to be governed by men, who sometimes can be morally competent. What developed in the modern period of Western philosophy was the *idea* that all (ordinary) persons do have the requisite capacities to be moral agents. This competency is their moral autonomy.[43] Despite this growing insight, however, Western culture during the modern period clung tenaciously to various forms of social hierarchy and moral subordination. Male dominance was only one of many such lingering forms of moral and social control. Thus the ideal of the moral equality of all persons has scarcely been realized in social practice.

Moral autonomy bears on personal autonomy, among other things, in the following way. The moral equality of all persons includes the idea that all persons count equally as moral agents. As moral agents, all persons are equally entitled to contribute to moral dialogue, to make up their own minds about what is morally right and what is morally good, and to try to act accordingly. Morally equal agents are also entitled to live the nonmoral aspects of their lives each as they see fit. Personal autonomy is that feature of a life that, with suitable qualifications, involves its being lived in accord with the wants and values of the person whose life it is. Any aspect of a person's behavior, however, may have moral significance. Only those persons possessing moral competence can reasonably be trusted by others to recognize and act in accord with the moral significances of the personal choices they make in their lives. Only those with (presumptive) *moral* competence are entitled to have others respect their *personal autonomy*.

Social hierarchy and patterns of dominance upset the order of the moral equality of persons by putting some persons in positions of moral and personal dominance over others. Subordinated persons are constrained and coerced by a combination of factors. First, they are overpowered by dominant others. Second, they are controlled by the enforcement power of social institutions, which frequently serves the ends of powerful persons. And, if my earlier argument is correct, then third, subordinate persons are constrained by their human psychological tendencies both to submit to dominating others for the sake of self-preservation and, in the process, to mold their own wants and values around the preferences of the powerful persons they can neither overcome nor escape.

Dominant persons are more able to act according to their own wants and values, since others will defer to them, submit to them, and even love them for it. When persons in positions of social dominance act autonomously, they often do so at the expense of the autonomy of subordinated persons. Suppressed and subordinated persons are denied some measure of social recognition and respect for their moral competence – that is, their competence to make personal choices in recognition of the moral significances that arise. The moral equality of those persons is thereby denied its due. Gender-related inequalities of strength and aggressiveness are among the conditions that enable some (stronger and more aggressive men) to take charge of social relationships in ways that obstruct the personal autonomy of others (including weaker and less aggressive women). As a result of gender-based (and other forms of) subordination, the equal *moral* competence of weaker and less aggressive persons fails to get the social expression, recognition, and respect it deserves.[44]

When subordinate persons manage to behave according to their own reflective wants and values, they overcome in some small way the moral imbalance involved in their subordination. They do so especially when acting for the sake of wants or values that were not adapted to mimic the wants or needs of those in control. Thus the personal autonomy of subordinated persons promotes social recognition of and respect for their equal moral competence, and thereby promotes the social *realization* of the moral equality of all persons. In that respect, its worth appreciates beyond the simple intrinsic value of autonomy as such.

In this discussion, I have assumed that male dominance will persist for the foreseeable future, and is partly rooted in men's statistically greater degrees of strength and aggressiveness compared to women. Female autonomy is reduced by this strength advantage in combination with women's *human* tendency to defer to inescapable, overpowering others. I then considered four ways to rethink autonomy in light of this difference between women and men. I concluded that under conditions of male dominance, female autonomy is more *valuable* than male autonomy because it better promotes social realization of the moral equality of all persons. Because it is more valuable, we all have good reason to advance women's autonomy whenever possible while at the same time restraining male aggression.

Notes

The earliest version of this chapter was presented at the Eastern Division meetings of the American Philosophical Association, Atlanta, Georgia, 28 December 2001. A later version prior to this draft was presented to the Society for Women in Philosophy meeting in conjunction with the Pacific APA, San Francisco, California, 28 March 2003.

1. Niccolo Machiavelli, *The Prince*, in *Modern Moral and Political Philosophy*. Robert C. Cummins and Thomas D. Christiano, eds. London: Mayfield, 1999 [1513]; 5–40 (chapter 17).
2. A familiar example of such truncated options is Joseph Raz's case of the "hounded woman," in *The Morality of Freedom* (Oxford: Clarendon Press, 1986), p. 374.
3. Felicia Pratto, "Sexual Politics: The Gender Gap in the Bedroom, the Cupboard, and the Cabinet" in David Buss and Neil M. Malamuth, eds. *Sex, Power, Conflict* (New York: Oxford University Press, 1996), pp. 179–230, at 179.
4. David M. Buss, "Sexual Conflict: Evolutionary Insights into Feminism and the 'Battle of the Sexes'," in *Sex, Power, Conflict*, pp. 296–318.
5. One may take a Hegelian tack and argue that the autonomy of the male "master" is compromised along with that of the female "slave." Even if this were true, however, it would not entail the notion that the autonomy of the slave is not diminished by the relationship. It is the loss of women's autonomy that concerns me. I leave it to others to develop the account of how men's autonomy is diminished by male dominance.

6. In this chapter, I use the terms "male dominance" and "male domination" interchangeably. They are not synonymous, however, and would need to be differentiated in other contexts.
7. Modern reproductive technologies eliminate this requirement, but the expense of such technologies makes them largely unavailable to most people of the earth. Since this chapter assumes a global context, I ignore the affects of technologies that reach only a small percentage of the earth's people.
8. See Joel Anderson, "A Social Conception of Personal Autonomy: Volitional Identity, Strong Evaluation, and Intersubjective Accountability." Ph.D. dissertation: Northwestern University, 1996; Marina Oshana, "Personal Autonomy and Society," *Journal of Social Philosophy* 29 (Spring 1998): 81–102; Catriona Mackenzie and Natalie Stoljar, eds. *Relational Autonomy: Feminist Perspectives on Autonomy, Agency, and the Social Self* (Oxford: Oxford University Press, 2000).
9. My point here is not to endorse war – far from it. My point is rather that women have sometimes been elected to offices that permitted them to exercise powers normally reserved for men.
10. Examples are scarcely needed, but here are two of them. In recent years, the "shantytown" neighborhoods of Rio de Janeiro, which contain over 1 million of Rio de Janeiro's 5.8 million residents, have become "gang fiefs." Gangs have gained control of these neighborhoods to such a degree that the police and legitimate levels of government are afraid to intervene, and are subject themselves to intimidation and violence. Gang rule, in the words of one Brazilian official, has created "parallel governments that threaten Brazil's democracy and the rule of law." One of the ways in which gang leaders exercise their power is by sexual assault directed at young women and girls. See Larry Rohter, "At Your Great Peril, Defy the Lords of the Slums," *New York Times*, 28 June 2002, p. A4.

    Another example: In Baghdad at the time of this writing, security and law enforcement are still broken down several months after the United States' invasion of Iraq was declared a victory by President George W. Bush. Rape, often accompanied by kidnapping, appears to be on the rise in Baghdad. The problem of rape in Baghdad is compounded by the code of "honor" to which many families subscribe. A woman or girl who is the victim of rape is regarded as a dishonor to her family. Thus, instead of getting support from her family, a rape victim is likely to be beaten by her father or male relatives. Sometimes these beatings are life-threatening. Because of this added danger, very few women or girls who are raped report these crimes to anyone. They are thereby deprived of any possible extra-familial protection that might be available. See Neela Banerjee, "Rape (and Silence About It) Haunts Baghdad," *The New York Times*, 16 July 2003, pp. A1, 9.
11. In English, at any rate.
12. Autonomy is not valued as such in many parts of the world. I have argued elsewhere, however, that even when not valued as such, autonomy may nevertheless figure implicitly as an ideal that governs the way people think about social practices and their justification; see Marilyn Friedman, *Autonomy*,

Gender, and Politics (New York: Oxford, 2004), especially chapter 9. Even if autonomy lacks that importance for a particular culture, people from elsewhere who do find value in autonomy may still try to understand that culture's practices in terms of autonomy, and then see what sorts of cross-cultural dialogue can be initiated on the basis of that understanding. That a particular culture lacks an explicit commitment to autonomy need not bring outsiders to that culture to an immediate full stop in their use of the concept.

13. Judith Herman, *Trauma and Recovery* (New York: Basic Books, 1992, 1997), 75 (page numbers in the next paragraph of the text refer to Herman's book).
14. D. Dutton and S. L. Painter, "Traumatic Bonding: The Development of Emotional Attachments in Battered Women and Other Relationships of Intermittent Abuse." *Victimology* 6 (1981): 139–55.
15. Dutton and Painter, 190–192
16. Dutton and Painter, 191.
17. J. Harvey, *Civilized Oppression* (Lanham, MD: Rowman & Littlefield, 1999).
18. See Christine Macleod, "The Politics of Gender, Language and Hierarchy in Mamet's 'Oleanna'." *Journal of American Studies* 29 (1995): 199–213, 211. Macleod is quoting from David Mamet, *A Whore's Profession: Notes and Essays* (London and Boston: Faber, 1994), p. 140.
19. Two exceptions in mainstream philosophy are Raz, *The Morality of Freedom*, and Oshana, "Personal Autonomy and Society." Feminist philosophical discussions of autonomy give ample attention to the social context of autonomy; see, for example, Mackenzie and Stoljar, *Relational Autonomy*, and Friedman *Autonomy, Gender, and Politics*.
20. Christman, "Liberalism, Autonomy, and Self-Transformation." *Social Theory and Practice* 27/2 (April 2001): 185–206.
21. These are not the only ways in which embodiment is relevant to autonomy; see Diana Tietjens Meyers, "Decentralizing Autonomy: Five Faces of Selfhood," Chapter 2 in the present volume.
22. See, for example, Anderson, "A Social Conception of Personal Autonomy"; Oshana, "Personal Autonomy and Society"; Mackenzie and Stoljar, *Relational Autonomy*; Oshana "Autonomy and Self-Identity," Chapter 4 in the present volume.
23. This is not to say that social relationships are always, or only, coercive or adversarial. Social relationships for those of us who are fortunate enough to avoid war, social unrest, and dysfunctional families are largely benign and cooperative. Yet coercive and adversarial relationships, when they do occur, may be so painful that even a small risk of them may exert a profound influence on attitudes and character.
24. We should also note that men are more vulnerable than women to violent assaults and battering by strangers. In either sort of case, however, the culprits are more likely to be men than women, so this point does not undermine the picture of male dominance sketched here.
25. Herman, 82.
26. Thomas Hobbes, *Leviathan*. Richard Tuck, ed. (Cambridge: Cambridge University Press, 1996 [1651]), 79; italics mine.

27. I do not claim that *all* religious attitudes have this motivation, merely some.
28. Jon Elster, "Sour Grapes – Utilitarianism and the Genesis of Wants," in Christman, ed., *The Inner Citadel: Essays on Individual Autonomy* (New York: Oxford University Press, 1989), 170–188.
29. Henry Richardson, "Autonomy's Many Normative Presuppositions." *American Philosophical Quarterly* 38/3 (July 2001): 287–303; see especially 292–3, 296–7.
30. Richardson, 292–3. Richardson talks interchangeably of self-respect (for example, 292) and self-esteem (for example, 298). It is not relevant to the present discussion to insist on the distinction between these notions.
31. These lyrics are from the song, "When I'm Not Near the Girl I Love," by Yip Harburg, 1947 (music by Burton Lane). A later version of the idea, more familiar to many readers, is: "If you can't be with the one you love, love the one you're with," by Stephen Stills from the song, "Love the One You're With" (1970). See *The Columbia World of Quotations* (New York: Columbia University Press, 1996).
32. Simone de Beauvoir, *The Second Sex*. Trans. and ed., H. M. Parshley (New York: Vintage Books, 1989 [Alfred A. Knopf, 1952]), 643.
33. Friedman, *Autonomy, Gender and Politics*.
34. Richardson, "Autonomy's Many Normative Presuppositions," 298.
35. Richardson, 298.
36. Raz, *The Morality of Freedom*, 373–74.
37. Dworkin, *The Theory and Practice of Autonomy* (Cambridge: Cambridge University Press, 1988), chapter 2; Jeff Spinner-Halev, *Surviving Diversity: Religion and Democratic Citizenship* (Baltimore, MD: Johns Hopkins University Press, 2000), 30.
38. Sigurdur Kristinsson, "The Limits of Neutrality: Toward a Weakly Substantive Account of Autonomy." *Canadian Journal of Philosophy*, vol. 30, no. 2 (June 2000): 257–86, 282.
39. Eva Feder Kittay, *Love's Labor: Essays on Women, Equality, and Dependency* (New York: Routledge, 1999).
40. Caregivers may come to depend emotionally on the subjects of their care, for example, by loving them or by deriving a sense of self-identity from the caretaking role.
41. Friedman, *Autonomy, Gender, and Politics*.
42. Thanks to Joel Anderson for comments on this chapter, originally presented as a paper at the Eastern Division meetings of the American Philosophical Association, Atlanta, Georgia, 28 Dec 2001, that helped me rethink the view presented in this section.
43. J. B. Schneewind, *The Invention of Autonomy: A History of Modern Moral Philosophy* (Cambridge: Cambridge University Press, 1998).
44. Some women acquire dominance over some men in virtue of social privileges such as those of race or class or in virtue of forms of aggressiveness that do not depend on physical strength, such as verbal alacrity. However male dominance over women is reinforced by social institutions, practices, and

ideals, something not true of female dominance. Male dominance is also redundantly marked by various linguistic conventions, all of which have no corresponding female-dominant equivalents. And female dominance over men typically incites scorn and ridicule. Male dominance is a *paradigm* of interpersonal dominance, whereas female dominance over men is exceptional.

PART III

THE SOCIAL

Public Policy and Liberal Principles

8

Autonomy, Domination, and the Republican Challenge to Liberalism

Richard Dagger

There was a time, not so long ago, when almost no one would have considered republicanism a challenge to liberalism. Conservatism, fascism, communism, and other forms of socialism were prominent on lists of liberalism's rivals, but not republicanism. Historians occasionally analyzed the classical republics of Greece and Rome, or the role of republican ideas in seventeenth-century England or the American founding period, but republicanism itself was not a live option in contemporary politics.[1] In recent years, however, the situation has changed dramatically. Among political theorists, at least, the question now is not whether republicanism presents a challenge to liberalism but what kind of challenge it is.

On this question there are, broadly speaking, two points of view. According to one, republicanism and liberalism are fundamentally different schools of thought, and the republican challenge is to be welcomed or resisted, depending on one's position, as an attempt to supplant or replace liberalism. Whole-hearted liberals thus condemn republicanism as a danger to individual liberties and free societies, while neo-republicans such as Michael Sandel and Philip Pettit maintain that republicanism is not only different from but superior to liberalism.[2] According to the other point of view, the features that liberalism and republicanism share are more telling than the differences that divide them. From this perspective, the republican challenge aims not at replacing or defeating liberalism but at correcting its course. It is in this spirit that Cass Sunstein has welcomed the revival of interest in republicanism 'as a response to understandings that treat governmental outcomes as a kind of interest-group deal, and that downplay the deliberative functions of politics and the social formation of preferences'.[3] The value of republicanism, on this view, is in its contribution to the development of a 'liberal republicanism' that promises to rescue American (and other) politics from the interest-group pluralism into which it has degenerated.

Like Sunstein and other advocates of 'republican' or 'civic' liberalism, I believe that it is historically unsound and politically unwise to insist on a sharp distinction between liberalism and republicanism.[4] Others disagree, however, and there is much to be learned from their position even if, ultimately, we should not adopt it. Those who take this more radical neo-republican view advance two main lines of argument: first, that the liberal emphasis on neutrality and procedural fairness is fundamentally at odds with the republican commitment to promoting civic virtue; and, second, that republicans and liberals conceive of liberty or freedom in incompatible ways. This second line of argument is my particular concern here, for it raises the question of whether republicans may attach the same value to autonomy that liberals do. My claim is that they may, and they must as republicanism and liberalism in the end are both theories of self-government. Before setting out and supporting that claim, though, it is necessary to examine briefly the first line of argument.

I Republicanism vs. Liberalism: Civic Virtue

What is republicanism, and how might someone see it as a rival of liberalism? Whole books have been written in the last few years to answer those questions, but a brief response might focus on the *public* in 'republic'.[5] Republicanism takes its name from the Latin *res publica* – the public thing or business – and contemporary republicans are quick to claim that this stress on the public betokens a significant difference between themselves and liberals. Liberals, they say, are preoccupied with liberating the individual from restraints on his or her liberty – a preoccupation that leads liberals into endless contortions as they strive to distinguish the private realm from the public and protect it against encroachment. Republicans, in contrast, recognize that individual liberty is secure only in a self-governing community, which means that individual rights must be balanced with public responsibilities if the community is to survive and prosper. Someone who takes these public responsibilities seriously is said to display *civic virtue*, or 'the disposition to further public over private good in action and deliberation'.[6]

This concern for civic virtue persists today in various forms, such as the exhortations to vote that regularly appear, at least in the United States, at election time. Another form is the suspicion that public officials are prone to corruption and conflicts of interest – conflicts that lead them to place their private interests ahead of the common good. But republicans do not take these signs of its persistence to mean that civic virtue is flourishing. If it were, there would be little point in exhorting people to vote; virtuous citizens would need at most a nudge to remind them to do their civic duty. The challenge today for those of a republican disposition is, as it usually has been, the challenge of finding ways to cultivate and sustain civic virtue. This challenge *for* republicans becomes a challenge *to* liberals because republicans believe that liberals, with their emphasis on the value of privacy, are either doing too little to foster civic virtue or are actively, if unintentionally, destroying it. In particular, liberals fail to stress the importance of overcoming *corruption* and *dependence*.

Corruption is the great enemy of civic virtue, on the republican view. In its active form, corruption occurs when people try to advance their personal interests at the expense of the common good, as when avarice leads to the looting of the public treasury or ambition to an attempt to seize power. In its passive form, corruption occurs when people shirk their civic duties in order to pursue personal pleasures, such as those found in indolence, luxury, and wealth. For civic virtue to thrive, such corrupting vices as ambition, avarice, and sloth must be, if not eliminated, at least contained.

In addition to worrying about corruption, republicans worry about dependence. For republicans, the good citizen is a responsible member of a self-governing polity – someone who, in Aristotle's terms, rules and is ruled in turn.[7] People who are almost completely dependent on others will likely be ruled, but they are surely in no position to rule. The rule of law is necessary, therefore, as a means of avoiding personal dependence. According to the old formula, 'a government (or empire) of laws, not of men', frees citizens by subjecting them to laws, not to the demands and whims of unchecked rulers. Republicans have also typically defended private property as a way of guaranteeing that citizens would not be dependent on others for their livelihood. To some, this has implied that citizenship must be confined to that minority of men who owned sufficient property to be independent; to others, such as James Harrington and Jean-Jacques Rousseau, it has suggested that property should be distributed so as to prevent anyone from being wealthy enough to dominate other citizens, thus rendering them dependent. As Rousseau put it, everyone should have something, but no one should have too much.[8] That is, everyone should have enough property to be able to speak and act independently – as a citizen. But no one should have so much property as to be corrupted by luxury or enabled to dominate others.

Liberals, of course, may well respond that they have never advocated corruption or dependence as proper forms of conduct or ways of life. But the republican point is that liberalism quite unintentionally promotes corruption, at least in its passive form, and dependence. Or perhaps I should say the republican *points*, as here we can begin to see how republicans have advanced two distinct lines of criticism against liberalism.

According to the first line of attack, liberals have promoted corruption by encouraging people to pursue their private interests at the expense of their public responsibilities. This criticism has been pressed forcefully, with special attention to the United States, by Michael Sandel. In *Democracy's Discontent* and other works, Sandel argues that liberals are now engaged in a self-defeating project because their concern for neutrality and procedure rules out 'a formative politics... that cultivates in citizens the qualities of character self-government requires'.[9] In their desire to remain neutral among competing conceptions of the good, liberals have devised a thin, insubstantial form of politics that aims only to 'provide a framework of rights that respects persons as free and independent selves, capable of choosing their own values and ends'.[10] Instead of producing virtuous citizens who are devoted to the common good, contemporary liberalism produces people who think of themselves as autonomous individuals – that is, individuals who jealously guard their freedom to live as they choose against the encroaching demands of state and society. Lacking any common ground other than their agreement to disagree, these individuals must count on a neutral government to maintain the procedural safeguards that will allow them to pursue their various, and even discordant, conceptions of the good life. Such a 'procedural republic', Sandel charges, cannot sustain the loyalty and sense of solidarity necessary to its own survival. As he argues:

The procedural republic that has unfolded over the past half-century can now be seen as an epic experiment in the claims of liberal as against republican political thought. Our present predicament lends weight to the republican claim that liberty cannot be detached from self-government and the virtues that sustain it, that the formative project cannot be dispensed with after all. The procedural republic, it turns out, cannot secure the liberty it promises because it cannot inspire the moral and civic engagement self-government requires.[11]

Is Sandel right?

He is certainly right, in my view, to insist on the need for a 'formative project' that will foster civic virtue; but he is wrong, as I have argued elsewhere, to oppose liberalism to republicanism as sharply as he does.[12] A strong dose of republican concern for inspiring civic virtue would be a valuable corrective to the tendency of many contemporary liberals to maintain that the state must be nothing more than an umpire or arbiter charged with protecting individual rights and insuring fair play. But that is not to say that we should throw out liberalism, root and branch, to replace it with republicanism. For a conception of civic virtue to prove compelling today, it must embrace tolerance, a sense of fair play, and respect for the rights of others – all of them virtues associated with liberalism, and none of them incompatible with republicanism. The challenge, then, is to devise a republican form of liberalism, or a liberal form of republicanism, that promises to support the 'formative politics' that will inspire a public-spirited citizenry.

There is, however, a second line of attack that aims at replacing liberalism with republicanism, and those who advance it are interested less in forming people for citizenship than in freeing them from dependence or domination. According to this criticism, as set out by Philip Pettit, Quentin Skinner, and Maurizio Viroli, liberalism and republicanism rest on fundamentally different conceptions of freedom, with the republican superior to the liberal.[13] As in Sandel's case, I believe that these authors exaggerate the difference between liberalism and republicanism. Indeed, Viroli himself holds that liberalism is not an alternative to republicanism but a form of it, albeit an 'impoverished or incoherent' form.[14] Nevertheless, the distinction these authors develop contains important insights about freedom and its place in the republican tradition – insights, I shall argue, that ultimately reveal autonomy to be a concern that republicans and liberals share, not one that divides them.

II Republicanism vs. Liberalism: Freedom

The neo-republican attempt to distinguish between republican and liberal conceptions of freedom has its antecedents in two earlier, much discussed distinctions. The first was the subject of Benjamin Constant's 'The Liberty of the Ancients Compared with That of the Moderns'. According to Constant, the liberty of the ancients consisted in the collective exercise of law-making power, but that of the moderns consists above all in the individual's right to go about his or her business. In Constant's words:

> The aim of the ancients was the sharing of social power among the citizens of the same fatherland; this is what they called liberty. The aim of the moderns is the enjoyment of security in private pleasures; and they call liberty the guarantees afforded by institutions to these pleasures.[15]

Constant does not connect his distinction to liberalism and republicanism, but it is easy to see how one might link ancient liberty to republican thinking and modern liberty to liberal thinking. When Constant goes on to condemn attempts to revive ancient liberty by insisting that 'none of the numerous and too highly praised institutions which in the ancient republics hindered individual liberty is any longer admissible in the modern times', moreover, it is easy to conclude that he is rejecting the republican view of liberty on essentially liberal grounds.[16]

Easy, perhaps, but wrong. Constant does believe that it is both foolish and dangerous to try to replace modern liberty with ancient liberty, and he has no sympathy for those who hope to revive such ancient 'institutions' as ostracism and censorship. But he also holds that the moderns are in danger of turning their backs entirely on ancient liberty. Ancient liberty 'might attach too little value to individual rights and enjoyments', but in words that anticipate de Tocqueville's apprehensions about 'individualism', Constant warns that the 'danger of modern liberty is that, absorbed in the enjoyment of our private independence, and in the pursuit of our particular interests, we should surrender our right to share in political power too easily'.[17] It is necessary, therefore, 'to learn to combine the two [forms of liberty] together'.[18] Far from renouncing ancient liberty, in fact, Constant concludes his speech with a paragraph that weaves together themes now regarded as republican with themes often considered liberal:

The work of the legislator is not complete when he has simply brought peace to the people. Even when the people are satisfied, there is much left to do. Institutions must achieve the moral education of the citizens. By respecting their individual rights, securing their independence, refraining from troubling their work, they must nevertheless consecrate their influence over public affairs, call them to contribute by their votes to the exercise of power, grant them a right of control and supervision by expressing their opinions; and, *by forming them through practice for these elevated functions,* give them both the desire and the right to discharge these.[19]

Whatever else it may do, in sum, Constant's distinction between ancient and modern liberty does not reveal the mutual hostility of republican and liberal liberty. On the contrary, it supports the claim that republican liberalism is both possible and plausible as a theory of politics.

The second distinction – that between positive and negative liberty – does not prove so helpful to the republican-liberal cause, but neither does it hurt it. This is because the distinction presents two problems for those who hold that republicanism is hostile to the liberal position on freedom.

The first is that the distinction itself is troublesome, even in its most celebrated and influential formulation by Isaiah Berlin, who generally defends the negative conception – that liberty is the absence of restraint – against the positive conception of freedom as self-mastery.[20] The second problem is that the positive/negative distinction does not correspond to or 'track' the distinction between republican and liberal conceptions of liberty. This second problem, furthermore, besets both sides of the distinction. For those interested in republicanism and liberalism, the tendency is to take negative liberty as the liberal conception and positive liberty as the republican. But that makes it difficult to account for T. H. Green, who was both a champion of positive freedom and a self-described liberal.[21] It is possible, to be sure, that Green was wrong – wrong to think that he was a liberal, or wrong to think that a liberal can conceive of liberty as 'a positive power or capacity of doing or enjoying something that is worth doing or enjoying ... in common with others'.[22] But even if Green were wrong in one or both of these ways, there is still the problem on the other side of the distinction. That is, negative liberty does not seem to be the exclusive property of liberals. According to Quentin Skinner, Machiavelli and other republicans 'never appeal to a "positive" view of social freedom'; instead, 'they work with a purely negative view of liberty as the absence of impediments to the realization of our chosen ends'.[23] Whether we look to the negative or the positive side of the distinction, then, the answer seems to be the same: republican and liberal conceptions of freedom simply do not match the negative/positive distinction.

This leaves us with the third and, for our present purposes, most straightforward distinction: republican versus liberal conceptions of liberty. In this case, the distinction drawing comes primarily from scholars sympathetic to republicanism, notably Philip Pettit and Quentin Skinner. Both Pettit and Skinner take the fear that personal dependence deprives people of their independence to be the heart of the republican idea of freedom, and both conceive of this as a form of negative liberty. For Skinner, republican, or 'neo-roman', liberty is 'absence of dependence'; for Pettit, 'the supreme political value' of the republican tradition is 'freedom as non-domination'. Against this republican conception of liberty they oppose not only positive liberty, understood as self-mastery, but also the 'classical liberal' form of negative liberty as 'absence of interference'.[24]

Freedom as non-interference is the liberal view, Pettit says, because Thomas Hobbes, Jeremy Bentham, William Paley, and other liberals have held that any and all interference with our actions deprives us of (some) freedom.[25] Pettit argues that this conception is unsatisfactory for two reasons. First, someone may suffer domination without suffering interference. If I were in someone's power, for instance, I might well see the need to shape my conduct to what I take to be his or her desires – and I might do so even if that person never interferes or even thinks of interfering with my actions. This kind of non-interfering domination happens all too often, according to Pettit, who provides numerous references to fawning, toadying, cap-doffing, forelock-tugging, and other forms of servile deference to demonstrate the evil of domination. The second objection is that freedom as non-interference ignores the distinction between arbitrary and non-arbitrary interference. It is not interference as such that is objectionable, but its arbitrariness. A slave who must bow to the will of the master, and a citizen who must bow to the force of the law, may both suffer interference; but it is a mistake to say that they both lose freedom as a result. The master holds arbitrary power over the slave because the master need not consider the slave's interests; but the law, at least in the ideal, must attend to the interests of the citizen even when it interferes with his or her actions. Because it protects the citizen against arbitrary power, the law is 'the non-mastering interferer' that ensures the citizen's freedom.[26]

Freedom as non-domination thus rests on 'the frankness of intersubjective equality'.[27] The law may happen to interfere with my conduct more than with yours, yet we stand eye to eye and are equally free as citizens. This independence from arbitrary power is so valuable, Pettit says, that it is a 'primary good' in the Rawlsian sense. Whatever else people may want, they will want to be free from domination because they then will have the ability to make plans, to speak freely, and simply to be *persons*; for 'everyone – or at least everyone who has to make their [sic] way in a pluralistic society – will want to be treated properly as a person, as a voice that cannot be generally ignored'.[28]

For Pettit, then, freedom as non-domination is the good to be secured and promoted by the neo-republican political institutions and practices he sketches in the second half of *Republicanism*; and, as goods go, it is better than the 'liberal' good of freedom as non-interference. If the choice must be posed in these terms, in short, I agree with him. Domination is always a threat to freedom; interference is not. But that is not to say that interference is no threat to liberty, nor is it to say that the republican and liberal conceptions of liberty are mutually exclusive and hostile. The key point is that both domination and interference threaten and limit freedom because both are at odds with *autonomy*. I say this for three reasons.

First, as the traditional republican opposition of dependence to independence indicates, the desire to be free from domination is rooted in the desire to be in some sense self-governing. Why else would we complain about being dominated by or dependent upon another person? Pettit says that people want to be free from domination so that they may enjoy 'the frankness of intersubjective equality' and be treated as voices 'that cannot be generally ignored'. To be on an equal footing with those who would dominate us, however, or ignore our voices, is to be in a position to govern our lives, just as they do theirs. That does not mean that a person can or should even want to be the complete master of his or her domain. The attempt to achieve that kind of self-mastery is likely to lead to the self-stifling 'retreat to the inner citadel' that Berlin rightly deplores in 'Two Concepts of Liberty'.[29] Instead, being in a position to govern our lives means, among other things, that we must be able to rely upon the impersonal force of the rule of law to secure our independence from the arbitrary power of others. And that implies, in turn, that we must rely on our fellow citizens, whose general cooperation and compliance makes the rule of law possible. It is as *inter*dependent citizens, then, that we can stand on an equal footing with others in making and following the laws that protect us from arbitrary power, and in that sense we can be self-governing. We want to be free from domination, in other words, so that we can exercise autonomy.

Second, Pettit's emphasis on non-domination leads to some odd conclusions about when a person gains or loses (some degree of) freedom. In the postscript to the paperback edition of *Republicanism*, Pettit declares that 'the republic does not take away the freedom of citizens when it legally coerces them, taxes them, *or even puts them in prison*'.[30] If the republic has rightfully imprisoned a culprit, then it is easy to see how his or her imprisonment does not in itself constitute domination. But this simply means that one may lose some *freedom* while remaining *free from domination*. Put in other terms – terms congenial to republicans and liberals alike – Pettit's point seems to be that people do not lose their autonomy when they are coerced, taxed, or imprisoned in accordance with laws that somehow issue from them as self-governing citizens. Identifying freedom with non-domination, however, leads him to hold that people in these positions do not suffer a loss of freedom – an embarrassment easily avoided by those who take autonomy to be the reason for worrying about both interference and domination.

The third reason to prefer autonomy to 'freedom as non-domination' relates to the distinction Pettit draws between ways in which freedom is *compromised* and ways in which it is *conditioned*. This distinction allows him to say 'that someone is *unfree* so far as their [sic] freedom is *compromised by domination*' and '*non-free*, though not strictly unfree... insofar as their [sic] freedom is subject to *conditioning* factors'.[31] I may be free from the domination of arbitrary power, yet various conditioning factors – physical handicaps, illness, ignorance, and so on – may nevertheless limit my freedom. This consideration leads Pettit to a priority rule. Republicans must act to promote non-domination first by abolishing or reducing arbitrary power; that done, they must then extend the range of *undominated choices* available to people: 'we ought to try and reduce influences that condition freedom as well as influences that compromise it'.[32] Again, I believe Pettit to be right on this point, but it is difficult to see how he is right if freedom is to be construed simply as non-domination. If that is what freedom is, then why should the republican do anything more than secure people from domination? There are no obviously republican grounds, that is, for wanting to remove or overcome those conditioning factors that render people 'non-free'. We do not face this problem, however, if we turn from non-domination to autonomy. We can then say that the conditioning factors limit or inhibit the ability to lead a self-governed life, which is reason enough to try to remove them. Extending the range of undominated choices is thus desirable for the same reason that eliminating domination is desirable: namely, both are ways of promoting autonomy.

On conceptual grounds, then, Pettit's way of distinguishing republican liberty from liberal liberty is suspect. The same must be said of its historical warrant. The distinction does underscore a signal feature of republicanism, but it also leads to a caricature of liberalism in which Hobbes, Bentham, Paley, and today's libertarians – all advocates of freedom as non-interference – are the principal liberals. In *Republicanism*, Pettit appeals more than once to Locke's observation (*Second Treatise*, §57) that the laws that hedge us in from bogs and precipices ill deserve the name of confinement, but he has to assign Locke to the commonwealth tradition to preserve the distinction between republican and liberal freedom.[33] Nor does he mention Green, John Dewey, or other liberals who have *not* defined freedom as non-interference, although he does admit in the postscript that John Rawls's conception of freedom 'is consistent with liberty requiring non-domination as well as non-interference'.[34] He would have done better to rely on what he says, in the Introduction to *Republicanism*, may be 'the best available' taxonomy: 'populist, republican/liberal, and libertarian'.[35]

In subsequent writings, in fact, Pettit retains and elaborates the distinction between 'freedom as non-domination' and 'freedom as non-interference', but he no longer explicitly associates the latter with liberalism. In *A Theory of Freedom,* he hints at the desirability of 'a liberal or inclusive form of republican theory', and he grounds his theory of freedom in the idea of *discursive control.*[36] The latter point is significant because Pettit's notion of a 'discursive subject' who enjoys 'discursive control' closely resembles the idea of an autonomous person. 'To enjoy discursive control', as he says, 'is to be proof against being silenced, or ignored, or refused a hearing, or denied the final say in one's own responses. It is, on the contrary, to be given recognition as a discursive subject with a voice and an ear of one's own'.[37]

These are salutary moves on Pettit's part. As he now seems to recognize, freedom as non-interference may be the view of freedom that many liberals hold, but it is hardly the only one available to them as liberals. There is another conception of freedom, encompassing the idea of non-domination but resting on the concept of autonomy, that is available to liberals and republicans alike.

Yet this conclusion, correct as I believe it to be, is too hasty. Pettit may no longer oppose the republican conception to the liberal conception of liberty, but his continued insistence on excluding non-interference from republican liberty stands in the way of an autonomy-based conception of republican freedom. 'Freedom just is non-domination', according to Pettit.[38] This claim puts him at odds with Quentin Skinner, who has his own reasons for resisting attempts to link republican, or neo-roman, liberty to autonomy. So, too, does Maurizio Viroli, who endorses Pettit's conception of 'freedom as non-domination' while holding that republicanism is incompatible with democratic autonomy. It will be necessary, then, to attend to the ways in which these neo-republicans have qualified and elaborated their views on freedom before proceeding to autonomy itself.

III Qualifications and Elaborations

IIIa Pettit vs. Skinner

Pettit and Skinner both acknowledge how much each one's analysis of freedom owes to insights gained from the other. It is hardly surprising, then, to find them agreeing on two fundamental points: first, that there is a distinctively republican or, as Skinner prefers, neo-roman conception of liberty; and second, that this conception is superior to its two rivals, freedom as self-mastery and freedom as non-interference. Nevertheless, there are three points of disagreement that separate them.

The first may be no more than an insignificant difference in terminology. Where Pettit takes republican liberty to be freedom from *domination*, Skinner defines it as freedom from *dependence*. Neither of them makes an issue of this difference, so far as I am aware, so I shall set it aside here.

The second point of disagreement arises with regard to Berlin's way of distinguishing negative from positive liberty. Skinner and Pettit agree that Berlin's two concepts are not enough, but they disagree on how to classify the republican conception. On Skinner's account, there is one concept of positive liberty, understood as self-mastery, but there are two competing concepts of negative liberty: the idea that 'negative liberty must be construed as absence of interference...' and 'the rival theory that negative liberty consists of absence of dependence'.[39] On Pettit's account, however, the republican conception of liberty

> is akin to the negative one in maintaining that what liberty requires is the absence of something, not necessarily the presence. It is akin to the positive conception, however, in holding that that which must be absent has to do with mastery rather than with interference. Freedom consists, not in the presence of self-mastery, and not in the absence of interference by others, but rather in the absence of mastery by others: in the absence, as I prefer to put it, of domination.[40]

Whether this is a significant difference is again not clear. Pettit does not refer to Skinner in this context, so there is no reason to think that he is trying to separate their positions here. And I suspect that Skinner would simply point out that Pettit's 'absence of mastery' is every bit as negative as his own 'absence of dependence', with freedom in both cases defined as the absence of something.

There is no question, though, that the third point of disagreement is significant. Indeed, Pettit has recently defended his 'simple' position against objections that Skinner presents in *Liberty Before Liberalism*. According to Pettit, the difference between them is clear: 'I hold that for republicans freedom means nondomination, period, whereas [Skinner] says that it means nondomination *and* noninterference'.[41] The question, then, is why do they disagree on this point, and who has the better position?

Skinner holds that Pettit's simple identification of freedom with nondomination is mistaken because it leads to the unacceptably paradoxical situations I have already discussed – situations in which someone's apparent loss of freedom cannot count as real because the interference was not the result of mastery or domination but of lawful procedures. According to Skinner, 'The [neo-roman] writers I am discussing never deal in such paradoxes. For them the difference between the rule of law and government by personal prerogative is not that the former leaves you in full possession of your liberty while the latter does not; it is rather that the former only coerces you while the latter additionally leaves you in a state of dependence'.[42] Thus the person who is jailed or otherwise coerced in accordance with the laws of a genuine republic suffers a real loss of freedom – freedom from interference or restraint – even if it is not as grievous or objectionable a deprivation as it would be if some arbitrary, unaccountable power were doing the jailing or coercing.

For Pettit, as we have seen, the person in question suffers no loss of freedom because there is a difference between having one's freedom *compromised*, which makes one *unfree*, and having it *conditioned*, which makes one *non-free*. Pettit rehearses this argument from *Republicanism* in his response to Skinner, stating that 'while the tax levy or even the term of imprisonment might not take away a person's freedom in an ideal world – they might not have the effect of a dominating agency – still they would leave the person nonfree: "while they do not compromise someone's freedom as non-domination they do allow us to say that the person is not free to spend or to travel as they [*sic*] wish"'.[43]

This argument, however, does not dispel the air of paradox that quite properly worries Skinner. How can it when Pettit tells us, in one sentence (emphasis added), that non-dominating interference 'might not take away a person's freedom', yet 'it would leave the person *nonfree*', and thus 'allow us to say that the person is *not free* to spend or travel' as he or she wishes? If enforcement of a non-dominating law deprives me of (some of) my freedom to spend or travel, and thus makes me non-free in these respects, then the enforcement of the law *must* take away my freedom – or at least some of it.

Pettit's argument here strikes me as insightful but unsuccessful in two ways. First, the distinction between forces that render us *unfree* by *compromising* our freedom and those that render us *non-free* by merely *conditioning* it does reflect common reactions to different kinds of experiences. In Pettit's example, the victim of a crime and the victim of an accident may both suffer an equal reduction in their range of choice, but we would hardly say that the evil they suffer is equivalent:

The evil of reduced choice is certainly important, but it is distinct from the evil involved in the assumption and exercise of domination by the criminal; it is this evil that explains why, intuitively, it is worse to have one's choices reduced by crime than by an unintended, perhaps purely natural, accident.[44]

We may grant Pettit this point, however, without granting that his unfree/non-free distinction captures the difference in question. We could even say that it is not freedom but *wrongdoing* that is at issue in these cases. It is worse, that is, to have one's choices reduced by crime than by accident not because the criminal's victim is made 'unfree' but because he suffers a greater wrong, *ceteris paribus*, than the victim of an accident. The unfree/non-free distinction thus seems to be Pettit's ad hoc way of trying to tie this point to considerations of freedom.

To be sure, Pettit might respond by saying that the wrong suffered by the crime victim is directly and inextricably connected to freedom as non-domination. He might invoke 'discursive control' or 'the frankness of intersubjective equality', pointing out that the criminal or dominating power wrongs the victim by treating him or her as less than an equal, or as someone other than 'a discursive subject with a voice and an ear of one's own'.[45] To take this line, however, is to say that people *ought* or *perhaps have a right* to be treated as free persons capable of leading their own lives. This is to build freedom from non-domination into the idea of being a *person*, so that the wrong the dominated person suffers is the wrong of not being respected as someone with a right to live, think, and speak for himself. In short, it is an implicit appeal to autonomy that is doing the work here, not the distinction between unfreedom and non-freedom.

Something similar happens with regard to the second way in which Pettit's argument is insightful but unsuccessful. In seeking to avoid the paradoxical situations that trouble Skinner, Pettit trades on the sense in which freedom is a threshold concept. That is, someone who has all the freedom it is possible to have is a free person; someone who completely lacks freedom, whether from domination or interference, is not; and between these poles is some vague, imprecise, and perhaps shifting point or range of points that forms a threshold of freedom. If I am above that threshold, I am a free person, no matter that I am not completely free, or free in all respects. I can be more or less free above the threshold, and more or less free below it, but if I am above it, I am free enough to count as a free person, all things considered. It is this threshold that enables us to make sense of Pettit's claim that the (non-arbitrary, non-dominating) tax levy both does and does not take away the tax-payer's freedom – in his terms, makes her non-free but not unfree. The tax payer is not as free to spend as she would be in the absence of the tax, but her loss of freedom is not great enough to make her an unfree person. If she goes to prison for tax evasion, it will be more difficult to make the case that she has not crossed the threshold that renders her an unfree person, but I will concede this point to Pettit for our present purposes. What should be noted, though, is that we could make the same point in the preceding two sentences if we were to substitute 'non-free' for 'unfree'. Someone who loses some degree of freedom, but not enough to drop below the threshold, remains a free person – that is, someone who is neither unfree nor non-free, all things considered. This tells us that it is the threshold that counts, not Pettit's distinction between compromising and conditioning factors that make us unfree and non-free, respectively.

Pettit's argument is insightful but ultimately unsuccessful, in sum, because he can dispel the paradox from the situations that worry Skinner only by trading implicitly on considerations that take him beyond his 'simple' conception of republican freedom as 'non-domination, period'. Indeed, Skinner could trade as effectively on these considerations as Pettit does. On the one hand, he could hold that someone who suffers interference but not domination loses (some) freedom while remaining a free person; on the other, he could hold that someone who suffers domination does not become *ipso facto* an unfree person. Like interference or restraint, domination comes in various forms and degrees, some of which will be sufficient to push one below the threshold of freedom and some of which will not. Skinner could trade on these considerations, moreover, without abandoning his claim that republican or neo-roman liberty involves the absence of domination (or dependence) *and* the absence of interference.

Nevertheless, Pettit has two more arguments against Skinner's position. Both of these follow from Pettit's belief that Skinner's neo-roman liberty places non-domination and non-interference on an equal basis. Hence Pettit argues, first, that domination alone ought to be considered the antonym of freedom, and, second, that Skinner's conception of liberty is unstable. Pettit is right, I think, to stress that non-domination is the distinctive aspect of republican freedom; and if 'freedom' must have a republican antonym, then I would only enter the quibble that there is something to be said for 'dependence' too. Otherwise, I readily accept the following claim:

What is bad about domination, and makes it a natural antonym of freedom, shows up in the three features of enforcing a restriction of choice, occasioning a distinctive uncertainty [because the dominated person is never sure of where he stands or what to expect,] and introducing an asymmetry of status [between dominator and dominated]. What is bad about interference-minus-domination is merely that it restricts choice.[46]

In accepting this claim, though, I note that one may still hold to the view that 'interference-minus-domination' remains a part of republican liberty. After all, there is a difference between saying that non-domination is the distinctively republican feature of republican liberty and saying that it is the whole of it.

Pettit's final argument concerns the purported instability of Skinner's conception. Here, Pettit identifies three possibilities: freedom as non-domination, freedom as non-domination and non-interference, and freedom as non-limitation (where limitation 'may come of natural inability or handicap or poverty or from the lack of resources available as the unintended result of the action or inaction of others'[47]). The middle view – Skinner's – is in danger of sliding into the third, Pettit says, because it cannot identify an evil that is common to domination and interference but not to non-intentional limitation.[48] If interference is on an equal footing with domination because both restrict people's choices, then non-intentional limitations may be on an equal footing with them too. We must therefore reject the second position in favour of simple freedom as non-domination, with its three features, if we are to avoid the slide down the slippery slope to freedom as non-limitation.

There are two problems with this argument. The first is that Pettit does not explain why it would be so dreadful to adopt or slide into the conception of freedom that counts non-intentional limitations as every bit as inimical to one's freedom as domination or interference. Presumably to do so would be to open the door to considerations that republicans should not want to count as compromising one's freedom; but to say that is simply to reaffirm Pettit's conviction that republican liberty is freedom from domination. Even if we grant this point, moreover, the second problem remains – namely, that Pettit's conception of republican liberty may be as likely to slide into non-limitation as Skinner's. Pettit acknowledges that domination shares one of its three features, the restriction of choice, with both interference and limitation; but it seems that domination also shares the other two features – 'a distinctive uncertainty' and 'an asymmetry of status' – with limitation. In fact, people limited by 'natural inability or handicap or poverty or... the lack of resources available as the unintended result of the action or inaction of others' are quite likely to feel a distinctive uncertainty as to how to conduct themselves; they are also likely to perceive an asymmetry of status in their relations with others. It is also true that some people see domination in what others regard as mere limitation. For example, the poverty that seems to some to be the unfortunate result of natural factors and innocent actions may appear to Marxists to be a consequence of capitalist domination. As this and many other possible examples illustrate, the slope leading to freedom as non-limitation seems as slippery for non-domination as it is for non-interference.

My conclusion, then, is that Skinner's conception of republican liberty is superior to Pettit's. Like Pettit's, Skinner's conception contains the distinctive feature that makes it *republican*: the emphasis on freedom as non-domination or independence. But Skinner's also allows that interference may sometimes 'compromise' freedom – indeed, that it may sometimes compromise freedom more severely than domination does. Such would be the case, I think, for the person who is wrongly convicted of a serious crime and imprisoned for many years, or perhaps even executed, even though his arrest, trial, and conviction proceeded fairly and in accordance with the republican ideal of the rule of law. Such a person would not be dominated, in Pettit's sense, but he would be less free by far than someone who must occasionally bow and scrape to the boss in order to keep his job.

There is an irony here, however. Pettit's recent writings, and especially his acknowledgment of the desirability of 'a liberal or inclusive form of republican theory', have brought him closer than Skinner to the position I favour. He may conceive of liberty more inclusively than Pettit, but Skinner does not regard this inclusive conception as evidence that republicanism and liberalism share a common foundation in autonomy. In this respect, he resembles Maurizio Viroli, another neo-republican who has his doubts about the relationship of republicanism to autonomy.

IIIb Republicanism vs. Autonomy?

Skinner's remarks on republicanism and autonomy are confined, so far as I know, to a footnote in *Liberty Before Liberalism*. There he states that one 'might say that the neo-roman and classical liberal accounts of freedom embody rival understandings of autonomy. For the latter, the will is autonomous provided it is not coerced; for the former, the will can only be described as autonomous if it is independent of the danger of being coerced'.[49] On this account, republicanism and liberalism both have foundations in autonomy, but not a common or shared foundation. What

Skinner's footnote does, in effect, is push the purported rivalry between liberal and republican conceptions of liberty up, down, or back a level to a rivalry between liberal and republican conceptions of autonomy.

Is this move justified? In the absence of a richer account of autonomy than Skinner provides, it is hard to see how it is. Of course, if we already believe that republicanism and liberalism are sharply distinct and incompatible, then we would expect either that one of the two theories lacks a conception of autonomy altogether or that their conceptions are quite different from each other. But that is to assume precisely what is in question here; and Skinner offers no evidence to show that 'neo-romans' and liberals really do differ as he says with regard to autonomy. Moreover, the 'rival understandings of autonomy' Skinner identifies both rest, like his neo-roman and liberal conceptions of liberty, on a common element – in this case, coercion. The 'liberal' view is that autonomy is the absence of coercion; the 'neo-roman' is that autonomy is the absence 'of the danger of being coerced'. Assuming that Skinner means to include the absence of coercion itself in the neo-roman/republican view, and not merely the danger of it, the result is an inclusive conception of autonomy. In this respect, neo-roman autonomy as the absence of coercion *and* of the danger of being coerced is like his neo-roman conception of liberty as the absence of interference *and* of dependence. But that is to say that in both cases, the neo-roman/republican position absorbs and extends the supposedly liberal position, not that it rejects it. If this is rivalry, then it is rivalry of a friendly and intramural nature.

As with Pettit, in sum, so with Skinner. Both have made valuable contributions to our understandings of republicanism and of freedom, but neither has shown that the republican conception of freedom is so different from or hostile to (what they take to be) the liberal conception as to demonstrate that liberalism and republicanism are fundamentally incompatible. But what of Viroli, who distinguishes republican liberty not only from the liberal but also from the *democratic* ideal of liberty as autonomy?

Viroli's understanding of republican liberty is in line with Pettit's: 'The central point for classical republican theorists is that dependence is a more painful violation of liberty than interference'.[50] Viroli extends Pettit's analysis, however, when he associates democratic liberty with autonomy. As he puts it:

The democratic ideal of political liberty, understood as a condition in which citizens have autonomy and are governed by laws that reflect their will, is in fact a radical version of the republican ideal of political liberty as absence of domination. If to be free means that one is not subject to the arbitrary will of a man or group, as republican theorists claim, we enjoy complete political liberty when we are dependent only on our own will – that is, when we live in a self-governing polity that permits us to approve or reject the rules governing the life of the collectivity.[51]

As stated here, the democratic ideal of political liberty may not seem to be a truly 'radical' departure from the republican ideal. As a citizen of 'a self-governing polity that permits us', my fellow citizens and me, 'to approve or reject the rules governing the life of the collectivity', I apparently enjoy 'complete political liberty' in both the republican and democratic senses. But Viroli has something much stronger in mind when he refers to approving or rejecting the rules governing the polity. To enjoy democratic autonomy in his sense of the term, I must be able not only to have a say or cast a vote, but to approve or reject each and every law of the polity – and so must every other citizen. The 'radical' nature of this democratic ideal emerges in the following passage:

The republican conception of political liberty approaches the democratic idea of liberty as autonomy of the will in that it, too, sees constraint as a violation of liberty; yet it is not identical, because it holds that the will is autonomous *not when the laws or regulations that govern my actions correspond to my will*, but when I am protected from the *constant danger* of being subjected to constraint.[52]

By implication, then, I am not autonomous according to the democratic ideal unless I have the power to veto any law or regulation that I disapprove. No wonder that this account of democratic liberty as autonomy of the will appears in a chapter entitled 'The New Utopia of Liberty'!

What are we to make of this conception of democratic autonomy? Viroli presumably wants us to reject it in favour of the more sensible republican ideal of liberty, but others may try to turn the tables on him by using it to reject republicanism. Robert Paul Wolff, for one, relies on much the same notion of autonomy – 'the refusal to be ruled' – yet Wolff argues for 'philosophical anarchism' because unanimous direct democracy is impossible to achieve, and anything less is incompatible with autonomy.[53] In any case, there is no reason to accept this radical view as *the* democratic conception of autonomy. None of the chapters in the present volume, for example, entails or even implies that a person is autonomous only when she is able to approve or reject every rule or law that applies to her; indeed, Rainer Forst's and Bert van den Brink's separate discussions of 'political autonomy' resemble Viroli's republican ideal much more closely than his 'democratic idea of liberty as autonomy of the will...' (see Chapters 10 and 11 in the present volume).

Nor does Viroli himself hold, in the end, that republicanism is thoroughly hostile to autonomy. As he says, the 'republican conception of political liberty *approaches* the democratic idea of liberty as autonomy of the will...' (emphasis added). It does this because freedom from domination or from dependence upon the arbitrary rule of others enables a person to be *self-governing* in a meaningful sense of that term even when that person must sometimes accept a rule or law that he or she did not approve. To see how such a person can be autonomous, however, and how autonomy underpins a republican-liberal political theory, requires, finally, a closer look at the concept of autonomy itself.

IV Autonomy

As the chapters in this and other volumes testify, autonomy is a rich and multi-faceted concept.[54] In the space remaining, I cannot even pretend to approach a comprehensive treatment of the subject, but I can offer remarks on four points that are especially pertinent to the republican challenge to liberalism.

The first point begins with the basic observation that autonomy is a matter of *self-government*. This observation may seem to be singularly unhelpful, as it leads to difficult questions about the nature of the self and how it may be said to govern – questions such as the nature of the relationship between *personal* and *moral* autonomy that Gerald Gaus and Jeremy Waldron explore in Chapters 12 and 13, respectively, in the present volume. Nevertheless, this basic observation provides a useful starting point, as it indicates that autonomy is something available only to people who have both a reasonably secure sense of self and the ability to govern their conduct. Someone who suffers from multiple-personality disorder cannot be autonomous; nor, as the film *Memento* illustrates, can someone who cannot remember whom he has just met, where he has just gone, what he has just said, or how any of these fit into his plans or purposes. Less dramatically, people who are unable to resist any impulse that strikes them also lack autonomy, for they are incapable of self-*government*.

It is equally important to notice that external forces can prevent someone who is quite capable of self-government from exercising this capacity. This may happen, for instance, when a person who could be autonomous is subject to constant interference or coercion; it may also happen when such a person is dominated by or utterly dependent upon others. This is why autonomy is a concern of liberals and republicans alike – and of those who believe that republican liberalism is an especially powerful political theory. Autonomy is the capacity to lead a self-governed life, but this capacity, like others, will atrophy if it is not exercised. Liberals, republicans, and republican liberals will all have an interest in protecting people, or enabling them to protect themselves, against interference or domination that threatens their ability to govern themselves. There will be disagreements and differences of emphasis among them, to be sure, but their fundamental concern for self-government demonstrates that republicans and liberals share a common foundation in their commitment to autonomy.

This claim leads to my second point about autonomy: it is not the peculiarly liberal concept that critics of liberalism sometimes take it to be. These critics are doubly mistaken, in my view, as they misconceive both liberalism and autonomy. Mark Tushnet provides a colorful case in point:

Liberalism's psychology posits a world of autonomous individuals, each guided by his or her own idiosyncratic values and goals, none of which can be adjudged more or less legitimate than those held by others. In such a world, people exist as isolated islands of individuality who choose to enter into relations that can metaphorically be characterized as foreign affairs.[55]

Setting aside the caricature of liberalism here, the pertinent question is whether autonomous individuals really are 'isolated islands of individuality'. The answer, quite clearly, is no. Autonomous individuals must be able to make choices, certainly, including the choice to enter into and break off various relations with others. But that is hardly to say that one is autonomous only if he or she takes part in nothing but self-chosen relationships.[56] We are born, most of us, with the capacity to lead self-governed lives, but we cannot develop or exercise this capacity without the assistance of other people, and it would be silly to think of our relations with all of them, even metaphorically, as 'foreign affairs'. Even as mature and presumably independent adults, we find ourselves entangled in relationships – with relatives, neighbors, co-workers, compatriots, and others – that we have not fully chosen. Yet we may still be reflective persons capable of judging the options available to us and making choices in light of those judgments. In short, we may achieve autonomy despite our inability to become 'isolated islands of individuality'.

As these remarks suggest, autonomy is not a simple on/off concept – something that one either does or does not have. On the contrary, one autonomous person may have more or less autonomy than another; or someone may be autonomous in one aspect of her life but not in another. In most discussions of personal autonomy, however, we are talking in global terms of whether this or that person or group of people should be deemed, all things considered, to be autonomous. We can do this – and this is my third point – because autonomy, like freedom, is a threshold concept. That is why someone who gives in to every impulse will not be autonomous, *ceteris paribus*, but someone who occasionally acts impulsively may be. One need not be perfectly autonomous, in other words, in order to be autonomous. It is only necessary to go beyond that vaguely defined threshold that distinguishes the autonomous from those who are not (quite) autonomous.

This is an especially important point in the present context because it helps to resolve those paradoxical situations that have worried Skinner and bedeviled Pettit. As we have seen, Pettit resorts to a distinction between 'unfree' and 'non-free' in his attempt to explain how someone who experiences non-arbitrary interference, such as the imposition of a tax levy, may not suffer a loss of freedom. In making this move, I argued, Pettit implicitly trades on the sense in which freedom is a threshold concept; and a more straightforward way to deal with the problem is to say that the person subject to the levy remains *a free person* even though she is not *as free* to spend as she was before the levy. An even better way to resolve the problem is to employ the concept of autonomy. Doing so certainly makes it easier to handle the case of the person whose imprisonment seems, almost by definition, to drop her below the threshold that separates the free person from the unfree. It is easier, at least, if we have reason to believe that the prisoner committed the crime of her own volition in full knowledge of the illegality of her act and of its likely consequences. To say that this prisoner remains a free person strains, at best, the concept of freedom. Yet there is little strain, if any, in describing the prisoner as *autonomous* but *not free*. That is because 'autonomy', unlike 'freedom' or 'liberty', is typically used to characterize persons in a global sense. I may ask whether you are free this weekend, but only in frivolity or in a philosophy seminar would I ask whether you are autonomous this weekend. The threshold element is stronger in autonomy than in freedom, in short, because autonomy is more of a global concept than freedom.

These considerations lead to my final point, which is that a commitment to autonomy does not also commit one to the populist or plebiscitary forms of democracy that Pettit and Viroli deplore. If we want our political arrangements to respect individual autonomy, or to acknowledge that people are 'discursive subjects' with voices and ears of their own, those arrangements will have to be in some sense democratic. But autonomy does not require unanimous direct democracy, for a person does not cease to be autonomous whenever a vote goes contrary to his wishes. Nor does autonomy require unbridled majority rule. Indeed, majority rule is both friend and foe of autonomy: *friend* because it is the only decision procedure that gives equal weight to everyone's vote, and *foe* because it may allow those who constitute the majority to dominate those in the minority. As Viroli remarks, a 'law accepted voluntarily by members of the most democratic assembly on earth may very well be an arbitrary law that permits some part of the society to constrain the will of other parts, *thus depriving them of their autonomy*'.[57]

Viroli's remark is important both for what it says about the threat that an excess of democracy poses to self-government and for what it implies about republicanism and liberalism. As the words I have italicized indicate, Viroli's defense of republican liberty against unchecked majoritarianism is entirely consistent with a commitment to autonomy. But it is also consistent with liberal fears that individual rights and liberties will fall victim to the tyranny of the majority. That is why the rule of law, separation of powers, checks and balances, and other devices for constraining the majority are neither peculiarly republican nor distinctively liberal. That is also why republicans and liberals alike should be concerned with problems such as permanent or persistent majorities, which inevitably lead the people who are on the losing side of almost every vote to ask whether they are really self-governing or merely subject to the domination of the majority. It is, in sum, the commitment to autonomy that unites republicans and liberals in their quest for political arrangements that protect and promote the individual's ability to be self-governing. In this, as in other respects, there is no reason to regard republicanism and liberalism as hostile or even sharply divided political theories.

V The Republican Challenge to Liberalism

What, then, is the nature of the republican challenge to liberalism? It is the challenge to take more seriously the commitment to individual autonomy. Liberals too often seem to think that respecting autonomy is simply a matter of leaving people alone to pursue their own conceptions of the good, at least as long as they do not harm or violate the rights of others. Many liberals are thus vulnerable to the two lines of attack that neo-republicans have brought against them: first, as Sandel and others have urged, that liberal societies give too little attention to the cultivation of the civic virtues necessary to sustain a self-governing polity; and second, as Pettit, Skinner, and Viroli insist, that freeing people from interference is not the same as enabling them to be free, self-governing persons. Anyone who hopes to foster autonomy will do well to take these criticisms seriously. For liberals, this means that they should correct their course where necessary to respond to the republican challenge.

Can this be done? The examples of Constant, John Stuart Mill, and other liberals who have displayed markedly republican tendencies indicate that it can. For Constant, as we have seen, the challenge is to cherish 'modern' liberty while guarding against the danger that, 'absorbed in the enjoyment of our private independence, and in the pursuit of our particular interests, we should surrender our right to share in political power too easily'.[58] For his part, Mill gave classical expression to the 'liberal' view of freedom: 'The only freedom which deserves the name, is that of pursuing our own good in our own way, so long as we do not attempt to deprive others of theirs, or impede their efforts to obtain it'.[59] But he also denied, in *Considerations on Representative Government*, that a truly benevolent despotism is the ideal form of government, and he called attention to the evil of domination in *The Subjection of Women*. That is not to say, of course, that Mill and Constant were always right, or that their writings exhaust the possibilities of republican liberalism or liberal republicanism. What these writings do show, however, in line with the arguments set out in this chapter, is that a republican liberalism is not only possible but, for anyone committed to the promotion of autonomy, remarkably attractive as a theory of politics.[60]

Notes

1. See, for example, Zera Fink, *The Classical Republicans: An Essay in the Recovery of a Pattern of Thought in Seventeenth Century England* (Evanston, IL: Northwestern University Press, 1945); Caroline Robbins, *The Eighteenth-Century Commonwealthman* (Cambridge, MA: Harvard University Press, 1959/1985); and Gordon Wood, *The Creation of the American Republic, 1776–1787* (Chapel Hill, NC: University of North Carolina Press, 1969).
2. Michael Sandel, *Democracy's Discontent: America in Search of a Public Philosophy* (Cambridge, MA: Harvard University Press, 1996); Philip Pettit, *Republicanism: A Theory of Freedom and Government* (Oxford: Clarendon Press, 1997). For liberals who reject republicanism, see, for example, Steven G. Gey, 'The Unfortunate Revival of Civic Republicanism', *University of Pennsylvania Law Review*, 141 (January 1993): 801–98; and, more temperately, Gerald F. Gaus,

'Backwards into the Future: Neorepublicanism as a Postsocialist Critique of Market Society', *Social Philosophy and Policy*, 20 (Winter 2003): 59–91.
3. Sunstein, 'Beyond the Republican Revival', *Yale Law Journal*, 97 (July 1988), p. 1590.
4. I develop this position in *Civic Virtues: Rights, Citizenship, and Republican Liberalism* (Oxford: Oxford University Press, 1997). Others who make a case for liberal republicanism or republican (or civic) liberalism include Shelley Burtt, 'The Politics of Virtue Today: A Critique and a Proposal', *American Political Science Review*, 87 (June 1993): 360–68; Stephen Holmes, *Passions and Constraint: On the Theory of Liberal Democracy* (Chicago: University of Chicago Press, 1985), especially pp. 5 and 28; Jeffrey Isaac, 'Republicanism vs. Liberalism? A Reconsideration', *History of Political Thought*, 9 (Summer 1988): 349–77; Alan Patten, 'The Republican Critique of Liberalism', *British Journal of Political Science*, 26 (1996): 25–44; Thomas A. Spragens, Jr., *Civic Liberalism: Reflections on Our Democratic Ideals* (Lanham, MD: Rowman and Littlefield, 1999); and Ronald Terchek, *Republican Paradoxes and Liberal Anxieties* (Lanham, MD: Rowman and Littlefield, 1997).
5. For book-length responses, see Bill Brugger, *Republican Theory in Political Thought: Virtuous or Virtual?* (London: Macmillan, 1999); Iseault Honohan, *Civic Republicanism* (London and New York: Routledge, 2002); and M. N. S. Sellers, *The Sacred Fire of Liberty: Republicanism, Liberalism, and the Law* (London: Macmillan, 1999).
6. Shelley Burtt, 'The Good Citizen's Psyche: On the Psychology of Civic Virtue', *Polity*, 23 (Fall 1990): p. 24. Cf. M. M. Goldsmith, 'Republican Liberty Considered', *History of Political Thought*, 21 (Autumn 2000), p. 555: 'The good citizen will develop the values of identification with the society, loyalty to it and public spirit – the willingness to put the good of the society above one's own good'.
7. Aristotle, *The Politics*, 1283b42–1284a3 (Book III, Chapter 13).
8. Rousseau, *Du Contrat Social*: note that ends Book I.
9. Sandel, *Democracy's Discontent*, p. 6.
10. Ibid., p. 4.
11. Ibid., p. 323.
12. Richard Dagger, 'The Sandelian Republic and the Encumbered Self', *The Review of Politics*, 61 (Spring 1999): 181–208. See also Sandel's response and my rejoinder in ibid., pp. 209–17.
13. Pettit, *Republicanism*, esp. chapters 1–4; Skinner, *Liberty Before Liberalism* (Cambridge: Cambridge University Press, 1998), and 'A Third Concept of Liberty', *London Review of Books*, 16 (4 April 2002): 16–18; and Viroli, *Republicanism*, trans. Antony Shugaar (New York: Hill & Wang, 2002).
14. Viroli, *Republicanism*, p. 61: 'From a theoretical point of view, liberalism can be considered an impoverished or incoherent republicanism, but not an alternative to republicanism'.
15. Benjamin Constant, *Political Writings*, trans. and ed. Biancamaria Fontana (Cambridge: Cambridge University Press, 1988), p. 317.
16. Ibid., p. 321.
17. Ibid., p. 326.

18. Ibid., p. 327.
19. Ibid., p. 328; emphasis added.
20. 'Two Concepts of Liberty', in Berlin, *Liberty*, ed. Henry Hardy (London: Oxford University Press, 1969/2002). For the distinction's troubles, see, for example, David Miller's introduction to Miller, ed., *Liberty* (Oxford: Oxford University Press, 1993), esp. pp. 9–15; Holmes, *Passions and Constraints*, p. 28f.; and Rainer Forst's Chapter 10 in the present volume.
21. Indeed, Green's chief defense of positive freedom is found in his "Liberal Legislation and Freedom of Contract," which he delivered as a lecture to the Leicester [England] Liberal Association in January 1881.
22. "Liberal Legislation and Freedom of Contract," in Miller, ed., *Liberty*, p. 21.
23. Skinner, 'The Paradoxes of Political Liberty', in Miller, ed., *Liberty*, p. 202. In his Introduction to *Liberty*, David Miller argues (p. 6) that Skinner goes too far when he describes Machiavelli's view of freedom as *purely* negative, 'since that overlooks the fact that a person's freedom consists [for Machiavelli] also in his membership in a self-governing state'. We need not settle this point here, however, for on neither Miller's nor Skinner's reading does republican freedom equate to Berlin's positive liberty.
24. Skinner, 'A Third Concept of Liberty', p. 18; Pettit, *Republicanism*, p. 80. See also Skinner, *Liberty Before Liberalism*, p. 84: 'What the neo-roman writers repudiate *avant la lettre* is the key assumption of classical liberalism to the effect that force or the coercive threat of it constitute the only forms of constraint that interfere with individual liberty. The neo-roman writers insist, by contrast, that to live in a condition of dependence is in itself a source and a form of constraint'.
25. The following discussion draws on my '*Republicanism* Refashioned: Comments on Pettit's Theory of Freedom and Government', *The Good Society*, 9: 3 (2002): 50–53.
26. Ibid., p. 41.
27. Ibid., p. 64.
28. Ibid., p. 91.
29. Berlin, 'Two Concepts of Liberty', §III (pp. 181–87 in Berlin, *Liberty* [2002]).
30. Pettit, *Republicanism: A Theory of Freedom and Government* (Oxford: Clarendon Press, 1999), p. 291; emphasis added.
31. Ibid., p. 76; emphasis added.
32. Ibid., p. 77.
33. See also 'Republican Freedom and Contestatory Democratization' (in *Democracy's Value*, eds. Ian Shapiro and Casiano Hacker-Cordón [Cambridge: Cambridge University Press, 1999]), where Pettit refers to '"old liberals" such as John Locke' (p. 166, with no explanation of the quotation marks), then subsequently designates him 'the hero of the later commonwealthman tradition, John Locke' (pp. 170–71).
34. Ibid., paperback edition, p. 301, n. 2.
35. Ibid., p. 10.
36. For the quoted passage, see Pettit, *A Theory of Freedom: From the Psychology to the Politics of Agency* (Oxford: Oxford University Press, 2002), p. 152. But also note the reference to 'the characteristically liberal ideal of non-interference' on p. 151.

37. Ibid., p. 140.
38. Pettit, 'Republican Freedom and Democratic Contestation', p. 165.
39. Skinner, 'A Third Concept of Liberty', p. 18.
40. 'Republican Freedom and Contestatory Democratization', p. 165.
41. Pettit, 'Keeping Republican Freedom Simple: On a Difference with Quentin Skinner', *Political Theory*, 30 (June 2002), p. 342; emphasis in original.
42. Skinner, *Liberty Before Liberalism*, p. 83, n. 54.
43. Pettit, 'Keeping Republican Freedom Simple', p. 347. The internal quotation is from Pettit, *Republicanism*, p. 56.
44. Ibid., p. 344.
45. Pettit, *A Theory of Freedom*, p. 140.
46. Pettit, 'Keeping Republican Freedom Simple', p. 351.
47. Ibid., p. 351.
48. Ibid., p. 352.
49. Skinner, *Liberty Before Liberalism*, p. 84, n. 57.
50. Viroli, *Republicanism*, p. 10. See also pp. 47–52, where he argues against Skinner's conception of republican liberty as absence of dependence *and* of restraint.
51. Ibid., p. 10; see also p. 41.
52. Ibid., p. 42; emphasis added to '*not when... my will*', but not to '*constant danger*'. See also ibid., p. 41: 'The republican conception of liberty differs from the democratic idea that liberty consists of the "power to establish norms for oneself and to obey no other norms than those given to oneself". This is liberty in the sense of autonomy'. Viroli does not give the source of the internal quotation, but it appears from the context to be Norberto Bobbio, *Politica e cultura* (Turin: Einaudi, 1974).
53. Wolff, *In Defense of Anarchism*, 3rd ed. (Berkeley, CA: University of California Press, 1998), p. 18 *et passim*. I criticize Wolff's argument in *Civic Virtues*, pp. 62–68.
54. See, for example, John Christman, ed., *The Inner Citadel: Essays on Individual Autonomy* (New York: Oxford University Press, 1989), and *Social Philosophy and Policy*, 20 (Summer 2003), which is devoted to autonomy.
55. Tushnet, 'Following the Rules Laid Down: A Critique of Interpretivism and Neutral Principles', *Harvard Law Review*, 96 (February 1983): p. 783.
56. It is worth noting that for all their differences, not a single essay in the present volume conceives of autonomous persons as 'isolated islands of individuality'.
57. Viroli, *Republicanism*, p. 43; emphasis added.
58. Constant, *Political Writings*, p. 326.
59. Mill, *On Liberty and Other Writings*, ed. Stefan Collini (Cambridge: Cambridge University Press, 1989), p. 16.
60. For very helpful comments on an earlier draft of this essay, I am grateful to Cécile Fabre and David Miller.

9

Liberal Autonomy and Consumer Sovereignty

Joseph Heath

There is obviously a very close affinity between the concept of *citizen autonomy*, which is identified with a liberal organization of the political sphere, and the concept of *consumer sovereignty*, which is used to justify certain sorts of free market arrangements in the economy. Depending upon whose stock is thought to be higher at any given time, politicians will appeal to economic metaphors in order to justify liberal political principles, just as business leaders will appeal to democratic imagery in order to justify economic freedom. Thus, citizens are often described as "consumers" or "clients," browsing through the "marketplace of ideas," deciding how to "spend" their votes. Similarly, consumers are said to "vote with their wallets," and that the success of firms reflects the "popular will." The very term "consumer sovereignty" borrows a concept from the political sphere in order to legitimate a certain sort of economic arrangement.

These parallels are not illegitimate. The doctrines of liberal autonomy and consumer sovereignty are usually grounded through appeal to very similar normative considerations. More specifically, the arguments that are given for the claim that the state should respect the autonomy of citizens are often identical to those made in favour of consumer sovereignty. If individuals are, by and large, the best judges of their own interests, then the society that leaves them free to pursue their own chosen plan of life will be superior to one that does not. Autonomy in the political realm gives individuals the legal freedom to pursue their goals, whereas sovereignty in the marketplace allows them access to the resources needed to achieve them.

However, whereas autonomy is a very popular political ideal among those of a broadly liberal persuasion, consumer sovereignty has not received a uniformly warm reception. The doctrine is often viewed with suspicion, if not outright hostility. This hostility runs highest among those who want to diagnose "consumerism" as one of the major flaws of capitalism. (In fact, the critique of consumerism is in many ways equivalent to a rejection of the doctrine of consumer sovereignty.) According to this sort of view, the doctrine of consumer sovereignty constitutes nothing more than a crude misappropriation of democratic vocabulary in order to justify callow corporate interests.

This is where the big question emerges. Is it possible to reject consumer sovereignty while endorsing liberal autonomy? Economists have an extremely strong tendency to simply equate the two doctrines – to assume that a democratic society must respect the wishes of consumers, and therefore that a laissez-faire economic system is a natural expression of the political ideals underlying western liberalism. This close tie between consumer sovereignty and liberal political ideals has been inadvertently reinforced by many critics of consumerism, who have had a lamentable tendency to develop their critique in a way that flagrantly disregards the principles of liberal autonomy. In particular, these critics have not been nearly careful enough to ensure that their critique of consumer sovereignty does not imply an unacceptably paternalistic attitude toward consumers. This has made it much easier to dismiss the critique of consumerism as fundamentally illiberal.

It is my conviction that one can consistently criticize consumerism without abandoning the liberal commitment to respecting the autonomy of consumers, but that doing so requires greater care in the formulation of the critique than is normally exercised. The key difference between the two doctrines, as traditionally conceived, is that a commitment to liberal autonomy does not preclude the possibility of legal remedy in cases where state intervention is able to resolve a collective-action problem. The doctrine of consumer sovereignty, on the other hand, has traditionally involved a commitment to market freedom under all circumstances, even in cases where consumers are clearly caught in a suboptimal equilibrium. Thus it is possible to violate consumer sovereignty in order to eliminate such equilibria, without thereby contradicting one's commitment to respect autonomy.

I Autonomy and Sovereignty

Many theorists regard the defining characteristic of a liberal political order to be an official commitment on the part of the state to remain neutral with respect to the different goals and projects pursued by its citizens. This strain of liberal thinking dates back at least to Hobbes, who argued that because each person's conception of the good is a function of that person's ever-changing desires, any attempt to establish a political order dedicated to the pursuit of one particular conception of the good would necessarily generate conflict and disorder. The solution was to create a state dedicated to providing only the enabling conditions needed for the pursuit of any conception of the good: personal security, enforcement of contracts, and so on. Because these sorts of services are of value to citizens regardless of the conception of the good that each one happens to endorse, such a state should be able to enjoy stable, universal support amongst the citizenry. Most importantly, the powers exercised by such a state should be ones that all citizens could agree to accept *ex ante*.

It is not difficult to derive from this commitment to neutrality the view that a liberal state should respect the autonomy of its citizens. One need only add the premise that the individual is, in general, best positioned to ascertain his or her own good, and also the most likely to carry out the pursuit of such good in a conscientious manner. From this, it is easy to infer a general non-interference principle. Not only should the state refrain from imposing some conception of the good upon an individual, the state should not even impose upon the individual when doing so is thought to promote that individual's own good. This is naturally subject to certain conditions: the action in question must not harm anyone else, the individual making the decision must be mature, well-informed and of sound mind, and so on. When these conditions are satisfied, it is then claimed that the best overall outcome is to be achieved by granting individuals whatever freedoms are needed for them to formulate and pursue their own particular conceptions of the good life. It is precisely in granting this freedom that the liberal polity is said to respect the autonomy of its citizens.[1]

This commitment to respect autonomy has a number of different political consequences. One of the most important is that it acts as a *prima facie* constraint on the enactment of paternalistic laws. If individuals are the best judges of what is good for them, then the state is not justified in making interventions that have as their primary intent thwarting a self-regarding, voluntary choice made by those individuals, even when it is thought that this is being done for their own good. The classic argument for such an anti-paternalism constraint – from John Stuart Mill – is that for every one or two times somebody is stopped from doing something that he or she truly would have regretted, there will be dozens of interventions that simply represent other people's imposing their own conceptions of how best to live. Thus the net effect of a policy of paternalistic intervention will be an overall reduction in social welfare.

Apart from this efficiency argument, it is also often argued on contractualist grounds that the power to make paternalistic interventions could never be grounded in consent (since the person whose decision is being overridden would always object), and so the state could not have the legitimate authority to engage in such interventions. Any interventions that do take place must therefore represent the unjust exercise of power by one individual or group over another.

The case for consumer sovereignty rests upon substantially similar grounds. Put crudely, the doctrine of consumer sovereignty states that individuals should be able to spend their money however they want. More generally, where "market transactions" are understood as contracts involving the exchange of rights over property, consumer sovereignty stipulates that individuals should be free to dispose of any property they have rights over through any market transaction they choose. They should not be forced to buy anything or hold anything they do not want.

The term "consumer sovereignty" is of relatively recent vintage. Its formal introduction is credited to William Harold Hutt, who in his 1936 book *Economists and the Public*, defined it as follows: "the consumer is sovereign when he has not delegated to political institutions for authoritarian use the power which he can exercise socially through his power to demand (or refrain from demanding)."[2] Of course, a commitment to consumer sovereignty is implicit in a lot of earlier work. Perhaps the reason it was not articulated more explicitly is that the set of liberties in question can easily be seen as simply a subset of those liberties accorded to all citizens within a liberal political regime. If market transactions are just contracts, and the state is simply in the business of enforcing contracts – not deciding which ones are wise or unwise – then it follows pretty closely that consumers can enter into whatever market transactions they like.

It is unsurprising, then, that the primary arguments for consumer sovereignty are substantially equivalent to the ones for liberal autonomy. First, in terms of the efficiency effects, consumer sovereignty gives consumers (indirect) control over the major decisions pertaining to the allocation of scarce resources within the society. This makes it far more likely that these resources will be employed in ways that promote human welfare than if the decisions are made by some other agency, such as the state. The details of how the price system accomplishes this are too well known to require repetition here. The second argument appeals to more principled concerns. If individuals are not choosing for themselves how to exercise their demand, then they are in effect being bound by contractual obligations that they have not freely chosen. The fact that they have not consented, again, suggests that the relevant exercise of power is not one that citizens could have unanimously agreed to delegate to the state. It therefore represents the unjust exercise of power of one group within society over another.

II Perfectionism

The most common objection to consumer sovereignty is that it leads to a social pathology known as "consumerism." This ailment is somewhat ill-defined. Obviously, prior to the twentieth century, the overwhelming majority of human beings lived at, near, or below the subsistence level. It is only in the past century, in the industrialized parts of the world, that any significant segment of a population has acquired what might reasonably be described as "disposable income." This has meant that for the first time, large numbers of people find themselves with actual consumption choices – that is, situations in which their choices are not directly dictated by economic necessity. People in our society – even many of the very poorest – now choose what they would like to eat for breakfast, choose what clothes to wear, choose what forms of entertainment to consume, and so on.

At first glance, this would seem to be a good thing. The fact that people have such choices is a direct consequence of the fact that they are no longer condemned to living out their lives in grinding poverty. Thus there is a clear sense in which consumerism, insofar as it is a problem, is something of a problem for happy people. Like obesity, it's not something that people have had to worry about too much over the course of human history. The concern, however, is that people may not be exercising this new-found freedom wisely. John Kenneth Galbraith put it best, at the beginning of *The Affluent Society*, when he suggested that people may not handle living under conditions of material affluence very well, simply because the human race has no prior experience dealing with this condition.[3]

There are in fact some striking parallels between obesity and consumerism. Both are understood as diseases of excess. However, unlike the case of obesity, where the damage done to the person's health is easily quantifiable, the impact of consumerism is much harder to diagnose.

There is the obvious fact that people often express dissatisfaction with their lives, regardless of how much money they make, or how many material possessions they have. But the underlying cause of this dissatisfaction is very difficult to determine, and tends to get expressed in a wide variety of different ways. As a result, critics of consumerism tend to define the pathology in a way that is quite intimately tied to what they happen to think is wrong with consumer society.

The most common objection to consumer sovereignty is simply that, according to the critic, consumers consistently make bad decisions. Of course, this objection would have very little force if it were expressed as simply a disagreement – or worse, a difference in taste – between the critic and the consumer. The standard strategy is rather to argue that consumption choices reflect a commitment to some broader set of values, or conceptions of the good, and that these values can be organized into some sort of evaluative hierarchy. It is then claimed that the choices made by consumers consistently reflect values that are found towards the bottom of this hierarchy

When formulated in terms of values, this critique of consumerism can be referred to as perfectionist. The perfectionist critique boils down to the claim that consumerism reflects a commitment to the wrong conception of the good. This claim is often derived quite explicitly from a more general perfectionist doctrine. Consider, for example, the reasoning of Pope John Paul II:

To call for an existence which is qualitatively more satisfying is of itself legitimate, but one cannot fail to draw attention to the new responsibilities and dangers connected with this phase of history. The manner in which new needs arise and are defined is always marked by a more or less appropriate concept of man and of his true good. A given culture reveals its overall understanding of life through the choices it makes in production and consumption. It is here that *the phenomenon of consumerism* arises. In singling out new needs and new means to meet them, one must be guided by a comprehensive picture of man which respects all the dimensions of his being and which subordinates his material and instinctive dimensions to his interior and spiritual ones. If, on the contrary, a direct appeal is made to his instincts – while ignoring in various ways the reality of the person as intelligent and free – then *consumer attitudes* and *life-styles* can be created which are objectively improper and often damaging to his physical and spiritual health. Of itself, an economic system does not possess criteria for correctly distinguishing new and higher forms of satisfying human needs from artificial new needs which hinder the formation of a mature personality.[4]

According to John Paul II, it is precisely the *neutrality* of the capitalist economy that generates the problem. Because it works to satisfy whatever needs people happen to have, it has no mechanism to promote the sorts of needs and desires that people *should* have. Unfortunately, people have a tendency to let themselves be governed by their "instincts," and so to assign greater priority to their lower material needs than to their higher spiritual ones. This tendency gets translated by the economic system into a pattern of production and consumption that overemphasizes the value of material goods.

Of course, this argument makes no pretence of respecting liberal political principles. It is self-consciously illiberal, insofar as it depends upon the view that society should privilege one particular conception of the good. The neutrality of economic institutions is what provides the primary grounds for the objection to the unrestricted exercise of consumer choice. Its rejection of consumer sovereignty and its rejection of liberal autonomy therefore go hand in hand.

There should be no doubt that the position articulated here is *consistent* (regardless of whether it is politically judicious). However, it is clearly not a view that is available to the liberal critic of consumerism, as least as far as those terms are being used here. Much more problematic are cases in which critics rely upon a tacitly perfectionist critique of consumerism, while still espousing liberal principles in the political realm. Consumerism as a social phenomenon is generally sustained through individual behavior that we condemn on moral grounds. In particular, consumerism is associated with character traits that we identify as vices: vanity, greed, narcissism, venality, to name just a few. Critics often suppose that if is wrong for individuals to engage in this sort of behavior, then clearly it is also wrong for society to set up the economic system that rewards this sort of behavior.

Much of this concern is clearly motivated by anxiety over the decline of the traditional virtues associated with the "Protestant work ethic," and the growing shift in emphasis away from production and toward consumption. For example, Daniel Bell's *The Cultural Contradictions of Capitalism* is motivated by the assumption that these virtues are somehow functionally essential for the reproduction of our society, and that without them we are condemned to civilizational decline.[5] But despite decades of hand-wringing, none of these dire predictions has come true. Capitalism appears to get along just fine without the old package of Christian virtues. Furthermore, it has scored some remarkable successes in parts of the world where "materialist" values are arguably even more prominent – various parts of Asia come to mind. So if there is any mileage to be had from this anxiety about the work ethic, it must be that the critic regards these values as somehow intrinsically superior to the ones that prioritize consumption.

The problem with such arguments is that the hierarchy of values that they hinge upon is extremely controversial. It is not like the case of health and obesity. There is no question that the way we are wired up gives us an impulse to gorge on fatty foods. This is an adaptation designed to help us survive conditions of material scarcity, and it is clearly a maladaptation in contexts of abundance. Thus there is very little objection when governments engage in public-health initiatives designed to counter these effects (promoting healthy diet and lifestyle, requiring nutritional information on food packages, and so on.) But the case of consumerist values is quite different. We could certainly use a more robust discussion in our society about how it is best to live. We may also agree that many people pursue forms of gratification that are ultimately self-defeating. But there is still room for a great deal of *reasonable* disagreement about the merits of these different projects. Thus it is entirely inappropriate for the liberal state to intervene in order to discourage "improper" lifestyles.[6]

III   False Consciousness

While the perfectionist critique of consumerism rejects the liberal commitment to autonomy either implicitly or explicitly, there are a number of other views that endorse the basic principle yet deny that the conditions needed for the exercise of autonomous choice by consumers are satisfied. In order to count as fully autonomous, a choice must be made by an agent who is sufficiently mature, well-informed, and rational. Many critics argue that one or another of these conditions is usually absent, and thus that the choices made by consumers will often not reflect their own best interests. According to this view, the pattern of action that results from such choices – consumerism – reflects a form of *false consciousness*. Consumerism is therefore diagnosed as a type of ideology.

Early versions of this argument were direct descendents of Marx's critique of "commodity fetishism." The original critique of ideology was intended to provide some explanation for why workers generally failed to agitate for the revolutionary overthrown of capitalism, given that the persistence of the capitalist order was supposedly so inimical to their interests. Marx's considered response was that the operations of the capitalist economy disguised what were essentially social relationships, making them appear as though they were a relationship between *things*. This gave the economy the appearance of being a natural order, when in fact it was artificial, and hence mutable.

This explanation became considerably less persuasive as the twentieth century progressed, simply because the occurrence of communist revolutions in Russia and elsewhere made it clear to almost everyone that a capitalist organization of the economy was merely one option among many. So then why did the workers not rebel? Part of the problem seemed to be that workers were overly content with the material goods afforded to them by the capitalist order. Thus "consumerism" was hit upon as a fallback explanation for the fact that the communist revolution did not occur. Consumer goods were identified as the new opiate of the people. Workers had been seduced into thinking that they liked living in suburban houses, watching television, and eating white bread. This caused them to overlook their real interests, which involved building a classless society, freeing themselves from oppression, and so forth.

Of course, this theory ascribes a pretty colossal self-misunderstanding to the working classes. As a result, it takes on a substantial burden of proof. The mere claim that the "objective interests" of the proletariat could be deduced from a correct understanding of their world-historical role is hardly sufficient to discharge this burden. What made the diagnosis more plausible was the development of *advertising*. The success of Nazi propaganda during the Second World War showed that modern techniques of manipulation, particularly when amplified through mass media like print and radio, could have an extraordinarily powerful effect upon individuals. Anyone who doubted that large numbers of people could be quite systematically misled about where their interests lay had only to look at the Nuremberg rallies in order to see quite dramatic counterevidence.

It is therefore not surprising that after the war ended, many people were quite disturbed to see exactly the same propaganda techniques applied with renewed vigor to the sale of consumer goods. It suggested the following line of reasoning: If Germans could be systematically brainwashed by the Nazis, why couldn't consumers be similarly brainwashed by corporations?

Thus the development of advertising lent a great deal of plausibility to the diagnosis of consumerism as a form of false consciousness. Vance Packard's 1957 bestseller *The Hidden Persuaders* provides a canonical formulation of this critique, and reflects quite clearly the alarm and anxiety that the introduction of these new techniques of persuasion created. Of course, *The Hidden Persuaders* was written at a time in which the intellectual credibility of Freudian psychoanalysis was still untarnished. This meant that people were far more likely to take seriously the suggestion that consumers might be subjected to total manipulation at a subconscious level. Packard cited studies, for example, that purported to show that consumers entered into a "hypnoidal trance" upon entering supermarkets. These poor shoppers, he reports, "were so entranced as they wandered about the store plucking things off shelves at random that they would bump into boxes without seeing them."[7]

But setting aside these more extreme claims, it must be admitted that there are some grounds to be concerned about the effects of advertising. If the widely-reported claim that we are exposed to approximately 3,000 commercial messages every day is correct, then this is bound to have a distorting effect upon our consciousness. It doesn't matter how "media-savvy" consumers have become, the idea that anyone could emerge from this sort of bombardment without at least some distorted perceptions is psychologically fantastic. Advertising must be having some effects, and there is no reason to think that these effects work to the interest of consumers – simply because advertising is not *designed* to promote the consumers' interest.

Thus, critics of consumerism have called for restrictions upon advertising, or on forms of consumption heavily promoted by advertising. Of course, their case is bolstered by the fact that we already have laws that prohibit certain types of misleading advertising. Advertisements that make false claims about a product are illegal, as is packaging that misrepresents its contents. All of these restrictions are designed to prevent consumers from being manipulated by advertisers. So why not just extend these laws further? We have had a tendency to focus legal efforts on the prohibition of deceptive advertising. (Of course, almost all advertising is deceptive to some degree – regulation is usually a matter of drawing the line somewhere.) We might consider extending these efforts in other directions as a way of combating consumerism.

However, as soon as this suggestion is made, it becomes clear that such a proposal runs into trouble with autonomy. Take first the case of advertising aimed it manipulating people's desires. It is common, among critics of consumerism, to suggest that there is a distinction between our "natural" desires and "artificial" desires. (Such a distinction is, of course, one of the oldest chestnuts in the literature on autonomy.) Advertising is often held responsible for inculcating the latter. Because the agent is manipulated into acquiring this desire, the conditions of autonomous choice were not satisfied. As a result, it is argued, a paternalistic intervention aimed at blocking the ad, or preventing the consumer from acting upon the desire, would be legitimate.

Among liberals, there is still considerable controversy over the question of whether actions based on imprudently formed desires count as autonomous. Some have argued that an intervention is only paternalistic if it prevents the agents from satisfyings desire that she would have had, under conditions of full information and complete rationality. Others argue that society has no business asking whether or not the agent has exercised due diligence in cultivating one or another of his desires – thus all of them should be taken at face value.

But without even getting into this issue, we can see that there are still greater problems with the idea that the desires formed through advertising can be discounted or overruled. The most basic problem is simply that for every one agent who acquires a desire through some purportedly "illegitimate" mechanism like advertising, there will be two or three more who acquire it in a way that cannot be so easily impugned. For example, people are far more influenced by word of mouth, along with the consumption habits of those around them, than they are by advertising.[8] How could anyone possibly separate out these cases? There is a clear sense in which all of our desires are "artificial," produced through a very complex interaction between individuals and their cultural environment. The idea that any one set can be privileged as somehow more authentic than some other is deeply implausible. What is more likely is that it reflects a mere difference in *values*. But if this is the case, then the critique of false consciousness turns out to be just a disguised form of perfectionism.

The major problem is that whatever diagnosis the critique eventually settles on is still likely to be deeply controversial. In the case of deceptive advertising, we at least have some widely accepted criteria that allow us to distinguish between false and true belief. One doesn't need to be a non-cognitivist about evaluative judgment to recognize that such criteria are lacking in the case of desires. Even if it makes sense to judge one desire to be more authentic, or natural, or even true, than another, there is no consensus about how this should be done. And as long as such disagreements exist, it would be unacceptably paternalistic to control advertising because of its ability to manipulate our desires. We may place restrictions on advertising aimed at children, but we cannot do so with respect to adults.[9]

IV   Cultural Homogenization

The argument for consumer sovereignty rests quite heavily on the assumption that markets are a relatively transparent mechanism for transmitting consumer demand to suppliers. If markets are transparent, then the fact that a particular commodity is being produced, in certain quantities, reflects the fact that there is approximately that much demand for it. So when you drive through the suburbs, past outlet malls, big-box retailers, and franchise fast-food joints, you can rest content in the knowledge that all is well; these places exist only because they are what the people themselves want most. And when McDonalds or Pizza Hut opens up shop in some new country somewhere in the world, putting a number of local restaurants out of business, one should rejoice because, after all, the people there obviously prefer to eat at McDonalds or Pizza Hut.

This story is, for better or for worse, one that many people have a hard time believing. Looking at the incredible diversity of cultures in the world, it is difficult to imagine that much of this was sustained only through the relative isolation of societies from one another – but that once they start trading, people turn out to all harbor a secret desire for Big Macs and Coca-Cola. But there does seem to be a strong *prima facie* connection between increased globalization – in particular, increased integration into the global capitalist economy – and increased cultural homogenization. It is tempting, however, to think that this homogenization, rather than reflecting an underlying, preexisting homogeneity of taste, is actually an *effect* of the global economy. The market economy, in other words, far from being neutral with respect to taste, is positively biased towards the satisfaction of certain sorts of tastes. In particular, it is often suspected that the market has a leveling tendency – reducing everything to the lowest common denominator.

If this is correct, then intervention in the market might not violate autonomy, because the market itself is not neutral. If the market is positively biased towards increased homogenization, selective interventions aimed at mitigating these effects need not privilege one particular set of values. In fact, such intervention would be necessary in order to ensure that the preexisting range of values and tastes are treated equally. Unfortunately, critics are often less than explicit about why markets have this homogenizing character. They also usually fail to take seriously the possibility that this homogeneity may reflect uniformity of taste (or more specifically, a uniform range of diverse tastes). Thus, many critics of consumerism do very little to free themselves from the suspicion that this cultural homogeneity simply offends *their* taste.

The closest thing to a stand-alone argument for limiting consumer sovereignty in order to stave off cultural homogenization is due to Tibor Scitovsky. Scitovsky points out that markets are only transparent under very restrictive conditions. One of these conditions is that there must be no economies of scale. But such economies do exist in the real world, and as a result, mass-produced goods are often cheaper to manufacture than others. This is what produces homogenization. Here is the argument:

> Economies of scale not only cheapen large-scale production but by raising wages they also raise the cost and diminish the profitability of small-scale production. This in turn raises the minimum volume of sales necessary to render production profitable and thus leads to an ever increasing narrowing of the range of variants of products offered and neglect of minority needs and tastes in the nature and design of goods produced and marketed. The increasing neglect of minority preferences is a bad thing, because it is illiberal, makes for uniformity, and destroys to some degree the principal merit of the market economy: its ability to cater separately and simultaneously to different people's differing needs and tastes.[10]

This argument moves a bit too quickly though. Suppose that, initially, goods are custom-ordered from a small-scale supplier, who produces items that are tailor-made to each individual customer. A large-scale producer comes along who makes the same type of product, but only in, say, three styles. By limiting the number of styles, this producer is able to sell the goods at much lower cost. Scitovsky infers that the large producer will drive the small producer out of business.

But this is not necessarily the case. One must assume, given the variety of products made by the small-scale producers, that the three mass-produced variants will not exactly match the taste of at least some consumers. This means that they will suffer a loss of welfare if they switch to the mass-produced goods. So if they do switch, it must be because they prefer the money they save to the inconvenience of purchasing goods not perfectly suited to their tastes. The small-scale producer would not go bankrupt if people with minority tastes were willing to *pay more* for the goods than those with majority tastes. Homogenization arises only because people are unwilling to pay the full cost associated with satisfaction of their preferences when low-cost alternatives that are "close enough" become available. There is nothing coercive or illiberal about this.

In any case, it is not really the market that is causing the problem here. People who have extremely mainstream tastes benefit from that fact, simply because these tastes take less effort and fewer resources to satisfy when mass-production techniques are available. This has nothing to do with the market; it has to do with the distribution of tastes in the population and with the productive technology that permits manufacture on a large scale. Consumer sovereignty is not to be blamed. Furthermore, it is not really unfair that people with minority tastes should have to pay more, since satisfaction of these tastes imposes greater costs upon society under such conditions.

The only case where Scitovsky's argument holds is when a special sort of feedback loop develops between production and purchasing decisions. For example, if some portion of the value of a good is determined by its anticipated resale value, people may purchase goods that are perceived to satisfy majority tastes, even if they themselves do not especially like them. If large numbers of people do this, it may become a self-fulfilling prophecy – most people will buy a good just because it seems like the sort of thing that most people will buy. But this is clearly a marginal phenomenon, and it is not clear that very much can or need be done about it.

Finally, despite all the rhetoric, it is not at all obvious that mass-production does generate homogenization. One hundred years ago, most people wore clothes that were made specifically for them by a tailor. But the overall variety of clothing was much narrower than it is now, especially in terms of the variety that one could see in public display. This is primarily because basic clothing has become so cheap that people can afford to spend more on various aspects of style that make clothes distinctive. The same can be said for food (which has become available in far greater variety even in the past thirty years), housing, music and entertainment, and so on.[11]

V Market Failure

So far, we have seen very little to suggest that the critique of consumer sovereignty is consistent with respect for the autonomy of citizens. However, of all the arguments canvassed so far, the most difficult one to fault in this respect is Scitovsky's. Despite its flaws, the argument does contain a valuable theoretical strategy. Scitovsky tacitly acknowledges that under conditions of perfect competition, there would be very little to be said against consumer sovereignty. But the world we live in is very far from meeting those conditions. As a result, the market will not function as a "transparent" mechanism for imposing consumer demand on firms. When the signals being sent by consumers are being distorted, it is possible that changing the pattern of demand will generate a new equilibrium that comes closer to satisfying the actual preferences of consumers. Thus, imposing certain constraints on the sovereignty of the consumer may in fact lead to a greater overall level of satisfaction of consumer welfare. Such an intervention, despite limiting the freedom of consumers, need not violate their autonomy.

Scitovsky's particular example – economies of scale – fails to motivate a policy of government intervention, simply because he is unable to show that the market outcome is unfair to anyone in particular. However, if the market imperfection is one that generates a Pareto-inefficient outcome, then there would be nothing wrong with a regulatory intervention aimed at remedying this inefficiency. Thus, if consumerism is identified, not as a system of values or as a type of false consciousness, but rather as a pattern of behavior that is symptomatic of *market failure*, then there is no reason that a liberal cannot seek legislative remedies that involve restrictions on consumer choice.

In order to see why legal intervention in such a case would not be inappropriate, it is important to realize that the liberal conception of autonomy has never been understood as preventing citizens from using state power to eliminate collective action problems (or "prisoner's dilemmas"). In fact, the primary justification for freedom of contract, since Hobbes, has been that it allows individuals to work out their own cooperative solutions to collective action problems, then to call upon the state to enforce them. Every economic exchange, for instance, creates a collective action problem, because both parties have an incentive to "free-ride" by eluding payment. Contracts of sale allow parties to work out the terms of a solution, then to bind themselves to these terms by licensing the state to punish any free riders. This sort of enforcement does not compromise anyone's autonomy, because the contract is mutually advantageous and subject to general consent.

John Kenneth Galbraith was the first to point out that the existence of market failure, along with missing markets, creates a serious problem for the doctrine of consumer sovereignty. Property rights are very effective at eliminating collective action problems when it comes to the exchange of medium-sized dry goods, like chairs and bags of wheat. They are also good at regulating the use of land. They are not so good when it comes to more intangible goods, like knowledge, or goods that must be delivered on a large scale, like bridges. They are not good at regulating the use of air or water either. In all of these cases, these limitations are due to enforcement problems that make it nearly impossible to eliminate free riders.

As a result, markets will systematically overproduce certain types of goods, especially material ones, and will underproduce others. Goods that have significant negative externalities will be overproduced, while those with significant positive externalities will be underproduced. (We are talking here about production levels relative to what consumer demand would be, at the price level that would obtain when all externalities were internalized.) Furthermore, consumers will be unable to correct this bias through voluntary action, because the relevant economic incentives all reinforce the biased outcome. Thus the presence of externalities locks consumers into a giant collective-action problem.

Galbraith observed that under such circumstances, it would be entirely reasonable for consumers to choose, collectively, to impose restrictions on their private purchasing behaviour. Consumer sovereignty, under conditions of "real existing capitalism," will generate overproduction of "private goods" – that is, goods of the sort that property rights are good at protecting. Thus, "vacuum cleaners to insure clean houses are praiseworthy and essential in our standard of living. Street cleaners to insure clean streets are an unfortunate expense. Partly as a result, our houses are generally clean and our streets generally filthy."[12] This is an enormous boon for those who happen to have a strong preference for the private goods, but it is unfair to everyone else. Thus neutrality requires that some of the resources that are being used to produce private goods be redirected into the production of non-market goods.

The primary mechanism through which this is done is the income tax. Taxes in a welfare-state society are best understood as a form of mandatory spending.[13] Consumers are prevented from spending some fraction of their income on private goods. The state takes this income and uses it to finance the provision of a wide range of goods that markets fail to provide, or that markets would not provide at the right prices. This must involve a restriction of consumer sovereignty, because given a choice consumers would choose to free-ride rather than pay for these goods. They want national defense, pest control, public education, and so on, but they simply have no incentive to contribute. Thus, as Cass Sunstein puts it, there are cases where "the force of law is necessary *in order to allow people to obtain what they want.*"[14] The consumer is only able to achieve satisfaction of his preferences through delegation "to political institutions for authoritarian use the power which he can exercise socially through his power to demand" – except of course that this use is "authoritarian" only in the sense that it is coercive. This does not preclude the possibility that the state remain democratically accountable for way that this spending power is exercised.

Galbraith's analysis also provides a useful insight into why consumerism is often diagnosed as a form of false consciousness. Imagine that each agent has two different preference schedules, one for market goods and the other for non-market goods. Supply of the latter is compromised by a collective action problem that markets fail to resolve, and so will either be delivered through a non-market mechanism, or will not be delivered at all. If one assumes that all consumption is subject to diminishing marginal satisfaction, this will mean that additional increments in the supply of either type of good will be used to satisfy increasingly unimportant needs. Thus consumers will first ensure that their basic needs are met – food, shelter, clothing, and so on – before they go on to purchase "frills" or luxury items. Now suppose that a society is doing a very bad job of supplying non-market goods. As a result, goods that are very high on everyone's list, like education or clean air, may not be provided in sufficient quantities. However, consumers who receive additional increments in income have no means of purchasing non-market goods, because of the unresolved collective action problem. As a result, they will wind up buying increasingly inessential market goods that produce miniscule increments in satisfaction, even when other very basic needs go unmet. From the outside, it looks as though consumers are investing their resources quite irrationally. It is important to see, however, that while this behavior is collectively self-defeating, it is not irrational. Consumers are merely responding to the existing set of economic incentives.

VI Conspicuous Consumption

The important feature of Galbraith's diagnosis of consumerism is that he treats it as a type of collective action problem. This is why his proposed remedy does not violate the autonomy of consumers. Upon closer analysis, however, one can see that these sorts of collective action problems are far more widespread than Galbraith imagined, and that they need not involve any sort of obvious market failure. In particular, certain forms of conspicuous consumption generate a negative-sum game, in which consumers "overspend" on goods that ultimately fail to produce any satisfaction. This is particularly common in cases where some significant fraction of the satisfaction consumers derive from a good depends upon a comparison with others.

Thorstein Veblen very clearly identified the problem more than a century ago.[15] Veblen observed that goods were sought for both their material properties and for the status they conferred upon their owner. The problem with status consumption, according to Veblen, is that it generates waste. It is not called "waste" simply because Veblen disapproves of the relevant sort of desires. He claims that his critique involves "no deprecation of the motives or of the ends sought by the consumer," and thus is not merely a value-judgement, in the perfectionist sense.[16] The problem with status goods, according to Veblen, is that they work by generating an "invidious comparison" between individuals. In other words, they increase one person's status only by lowering someone else's. Thus the consumption of status goods does "not serve human life or human well-being on the whole."[17] Nowadays, we would say that status is a zero-sum game, and thus status competition, insofar as it consumes other resources, is a negative sum. Conspicuous consumption is, in short, a prisoner's dilemma.

Contemporary neo-Veblenians have formulated this basic critique at a greater level of generality, in order to distinguish it more clearly from the moralizing perfectionist critique. Consider Robert Frank:

Much has been written about our failure to achieve better balance in our lives, which authors almost invariably attribute to dark forces of one kind or another – some rooted within us, such as greed, impatience, or stupidity, and others that work on us from the outside, such as exploitation by powerful corporate interests. Yet these forces could be swept aside entirely and the fundamental problem would remain, for its primary source lies not in individual or corporate imperfection, but in the cold, impersonal logic of competition.[18]

Frank is at pains to emphasize that it is the comparative nature of our preferences that generates this competitiveness. Comparativeness is often difficult to detect, however, simply because people are in general highly adaptive. We tend to judge things big or small, beautiful or ugly, dirty or clean, relative to what we are used to. When standards of cleanliness in our environment go up, we adapt quickly, which in turn affects our future judgments. Things are no different in an economic environment. Frank uses a very telling example, involving the desire to live in a spacious home. What counts as spacious is very much dependent upon the size of everyone else's house. Extremely rich people in New York live quite happily in apartments that would seem impossibly cramped by the standards of Palo Alto. These apartments actually *feel* quite spacious when one is in New York, simply because they are quite large relative to what other people have. But because of this comparison, the desire to live in a spacious home generates a prisoner's dilemma. The only way to satisfy such a preference is to buy a home that is of above average size, but when everyone does this, the average size creeps upwards. Thus, more resources are invested in home construction and maintenance, while the increase in satisfaction associated with the feeling of spaciousness is quickly eroded.

One could describe the problem here as a sort of market failure. If the value of a good is based on a comparison with what others are consuming, then all of the consumption choices made in this domain generates externalities for other consumers. (And, of course, if one defines market failure as any circumstance in which markets do not achieve Pareto-optimal outcomes, then it becomes true by definition that these are all cases of market failure.) The important point is that these effects can occur even in markets that are well-structured, according to the standard economic criteria – where there is robust price competition, property rights are well-defined, there are few information asymmetries, and so on. As a result, the critique of competitive consumption can license interferences in consumer sovereignty even in domains where markets are doing a good job of producing goods in ample quantity. This may seem counterintuitive, until one recalls that it is not the sheer quantity of goods produced by the economy that counts, from a normative point of view. What matters is the satisfaction that these goods generate. When consumers get locked into competitive consumption, huge amounts of resources get funneled in to feeding a competition that ultimately generates no increase in satisfaction.

Frank's solution to this problem mirrors Galbraith's. His proposal is for a progressive consumption tax (to be levied as a tax on income minus savings). This is based on the observation that while increased income is initially quite strongly correlated with increased happiness, the correlation tapers off quickly once a certain basic level of need has been met. The reasons for this must certainly be complex, but clearly one contributing factor must be that most of the high-priority items on people's general preference schedules over consumer goods are items valued primarily for their intrinsic properties, but that as one moves along to less important items, the comparative dimension begins to loom larger.

Of course, there would be no point to such a tax if there were nothing else that the money could be spent on (that is, nothing else that society could commit its resources to). But this is not the case. Apart from the market goods that people spend their money on, there is the full range of goods that are *not* delivered through the market. Even if the progressive consumption tax does no more than discourage work effort, it might still generate an efficiency gain. This is because people value the non-market good of leisure. Thus a tax, insofar as it simply dampens down consumption in the upper disposable income range, will increase the welfare of everyone – including those who pay the bulk of it. The most exclusive clubs will still be just as exclusive, and belonging to them will still confer just as much prestige. It is just that they will cost less to join (because everyone will have less money). The difference, however, is that people will have more free time. Thus the satisfaction that people derive from their consumption of private goods will be unaffected, while their consumption of non-market goods will increase.

VII Conclusion

Critics of consumerism are constantly subjected to charges of elitism, Puritanism, paternalism, and so forth. The reasons for this are not hard to find. After all, given the absence of overt coercion in the supermarkets and malls, criticizing consumerism must involve criticizing the choices made by consumers. But it is difficult to see why the social critic should be better positioned than the consumer herself to decide what she should be buying – hence the suspicion that the critic is simply trying to meddle in the private affairs of others. And since important features of our political institutions were put in place precisely to prevent this sort of meddling, it is no surprise that the critique of consumerism so easily runs afoul of liberal democratic principles.

At the same time, it is very hard to avoid noticing that there is a genuinely perverse inversion of priorities at work in the way our society allocates its resources (more money for SUVs, less money for schools...). Hence the problem facing the critic of consumerism: How to articulate the perversity underlying these consumption choices, without simply attributing it to the ignorance or venality of consumers? And how to formulate remedies that do not constitute illegitimate interferences with their autonomy?

The clearest solution lies in the observation that the lopsided investment of resources into market over non-market goods constitutes a Pareto-inefficient consumption pattern, generated by an underlying collective action problem. Using the force of law to correct such collective-action problems does not require any infringement on the autonomy of consumers. If one takes the term "consumer sovereignty" to refer to a blanket prohibition on legislative measures that limit individuals' ability to spend their income however they like, then the elimination of such a collective-action problem will be inconsistent with consumer sovereignty. Thus liberal autonomy and consumer sovereignty will not coincide – in fact, one might reasonable expect citizens to *exercise* their autonomy in order to enact legislative measures that limit their own freedom of choice as consumers.

Such measures may not do justice to all of the complaints that have been made about the consequences of consumer sovereignty. It will do nothing to encourage traditional virtues, like moderation in the satisfaction of one's desires. Nor will it do anything to cure the masses of their inveterate bad taste. And it is very unlikely to diminish the popularity of Big Macs and Coca-Cola. But the reason this kind of anti-consumerist program – the kind that diagnoses consumerism as a collective action problem – leaves these features of our society intact is that any effort to use the force of law to remedy these supposed problems would be inconsistent with the respect for autonomy and pluralism that is such an important feature of civic life in democratic societies.

Notes

1. This statement of principle is, of course, merely the point of departure for reflections on the role of autonomy in a liberal polity. I am using the term autonomy here to refer only to what Forst calls *legal autonomy*. The chapters in the present volume provide a good sense of the complexities that develop, and the number of further distinctions that are required, when one begins to explore the ramifications of this commitment in more detail.
2. William Harold Hutt, *Economists and the Public: A Study of Competition and Opinion* (London: Jonathan Cape, 1936), p. 257.
3. John Kenneth Galbraith, *The Affluent Society* (Boston: Houghton Mifflin, 1976).
4. Pope John Paul, *Encyclical Letter: Centesimus Annus* (1991), p. 75.
5. Daniel Bell, *The Cultural Contradictions of Capitalism* (New York: Basic Books, 1976).
6. Of course, there are some cases that are quite borderline. For instance, people have a well-documented tendency to discount the future quite sharply, and thus to adopt savings policies that are inconsistent with their own considered judgments about how they would like to distribute consumption opportunities over their own lifetimes. This is analogous to the "fatty foods" case, insofar as our capacity to defer gratification has an obvious biological dimension. Thus there may be grounds for the government to adopt measures designed to promote higher savings rates (and thus to reduce short-term consumption). However, this should not be thought of as partiality to one particular value, such as "frugality." A program to encourage savings is neutral with respect to what these savings will eventually be spent on. It only forces consumers to defer some portion of their consumption; it doesn't *privilege* one form of consumption over another.
7. Vance Packard, *The Hidden Persuaders* (New York: David McKay, 1957), p. 107.

8. For a very sober discussion of these issues, see Michael Schudson, *Advertising, The Uneasy Persuasion* (New York: Basic Books, 1986).
9. There are certain special cases, such as addictive substances, where the consumer's behavior can be clearly at variance with his or her expressed preferences. The fact that even many of these cases remain controversial, however, shows just how significant a burden of proof one must meet in order to justify restrictions on the market aimed at redressing consumer irrationality. A lot of anti-consumerism fails to meet this threshold, and doesn't even try.
10. Tibor Scitovsky, "On the Principle of Consumer Sovereignty," *American Economic Review*, 52 (1962): 262–268 at 265.
11. See Tyler Cowen's two books, *In Praise of Commercial Culture* (Cambridge, MA: Harvard University Press, 1998), and *Creative Destruction* (Princeton, NJ: Princeton University Press, 2002).
12. Galbraith, *The Affluent Society*, p. 134.
13. This is most obvious when it forms part of the classic Keynesian strategy for counteracting the business cycle. During a recession, consumers have an incentive to defer purchases until others have made their purchases. This is collectively self-defeating, and perpetuates the recession. The Keynesian prescription is for the state to correct this by taking money and spending it on everyone's behalf.
14. Cass Sunstein, *After the Rights Revolution*, (Cambridge, MA: Harvard University Press, 1999), p. 43.
15. Thorstein Veblen, *The Theory of the Leisure Class* (New York: Penguin, 1979).
16. Ibid. See pp. 97–100. His view is often misunderstood on this point. See, for example, James Twitchell, *Lead us into Temptation* (New York: Columbia University Press, 1999), p. 37.
17. Ibid., p. 100.
18. Robert H. Frank, *Luxury Fever* (New York: The Free Press, 1999), p. 146.

10

Political Liberty

Integrating Five Conceptions of Autonomy

Rainer Forst

1. Although "liberty" today is generally recognized as a fundamental criterion for the legitimacy of a society's basic institutional structure, disputes over its content continue unabated. Within the history of political philosophy as well as in contemporary debates, a wide variety of theories provide competing accounts, ranging from republicanism to Marxism, from libertarianism to various forms of liberalism ("perfectionist" or "political").[1] In the following, I want to suggest that the best way out of these controversies can be found in an *intersubjectivist concept of political liberty* comprised of an adequate integration of *five different conceptions of individual autonomy*.

2. The term "political liberty" is used here in a rather broad sense, including both the republican "liberty of the ancients" and the liberal "liberty of the moderns."[2] In contrast to the more narrow notion of "political autonomy" – the participation in the exercise of political self-rule – "political liberty" is understood as the liberty that persons have as citizens of a political community – that is, the liberty that they can claim as citizens and that they must grant each other as citizens.

3. The "intersubjectivist" approach I defend is not to be confused with communitarian approaches, according to which a person can be free only if his or her individual life is part of and constituted by the "larger life" of a political community that provides its citizens with a sense of the good and virtuous life.[3] Rather, what I mean by "intersubjective" lies on a different plane from that of the quarrel between individualistic and communitarian notions of personal freedom. It is to be explained by the terms "reciprocity" and "generality": political liberty is the form of liberty that persons as citizens grant each other reciprocally and generally. It is not "the state" or "the community" that "distributes" rights and liberties to citizens; rather, the citizens themselves are at the same time the *authors* and the *addressees* of claims to liberties (usually in the form of rights claims). As citizens, persons are both *freedom-claimers* (or *freedom-users*) and *freedom-grantors*. And by analyzing this double role, we will find that it implies different conceptions of individual autonomy.

On this approach, the question of *liberty* is part of the larger question of *justice*; for the relevant criteria of (reciprocal and general) justification are criteria of procedural justice.[4] In a phrase: All claims to political liberty need to be justified as claims to justice, yet not all claims of justice are claims to liberty.

4. In speaking of "a" concept of political liberty, I am diverging from Isaiah Berlin's well-known view that there are "two concepts of liberty," one positive and one negative.[5] I cannot go into the details of Berlin's text here, but a few remarks are necessary. First, Berlin is by no means clear in his analysis of these concepts. For example, terminologically, he speaks not only of two "concepts" but also of two different "notions" as well as "senses" of liberty. This suggests that there is an ambiguity between the thesis that there are two incompatible concepts of political liberty and the thesis that there is only one concept with two different and contradicting interpretations that constitute two different conceptions of that single concept.[6] In Berlin's text, we find support for both of these readings. At one point, it seems that there really are two concepts of political liberty: "The former [i.e. those who defend negative liberty] want to curb authority as such. The latter [i.e. those who defend positive liberty] want it placed in their own hands. That is a cardinal issue. These are not two different interpretations of a single concept, but two profoundly divergent and irreconcilable attitudes to the ends of life."[7] In other passages, Berlin underlines the common core of both notions of liberty: "The essence of the notion of liberty, both in the 'positive' and in the 'negative' senses, is the holding off of something or someone – of others who trespass on my field or assert their authority over me, or of obsessions, fears, neuroses, irrational forces – intruders and despots of one kind or another."[8]

Second, and more importantly, Berlin's characterization of negative liberty implies a particular notion of positive liberty. For the question of negative liberty – "How much am I governed?" or "Over what area am I master?" – presupposes an answer to the positive question – "By whom am

I governed?" or "Who is master?" It is only the answer that some notions of positive liberty give – "Master should be the higher, more rational self, i.e. what we, who hold power, know is more rational given our common higher ends and duties!" – that Berlin rejects.[9] Yet there is no question that negative freedom implies a certain conception of the autonomy of a person as "a being with a life of his own to live"[10] – that is, as having the capacity of reflection and meaningful choice between options in his or her life. One can even say that securing this kind of autonomy is the point of negative liberty. Thus Berlin says that the extent of liberty depends not only on the number of options open to somebody and the difficulty of realizing them, but also on how important these options are "in my plan of life, given my character and circumstances."[11] (Two further criteria are (1) how far options are opened up or closed off by the deliberate action of others, and (2) the importance generally attributed to these options by society.) Thus negative liberty serves autonomy, yet an autonomy that is not defined by "higher" values (which would allow for external ethical judgments about what is good for a person): "I wish to be a subject, not an object; to be moved by reasons, by conscious purposes, which are my own, not by causes which affect me, as it were, from outside."[12]

This suggests, third, that Berlin's thesis is not that there are two irreconcilable concepts of liberty, but that there is *one* core concept and two interpretations of it that historically diverged and opposed themselves to one another. Berlin's thesis is primarily historical, not conceptual: "The freedom which consists in being one's own master, and the freedom which consists in not being prevented from choosing as I do by other men, may, on the face of it, seem concepts at no great logical distance from each other – no more than negative and positive ways of saying much the same thing. Yet the 'positive' and 'negative' notions of freedom historically developed in divergent directions not always by logically reputable steps, until, in the end, they came into direct conflict with each other."[13] Thus there is one *concept* according to which it is the task of political liberty to enable and secure personal *autonomy*, but there are different *conceptions* of political liberty, depending upon *which* notion of autonomy serves as the basis. Every "freedom from" is a "freedom to," yet it is a matter of dispute which kind of self-determination or self-realization is to be the aim of political liberties. "If it is maintained that the identification of the value of liberty with the value of a field of free choice amounts to a doctrine of self-realization, whether for good or for evil ends, and that this is closer to positive than to negative liberty, I shall offer no great objection; only repeat that, as a matter of historical fact, distortions of this meaning of positive liberty (or self-determination) ... obscured this thesis and at times transformed it into its opposite."[14]

One may, therefore, understand the core concept of liberty according to the formula suggested by MacCallum: "x is free from y to do or be (or not to do or be) z."[15] Yet this formula is far too abstract; what matters is how one fills out x, y, and z in a *political* context. What is a "truly" self-determining actor (the empirical or a "true" self)? What counts as a constraint of liberty (external or internal constraints)? Which actions and aims are characteristic of a self-determining (or "self-realizing?") actor? What is needed is an analysis of the forms of autonomy that are at the center of a concept of political liberty.

5. The objection could be made that it is not very useful to try to explain a difficult concept like political liberty with the help of another, no less contested concept like individual or personal autonomy. For while it is true that many political philosophers applaud the idea that political liberty is needed for its value to us as autonomous "purposive beings,"[16] for its service to our well-being as autonomous agents choosing "valuable options,"[17] as an expression of the "full autonomy" of citizens in a liberal well-ordered society,[18] or as ensuring the "equiprimordiality" of both "private" and "public" autonomy[19] – it is equally true that these theorists mean very different things by "autonomy." But it seems to me that if one starts from the basic idea that persons are simultaneously the authors and the addressees of claims to liberty in a given political community, one can develop a differentiated concept of political liberty that allows for a critical perspective on the diverse conceptions of autonomy employed by the theories mentioned here.

6. I suggest the following definition: The concept of political liberty is comprised of those conceptions of autonomy that persons as citizens of a law-governed political community must reciprocally and generally grant and guarantee each other – which means that political liberty includes all those liberties that citizens as autonomous freedom-grantors and freedom-users can justifiably claim from each other (or, negatively, that they cannot reasonably deny each other) and for the realization of which they are mutually responsible. To spell this out, five different conceptions of individual autonomy have to be distinguished: *moral, ethical, legal, political,* and *social* autonomy. All of these play a certain role in the concept of political liberty, yet none of them should become – as is so often the case – paramount and dominant at the expense of the others. This is the problem of most one-sided "negative" or "positive," individualist or communitarian conceptions of political liberty: They make a certain conception of autonomy absolute. To avoid this, a multi-dimensional single concept of political liberty is necessary.

7. Talk of *conceptions* of autonomy presupposes an underlying *concept* of autonomy. According to this concept, a person acts autonomously – that is, as a self-determining being when she acts intentionally and on the basis of reasons. She is aware of the reasons for her action, can "respond" when asked for her reasons, and is thus "responsible" for herself. Autonomous persons in this sense are accountable agents – accountable for themselves to both themselves and others; they can reasonably explain and justify their actions. Yet what do "accountability" and "reasonable justification" mean here? To whom – beside herself – is a person accountable and to whom must the reasons for action be justifiable if she is to count as autonomous? This question necessitates a distinction between different conceptions of autonomy, depending on the practical contexts in which the justification of actions is required. All of these contexts of justification are intersubjective contexts of communities, yet of very different kinds, implying different kinds of reasons for accountable action. Persons are autonomous, then, to the extent to which they can recognize and act on good reasons in these diverse contexts. We should always consider persons to be "situated" in certain contexts, yet we should not think that there is only one kind of "situation" in which persons find themselves.[20] Thus I propose the following set of distinctions, which, however, I can only spell out insofar as it is necessary for the question of political liberty.

8. In a *moral* context, a person can be called autonomous only if he or she acts on the basis of reasons that take every other person equally into account, so that these reasons are mutually justifiable. Wherever the actions of a person affect others in a morally relevant way, they must be justifiable on the basis of reciprocally and generally binding norms, and therefore all those affected – individually – can demand that the agent justify his action on the basis of reasons that are "not reasonable to reject"[21] – that is, that are not reciprocally and generally rejectable. The criteria of reciprocity and generality then are recursively arrived at, starting from the validity claim implied by moral actions and norms.[22] The criterion of reciprocity means that none of the parties concerned may claim certain rights or privileges it denies to others, and that the

relevance and force of the claims at issue is not determined one-sidedly; generality means that all those affected have an equal right to demand justifications. Every moral person has a basic *right to justification*, a right to count equally in reflections regarding whether reasons for action are justifiable.[23] This is what, in my view, is implied by the Kantian idea of the dignity of a person as an "end in itself," as a justificatory being. A moral person can demand to be respected as an autonomous author and addressee of moral claims; he has the freedom to say "no" to claims made by others that violate the criteria of reciprocity and generality.[24] Morally autonomous persons recognize the community of all moral persons as the relevant context of justification and do not restrict the community of justification in any other way. Yet even though this context is one that transcends all other local communal contexts, it is not a worldless, "transcendental," or "acontextual" context, so to speak. It is, rather, the very concrete context in which persons respect each other as human beings, whatever else they may or may not have in common with regard to other contexts such as a culture, a state, a family, and so on.

For the present question of political liberty, it is important to see that the conception of moral autonomy plays a fundamental role in the determination of that concept. For especially as freedom-grantors, but also (in a certain sense) as freedom-users, citizens must view themselves and each other as morally autonomous. To the extent that they are freedom-users, citizens consider it to be one of the tasks of political liberty to help create a society in which they can be responsible moral agents, in which they can rely on each other in everyday life and have the chance to develop moral capacities; as freedom-grantors, citizens first and foremost have to be able to justify their freedom-claims to each other mutually and generally and must grant them on the basis of sharable (that is, non-rejectable) reasons. The basic liberties that will become part of positive law are those that morally responsible and autonomous agents cannot reasonably deny each other. Thus they have a certain moral content as "human rights" – a content, however, that remains abstract and indeterminate as long as it is not put into a concrete form, institutionalized and interpreted in fair procedures of legislation and adjudication. These liberties constitute the abstract core of basic legal principles and rights; yet their content is not a priori given by substantive moral norms or "natural rights"; rather, it is determined by the *criteria* for justifiable claims to liberty. The basic moral "right of justification" corresponds to a veto-right of all those whose claims are in danger of being ignored or silenced. Without this basic form of moral, mutual respect there can be no political liberty.

9. Since the abstract moral core of basic rights has to be determined and institutionalized in legal and political contexts, what is needed, beside the conception of the "moral person," are the conceptions of the "legal person" (as the concrete, positive form of personal rights and duties and as the addressee or subject of the law) as well as the conception of the "citizen" (as the author of the law, who in democratic procedures of deliberation and decision-making determines the concrete form the legal person should take). This gives rise to the conceptions of legal and political autonomy, but before discussing them, I want to mention another conception of autonomy that is basic to understanding the role that legal and political autonomy play – namely, *ethical* autonomy.

As I have explained, moral autonomy refers to the capacity of agents to act on morally justifiable reasons in cases in which one's actions morally affect other agents. The moral context, however, is not the only one in which a person has to answer the practical question of what she should do. For as an "ethical person" – that is, as the person she is in her qualitative, individual identity, she has to find meaningful and justifiable answers to questions of the good life – *her* good life – that are not sufficiently answered by taking moral criteria into account (and that can come into conflict with moral answers). Ethical questions are those a person must answer as somebody who is "constituted" by relationships, communities, values, and ideals that serve as the (reflectively affirmed) "fixed points" or "strong evaluations" of her life[25]; they are questions concerning "my life," the life one is responsible for as its (at least partial) author. A person is ethically autonomous when she determines what is important for herself on the basis of reasons that most fully and adequately take her identity into account – as the person she has been, as she is seen, as she wants to be seen and to see herself in the present and the future; ethical reflection is retrospective and prospective at the same time. Thus, even if an autonomous person is not the single author or creator of her life, she is, in the final analysis, more responsible than anybody else for her life choices. An ethically autonomous person answers ethical questions – "what is good for me?" – *for herself with others*, but she herself is responsible for such answers. Thus the reasons that ultimately count as good ethical reasons are those she can explain, on due reflection, to those "concrete others" that are significant to her – although every meaning these reasons have for others might fall short of the existential meaning they have for the person whose life is in question.

These very general remarks move on the surface of a large debate in ethical theory about the problem of what constitutes a good answer to the question of the good life. Even apart from the issue of the relationship between ethical and moral reasons, there have been many different theories of the form of ethical life as well as a plurality of conceptions of its content. Should one realize oneself in the pursuit of one's "authentic" wishes or in striving to achieve "originality," or in the pursuit of objective values or of duties to God? Should one live a coherent life, as a narrative or even a fixed "life-plan," or should one constantly liberate oneself from fixed identities and the social meanings that encroach on one's ethical autonomy? What distance from others or communities is necessary?

As it seems to me, one would not just burden a theory of political liberty with an insoluble task if one expected it to decide these questions and choose the "right" answer; one would also misunderstand a central point about political liberty. For as soon as one understands that one of the main reasons why personal liberty is so important is that there can be, and will be, very different and incompatible answers given to the question of the good life, and that there is no generally agreed upon objective yardstick to evaluate them, one understands that one of the main characteristics of a plausible concept of political liberty is that it should *not* be based on one particular ethical answer. Rather, in this context one can say that political liberty is the freedom of persons from being forced to live according to one of these specific answers (and the freedom to live according to the answers one thinks most meaningful).

But one may object that this argument itself is based on a quite specific version of ethical autonomy. To answer this, it is necessary to distinguish between *first-order conceptions* and a *second-order conception of ethical autonomy*. First-order conceptions follow particular ethical doctrines about the form and content of the good life, such as those mentioned; the second-order conception allows persons to live according to one or the other first-order conception and to reflect on and decide between these conceptions autonomously. This does *not* mean that it is the ("unencumbered") higher-order choice between them that makes one ethically autonomous; rather, the leading insight is that one of these first-order answers can be absolutely sufficient for an autonomous and a good life, but that, given that there can be reasonable disagreement about the right answer,[26] the political community cannot choose one of the first-order conceptions as the basis for answering the question concerning the extent to which law and politics should guarantee the exercise of ethical autonomy. It is true that an important purpose of political liberty is to enable persons to lead an ethically autonomous life, but it is not its purpose to "make" people lead an autonomous life according to one of the first-order conceptions *or* according to the second-order conception. Ethical autonomy is one of the main points of legally guaranteed autonomy, but the legally secured space of personal life is determined by the *moral* criteria of reciprocity and generality alone, not by *ethical* judgments about the good and autonomous life.[27] Contrary to what many (liberal or communitarian) theorists think, citizens need not believe that a specific version of ethical autonomy is a necessary precondition for the good life in order to institutionalize the possibilities to live according to first- or second-order conceptions of ethical autonomy, because not granting and securing this kind of freedom is a violation of a person's dignity as a morally autonomous being with a right to reciprocal justification. Political liberty essentially rests on the respect for moral autonomy, and the respect for ethical autonomy in a comprehensive sense is an implication of this.

10. The conception of *legal* autonomy can thus be introduced as a matter of not being forced to live according to a specific conception of ethical autonomy. Here lies the truth of the liberal defense of "negative" liberties,[28] although this entails no absolute priority of individual liberties beyond their reciprocal-general legitimacy. Respecting legal autonomy thus implies respecting the freedom of persons to live according to their ethical convictions – a form of respect not just due between ethical communities, so to speak, but also within them. None of these communities may force its members to live according to a traditional way of life – and, likewise, the legal community may not force someone not to live according to such a way of life, for that would make the second-order conception of autonomy into a first-order conception.[29] The goal of legal autonomy – to enable persons to live a life that *they* can regard as being worthy to live – can only be reached if the parameters of legally secured ethical spaces and options are not themselves of a particular ethical nature, but are justifiable in a more general, "reasonable" way. But how can this "reasonable" limit be drawn?

The autonomy of a "legal person" is constituted by the legal definition of the boundaries around the area of personal freedom (*Willkür* in the Kantian sense) granted to each individual. From the discussion of moral and ethical autonomy so far, it follows that the limit to be drawn between permissible and unacceptable uses of personal freedom cannot legitimately be determined by substantive ethical values, since these values favor one conception of the good life over the other. Legal autonomy should legally guarantee the possibility of second-order ethical autonomy, though not on the basis of an ethical judgment about what is "good" for persons but on the basis of norms justified by the moral criteria of reciprocity and generality. In determining these norms, every person is taken into account as a person with equal rights to legal recognition precisely because he or she is at the same time a particular ethical person. Only in this way can the legal person, constituted by general norms, be a *protective cover* for ethical persons and their "thick" identities; only in this way can it be fair to different conceptions of ethical life.

Thus the formula of "reciprocal and general justification" can be used to answer the question as to what a "reasonable" basis for the mutual respect of personal freedom can be. Only those claims to liberty (or those claims to restrict certain liberties) are justified that cannot be rejected on the basis of reciprocally and generally acceptable reasons. And to find these reasons, the participants must find ways to "translate" their arguments into a language that others can understand and accept – at least accept in the sense that they see that the claims being made do not violate reciprocity. If a particular ethical community then tries to generalize its specific values and present them as a legitimate basis for general legislation, it must be able to explain why this is *morally* justified, given its legitimate interests and the interests of all others. If the members of that community succeed in showing that they do not just argue in favor of their ideas of the good that they want to become socially dominant, but in favor of moral goals others can agree to, their claim is justified. Persons do have a right to have their ethical identity respected equally, yet they do not have a right to have their ethical views become the basis of general law.[30] The general law is not neutral in the bad sense of ignoring ethical values as such; it is neutral only in giving equal respect to ethical identities, trying to avoid the danger of marginalizing some through a kind of "ethical law."[31] No unquestioned ethical, objective values are available *a priori* to determine the legitimate uses of personal freedom in a political community. As a result, a space opens up for a plurality of ethical conceptions and ways of life – ways of life that by no means have to be "liberal" in a substantive sense or those of "unencumbered selves" beyond "constitutive commitments."[32] The autonomy of legal persons does not imply a specific conception of the good life "free from" duties, commitments, communities or traditions of, say, a religious kind. It is a fallacy to see legal and ethical contexts connected in that way; individual rights are not based on the idea of individualistic or "atomistic" life-plans.

Legal autonomy implies that a legal person is accountable and responsible only to the law, not to certain ethical values. Since positive law regulates only the external behavior of persons, abstracting from their motives, it opens a space of personal arbitrariness in which persons have the right "not to be rational," to use Wellmer's phrase,[33] understood in the sense of ethical nonconformity and the freedom not to take part in public or political discourses,[34] not, however, understood as the absolute freedom from the need to justify one's actions morally to others affected. Intersubjectively justified rights to personal liberty have to be reciprocally and generally acceptable; thus, even if legal persons need not act out of specific ethical or moral motives, they have no rights to the exercise of any form of liberty that violates the legitimate claims of others.[35]

11. The relation between moral, ethical and legal autonomy within a concept of political liberty necessitates the following step: the principle of reciprocal and general justification must be translated into procedures of "public justification" among citizens as the authors of the law. Only if such procedures embody the criteria of reciprocity and generality can their outcomes be justified and claim to ensure the most adequate and fair amount of personal liberties. As participants in these justificatory procedures and as members of a political community responsible for their outcomes, citizens are *politically* autonomous.

While legal autonomy means that a person is responsible *before* the law, political autonomy means that a person is, as part of a collective, responsible *for* the law. This alludes to the classic republican idea of political autonomy as participation in collective self-rule[36] – an idea, however, that too often has been interpreted as just another ethical conception, so that the political life becomes the most important constituent of the good life or that citizens, as "citoyens," undergo a personal transformation and receive a new ethical identity apart from their more narrow private interests.[37] Such a conception of the good should certainly not be ruled out, yet it is not how political autonomy in general should be understood. More important is the argument – neglected by liberal thinkers like Berlin – that if personal liberty is to be secured by legitimate law, then legitimate law needs to be justified by certain criteria of generality and reciprocity, and, furthermore, procedures of democratic law-making are necessary in which the claims and arguments of all those subject to the laws can adequately be raised and considered. A concept of political liberty does not imply the duty of citizens to participate in such processes, but it does imply the formal and material existence of equal rights and opportunities to do so. In this sense, legal and political autonomy are inextricably linked conceptually in the idea of persons as addressees as well as authors of the law.[38] Without the democratic institutionalization and exercise of political *power*, political liberty will not be possible.

Political autonomy is thus a form of autonomy that can be exercised only jointly with others as members of a political community. Autonomous citizens understand themselves to be responsible for and with each other; they "respond" to each other with mutually and generally acceptable (or at least *tolerable*)[39] reasons and consider themselves "responsible" for the results of collective decisions – a responsibility they not only have for each other but also towards others who are not members of their political community but who are still affected by their decisions. Regarding the latter, one must not forget that the moral and political responsibility of citizens does not stop at the borders of their political context.[40]

12. From the discussion so far, it is obvious that the multi-dimensional concept of political liberty implies quite demanding forms of autonomous action, especially on the part of citizens as authors of the law. Thus, part of the question of political liberty is the question of the social conditions necessary for the development of the capacity of autonomy and for the possibility of its exercise. In this respect, any constraints on the exercise of the forms of autonomy necessary for the equal and full participation in political and social life that could be reduced or removed by justifiable political action fall within the reach of the social and political responsibility of citizens for the creation of a regime characterized by political liberty.[41] Such constraints are not reciprocally and generally justifiable. *Social* autonomy thus means that a person has the internal[42] and external means of being an equal and responsible member of the political community – that is, being autonomous in the four senses discussed so far. It lies in the responsibility of all citizens to grant and guarantee each other rights to a life without legal, political, or social exclusion – and the standards by which one could measure social autonomy would be social standards of a non-stigmatized, fully participating life (not specific ethical ideas about the good life).[43] Rather than assuming that political liberty consists in having certain rights, while the "value of liberty" lies in the material possibilities of using these rights,[44] it is more coherent to regard this material possibility of realizing one's liberties in the form of a conception of social autonomy as an integral part of a concept of political liberty.

The fact that this conception of autonomy results from a reflection on the conditions for the possibility of realizing the four fundamental forms of autonomy mentioned previously, and is thus conceptually dependent upon them – and therefore located on a different theoretical level in that respect – does not mean that it does not refer to a distinct, normatively no-less-important dimension of liberty. There is no political liberty where citizens do not have the opportunity to be fully equal and autonomous members of the political community.[45]

13. In conclusion, one can say that the analysis of the concept of liberty comprised of the five conceptions of individual autonomy offers a theoretical synthesis beyond the opposition between "negative" and "positive," and one-sided libertarian, liberal (perfectionist or not), republican, or strictly egalitarian conceptions of liberty. It provides a comprehensive answer to the question of how to conceptualize a political and social structure that could claim to grant political liberty: citizens are politically free to the extent to which they, as freedom-grantors and freedom-users, are morally, ethically, legally, politically, and socially autonomous members of a political community.

On a more concrete level, the fruitfulness of the preceding analysis hinges on whether it allows for a differentiated understanding of the justification, importance, and priority of specific liberties. Since it is the point of political liberty to enable and protect individual autonomy, every right to a certain form of liberty, every combination of such rights, and every restraint of certain liberties must be seen in light of whether autonomous persons can recognize and justify this as conducive to the form of autonomy they think most important in a certain context.[46] Rights and liberties therefore have to be justified not only with regard to one conception of autonomy but with respect to a complex understanding of what it means to be an autonomous person. Integrating different interpretations of autonomy in this way gives rise to a concrete, balanced *conception* of political liberty that can be developed in a particular political and social context – as an *autonomous project* of citizens themselves. And that, in turn, is the essential meaning of political liberty.

Notes

This chapter is a revised version of an essay that appeared as "Politische Freiheit," in *Deutsche Zeitschrift für Philosophie* 44 (1996): 211–27.

1. For an overview of the history of theories of political liberty, see Zbigniew Pelczynski and John Gray (eds.), *Conceptions of Liberty in Political Philosophy* (London: Athlone Press, 1984). Important contemporary discussions can be found in David Miller (ed.), *Liberty* (Oxford: Oxford University Press, 1993), Tim Gray, *Freedom* (London: Macmillan, 1990), and George G. Brenkert, *Political Freedom* (London and New York: Routledge, 1991).

Political Liberty

2. Benjamin Constant, "Liberty of the Ancients Compared with that of the Moderns," in Constant, *Political Writings*, trans. and ed. by Biancamaria Fontana (Cambridge: Cambridge University Press, 1988).
3. On the difference between "individualistic" and "communalist" notions of freedom, see Albrecht Wellmer, "Models of Freedom in the Modern World," in Michael Kelly (ed.), *Hermeneutics and Critical Theory in Ethics and Politics* (Cambridge, MA: MIT Press, 1990).
4. For a fuller account of the conception of justice that serves as the background for the following discussion, see my *Contexts of Justice: Political Philosophy beyond Liberalism and Communitarianism*, trans. by J. Farrell (Berkeley, CA: University of California Press, 2002; German original 1994).
5. Isaiah Berlin, "Two Concepts of Liberty," in Berlin, *Four Essays on Liberty* (London: Oxford University Press, 1969/2002).
6. On this distinction, cf. John Rawls, *A Theory of Justice* (Cambridge, MA: Harvard University Press, 1971), 5.
7. Isaiah Berlin, "Two Concepts of Liberty," 166.
8. Ibid., 158.
9. For a critique of the connection between positive liberty and political coercion that Berlin draws here, see Raymond Geuss, "Freedom as an Ideal," in *Proceedings of the Aristotelian Society*, Suppl. Vol. LXIX (1995), 90f.
10. Isaiah Berlin, "Two Concepts of Liberty," 127.
11. Ibid., 130, fn. 1.
12. Ibid., 131.
13. Ibid., 131f.
14. Isaiah Berlin, "Introduction," in Berlin, *Four Essays on Liberty*, LXI.
15. For this formula, which I have altered slightly, see Gerald MacCallum, Jr., "Negative and Positive Freedom," in David Miller (ed.), *Liberty*. See also Joel Feinberg, "The Idea of a Free Man," in Feinberg, *Rights, Justice, and the Bounds of Liberty* (Princeton, NJ: Princeton University Press, 1980), and Tim Gray, *Freedom*, for similar views.
16. Charles Taylor, "What's Wrong With Negative Liberty?" in Taylor, *Philosophy and the Human Sciences. Philosophical Papers 2* (Cambridge: Cambridge University Press, 1985), 219.
17. Joseph Raz, *The Morality of Freedom* (Oxford: Clarendon Press, 1986), 410.
18. John Rawls, *Political Liberalism* (New York: Columbia University Press, 1993), 18f., 72ff.
19. Jürgen Habermas, *Between Facts and Norms. Contributions to a Discourse Theory of Law and Democracy*, trans. by William Rehg (Cambridge, MA: MIT Press, 1996), chapter III.
20. On this point, see my *Contexts of Justice*, especially chapter V, and the debate with Seyla Benhabib: R. Forst, "Situations of the Self: Reflections on Seyla Benhabib's Version of Critical Theory," and Seyla Benhabib, "On Reconciliation and Respect, Justice and the Good Life: Response to Herta Nagl-Docekal and Rainer Forst," *Philosophy and Social Criticism* 23 (1997).
21. I am using Thomas Scanlon's phrase here, but suggest my own explanation of the criteria of "reasonable rejection." Cf. Thomas M. Scanlon, "Contractualism and Utilitarianism," in Amartya Sen and Bernard Williams (eds.),

Utilitarianism and Beyond (Cambridge: Cambridge University Press, 1982), and Scanlon, *What We Owe to Each Other* (Cambridge, MA: Harvard University Press, 1998), chapter 5, where the notion of "fairness" comes close to my view.

22. I have developed this in my "Praktische Vernunft und rechtfertigende Gründe. Zur Begründung der Moral," in Stefan Gosepath (ed.), *Motive, Gründe, Zwecke. Theorien praktischer Rationalität* (Frankfurt am Main: Fischer, 1999).

23. On this right, see my *Contexts of Justice*, chapters II and V.2 especially, and "The Basic Right to Justification: Toward a Constructivist Conception of Human Rights," *Constellations* 6 (1999).

24. This notion of a moral right to justification seems to be the basis for the idea of a "presumption in favor of liberty" that Gerald Gaus, ["The Place of Autonomy Within Liberalism" (Chapter 12 in the present volume)], following Feinberg, argues for as a "basic liberal principle." There is, however, more than a "presumption" and more than "liberty" in an abstract sense at issue here: a non-deniable right to demand moral justification for morally relevant actions, not a claim to "liberty" that lacks a criterion for what kind of liberty is justifiable. Hence the presumption Gaus argues for would at least have to be one of "equal liberty," and more so one of "equally *justifiable* liberty." Of the two components of Gaus's liberal principle (MS p. 274), the first one – "a person is under no standing obligation to justify his actions" – is too broad, for there is a standing duty to justify morally relevant actions. The second component – "interference with, or restriction of, another's action requires justification; unjustified interference or restriction is unjust, and so morally wrong" – is correct but builds upon the basic moral right to justification. This I also take to be more in line with the Kantian conception of moral autonomy that Gaus stresses but that he does not sufficiently connect with the other forms of autonomy I distinguish, especially legal and political autonomy.

25. Cf. Charles Taylor, "What is Human Agency?" in Taylor, *Human Agency and Language. Philosophical Papers 1* (Cambridge: Cambridge University Press, 1985) on the notion of "strong evaluations." On the question of ethical ends, see Harry Frankfurt, "On the Usefulness of Final Ends," and "Autonomy, Necessity, and Love," in *Necessity, Volition, and Love* (Cambridge: Cambridge University Press, 1999). See also the discussion in Joel Anderson, "Starke Wertungen, Wünsche zweiter Ordnung und intersubjektive Kritik: Überlegungen zum Begriff ethischer Autonomie," *Deutsche Zeitschrift für Philosophie* 42 (1994).

26. Cf. Charles Larmore, "Pluralism and Reasonable Disagreement," in *The Morals of Modernity* (Cambridge: Cambridge University Press, 1994).

27. This is the main difference between the approach suggested here and Raz's "perfectionist" conception of political liberty. See Joseph Raz, *The Morality of Freedom*, especially chapters 14 and 15.

28. For example, Ronald Dworkin, "Rights as Trumps," in Jeremy Waldron (ed.), *Theories of Rights* (Oxford: Oxford University Press, 1984).

29. On this point, see my critique of Will Kymlicka's notion of personal autonomy as the basis of a conception of multicultural citizenship. Rainer Forst,

"Foundations of a Theory of Multicultural Justice," and Will Kymlicka, "Do We Need a Liberal Theory of Minority Rights? A Reply to Carens, Young, Parekh and Forst," *Constellations* 4 (1997), reprinted in Kymlicka, *Politics in the Vernacular* (Oxford: Oxford University Press, 2001), chapter 3.

30. This leads to the important question of toleration. See my "Toleration, Justice, and Reason," in Catriona McKinnon and Dario Castiglione (eds.), *The Culture of Toleration in Diverse Societies: Reasonable Tolerance* (Manchester: Manchester University Press, 2003), and "Tolerance as a Virtue of Justice," *Philosophical Explorations* 2 (2001). I develop a comprehensive, historical, and systematic theory of toleration in *Toleranz im Konflikt. Geschichte, Gehalt und Gegenwart eines umstrittenen Begriffs* (Frankfurt am Main: Suhrkamp, 2003).

31. An example of a one-sided "ethical law" is the construction of a "positive freedom of religion," according to which the strict principle of the religious neutrality of the state deprives members of a dominant religion of the possibility to express their beliefs. To remove, for example, crosses and crucifixes from classrooms in public schools would violate that right, as the "Verwaltungsgerichtshof München" (the highest Administrative Court in Bavaria) (NVwZ 1991, 1099) decided in 1991. Contrary to this, the "Bundesverfassungsgericht" (German Supreme Court) found in 1995 that the law according to which crosses and crucifixes had to hang in classrooms in Bavarian public schools was unconstitutional and violated the basic right to freedom of religion and conscience of persons with different beliefs (1BvR 1087/91). On this, see my "A Tolerant Republic?" in Jan-Werner Müller (ed.), *German Ideologies Since 1945* (New York: Palgrave, 2003).

32. This is the fear of Michael J. Sandel, "The Procedural Republic and the Unencumbered Self," *Political Theory* 12 (1984), and Alasdair MacIntyre, "Is Patriotism a Virtue?" in Ronald Beiner (ed.), *Theorizing Citizenship* (Albany, NY: State University of New York Press, 1995).

33. Albrecht Wellmer, "Models of Freedom in the Modern World," 241, 245.

34. Cf. Klaus Günther, "Die Freiheit der Stellungnahme als politisches Grundrecht," *Archiv für Rechts- und Sozialphilosophie*, 54 (1992), 58–73.

35. Thus I disagree with Albrecht Wellmer's thesis ("Models of Freedom in the Modern World," 245ff.) that the "principle of equal liberties" and the "principle of communicative rationality" derive from two different normative sources. Rather, they are united in the principle of reciprocal and general justification.

36. See the important recent interpretations of that idea by Philip Pettit, *Republicanism: A Theory of Freedom and Government* (Oxford: Clarendon Press, 1997), and Quentin Skinner, *Liberty Before Liberalism* (Cambridge: Cambridge University Press, 1998).

37. See, for example, Benjamin Barber, *Strong Democracy. Participatory Politics for a New Age* (Berkeley, CA: University of California Press, 1984) and, in a different, less Rousseauian sense, Hannah Arendt, "What is Freedom?" in Arendt, *Between Past and Future* (Harmondsworth: Penguin Books, 1985).

38. See Jürgen Habermas, *Between Facts and Norms*, chapter III, on the "equiprimordiality" of "private" and "public" autonomy. Whereas I try develop the argument for the conceptual linkage of legal and political autonomy on the

basis of the principle of reciprocal and general justification and its meaning in different contexts, Habermas argues that the equiprimordiality thesis derives from a combination of the "discourse principle" (of the general justification of norms) with the "legal form" of the institutionalization of the "communicative liberties" that are necessary for political self-determination. The problem with the latter approach is that it does not adequately reconstruct or underscore the (independent) *moral* core of basic rights. On this, see my "Die Rechtfertigung der Gerechtigkeit. Rawls' Politischer Liberalismus und Habermas' Diskurstheorie in der Diskussion," in Hauke Brunkhorst and Peter Niesen (eds.), *Das Recht der Republik* (Frankfurt am Main: Suhrkamp, 1999), section 4.

39. On this point, see my "The Rule of Reasons: Three Models of Deliberative Democracy," *Ratio Juris* 14 (2001).
40. Three problems that I cannot go into arise here. First, to what extent this responsibility reaches back into the past; second, to what extent claims of third parties have to be taken into account in political decisions; and third, how "independent" a political community needs to be politically and economically in order to count as politically autonomous. On the second point, see my "Towards a Critical Theory of Transnational Justice," in T. Pogge (ed.), *Global Justice* (Oxford: Blackwell, 2001).
41. For a discussion of such a wide criterion of constraints, see David Miller, "Constraints on Freedom," *Ethics* 94 (1983), 66–86.
42. Constraints on "internal" means of being socially autonomous are those that result from a lack of social means of acquiring knowledge, capacities, and qualifications that could be avoided by an alternative, reciprocally justifiable distribution of resources.
43. Cf. Amartya Sen, *The Standard of Living*, G. Hawthorn (ed.) (Cambridge: Cambridge University Press, 1987), and Sen, *Inequality Reexamined* (Cambridge, MA: Harvard University Press, 1992).
44. Cf. John Rawls, *A Theory of Justice*, 204f., 224f; Rawls, "The Basic Liberties and Their Priority," in *Political Liberalism*, 356ff.
45. It should be stressed here, as I said at the beginning, that arguments for political liberty, although they are arguments for justice, do not exhaust *all* the arguments for justice. Thus the notion of social autonomy discussed here highlights just *one* aspect of social justice from the viewpoint of a theory of political liberty. For a more comprehensive discussion of distributive justice based on the principle of reciprocal and general justification and the notion of "full membership," see my *Contexts of Justice*, chapter III.4. I am grateful to Stefan Gosepath for asking me to clarify my understanding of the relationship between justice and liberty.
46. One can, for example, justify the exercise of the right to freedom of expression via its relevance for the free development of one's ethical identity as well as via its importance for political communication or as a basic demand of the respect of an individual's moral autonomy – and thus possible restrictions of the exercise of this right will have to be evaluated in light of those dimensions of autonomy that would suffer from the restriction that is proposed, with priority given to moral considerations.

PART IV

THE POLITICAL

Liberalism, Legitimacy, and Public Reason

11

Liberalism without Agreement

Political Autonomy and Agonistic Citizenship

Bert van den Brink

In recent years, liberal political theory has been revolutionized in a number of ways.[1] First, initiated by John Rawls, mainstream liberalism has dropped its self-understanding as a comprehensive moral in favor of a purely political self-understanding. Second, several authors have started criticizing this now widespread "political" self-understanding of liberalism in a number of ways. Some claim that liberalism is not a purely political doctrine at all. Others argue that, irrespective of the question whether it is or is not, it cannot claim to be based in the hypothetical agreement of all reasonable citizens. As Marilyn Friedman puts it: "... political liberalism is simply one more political doctrine among many, freestanding or not, with no greater politically independent, *consent-based* claim to anyone's allegiance than many of its political rivals."[2]

Of course, it is not at all clear that this conclusion is warranted. But suppose it is. And further suppose that in a pluralistic social world, ongoing interpretative conflicts over the requirements of a just and well-ordered society, its constitutional essentials, and its principles of justice are more characteristic of political cooperation than fundamental agreements as to these requirements are. We then arrive at a starting point for normative political theory that is strikingly different from that of political liberalism. For our main question would no longer be: which substantive agreements among reasonable citizens would help warrant political legitimacy, and appropriate understandings of political autonomy and civic responsibility? Rather, it would be: which ways of conducting interpretative conflicts over what these notions mean to and require of citizens are able to inform us about legitimacy, autonomy, and civic responsibility in societies that are not characterized by firm agreements on constitutional essentials and principles of justice? Think of the famous picture that can be seen both as a duck and a rabbit. See the duck as a political theory that builds on the importance of informed consent. See the rabbit as a political theory that builds on the importance of informed dissent. Now think about politics as a pluralistic practice in which finding a civilized way of *shaping* informed dissent is at least as important as finding a civilized way of *overcoming* it. Finally, read this chapter as an attempt to see, for once, the rabbit rather than the duck in the landscape of politics – that is, to see civic practices that *shape* fundamental political disagreements in legitimate ways as more informative for a normative political theory for a pluralistic society than civic practices that *overcome* fundamental disagreement.

I will start with a discussion of the accounts of political legitimacy of agreement-based liberalism and what I will call "liberalism without agreement" (Section I). Subsequently, I will consider the accounts of political autonomy of both versions of liberalism and argue for an agonistic understanding of political autonomy, central to which is the moral right to contest arbitrary claims to sovereignty, rather than to act in accordance with ideal-theoretical objective principles of fairness and political justice (Section II). Assuming that liberalism without agreement and its agonistic understanding of citizens' autonomy are viable aspects of a political doctrine, I will then go on to sketch some general aspects of the understandings of public reason and civic virtue this doctrine must embrace (Section III). Finally, I will focus on two general civic dispositions – a disposition for *responsiveness to* and *endurance of* the burdens of citizenship under conditions of disagreement – that I consider preconditions for the adequate exercise of citizens' political autonomy under non-ideal conditions of political cooperation (Section IV).

I Liberalism With and Without Agreement

How do political theorists and political philosophers, liberal ones especially, perceive the relationship between social and political cooperation and the necessity of a substantive *agreement* on a shared framework for such cooperation? Authors influenced by contractarian political thought hold that a just and well-ordered society would be one in which citizens are united by their hypothetical agreement to essentials of a fundamental framework or contract – specifying principles, rights, and goods – for their cooperation. As John Rawls famously put it:

> ... our exercise of political power is fully proper only when it is exercised in accordance with a constitution the essentials of which all citizens as free and equal may reasonably be expected to endorse in the light of principles and ideals acceptable to their common human reason.[3]

As a principle of legitimacy, there is not much that can be held against this. It is important to see that the principle does not inform us about the requirements of ordinary, non-ideal social and political cooperation, in which the exercise of political power is hardly ever "fully proper." Since it does not aim to do so, at first sight it may seem that this cannot generate problems for our understanding of everyday cooperation. Yet the principle of legitimacy is said to be of use for a normative political theory that is supposed to inform the members of actually existing liberal societies.[4] As such, it seems to be confronted with a considerable gap between its idealized agreement-based understanding of social and political cooperation and the dynamics of non-ideal, everyday such cooperation.

Many liberal authors, Rawls among them, think about the way to reach fair social and political cooperation roughly in terms of the following four-step program: First, we determine, through a principle of legitimacy, what would make political institutions and the exercise of political power legitimate. Second, we determine, through detailed accounts of justice, the use of reason, and social circumstances such as the "fact of pluralism," that possible arrangement A (rather than possible arrangements B, C, D, and so on) is the best arrangement we can arrive at. Third, in a practical step, we ask how arrangement A can be realized. Fourth, we think about fair social and political cooperation as a practice that ideally takes place within the framework set by arrangement A – that is, a practice that only comes into its own under conditions of the "fully proper" exercise of power.

The first step is usually accounted for either in terms of consent of the governed[5] or in terms of some consent-independent notion of the well-being of the governed.[6] Whatever method is chosen, it is correctly assumed that, on principle, constitutional-democratic institutions and the exercise of political power should respect the legitimate needs and interests of all citizens. The second step depends on an assumption that is more problematic. Political philosophers who spell out detailed lists of social primary goods, principles of justice, and institutional arrangements that should be accepted from common human reason make themselves vulnerable to often quite justified critiques of their substantive proposals and the methods used to formulate them. This is, of course, what has happened to Rawls's principles of justice, his list of social primary goods, and thus his interpretation of basic needs and interests time and time again.[7] Since Rawls never stopped reformulating both his substantive ideas and his methods and taught us much in the process, this is certainly not something we should regret. But we may want to ask whether the assumption is really warranted, that by discussing substantive accounts of justice, reason, and social facts that have to be taken into account, theorists and citizens will one day reach an overlapping consensus on these issues – that is, will all agree, although for different reasons, that substantive (politically liberal) arrangement A should be preferred to arrangements B, C, and D?[8] Maybe it is more important that we always keep that discussion open in light of our competing accounts of justice, reason, and the circumstances of politics.

Here it is interesting to take a look at the work of the growing number of theorists who state that a firm agreement on principles of justice and constitutional essentials is not a necessary condition for reasonable cooperation at all. James Tully defends such a view:

Principles, rights, goods and identities are...constituents of the 'framework' [for civic cooperation] in a special sense. Politics is the type of game in which the framework – the rules of the game – can come up for deliberation and amendment in the course of the game. At any one time, some constituents are held firm and provide the ground for questioning others, but which elements constitute the shared 'background' sufficient for politics to emerge and which constitute the disputed 'foreground' vary.[9]

If this understanding of politics is correct, then the consensus-based "four-step program" for reaching political legitimacy I sketched earlier must be mistaken. Agreement is an important aim in politics, and we should try to strive for it whenever this is necessary. But disagreement is important, too, and the right to withdraw one's consent, to contest the political authority's account of one's needs and interests, is as important in an account of politics as is the right to consent. If we focus on the importance of an agreement to the political conception of justice of some ideal model too strongly, then this insight may be lost from view. Politics is not a practice that truly comes into its own under conditions of the fully proper, agreement-based exercise of power (step four). Rather, in the non-ideal social and political world we inhabit, it is a practice that – in lack of full legitimacy – continually goes back and forth between the different steps in light of new insights, theoretical breakthroughs, and social and political developments. The main reason why this alternative view includes all steps equally in its account of politics (while dropping the "comes into its own" claim of the fourth step) is that it is based on a more radical understanding of the consequences of ethical and political pluralism for our best account of politics. Most importantly, it does not try to transcend the empirical circumstance under which, in pluralistic societies, deep disagreements as to what is right and good do not just concern questions of "the good life." They also concern the question as to which principles of justice and constitutional essentials we should accept, and what they require of us.

What is the exact difference here? Although Rawls, like most liberals, is a master at acknowledging the diversity of often incompatible and irreconcilable comprehensive ideas about the good in society, he is very hesitant to admit that this diversity may run so deep that citizens may have fundamental disagreements about the requirements of justice and political morality. But this is not seen as a convincing move by all liberal authors. As Jeremy Waldron, a prominent liberal *and* critic of Rawls's work, puts it:

> John Rawls insists that 'a diversity of conflicting and irreconcilable comprehensive doctrines' is 'not a mere historical condition that may soon pass away; it is a permanent feature of the public culture of democracy.' And he says it is therefore fortunate that we do not need to share a common view in society about religion, ethics, and philosophy. But liberals have done a less good job of acknowledging the inescapability of disagreement about the matters on which they think we *do* need to share a common view, even though such disagreement is the most prominent feature of the politics of modern democracies.[10]

The things liberals such as Rawls think we do need to share a common view about are, of course, principles of justice, social primary goods, certain political goods, the fact of pluralism, the burdens of judgment, and so on.[11] Waldron does not dispute that, in practice, we often "need to act together on the basis of a common view." But he does dispute the assumption that the need for a common view as, for instance, represented by decisions and actions of the legislative, the executive, and the legal branches of government, makes "the fact of disagreement evaporate." A common view, Waldron claims, "... has to be forged in the heat of our disagreements, not predicated on the assumption of a cool consensus that exists only as an ideal."[12] In other words, the felt need for a common view is often purely practical and cannot realistically be based on the assumption that reasonable citizens, if only they were adequately placed to make the right normative judgments, would necessarily reach a substantive agreement on principles, rules, policies, and so on.[13]

If, in the light of these alternative views, we go back to the "four-step program" for reaching political legitimacy and fair civic cooperation, we can conclude the following. Liberalism without agreement, as represented here by Tully and Waldron, does not hold that legitimacy cannot at all be accounted for in terms of either the consent of the governed or some consent-independent notion of the well-being of the governed at all. As "ideas of reason,"[14] both ideas are of extreme importance. But although consent and accounts of well-being are important, liberalism without agreement recognizes that the normal "circumstances of politics" are "action-in-concert in the face of disagreement" – and that the liberal tradition has not taken this circumstance seriously.[15] This is a problem for the liberal tradition to the extent that we can reasonably assume that its methodological foundations – which make so much of the idea of an agreement-based framework for social and political cooperation – make it vulnerable to false assessments of the actual necessity of agreement in flourishing liberal-democratic societies. The other side of the coin of orientation to fundamental agreement is that those who do not agree (even when they do so for good reasons) will not be taken entirely seriously for fear of the possibility that by granting their claims, the agreement-based foundations of political legitimacy may evaporate. That psychologization is not as far-fetched as it may seem at first sight. Claims to the lack of legitimacy of existing political arrangements by women, working classes, and cultural minorities have too often been confronted with this indefensible reaction.[16] Although informed agreement *is* a condition of the fully legitimate exercise of power, understanding it as a realizable ideal at the institutional level of practical politics threatens to make our civic practices blind to the circumstance that the constitutional essentials and understandings of justice of even the most decent societies we know are not in any narrow way based in substantive agreements among all reasonable citizens. Disregarding that circumstance in our theoretical accounts may well result in normative theories that are blind to the need for an analysis of the ways in which members of such societies cope with the constitutive circumstance of politics that agreed upon common courses of action are often rather necessitated by the need for clarity, consistency, and the sheer need for an authorized normative framework for cooperation, than by any deep agreement based in the ideal conceptions of justice and civic cooperation among those members.

II Political Autonomy With and Without Objective Principles

Both accounts of a liberal politics at issue here are thoroughly democratic. This means, among many other things, that these accounts greatly value the political autonomy of the citizen. Narrowly understood, political autonomy is the capacity of the citizen to have an equal voice in the democratic process by which the political community she is a member of gives itself the law. It involves (1) having the formal right to participate, (2) possessing certain cognitive capacities for making reasonable political judgments and having a sufficiently democratic disposition (in which *moral* capacities such as a sense of justice, openness to the needs and interests of others, and willingness to accept the better argument play a crucial role[17]), and (3) taking an authentic stance on the political proposal one makes – that is, proposals one genuinely identifies with.[18] More broadly understood, political autonomy is defined by one's status as a bearer of rights under a constitutional regime. In that broader interpretation, characteristic of classical liberalism, political autonomy is primarily understood as freedom from unwarranted political intervention in one's private affairs. I am here mainly interested in the first, narrow understanding of political autonomy, which understands the citizen as a competent source of practical reasoning as to questions that concern the common good.

Agreement-based liberalism starts from a conceptualization of political autonomy that is arrived at through a method of deduction from the agreement-based framework for cooperation it proposes. In *A Theory of Justice*, for example, Rawls claims that if in moral education, future citizens are made to act according to certain principles of fairness or political justice, they are acting autonomously *insofar as* these principles are ones that "they would acknowledge under conditions that best express their nature as free and equal beings."[19] These principles, which determine whether we are autonomous, "... are objective. They are the principles that we would want everyone (including ourselves) to follow were we to take up together the appropriate general point of view."[20]

An important practical point of this understanding of autonomy is to protect social and political cooperation from the potentially divisive consequences of more loosely formulated conceptions of autonomy that are less bounded by objective principle:

The essential point here is that the principles that conform best to our nature as free and equal rational beings themselves establish our accountability. Otherwise autonomy is likely to lead to a mere collision of self-righteous wills, and objectivity to the adherence to a consistent yet idiosyncratic system.[21]

Of course, this liberal conception of political autonomy does not in any way force citizens to accept principles they do not recognize as objective. Rather, the idea is that the principles being proposed conform best to our reasoning abilities. We make them *our own* – and ourselves politically autonomous and authentic – by recognizing this and by wholeheartedly accepting them as principles we would choose ourselves. The autonomous person may believe that the principles that the liberal doctrine proposes are not really objective because she genuinely believes that she has good reasons not to identify with them. She may be right about this and thus have a reason for no longer embracing them and for proposing better principles – ones that she believes fit better with the legitimate interests of all citizens. In the end, it is the autonomous person and her reasoning abilities, not the content of some set of principles of justice, that remains the normative anchor of this view. The autonomous person makes conscious decisions as to the best morally defensible, universalizable principles she can arrive at. Finally, it is a sign of her autonomy that she wholeheartedly sticks to these principles and is willing to defend them in democratic deliberation.[22]

Now let me gradually introduce the alternative view by pointing to an unresolved issue in Rawls's work since *Political Liberalism*. Rawls sometimes presents agreement on "the very same principles of justice" as a condition of reasonable social and political cooperation. On other occasions, however, he states that people can reasonably disagree about the exact understanding of those principles and what they require.[23] But this causes a problem for agreement-based liberalism. For if it is the case that "full autonomy" is "realized by citizens when they act from principles of justice that specify the fair terms of cooperation,"[24] then we either have to conclude that political liberalism is not always interested in full autonomy or that it admits that, relative to different authentic, reasonable, but irreconcilable conceptions of a just society, competing understandings of full autonomy can be found in pluralistic societies. For we may conjecture that different conceptions of a just society come with different conceptions of the principles of fairness and political justice that citizens would "acknowledge under conditions that best express their nature as free and equal beings." Such principles have consequences for the conceptualization of citizens' public accountability and thus their autonomy. Since Rawls in his writings since *Political Liberalism* had become more consistent in stating that agreement on the very same principles is not a condition of fair social and political cooperation, the latter conclusion – that competing understandings of full autonomy can be found in pluralistic societies – seems to be the one that is intended. This development pushes political liberalism in the direction of what I call "liberalism without agreement": a version of liberalism that does not require a firm agreement as to an "objective" framework for social and political cooperation.

But what *does* it require? To start with, it requires a firm conceptual distinction between non-ideal and ideal understandings of the basic framework for social and political cooperation. On the one hand, it recognizes the importance of a non-ideal, contingently given, and still developing constitution and basic structure of society, the essentials of which are contested in the sense, again, that Tully suggests: elements of it, including elements of the basic structure of society, "come up for deliberation and amendment" in the course of democratic practices. On the other hand, it recognizes that citizens need ideal conceptions of the constitution and the basic structure in order to evaluate the legitimacy of the contingently given framework for cooperation. And just as Rawls seemed to accept in his work since *Political Liberalism*, liberalism without agreement accepts that a diversity of reasonable ideal conceptions does not necessarily constitute a threat to political cooperation. These ideal conceptions are the ones that citizens remain faithful to when they say, with Jeremy Waldron, that they accept the circumstances of politics: the practical need for "action-in-concert in the face of disagreement" (over ideal interpretations). Their action-in-concert concerns their prudential acceptance of the non-ideal, but in practice authoritative, framework; their disagreements concern their competing political ideals as to a better framework. In this way, liberalism without agreement retains the tension between ideal and non-ideal accounts of politics and makes it the basis of its theoretical account of politics. Non-ideal agreements warrant stability and limited legitimacy; disagreements as to the options open to the political community for improving stability and legitimacy warrant a practice of reflexive political deliberation that makes a pluralistic democratic society aware of its own limitations.

Both the non-ideal basic framework for social and political cooperation and the various ideal conceptions of political justice held by citizens have a formative force in constituting practices of political autonomy. By law, the non-ideal framework defines freedoms, opportunities, and limits that constitute a practice of self-government. This can be done along lines of representative democracy, radical democracy, classical republicanism, and so on. These doctrines have different ideal understandings of political autonomy. Some understand it against the background of a "negative" conception of liberty;[25] others understand it in light of a "positive" conception of liberty;[26] still others work from a republican conception of freedom as "non-domination."[27] Furthermore, these doctrines contain different ideas as to the institutional ordering and the forms of political participation a practice of self-government requires. In non-ideal practices – the only kind of practices in which political cooperation is really necessary – a mixture derived from these and other traditions will be held in place by positive law. At its best, such a non-ideal mixture will be seen by all citizens as a "good enough" practice of democracy, even though most of them may well believe that arrangements would be much better if only their ideal conceptions of political justice were taken more seriously.

This is where the duck and the rabbit become visible again. Agreement-based liberalism may want to say: the "good enough" practice will be based in some kind of agreement, if only an agreement to disagree. And that may well be true. But liberalism without agreement may want to respond: to the extent that the good enough practice is not endorsed by all in light of principles and ideals they wholeheartedly identify with, it is not the kind of agreement that agreement-based liberalism is after at all. If my account of political autonomy is derived from classical republicanism and yours from classical liberalism, then our both agreeing that a good enough constitutional compromise is more beneficial to a democratic practice and more legitimate than the lack of any such compromise does not imply that our agreement makes a truly legitimate exercise of political power possible. From our respective ideal-conceptions, we will both be unsatisfied with the constitutional compromise's understanding of the public role and responsibilities of both the autonomous citizen and the state and therefore not give it our wholehearted consent. But if we take our own political ideal conceptions of society seriously, and grant others – as we must – the right to do the same, then we will have to keep the field open for democratic encounters in which we try the find better solutions, which are to be laid down in law, which will be more legitimate (and agreement-based) than the current ones. Keeping the field open, going back and forth through the four steps of debating criteria of legitimacy, ideal arrangements, the connection between the ideal and the non-ideal conceptions before us, and the question under what circumstances politics comes to its own, is a *constitutive aspect* of political interaction, not just a *means* to reach what agreement-based liberalism thinks would be a proper political order: an order in which the basic framework would be uncontested because it coincides with the conceptions of justice of all reasonable citizens.

Liberalism without agreement cannot deduce its understanding of political autonomy from objective principles. But the picture I have sketched so far does leave room for an account of political autonomy. In democratic politics, the interpretation of constitutional essentials and the basic structure that individual citizens favor, as based in contested but reasonable conceptions of political justice, and the interpretation laid down in positive law, are not necessarily identical. This, liberalism without agreement says, is and always will be a normal circumstance of politics. Indeed, in democratic thought, it is a condition *sine qua non* of the political autonomy of citizens.

The point has often been made by theorists who adhere to a so-called "agonistic" understanding of politics. The adjective "agonistic" stems from the Greek noun *agon*, which refers to a game,[28] a struggle, a contest, and to "the conflict of character in classic drama."[29] Agonistic accounts of politics see politics primarily as a free activity of *contestation* of claims to a will-uniting sovereignty as upheld by positive law, not so much as an institutionalized and proceduralized practice of reasonable opinion formation and decision-making through which the political autonomy of the subject and the authority of positive law can ultimately be reconciled. When Hannah Arendt and Michel Foucault, independently of each other, claim that "... it is precisely sovereignty [that citizens] must renounce" (Arendt), and that we need "... a political philosophy that isn't erected around the problem of sovereignty"[30] (Foucault), they mean that the expectation of identity of the political will of "the people" and the political will of individual citizens should be renounced.

Of course, this does not mean that the authentic political conceptions of justice of individual members of society should by definition overrule the will of the people. After all, authentic political conceptions of justice can be wrong.[31] It rather means that the political conceptions of individual citizens should not be overruled by the will of the people or a purportedly "objective" framework of cooperation *simply because* they diverge from it. As seen from this perspective, state-centered *ideals* of legitimate political power such as the general and sovereign will and a basic structure of society founded on purportedly "objective" principles may in *political practice* become instruments of political repression. This will happen as soon as they are thought of in terms of *true representations* of the objective and sovereign will of all members of society at what is no more than the practical, *non-ideal level* of political cooperation. In practice, democratic decision procedures are simply not precise enough to warrant the assumption that their outcomes truly represent the legitimate needs and interests of all. At best, they are good enough outcomes, which have a limited and thus always contestable claim to legitimacy.

If we take this analysis of political power and its relation to democracy as our starting point, then the citizen's political autonomy should not be defined in terms of her status as a bearer of a specific set of legal rights as derived from ideal-theoretical objective principles,[32] but rather in terms of her *moral* right either to consent to or to contest any empirical definition of what defines her *as* a citizen, including her legal status, in an intersubjective search for more adequate, morally acceptable definitions. Especially by disagreeing, by breaking open set frameworks and routines *for the sake of the integrity of the civic association*, the citizen asserts her political autonomy.[33]

It is important to note that in liberalism without agreement, just as in the Rawlsian brand of political liberalism, political autonomy is conceptualized as a form of *moral* autonomy. When I said in the preceding paragraph that agonistic autonomous action is engaged in "for the sake of the integrity of the civic association," I implicitly introduced the idea that a politically autonomous person is not just guided by her own interests, but by "a universalized concern for the ends of all rational persons."[34] Political liberalism and agonistic liberalism without agreement both embrace that ideal of autonomy. But according to the agonistic view, the autonomy of the citizen consists in her ability to give herself and her fellow citizens the law in an open-ended practice that is not guided by objective principles of justice, but by a shared moral orientation towards the good and integrity of the civic association, which – as a *civic* form of association – is understood as an attempt to specify, correct, and adjust principles of justice time and time again in light of ever-changing challenges to the ideal of civic association. Citizens who participate in this project are politically autonomous insofar as they wholeheartedly endorse the ideal conceptions of political cooperation they defend, accept accountability for their consciously made choices (that may be wrong) for what they regard as morally defensible political options, and are willing to defend these choices as long as they wholeheartedly agree with them. The main difference with agreement-based liberalism is that this account of political autonomy is not derived from shared objective principles, but rather from the circumstance of the lack of such principles and the challenges to political cooperation associated with that fate of the political community.

As a moral conception of political autonomy, the agonistic view is not without guidance. It stresses the requirement of reciprocity in political discourse and in the granting of equal rights. It therefore evades the consequence that Rawls fears so much – that the practice of political autonomy will succumb to "a mere collision of self-righteous wills" and that the lack of objective principles will lead to the dominance of a "consistent yet idiosyncratic system" of political cooperation. The non-agreement-based agonistic view recognizes the danger that self-righteous wills may collide and that idiosyncratic systems of political thought may gain much influence in society. But it assumes that the collision of self-righteous wills and the influence of idiosyncratic systems can be controlled as long as enough citizens aim to defend the *integrity* of the civic association. For although reasonable citizens of pluralistic societies tend not to reach full consensus with regard to their exact understandings of the nature and requirements of justice, freedom, equality, mutual respect, solidarity, toleration, civility, and indeed autonomy, they are joined by the shared belief that these values are important and should somehow be incorporated in all reasonable political conceptions of society. A shared, if general, disposition towards democratic civic cooperation rather than a substantive agreement on constitutional essentials binds them together. Self-righteousness cannot be reconciled with such a disposition. If democracy has agonistic aspects – that is, is a game – then respect for and openness to one's political opponents is a necessary condition of competent autonomous citizenship. Idiosyncratic political systems do not respect the moral and political autonomy of their members. But since moral autonomy and civic responsiveness are of central importance to agonistic democratic thought, lack of objective principles of fairness and political justice need not lead to a derailed political association.

So at the theoretical level, some of the dangers that may seem inherent in the agonistic view can be evaded even at the level of definitions. At the practical level, however, the dangers are great indeed. If political cooperation among autonomous citizens can no longer be conceptualized as a practice that is embedded in a fixed and objective framework for cooperation, then questions as to the stability and the legitimacy of agonistic political cooperation arise. In the remainder of this chapter, I will address some of these questions, especially with regard to the use of public reason and the role of basic civic dispositions.

III   A Brief Reflection on the Use of Public Reason

The notion of public reason, understood as an intersubjective reasoning practice in which citizens deliberate on the courses of action open to the political community, seems to have taken the place of objective principles of justice in recent liberal theory.[35] This move should be applauded. For through the use of public reason, the danger that principles of justice or frameworks for cooperation that are taken to be objective will *in practice* turn into instruments of heteronomous domination can be identified and, perhaps, repaired.

I will not attempt an overview of the debate on the requirements of public reason here.[36] Rather, I will briefly discuss two possible ways of thinking about the use of public reason in order to make a point about the importance of shared democratic dispositions for the non-agreement-based view. The first way concentrates on the *reasonableness of opinions and arrangements* that issue from public deliberation. The second way concentrates on the *reasonableness of basic deliberative capacities and dispositions* that are needed in order to make adequate use of public reason. I will argue that a focus on *deliberative capacities and dispositions* is demanded by the idea of liberalism without agreement.

If we concentrate on the reasonableness of deliberative capacities and dispositions, autonomous participation in practices of public reasoning presupposes wholehearted commitment to basic civic values of freedom, equality, rule of law, peaceful social and political cooperation, the burdens of judgment, and an understanding of the circumstances of politics. Although it requires that one, in practice, be loyal to a good enough framework for cooperation, it does not require that one be committed to a *publicly favored interpretation* of the civic practices it holds in place. It rather requires that one develop capacities and dispositions that enable one to recognize and be loyal to the authority of non-ideal solutions, to express competently one's own interpretation of civic ideals in reciprocal democratic deliberation over problems generated by non-ideal solutions, and to be critical of and willing to learn from one's own and others' political conceptions in reciprocal deliberative exchanges in light of the general civic ideal to let the needs and interests of all citizens matter equally in social and political affairs. Again, given the circumstances of politics, there need not be substantive agreement on the exact requirements of this general civic ideal. But liberalism without agreement has to admit that a minimal agreement on its importance as a condition of a reasonable civic disposition is necessary.

According to the reasonableness-of-opinions-and-arrangements understanding, to be reasonable is to be committed to a "thick" set of values and principles that specify a canon of reasonable opinions and arrangements. On this view, it is assumed that public culture is shaped by substantive values, institutional arrangements, and ways of reasoning that have proved themselves in a historical, consensus-oriented process of trial and error and must be regarded as legitimate outcomes of the use of public reason. These outcomes of the use of public reason over time will undoubtedly specify an understanding of capacities and dispositions, too, but they will do so in a way that is more restrictive – and possibly backed up by a claim to the objectivity of the canon of opinions and arrangements – than the capacities-and-dispositions view thinks necessary.

The opinions-and-arrangements view does not recognize the fundamental tension between non-ideal but authoritative solutions and a plurality of ideal conceptions of justice. It makes the mistake of understanding dominant interpretations of political cooperation that are backed up by democratic majority decision as interpretations that all reasonable citizens should wholeheartedly accept. It confuses the need for practical and authoritative solutions to empirical problems of political cooperation with the aim for objective principles that can function as yardsticks for reasonable and autonomous political action. For that reason, this view runs the risk of excluding from view the political vocabularies, needs, and interests – and therefore the *agonistic political autonomy* – of those citizens who hold ideal conceptions that do not fit with the authoritative practical solutions to problems of cooperation. It lacks what John Christman calls "emphatic respect" for all authentic articulations of political values and conceptions that citizens judge to be important input to reasoning practices – that is, it lacks "an attempt at emphatic grasping of the subjectivity and motivations of others."[37]

Agreement-based political liberalism has in recent years often been criticized for defending a notion of public reason and political autonomy that is too substantive to live up to its aspirations as a freestanding political doctrine. Often, political liberalism has been criticized for silently presupposing individualistic, post-traditionalist lifestyles that easily fit with the normative framework that political liberalism proposes to be inherently better than other lifestyles. The claim is that, inadvertently, political liberalism formulates criteria of autonomy and reasonableness that those who hold individualist and post-traditionalist opinions, and favor attendant legal and political arrangements, can answer to far more easily than citizens with more collectivist and possibly traditionalist ideas of the good.[38] The best way in which political liberalism can answer this criticism is by firmly stating that a notion of public reason should be understood from a capacities-and-dispositions view rather than from an opinions-and-arrangements view. The most important criterion for living up to requirements of the use of public reason is that citizens – irrespective of their conceptions of the good – be disposed to engage in reciprocal democratic deliberations that will result in good enough democratic decisions, not that they will in the end come to favor this or that opinion or arrangement that issues from public deliberation. That general disposition – the requirements of which I spelled out earlier – is a necessary condition for civilized ways of engaging in interpretative conflict over both ideal and non-ideal understandings of constitutional essentials and justice. The point is as simple as it is demanding. Yet it is crucial to our understanding of liberalism without agreement.

IV Civic Virtue and the Need for Endurance and Responsiveness

In a liberal society without agreement, in which objective principles for right action are lacking, the stability and justice of political interactions becomes strongly dependent on the civic dispositions citizens act from. But in such a society, the exercise of civic virtue cannot be understood as following pre-given rules of civic conduct or as derived from an uncontested view of human excellence. Where there is no fixed and stable set of fully just political principles, the question as to what it means in practice to act as an autonomous, competent citizen who aims to foster the common good of all citizens has no definitive answer. Acting for the common good cannot be understood as acting according to one's own or dominant legal understandings of the common good. For, as was noted before, one cannot be sure that these understandings are correct. One of the consequences of this is that acting autonomously is not just about giving oneself and others acceptable laws in light of clear criteria of what one considers to be right; it is also about discovering time and time again, in interaction with others, what one really believes and what one can or cannot accept about those beliefs.[39] Finding out which dispositions and virtues are required in which situation becomes a continuous self-critical task for citizens who aim to make competent autonomous use of their reasoning capacities. Citizens' civic dispositions and the autonomy of their actions will be expressed, tested, and revised in their encounters over practical questions of distribution and opportunity (justice), of mutual respect (recognition), of the ordering of public debates (reasonableness), of giving all parties their due in political decisions (reaching compromises), of accepting or rejecting utterances and actions of their fellow citizens (tolerance), and so on. In such encounters, citizens will test the acceptability of (1) their own civic competencies and ideals in light of (2) the competencies and ideals of fellow citizens and (3) predominant but contestable interpretations of civic competencies and ideals as laid down in law. As a result, revisions of all three dimensions may become necessary. The citizen who contests alternative interpretations of civic competencies and ideals will entice a critical test of her own interpretations. Her allowing such a test to take place is a sign both of her reasonableness and of her civic virtue; it will warrant that interpretative conflicts will be more than a mere collision of self-righteous wills.[40] Furthermore, allowing the test to take place is a condition of developing a civic attitude that is conductive to learning processes that enable the internalization of authentic civic dispositions that are more than functional requirements of an existing political order. For good reasons, liberal theory has always been wary of such functionalistic understandings of virtue, which require citizens to subordinate their action to quasi-unquestionable but arbitrary forms of power. Given its suspicion of arbitrary claims to sovereignty, the agonistic account of civic virtue does not involve that requirement.

Agreement-based liberalism has often tried to free citizens from the burden of developing good political dispositions (most famously perhaps in Kant's reflections on the nation of devils). However, for lack of a substantive agreement that would make the near total proceduralization of virtue (justice, reciprocity, reasonableness, tolerance, and so on) in strong institutions a viable option, liberalism without agreement cannot do that. Indeed, it is exactly because of the lack of an agreement-based common framework that much responsibility for the quality of political cooperation in a society falls on the shoulders of citizens and their associations.

What is remarkable about many liberal accounts of civic virtue is that although they are quite detailed, they do not say much about how they may guide citizens through a pluralistic condition in which aspects of the very basic framework of cooperation comes up for deliberation and amendment time and time again. Liberal theorists of civic virtue are surely right that all citizens at times need to exercise virtues such as courage, justice, loyalty, law-abidingness, tolerance, self-restraint, conscientiousness, perseverance, and independence of thought.[41] But because these theorists think about these and other virtues against the background of quite substantive understandings of an inherently stable and nearly just, agreement-based liberal society, they do not stress sufficiently that the exercise of these virtues within a liberal framework does not require the same kinds of attitudes and actions from all citizens. Let me elaborate on this point by introducing to the debate over civic virtues two general civic dispositions that I believe help citizens who are positioned on the map of society in specific ways to exercise political autonomy and civic virtue in their own ways – ways that do not surrender to arbitrary power relations. The first of these I label "civic endurance" and the second, "civic responsiveness."[42]

Civic endurance is the disposition of being willing to carry the burdens of citizenship that come with being a member of a political community the given principles and concrete policies of which one cannot wholeheartedly agree to. Civic responsiveness, on the other hand, is the disposition of being forthcoming to those who tend to carry these burdens – in our societies, members of cultural and religious minority groups, citizens in vulnerable socioeconomic positions, and citizens with "alternative" tastes and lifestyles, especially. We may call these dispositions general virtues of civic cooperation, since – or so I claim – they are crucial to the general civic competencies that decide whether or not citizens are able to act from more specific civic competencies and virtues in ways that fit well with the circumstances of politics in pluralistic societies.

Although in some way or another, all citizens at times need to exercise civic endurance, it is likely that the members of social, cultural, and political minorities in society will experience the burdens of endurance most strongly. Let us assume that members of such minorities, as citizens, often have the experience that their prospects of leading a good life in light of their own political and more comprehensive conceptions of the good are somewhat under threat because of their lack of effective political power. They may have equal political rights, but may at the same time feel that the dominant liberal-democratic terms of civic cooperation and dominant but discriminatory informal standards of evaluation in society make it impossible for them to effectively claim their legitimate needs and interests in political deliberation. They may also feel that they lack the social and educational resources they need in order to stand up for themselves and to gain information that is relevant to gaining sufficient insight in the reasons for their condition. Such claims, which are hardly ever claims to the total illegitimacy of political arrangements (and all the more reasonable because of that), are of course familiar from the debates over feminism, multiculturalism, and special political and cultural rights.[43] Depending both on the seriousness of their condition and the level of their own civic-mindedness, citizens who endure the consequences of being in a less favorable position in society may respond in a number of ways.[44] First, they may *passively endure* the consequences of their position in society – that is, regard it as an unchangeable condition. Second, they may *actively endure* their situation – that is, regard it as a condition that is caused by a mistaken, contestable, but in principle alterable interpretation of civic ideals in their society. Third, they may *not want to endure their situation at all* and, for instance, resort to the use of civil disobedience or even political violence.

I call the middle position of active endurance of one's position in society one of *civic endurance* – the endurance of burdens that come with civic cooperation in a mode that still relies on the possibility of repairing certain aspects of these burdens through civic interaction within the limits set by the law. Note that the other two attitudes are not always to be condemned: passive endurance may be a prudent strategy of sheer survival in a totalitarian society, and resort to civil disobedience and even political violence is not necessarily morally illegitimate. They are to be condemned only to the extent that they are engaged in by members of a civic community that is sufficiently *responsive* to the claims of those who endure actively (I will come to that shortly). Those who endure actively still rely on their perhaps threatened, but not wholly absent, political autonomy as defined both by their legal status and by the not self-righteous acknowledgment of their moral and legal right to political autonomy by at least some of their fellow citizens who have the power to change, through political action, the condition of those who endure arbitrary but repairable burdens of membership of the political community.

As Russell Bentley and David Owen put it, civic endurance is "a *dynamic* political way of being that captures an agonistic sense of belonging."[45] On the one hand, this way of being is directed at *making oneself heard to one's fellow citizens* with the intention of repairing unequally distributed civic burdens, and thereby repairing the integrity of the civic community as a whole. It captures an agonistic sense of belonging and of autonomous membership because it necessitates a reciprocal civic competition over the best evaluation of the situation at hand and the best options for repairing the shortcoming of the civic order. On the other hand, it is directed, for each of the participants in the political encounter at hand, at discovering a political *self-understanding* that fits with one's specific position within the civic order. So civic endurance may be said to be a matter of productively shaping one's civic relations to others as well as one's self-understanding as a citizen. The citizen who actively endures civic burdens understands that the civic order as a whole, in its current arrangement, is by nature contested and non-ideal, and that this exact circumstance makes it possible (and necessary) to contest the constellation that is responsible for the arbitrary but repairable civic burdens she carries.

Like civic endurance, civic responsiveness is a virtuous civic disposition that must be delimited from two possible reactions to the claims for fairer distribution of civic burdens: *blindness to* and *repression of* such claims. Just as is the case with civic endurance, civic responsiveness concerns one's relation to the civic order as a whole, one's civic relations with others, as well as one's own self-understanding as a citizen. As to the relation to the civic order as a whole, the responsive citizen understands that this order is, by its very nature, a contested one. By recognizing this, she also recognizes, first, the contested nature of her own civic beliefs and ideals and those of others; second, the gap that is to be expected between "pure" civic ideals and actual civic practices; and, third, the circumstance that for some groups in society this gap – and the burdens that come with it – will be bigger than for others. For her relation to other citizens, this implies that the responsive citizen – let us say, a civically minded member of the majority culture in society – will investigate to what extent other citizens' political claims may be justified even though they do not fit well with dominant arrangements and opinions in society (remember the section on the use of public reason). With respect to her own civic self-understanding, this implies that the responsive citizen is willing to accept that not only the current state of society, but also her own political conception of it, may well be blind to legitimate needs and interests of citizens whose political voice is not easily heard.[46] In this threefold sense, civic responsiveness enables the citizen to make better political judgments – that is, to exercise her political autonomy in a way that is true to the actual circumstances of politics in her society instead of being true to a powerful but partly arbitrary interpretation of core civic ideals.

Together, civic endurance and civic responsiveness warrant a political *sense of reality* and *flexibility* of the citizen that, like a sense of justice and a sense of the good, are preconditions of autonomous political judgment. The citizen who civically endures the burdens that come with citizenship recognizes that her lack of consent to the way in which her position in society is arranged fits with normal circumstances of politics. Instead of giving up her reliance on the normal circuits and routines of civic cooperation, she still trusts that she will be able to thematize – through the help of social movements, political representatives, the courts, and so on – her condition in a way that will eventually meet with a responsive and self-critical attitude of her fellow citizens. Civic responsiveness is a similarly flexible and generous disposition in face of disagreement. It enables one to withstand the huge attraction of simply not reflecting on the uncivil or even immoral consequences of one's position of power in society. The responsive citizen is generous enough to admit, in light of a critical evaluation of her civic ideals and *vis-à-vis* the burdens of cooperation carried by some of her fellow citizens, that she cannot accept the legitimacy of the very civic order that privileges her. Seen in this way, the citizen's disposition to act from civic responsiveness and civic endurance is a sign of her civic integrity – that is, of her testing her own, others, and legally sanctioned civic interpretations in light of the ideal to let the legitimate needs and interests of all citizens matter equally. This civic integrity presupposes a considerable amount of self-restraint and self-sacrifice.[47] For the citizen who acts from the virtue of civic endurance, it presupposes the willingness to remain patient and civil in her political conduct even when the limits of loyalty are well in sight. For the citizen who acts from responsiveness, it presupposes the willingness to live up to insights that may result in her having to give up some of the privileges she enjoys. Finally, where democratic majorities are not responsive to the needs of minorities, it is not morally in order to expect these minorities to exercise civic endurance. And where minorities do not want to endure even perfectly reasonable burdens of citizenship, there is a clear limit to the responsiveness they can expect from majorities – a limit that is defined by the lack of the very disposition towards civic cooperation that is a condition of all fruitful civic interactions.[48]

One last word on more specific civic virtues. Where laws and regulations that are supposed to protect the civil peace become subject to interpretative conflict themselves, citizens and their political representatives are often asked to remain tolerant, just, exercise self-restraint, loyalty, law-abidingness, and so on. Given the importance of stability and social order, this is understandable. However, such appeals to the exercise of civic virtue remain quite empty if they do no make it clear what the call for civic virtue implies for differently positioned citizens. A reflection on the requirements of civic endurance and responsiveness can help answer that question. The point is easily made through dramatic examples: during racial riots, a call for tolerance implies very different concessions and future courses of actions for different persons and groups involved; in a situation of unequal distribution of basic goods such as food, water, and medical care, calls for restraint and justice imply different courses of action for different people. But if one thinks of less dramatic examples from political struggles over socioeconomic and identity-related issues, the same point goes for virtues such as courage, loyalty, law-abidingness, perseverance, and so on. It is through our dispositions for civic responsiveness and endurance that we learn to exercise civic virtue and autonomous political judgment and action in ways that are appropriate to our own and others' situation as members of internally conflicted political communities that are not, but often aim to be, well-ordered and just.

V Conclusion

I have argued that liberalism without agreement is a viable alternative to variants of liberalism based on the assumption that a firm agreement on the requirements of a common framework for social and political cooperation is a necessary condition for civic cooperation. The need to make this argument arises from the many serious doubts that liberal and other political theorists have raised as to the appropriateness of agreement-based liberalism in a pluralist age. In particular, an understanding of the deeply pluralistic "circumstances of politics" (Waldron) provides us with good reasons to leave agreement-based liberalism and its understanding of the requirements of civic cooperation behind. I have shown that liberalism without agreement is based on quite different ideas about the legitimacy of the civic order, the nature of political autonomy, the use of public reason, and civic virtue than agreement-based liberalism is. Finally, I have introduced two general civic dispositions – civic endurance and civic responsiveness – and explained how these may help us to understand the requirements of the exercise of civic virtue and political autonomy. Although the story I have told is quite general in nature, and calls for further elaboration, I hope that it has made it clear that liberalism without agreement may well be a viable alternative to the immensely important, but in its theoretical self-understanding mistaken, tradition of agreement-based liberalism.

Notes

1. I have benefited from comments on earlier drafts of this chapter by members of audiences in Frankfurt am Main, Tilburg, and Southampton. Special thanks are due to Russell Bentley, Rainer Forst, Axel Honneth, Bart van Klink, David Owen, Hildegard Penn, Morten Raffnsøe Møller, Sanne Taekema, Bertjan Wolthuis, the editors of the present volume, and four anonymous referees for Cambridge University Press.
2. Marilyn Friedman, "John Rawls and the Political Coercion of Unreasonable People," in: *The Idea of a Political Liberalism: Essays on Rawls*, ed. by Victoria Davion and Clark Wolf (New York: Rowman & Littlefield, 2000), pp. 16–33; here: p. 31. Emphasis in the original.
3. John Rawls, *Political Liberalism* (New York: Columbia University Press, 1993), p. 137.

4. Rawls's "hermeneutical turn" in *Political Liberalism* clearly serves the purpose of developing a normative political theory for members of contemporary Western, liberal constitutional democracies (or even narrower: the United States).
5. This is, of course, John Rawls's method. The most fundamental account of the role of consent in constitutional-democratic political thought is probably Jürgen Habermas, *Between Facts and Norms: Contributions to a Discourse Theory of Law and Democracy*, trans. by William Rehg (Cambridge, MA: MIT Press, 1996).
6. Joseph Raz, "Government by Consent," in: Raz, *Ethics in the Public Domain: Essay in the Morality of Law and Politics* (Oxford: Clarendon, 1994), pp. 339–353.
7. Most famously, of course, by Michael J. Sandel in *Liberalism and the Limits of Justice* (Cambridge: Cambridge University Press, 1982).
8. One of the main problems with the notion of an overlapping consensus is that although you and I may agree that liberty, equality, solidarity, equity, and pluralism should be core values in our society, we may hold radically different views about all these values. One politically liberal author who sees this problem very clearly is J. Donald Moon, *Constructing Community: Moral Pluralism and Tragic Conflicts* (Princeton: Princeton University Press, 1993), pp. 75ff.
9. James Tully, "The Agonic Freedom of Citizens," *Economy and Society*, 28/2 (1999): 161–182; here: 170.
10. Jeremy Waldron, *Law and Disagreement* (Oxford: Oxford University Press, 1999), pp. 105–106. The quotation from Rawls is from "The Domain of the Political and Overlapping Consensus," in *The Idea of Democracy*, ed. by D. Copp, J. Hampton, and J. Roemer (Cambridge: Cambridge University Press, 1993), p. 246.
11. To be fair, it is not easy to determine to what extent Rawls thinks agreement on the substance of, for instance, principles of justice, primary goods, and the requirements of the burdens of judgment is important. It seems that, over the years, agreement on substance became less important for him, while a conscious use of public reason had become ever more important.
12. All quotations from Waldron, *Law and Disagreement*, p. 106.
13. See, for the metaphysical issues looming behind this assumption, Bernard Williams, *Shame and Necessity*, Berkeley: University of California Press, 1993, pp. 161ff. Williams may be said to give a genealogy of the historically contingent core idea of Enlightenment political thought "... that the relations of human beings to society and to each other, if properly understood and properly enacted, can realize a harmonious identity that involves no real loss" (p. 162).
14. See, on this point, Immanuel Kant, "On the Common Saying: That May Be Correct in Theory, but It Is of No Use in Practice," in: Kant, *Practical Philosophy*, trans. and ed. by Mary J. Gregor (Cambridge: Cambridge University Press, 1996), pp. 296–297 especially.
15. Waldron, *Law and Disagreement*, p. 108.

16. See, for a feminist analysis of the dangers involved, Marilyn Friedman's contribution to the present volume (Chapter 7), "Autonomy and Male Dominance."
17. I stress the moral capacities since they are of crucial importance to both the conception of political autonomy of the Rawlsian brand of agreement-based liberalism I discuss and liberalism without agreement. See, for several accounts of the importance of moral autonomy in liberalism in the present volume, Rainer Forst, "Political Liberty: Integrating Five Conceptions of Autonomy" (Chapter 10); Gerald Gaus, "The Place of Autonomy Within Liberalism" (Chapter 12); Jeremy Waldron, "Moral Autonomy and Personal Autonomy" (Chapter 13); and John Christman, "Autonomy, Self-Knowledge, and Liberal Legitimacy" (Chapter 14). Of course, other cognitive capacities relating to rationality, self-control, freedom from pathology, adequate information, and motivational effectiveness of one's beliefs are relevant to the exercise of political autonomy as well. See Christman, Chapter 14 in the present volume, Section I.
18. As to the question of authentic identification, I agree with John Christman that in political reasoning, the authority of an individual citizen with respect to her authentic beliefs is not of an "epistemic" but of a "personal" or "normative" nature (see John Christman's Chapter 14 in the present volume, Sections III and IV). We accept the authority of someone expressing her "own" beliefs not because we have reason to assume that she is the best judge of the truth of what she believes, but because she is in the best position to express her own value commitments, which she considers to be of importance to public deliberations over political matters. The epistemic authority in these matters falls to intersubjective deliberation over the appropriateness of her beliefs. This is an important point with respect to a question posed by John Rawls that will be discussed later – namely, how autonomous political action can be prevented from being too self-righteous.
19. John Rawls, *A Theory of Justice* (Cambridge, Mass.: Harvard University Press, 1971), p. 515.
20. Ibid., p. 516.
21. Ibid., p. 519. Similarly, in *Political Liberalism*, p. 77, Rawls states that it "... is in their public recognition and informed application of the principles of justice in their political life, and as their effective sense of justice directs, that citizens achieve full [political] autonomy. Thus, full autonomy is realized by citizens when they act from principles of justice that specify the fair terms of cooperation they would give to themselves when fairly represented as free and equal persons."
22. See, for the several aspects of autonomy mentioned here, Jeremy Waldron's reconstruction of autonomy in Section III of his contribution to the present volume, "Moral Autonomy and Personal Autonomy" (Chapter 13). His reconstruction there focuses on similarities between the notions of personal and political autonomy, especially the importance of moral autonomy to both these notions. I agree with him that in political theory, a radical separation between personal and political autonomy cannot be made. See also Bert van den Brink, *The Tragedy of Liberalism: An Alternative Defense of a*

Political Tradition (Albany, NY: State University of New York Press, 2000), Part 2, where I argue that John Rawls's notion of political autonomy presupposes that citizens orient themselves to certain moral values even in their personal, "pre-political" lives.
23. The change in position is most obvious in "The Idea of Public Reason Revisited," in: *The Law of Peoples*, Cambridge, Mass.: Harvard University Press, 1999.
24. See note 21.
25. Isaiah Berlin, "Two Concepts of Liberty," in: *Four Essays on Liberty* (Oxford: Oxford University Press 1969), pp. 118–172.
26. Charles Taylor, "What's Wrong with Negative Liberty," in: *Philosophy and the Human Sciences. Philosophical Papers Vol. 2* (Cambridge: Cambridge University Press, 1985), pp. 211–229.
27. Philip Pettit, *Republicanism: A Theory of Freedom and Government* (Oxford: Clarendon Press, 1997).
28. Tully stresses this game element of the agonistic understanding of politics in "Agonic Freedom," *passim*.
29. John Gray, "Agonistic Liberalism," *Enlightenment's Wake* (London: Routledge, 1995), p. 68.
30. Hannah Arendt, "What is Freedom?" in: Arendt, *Between Past and Future* (Harmondsworth: Penguin, 1985), p. 165. See Michel Foucault, "Truth and Power," in: Foucault, *Power/Knowledge: Selected Interviews and Other Writings, 1972–1977*, ed. by Colin Gordon (New York: Pantheon Books, 1980), pp. 109–133; here: 121. See Tully, "Agonic Freedom" for a detailed account of the similarities and differences of Arendt's and Foucault's accounts of agonistic freedom.
31. See note 18.
32. John Tomasi, *Liberalism Beyond Justice* (Princeton: Princeton University Press, 2001), p. 54.
33. See Arendt, "What is Freedom?" pp. 165ff.; Tully, "Agonic Freedom," p. 162.
34. Jeremy Waldron, "Moral Autonomy and Personal Autonomy," Chapter 13 in the present volume (p. 307).
35. Rawls, *Political Liberalism*, p. 226: "Accepting the idea of public reason and its principle of legitimacy emphatically does not mean . . . accepting a particular liberal conception of justice down to its last details of the principles defining its content. We may differ about these principles and still agree in accepting a conception's more general features. We agree that citizens share in political power as free and equal, and that as reasonable and rational they have a duty of civility to appeal to public reason, yet we differ as to which principles are the most reasonable basis of public justification." In *Political Liberalism*, Rawls seems torn between this view and what is probably his older and more static view that a well-ordered society "is a society in which everyone accepts, and knows that everyone else accepts, the very same principles of justice . . . " (p. 52).
36. See Russell Bentley and David Owen, "Ethical Loyalties, Civic Virtue and the Circumstances of Politics," *Philosophical Explorations* 4 (2001): 223–239; Friedman, "Rawls and Political Coercion"; J. Donald Moon, *Constructing*

Community; David Archard, "Political Disagreement, Legitimacy, and Civility," *Philosophical Explorations* 4 (2001): 207–222; van den Brink, *The Tragedy of Liberalism.*
37. Christman, "Autonomy, Self-Knowledge, and Liberal Legitimacy," Chapter 14, Section III, in the present volume.
38. See, for instance, the literature mentioned in note 36.
39. Cf. Diana T. Meyers' distinction between self-definition and self-discovery in her contribution to the present volume, "Decentralizing Autonomy: Five Faces of Selfhood," Chapter 2, Section V.
40. For a similar point, see David Owen, *Nietzsche, Politics and Modernity* (London/Thousand Oak, CA: Sage, 1995), pp. 142ff.
41. Stephen Macedo, *Liberal Virtues: Citizenship, Virtue, and Community in Liberal Constitutionalism* (Oxford: Clarendon Press, 1990), pp. 275–276; William A. Galston, *Liberal Purposes: Goods, Virtues, and Diversity in the Liberal State* (Cambridge: Cambridge University Press, 1991), pp. 221ff.
42. To my knowledge, Bentley and Owen, in their essay "Ethical Loyalties, Civic Virtue and the Circumstances of Politics" (note 36), are the only other authors who use those terms in roughly the same way as I do. I thank them for acknowledging the influence of my lecture "Endurance as a Civic Virtue" (University of Southampton, December 2000) on their work. In return, I want to acknowledge the way in which their discussion of civic endurance and responsiveness has shaped the ideas I present here, especially the suggestion to delimit what they call the "virtues" of endurance and responsiveness from attendant vices.
43. For quite different analyses of the exact forms of repression and lack of political voice see, for instance, James Tully, *Strange Multiplicity* (Cambridge: Cambridge University Press, 1994) and Will Kymlicka, *Multicultural Citizenship,* (Oxford: Oxford University Press, 1995).
44. See also Bentley and Owen, "Ethical Loyalties," p. 236.
45. Ibid.
46. I cannot go here into the interesting parallels between responsiveness as a civic disposition and as a virtue of "responsive" law, as developed by Philip Selznick in *The Moral Commonwealth: Social Theory and the Promise of Community* (Berkeley: University of California Press, 1993), pp. 463–471.
47. See Philip Selznick, "Civilizing Civil Society," in: Anton van Harskamp and Albert W. Musschenga, eds., *The Many Faces of Individualism* (Leuven: Peeters, 2001), pp. 171–185.
48. Although I cannot argue for this here, I think that my account of endurance and responsiveness fits with some of the normative consequences that seem to follow from Axel Honneth and Joel Anderson's quest for an understanding of civic freedom and equality in terms of a multivocal model of interpersonal communication and mutual recognition. With the help of the notions of civic endurance and responsiveness, I try to gain insight into situation-dependent forms of concrete mutual recognition that can help restore the multivocality and effective freedom and equality of the members of a pluralistic and less than just political community. See Anderson and Honneth's contribution

to the present volume, "Autonomy, Vulnerability, Recognition, and Justice" (Chapter 6). For a partly recognition-theoretic argument regarding civic respect among members of majority and minority cultures see my "Democratic Reasoning and Reasons of One's Own," in Maureen Sie, Marc Slors, Bert van den Brink (eds.), *Reasons of One's Own* (Aldershot: Ashgate, 2004), pp. 69–86.

12

The Place of Autonomy within Liberalism

Gerald F. Gaus

I Introduction

My concern in this chapter is the place of autonomy within liberalism, understood as a public morality.[1] To what extent is liberal morality necessarily committed to some doctrine of autonomy, and what is the nature of this doctrine? I begin (Section II) by briefly explicating my understanding of liberalism, which is based on *the fundamental liberal principle* – that all interferences with action stand in need of justification. Section III then defends my first core claim: given a certain compelling view of the nature of moral reasons, the fundamental liberal principle presupposes a Kantian conception of morally autonomous agents. I then consider (Section IV) an implication of the fundamental liberal principle when applied to public morality and the law – that an interference with liberty must be justified to everyone. This *public justification principle*, I argue, constitutes a version of Kant's categorical imperative; thus liberalism is committed to not only autonomy of the will (Section III) but a substantive morality of autonomy. By the end of Section IV, I will have shown that liberal morality is committed to what may be broadly deemed a "Kantian" conception of moral autonomy.

In Section V, I show how this necessary presupposition of moral autonomy in liberal public morality implies a further commitment to one interpretation of the much-discussed ideal of "personal autonomy." It is often maintained that the ideal of personal autonomy is independent of moral or "Kantian autonomy": the commitment to one is said not to entail a commitment to the other. Kantian autonomy is understood as a metaphysical idea concerned with free will, or more generally a presupposition of the very possibility of moral responsibility, while personal autonomy is typically understood as a character ideal, focusing on the value of critical self-reflection on one's desires, values and plans, or the value of choosing one's way of life for oneself, or perhaps the value of self-control.[2] To be sure, most acknowledge that Kantian moral autonomy and personal autonomy are in some way related – after all, they both go by the label of "autonomy." Both are about self-direction or self-government.[3] Nevertheless, most advocates of what we might call "liberal autonomy" – according to which the justification of liberalism is grounded on the notion of personal autonomy – seem more intent on distinguishing the two ideas of autonomy than showing their connections. Section V challenges this: the case for personal autonomy, I argue, derives from the case for moral autonomy. They are distinct, but by no means independent, notions of autonomy – a position not unlike Ranier Forst's in Chapter 10 of the present volume. My claim is, I think, less radical than the thesis Jeremy Waldron defends in Chapter 13: while I wish to stress the connections between moral and personal autonomy, I nevertheless rely on the distinction between them.[4]

Insofar as a commitment to autonomy is bound up with liberal public morality, many liberal autonomists appear to think that it is personal autonomy that is really crucial. Distinguishing personal autonomy from Kantian autonomy is typically part of a project claiming that a liberal political morality can be based on the former.[5] By and large, those who would construct liberal political morality on autonomy seek to build on personal autonomy.[6] Thus, for example, one commentator tells us that although "Kant's strong and metaphysically controversial conception of autonomy" seems unable to "play the role of providing a sufficiently non-sectarian basis for liberalism," those "conceptions connected with the value of self-reflection" are much more widely accepted, and may well provide the basis of non-sectarian liberalism.[7] To be sure, some who advance personal autonomy justifications of liberal morality and the liberal state give at least a passing acknowledgment to Kant's conception of autonomy.[8] More importantly, Rawls is, on the whole, an exception to this common privileging of personal autonomy: Kantian autonomy, understood as a type of moral power, plays a fundamental role in Rawls' liberalism (though it is certainly also true that he moved away from a Kantian "comprehensive" view as his political liberalism evolved).[9] In any event, I aim to show in this chapter that though Kantian and personal autonomy are related, and commitments to both are part of liberal public morality, the Kantian notion is more fundamental than the ideal of personal autonomy.

II The Fundamental Liberal Principle

Stanley Benn asks us to

> Imagine Alan sitting on a public beach, a pebble in each hand, splitting one pebble by striking it with another. Betty, a causal observer, asks him what he is doing. She can see, of course, that he is splitting pebbles; what she is asking him to do is to explain it, to redescribe it as an activity with an intelligible point, something he could have a reason for doing. There is nothing untoward about her question, but Alan is not bound to answer it unless he likes. Suppose, however, that Betty had asked Alan to justify what he was doing or to give an excuse for doing it. Unlike explanations, justifications and excuses presume at least prima facie fault, a charge to be rebutted, and what can be wrong with splitting pebbles on a public beach? Besides, so far as we can tell, Alan is not obliged to account to Betty for his actions. . . .
>
> Suppose Betty were to prevent Alan from splitting pebbles by handcuffing him or removing all the pebbles within reach. Alan could now quite properly demand a justification from Betty, and a *tu quoque* reply from her that he, on his side, had not offered her a justification for splitting pebbles, would not meet the case, for Alan's pebble splitting had done nothing to interfere with Betty's actions. The burden of justification falls on the interferer, not on the person interfered with. So while Alan might properly resent Betty's interference, Betty has no ground for complaint against Alan.[10]

Benn observes a basic asymmetry between acting and interfering with the actions of another. Alan does not have to justify his pebble splitting to Betty: he is under no standing requirement to show Betty that he has good reasons for what he is doing. On the other hand, it is required of Betty that she justify to Alan interfering with his actions, or stopping him from what he is doing, or in some way restricting his actions. This is essentially what Joel Feinberg has called the "presumption in favor of liberty": "liberty should be the norm, coercion always needs some special justification."[11]

The liberal tradition in moral and political philosophy maintains that each person has a moral claim to do as he wishes until some justification is offered for limiting his liberty.[12] As liberals see it, we have liberty to act as we see fit unless reason can be provided for restriction. Call this *the fundamental liberal principle*:

1. A person is under no standing obligation to justify his actions;
2. Interference with, or restriction of, an other's action requires justification; unjustified interference or restriction is unjust, and so morally wrong.

The presumption underlying the liberal principle is essentially justificatory: it regulates justificatory discourse about the morality of action, and ties moral wrongness to the lack of required justification. (This is not to say that this justificatory presumption in favor of liberty itself does not have to be defended; that indeed would be a question-begging error.) It matters greatly, then, on whom the onus of justification is placed: who must bear the justificatory burden? As Benn says, "justifications and excuses presume at least prima facie fault, a charge to be rebutted." If I have no justificatory burden I am permitted to act without justification, for I have no charge to rebut, no case to answer. If the onus is on you, the failure to justify condemns your act. Conceivably, a conception of morality might place the onus on the actor: "never act unless one can meet the justificatory burden by showing that one is allowed to act." The liberal insists that moral persons have no such general burden to bear, though of course they may in special contexts in which a restriction already has been established (say, in contexts of trusteeships). Thus, unless you occupy a special role, such as a trustee, if I object to what you are doing, it is of no avail to demand, "Show me why you should be allowed to act." As Locke said, all men are naturally in "a State of perfect Freedom to order their actions ... as they see fit ... without asking leave, or depending upon the Will of any other Man."[13] My objection must take the form of a claim that your action is immoral, or inconsiderate, or dishonorable – you must answer the case that your act is not eligible. But I bear the justificatory burden of establishing this case. Ranier Forst objects that, contrary to the fundamental liberal principle, "there is a standing duty to justify morally relevant actions" (see Chapter 10 of the present volume, fn 24). However, by the time we have established that an action α is morally relevant we have, *ex hypothesi*, justified a limitation on freedom (or, alternatively, a case to be answered). That there is a *justified* moral rule prohibiting or regulating α implies, of course, that the justificatory burden has already been met. Morality, for the liberal, is as much in need of justification as any other restriction on action,[14] but once justified, moral prescriptions shift the onus back to the agent (he now has a case to answer), as Forst rightly observes.

My main aim in this chapter, however, is not to defend the fundamental liberal principle (but see Section Va); rather, I seek to examine its presuppositions. More precisely, I am concerned with what must be the case about reasons for actions and agents if the fundamental liberal principle is to serve as a moral principle for governing social life.

III The Liberal Principle and Moral Autonomy

IIIa What Reasons Do We Have? The Radical Instrumentalist Model

My concern, then, is the sorts of agents and their reasons that are presupposed by the fundamental liberal principle. What must be true for the fundamental liberal principle to be the basic moral principle? To begin, suppose that all reasons for action are instrumental reasons.[15] The core of the instrumental model is the intuition that in rational action, an agent necessarily seeks the best available result, with "best" being understood in terms of what she cares about, her goals, her purposes, and so on. This is the idea behind one conception of rational action qua utility maximization, which is often taken to be much the same as saying that an agent has "purposes that her action is designed to promote."[16] I shall follow Robert Nozick in taking the idea of goal pursuit as the core of instrumental rationality; indeed, as Nozick observes, "it is natural to think of rationality as a goal-directed process." So according to the basic "instrumental conception, rationality consists in the effective and efficient achievement of goals, ends, and desires. About the goals themselves, an instrumental conception has little to say."[17] I explicitly do not refer to "preferences" here, as the idea of a preference is ambiguous between something akin to a goal, purpose, or end (in which case "preference" would be suitable) and something akin to an overall reason for action, in which case it is axiomatic that all reasons for action are intended to satisfy preferences (which is a broader idea than instrumental rationality).

Elsewhere I have specified this instrumental model in more detail.[18] For now, let us work with a straightforward formulation:

Instrumental Rationality: Betty has a (good) purely instrumental reason to β if and only if given her option set, β best secures her goals (ends, etc.).[19]

Therefore, if Betty performs some alternative action β^*, β^* cannot be justified by appeal to instrumental rationality.

Suppose, then, not only a world in which each is always guided by, and only by, her instrumental rationality, but a conceptual world in which there simply is no other type of reason for action. The only reason for action that anyone ever has or could have, given a set possible acts, is a reason to do that which best promotes her goals, achieves her ends, and so on. Many think we live in such a world: they are convinced that instrumental rationality subsumes all of rationality. This is the world of orthodox rational-actor theory and, through that theory, many moral theories, such as David Gauthier's.[20] It is, I shall argue, an illiberal world.

IIIb The Basic Case

Suppose in this world of purely instrumental reasons, Betty interferes with Alan's actions. Betty is a successful predator, and manages to force Alan to do what she wants. She gains; he loses. She does not seek to justify her actions to him, nor is she concerned that he is harmed; her instrumental reasons unambiguously instruct her to invade. Given all she cares about, the act "invade Alan" best promotes her goals, so she follows her best reasons and invades. This is a manifest injustice; it is a considered judgment of liberals that Betty does wrong. Our question is this: in such a world, can Alan invoke the basic liberal principle, insisting that unless Betty justifies her intervention, she acts unjustly? If he cannot do so, then the fundamental liberal principle presupposes some world other than the world of purely instrumental reasons.

IIIc The Rejection of a Radical Externalist Account of Moral Obligation

For Alan to sensibly invoke the fundamental liberal principle in the world of purely instrumental reasons, it would have to be possible for him to claim that Betty's unjustified invasive action is *ipso facto* wrong, even though she has no reason to refrain from her invasion. That is, he (and we) would have to accept:

Radical Externalism: Betty can have a moral obligation to refrain from act β even if there is no reason for her not to β.[21]

Radical Externalism should be rejected: it denies a necessary connection between a moral obligation to not β and a reason to not β. If Radical Externalism holds, then even if Betty has no reason at all to refrain from invading Alan, she still can have a moral obligation to refrain; the moral obligation itself provides no reason for her to refrain. It should be stressed that Radical Externalism is indeed a truly radical form of externalism. It goes considerably further than would those externalists who would insist that Betty can have a moral obligation to refrain from β even if she does not have a *motivating* reason to refrain from β (for an externalist can admit that her *lack of motivating reason* to β does not itself show that *there is no reason* for her to β; see, however, Section IIIe). Indeed, Radical Externalism goes beyond the typical externalist claim that Betty can have a moral obligation not to β even if there is no way that, given her epistemic position, desires, and so on, she could have access to a reason not to β.[22] In fact, most externalists, as well as all internalists, deny Radical Externalism – that is, they deny that Betty can have a moral obligation to refrain from β when there is no reason whatsoever for her to refrain from β. They thus accept:

Modest Internalism: Betty has a moral obligation to refrain from β only if there is a reason for her not to β.

Strong conceptions of externalism are consistent with accepting Modest Internalism (which goes to show just how modest a form of internalism it is). On these more plausible externalist accounts, just as there can exist a moral obligation whether or not a person knows about it or is motivated to act on it, so too can there be a reason to act on this obligation whether or not a person is aware of it, or is motivated to act on it.[23]

Radical Externalism denies, to use Michael Smith's term, a "platitude" about morality: that morality is part of practical reason in at least the weak sense that an ideally rational agent, who was aware of all the reasons for action that there are, would necessarily have reasons to act on her moral obligations.[24] To accept Radical Externalism is to hold that correct moral judgments need not imply reasons of any sort – motivating or otherwise – to do anything about them. Of course, some do think this. Radical expressivists seem to believe that moral judgments are simply affective expressions that have no tie to practical reason; radical realists conceive of moral judgments as simply claims about certain moral facts that have no implications for what agents have reason to do. But these are strange views, which are not even embraced by most expressivists and realists. If morality is not about what agents have reasons to do, it is hard to understand what it is about.

Now if we accept, as we should, Modest Internalism, Alan – in our world of purely instrumental reasons – cannot coherently claim that Betty is under a moral obligation or duty to refrain from interfering with him without justification. More simply, he cannot claim that Betty acts wrongly in our case, for, *ex hypothesi*, Betty's only reasons are to advance her own goals, and these are reasons that unambiguously endorse invading him. Thus, according to Modest Internalism, if Betty has no reason to refrain from invading, she cannot have an obligation to refrain, and so she does not act wrongly. If that is so, we have a contradiction: the fundamental liberal principle deems Betty's act wrong, but on the supposition that all reasons are instrumental reasons, she does not act wrongly. Given Modest

Internalism, we need to give up either the fundamental liberal principle or the purely instrumental view of practical reason.

IIId A Challenge to an Assumption: The Convergence Thesis
Some may seek to remove the apparent contradiction by challenging the assumption that, all things considered, instrumental reasons endorse Betty's unjustified invasion. Following Hobbes, a number of contemporary moral and political philosophers have argued that agents such as Betty would find themselves in intractable conflict, which would frustrate the pursuit of their goals, and so our assumption is false. The contradiction, then, might be said to depend on a false assumption that instrumental reasons endorse unjustified interference.

For this reply to be effective there must be *no case* in which instrumental reason instructs Betty to wrongly invade Alan simply to effectively advance her goals. If there is just one case in which such predation is instrumentally rational, the inconsistency we have been discussing arises. Thus we need an argument for the universal convergence of instrumental reason and applications of the liberal principle. It seems pretty doubtful that a successful argument along these lines will be forthcoming, but let us grant the convergence assumption. Let us suppose that a project such as Gauthier's succeeds in showing that, given facts about human society and human nature in world *W*, for all individuals in *W* of purely instrumental reasons, it will always be the case in *W* that one will have reason to refrain from interference (unless that interference can be justified to the person being interfered with). This, though, would still only show that within *W* the contradiction would not arise. But our conception of liberal morality is not limited to *W*. Our understanding of morality commits us to some (I am assuming for now) counterfactual judgments (think of Judith Thomson's trolley cases, or her violinist case).[25] That those cases do not arise in our world does not show that our moral concepts need not apply to them. Now so too with the fundamental liberal principle: even if we live in *W*, the principle covers at least proximate possible worlds, including those in which instrumental reasons lead us to invade others without justification. If in these counterfactual cases the contradiction arises, we can conclude that our understanding of the liberal principle still presupposes that not all reasons are instrumental reasons. The conceptual point about the presuppositions of the fundamental liberal principle thus cannot be met by showing that there exists a world *W* in which the problem does not arise, even if we happen to live in *W*.

To be sure, as we entertain more and more outlandish counterfactuals – consider possible worlds that are further and further from our own – our concepts loose their grip, our ability to apply them becomes attenuated, and we become confused about what to say. This is certainly a severe problem with many of the so-called "mental experiments" designed to "test" our "moral intuitions," or, more accurately, the criteria for applying moral notions. In these worlds of incredible machines where hitting one button or the other causes amazing chains of events, our normal concepts are apt to leave us unsure about what to say.[26] Surely, though, that is not a relevant objection here. *Our* empirical world is one in which what best advances people's goals often enough conflicts with refraining from interfering with others; it is the assumption of universal convergence that pushes us into unfamiliar territory.

This criticism of the convergence assumption could be avoided by showing that the tie between the fundamental liberal principle and agents' goals is not contingent. Drawing on a theory of value, it might be suggested, say, that because everyone's true goal is to respect others, and because the fundamental liberal principle is an expression of this (or, perhaps, a means to it), in all relevant possible worlds – those with the correct theory of value – there will always be an instrumental reason not to unjustifiably interfere with others. Serious problems confront this proposal. As I have argued elsewhere, goal-based and principled-based reasons are not the same, nor can one be reduced to the other.[27] If this is so, then converting the fundamental liberal principle into a goal would not account for the types of reasons it implies. I will not, however, insist on this somewhat complicated point here. For our present purposes, we can reject the suggestion as it is clearly inconsistent with liberal theory. Liberalism denies that each of us has the overriding goal of being a good liberal, or that our overriding goal is to abide by liberal principles. (It should be stressed that for the present suggestion to work, abiding by the liberal principle must be one of our highest ranked goals, capable of giving instrumental reasons to forgo our other goals by refraining from interfering with others.) Although liberals do indeed insist that individuals are capable of putting aside their various goals to abide by the principle of non-interference, this is not because they believe that our primary goal is not to interfere with others. Liberals conceive of individuals as possessing a diverse array of goals and ends; they *do* not – certainly *need* not – advance a theory of value according to which an overriding goal of everyone is to abide by the fundamental liberal principle.

IIIe Acting upon Reasons for Action: A Standard Internalist Claim About Reasons to Act

We must conclude that, given Modest Internalism, the fundamental liberal principle is incompatible with a world in which all reasons to act are instrumental. Liberalism supposes that there are moral reasons (to refrain from interfering with others) that are not ways to achieve goals. Now to accept that there exists a reason R to refrain from β commits one to also accepting that, supposing no competing reasons outweigh R (are more important than R, rank higher than R, and so on[28]), a rational agent who is aware of R will refrain from β on the grounds of R, or because of R.[29] Reasons for action are part of practical rationality, and practical rationality guides the action of rational agents. A form of internalism that goes beyond Modest Internalism (Section IIIc) about reasons for action is compelling: there is an internal – necessary – connection between R's status as a reason and R's being acted upon. Let us call this:

Standard Internalism: If R is a reason to refrain from act β, it must be the case that, barring overriding reasons, a rational agent who is aware of R will refrain from β because of R.

Philippa Foot apparently rejects this; as she sees it, "an agent may fail to be moved by a reason, even when he is aware of it."[30] On her view, one can be aware that R is a reason to β, and yet not β. Now of course this can be the case if the agent is characterized by a failure of practical rationality; what is called "weakness of will" can be understood as a failure to act on one's best reasons.[31] However, one who fails to be moved by the best reasons for action of which she is aware always suffers from a defect of rationality: a practically rational person's actions are guided by her reasons. This is not merely asserting the definition that one is practically rational if and only if one is moved by one's reasons. We possess an implicit concept of rational agents,[32] and according to this concept, someone who asserts that "Yes, R is a reason to β that applies to me in the present context, but what does that have to do with my actually being moved to β?" does not understand what it means to say that R is a reason for action. "Yes, I have a reason not to steal, but what does this have to do with my actually refraining from stealing?" is not to exploit a distinction in our understanding of reasons for action and motivation; it expresses conceptual confusion.[33] (To make it intelligible, we might suppose that the speaker is claiming that though R is typically taken as a reason, she is actually denying it.) It is thus mistaken to assert that one may, without inducing conceptual puzzlement, claim that one just happens to be unmoved by one's reasons, say, because one lacks the desire to be rational.[34] Once we have established that a person acknowledges that R is her best reason, and it is a reason to β, we do not need additional premises to explain her β-ing. Indeed, her *not* β-ing is what calls for further explanation: we are apt to invoke a special account of breakdowns of rationality to make not β-ing intelligible.

IIIf Moral Autonomy as a Property of the Rational Will

We thus arrive at our first conclusion: given a plausible internalist conception of reasons for action, the fundamental liberal principle presupposes that there are reasons for agents to set aside their instrumental reasons and abide by the principle (Sections IIIa–d), and that (when they are the best reasons) rational agents act on these reasons (Section IIIe). This is to endorse a Kantian – though, of course, not Kant's – conception of moral autonomy.

As in Kant's view, autonomy is analytically connected with practical reason. As Kant understood it, to attribute autonomy to an agent just is to attribute to her the capacity to be moved by a practical principle, endorsed by practical reason, which does not make reference to her needs or interests.[35] To be autonomous is to have the capacity for one's will to be determined by moral practical reason.[36] Autonomy, then, is a property of the will. Our analysis of the presupposition of claims based on the fundamental liberal principle has led us to conclude that the principle is intelligible only if individuals have the capacity to be guided by practical reasons that do not derive from promoting their goals, ends, and so on. Again following Kant, only because we are cognizant of the demands of morality do we know that we are able to be guided by reasons for action that do not derive from furthering our goals or ends – that is, we possess moral autonomy.[37]

Susan Wolf seems to pose an objection. She has argued that the ability to act on reason is to be distinguished from a conception of freedom as autonomy.[38] As I understand her, she would depict the view endorsed here as a "Reason View," not an "Autonomy View," of moral responsibility. Whereas an Autonomy View locates moral freedom and responsibility in one's option to do or not do one's moral duty, for the Reason View "[w]hat matters is rather the availability of one very particular option, namely the option to act in accordance with Reason."[39] Certainly my position has much in common with Wolf's Reason View. And it is certainly true that claims about counter-causal freedom are important in Kant's thinking about autonomy. The argument presented here is silent about such freedom, so it does not capture all of what Kant meant to include in the concept of "autonomy." Acknowledging all that, it should be noted that interpretations of Kant, and Kantian conceptions of morality, differ in the ways they relate the will to reason, and the relative priority they assign to one or the other. For example, in contrast to my account, Christine Korsgaard appears to give a much more central place to the idea of the will; in some ways, reason seems secondary to the idea of the will in her interpretation.[40] The Kantian view defended here, in contrast, takes as central to Kant's conception of autonomy the idea that an autonomous will is one determined by moral reason, and that we are free when we act rationally in this way. That, in my view, is the central feature of the concept of moral autonomy.

It is worth stressing just how important to Kant's understanding of autonomy is what we might call the "metaphysics of reasons." Kant distinguished between, on the one hand, reasons of morality and, on the other, reasons that might be variously described as those of prudence, reasons concerned with one's subjective interests as a sensuous being, or reasons of self-love.[41] As is commonly observed, Kant conceived of the latter category too narrowly: we need not suppose that the reasons potentially opposed to moral reasons are necessarily selfish or self-centered. A more adequate contrast is between reasons devoted to pursuing that which we see as good, and so endeavor to obtain (valued states of affairs, cherished objects, goals, ends), and those moral reasons that demand we set aside our pursuit of the good or valuable.[42] In contrast to instrumental reasons, moral reasons do not confront us as hypothetical, because they do not depend on our affirmation of a goal or an end. They confront us as imperitival and categorical.[43] Regardless of our ends or goals, they demand that we do the right thing.

I follow Kant in distinguishing heteronomous moralities from autonomous moralities.[44] Attempts to derive the moral from the rational, where the latter is understood simply in terms of instrumental rationality, are heteronomous.[45] On such views, morality is simply a device for efficient goal pursuit. Such moral theories are ultimately unsuitable; their denial of autonomy renders them at a loss as to how to account for our ability to refrain from pursuing our concerns and values, and our demands that others do so as well. Rational agents approach being psychopathic when their reasons are consumed by their own ends.[46]

IIIg The Moral Autonomy of the Claimant

Thus far I have argued that in appealing to the fundamental liberal principle, Alan necessarily supposes that Betty possesses moral autonomy. Can Alan, though, insist that while he supposes that Betty possesses moral autonomy, he is simply an instrumental reasoner, and so non-autonomous? No: not only must Alan suppose that Betty is an autonomous agent, he must also suppose that he possesses moral autonomy.

To continue our example, assume that Alan invokes the fundamental liberal principle against Betty. We have seen that he supposes that she possesses moral autonomy, in the sense that she can act on moral reasons rather than on her goal-based ones. The basic liberal principle, though, does not prohibit all interference; it puts the onus of justification on Betty, who would interfere with Alan. Now assume that she meets this burden. Betty offers a justification for interfering with Alan's act α of the form: "Reason R justifies a moral prohibition of your act α; you ought not to α, and if you seek to α, I may legitimately β – that is, stop you." What can we say about the nature of this reason?

1. Well, it could be claimed that for the true liberal, there really are no such reasons as R purports to be. One might think that the genuinely liberal view is that it is never permissible to interfere with a person's liberty. Call this *the absolutist interpretation of the fundamental liberal principle*: the onus of justification can never be met. On the face of it, the absolutist interpretation appears too strict, as it apparently prevents liberals from endorsing a right to private property, or rights to bodily integrity. It would seem that the liberal would want to claim that it is justifiable when I interfere with your liberty by asserting my rights to private property or bodily integrity. If you are using your liberty to hit me on the head, or steal my acorn, it would appear that the liberal must think interference with your liberty is justifiable. Yet, if the absolutist interpretation excludes interference with liberty, it would appear to exclude such liberal rights and their defenses. Some seek to rescue the absolutist interpretation from this criticism, though, by insisting that one's property rights *define* one's liberty rights. As Jan Narveson argues, you own your eyes, and that is why they cannot be removed, and because you own your arm, it is up to you to decide whether to lift it or not. To be free to do something is just to be free to use what is yours – your property; so all your freedom rights concern your property. Indeed, Narveson claims, "it is plausible to construe all rights as property rights."[47] If so, then a person's liberty is interfered with if and only if his property rights are infringed.

Not only does this absolutist interpretation depend on the identification of liberty with property rights – which, I think, can be shown to be implausible[48] – but, in addition, it requires a claim about the compossibility of property-liberty rights.[49] If it were possible for my valid property right to X to conflict with your valid property right to Y, then somebody must interfere with someone else's property right (and, so liberty); but since, on the absolutist interpretation, there are no reasons that could justify an interference, it would follow that someone must do wrong.[50] I shall not pursue this option further. Unless one can show that all liberty rights are property rights *and* that property rights are compossible (or else accept that in some cases wrongdoing is unavoidable) – and I do not believe these can be shown – the absolutist interpretation is not compelling.

2. Betty might justify a prohibition of Alan's α on paternalistic grounds, claiming that her present interference can be justified because it better promotes Alan's own values, goals, projects, and so on. That is, Betty might appeal simply to Alan's instrumental reasons. Now if Betty takes this route, and shows that Alan's instrumental reasons endorse the prohibition, she advances a paternalist justification; the justification of the prohibition of α (and/or her interference, β) is that it advances Alan's goals.[51] This is worthy of note. If we accept (a) a world of purely instrumental reasons along with (b) Modest Internalism, the only justifying reason we could give another for limiting his freedom would be paternalistic. Suppose the convergence thesis held (Section IIId): moral principles are justified on the ground that everyone's instrumental reasons support following them. Everyone's goals are advanced by following the principles. Now suppose that Betty seeks to restrict Alan's liberty by appealing to these principles; she wants to claim that he is acting wrongly, and so morality justifies stopping him. Given Modest Internalism, her justification must be that his reason for accepting her interference is that his own ends are advanced by the interference. Thus, in a Gauthierish moral world, all justifications meeting the burden of the fundamental liberal principle collapse into paternalistic reasoning. To be sure, it would also be the case that the regulation would advance Betty's goals (*ex hypothesi*, which is why *she* has a reason to β), but her claim that Alan's action is wrong, and so that *he* has a reason to refrain from α, must be a claim that his reason for not α-ing is that it fails to advance his own goals.

It is certainly an odd account of liberal morality that would collapse all moral justifications into paternalism. Paternalism is, at best, an uncomfortable fit with liberalism.[52] Only those under the spell of a theory of practical reasoning according to which all reasons are instrumental would even attempt to construe liberal morality in this way. Typically, when one seeks to justify interfering with the liberty of another, it is not being claimed that the action is bad for him, but that even if it is the best thing he can do to advance his own goals, this use of his liberty is wrong, typically because it unjustifiably *harms others*.

3. Suppose, then, that Betty justifies her interference (β) on the ground that Alan's act (α) frustrates *her* goals, and that is her reason for stepping in. But suppose that, under the sway of the purely instrumental theory of practical reasons, Betty accepts that in a case in which α advances Alan's goals but thwarts hers, he has reason to α, and she has reason to β – that is, interfere with his α. Notice that in this case, Betty only justifies an interference with Alan: she does not justify the claim that Alan ought to refrain from α, or that it is wrong to α. So she asserts simply a Hohfeldian liberty to interfere.[53] According to Wesley Hohfeld, Betty has a liberty to β if and only if Alan has no claim against Betty that she not β. It also follows that if Alan has no claim that Betty refrain from β, then she has no duty to Alan to not β. For Hohfeld, when we talk about a person having a right to do something, we sometimes mean that she is merely at liberty to do so; she has no duty to refrain. But merely to have a liberty to do something does not imply that you have a claim that others not interfere. The classic example is the liberty of two pedestrians to pick up a dollar bill laying on the sidewalk. Neither has a duty to refrain from picking it up, but neither has a claim on the other to stand aside and let her pick it up. Such "naked liberties" often characterize competitions; people have the liberty to win, but no one has a claim to win. So Betty could simply be asserting a moral liberty to β (that is, interfere with Alan's α), while also accepting that Alan has a moral liberty to α.

Could it be the case that all justifying reasons are such permissions? If so, liberal morality would contain simply one moral duty, the duty not to interfere with the actions of another without justification. In specific cases, this moral duty would be met by justifying reasons that give one permission to intervene, though the person interfered with would have permission to resist. This certainly wouldn't be much of a morality. Every justification of an interference would be a justification of a competition or struggle. But liberals endorse rights to property, and rights to bodily integrity – and these are not plausibly understood as mere permissions, but as claims on others to act or refrain from acting. In contrast to liberties, claim rights imply duties on the part of others not to interfere (or to act); we might call them rights in the strict sense. To have a right in the strict sense is to be able to *demand* that others respect it: they have a duty to respect it, and so are not at liberty to ignore it. One's rights, then, concern what is owed to you, and so people are not free to decline honoring your claims.

4. By far the most compelling view, then, is that liberalism recognizes reasons that (a) justify interference with Alan's liberty, (b) do not simply appeal to his own instrumental reasons, and (c) justify claims on Alan that he has a duty to honor, not mere permissions to interfere. Again, insofar as reasons are practical (Section IIIe), it follows that fully rational agents will act on these reasons. Thus, when invoking the fundamental liberal principle against Betty, Alan not only supposes that as a rational moral agent she possesses moral autonomy, and can act on reasons to set aside her values, but he must also conceive of himself as a morally autonomous agent: one that accepts, and acts upon, reasons for action that Betty may give him that justify her interference, and this not only in the weak sense that Betty may show that she is at liberty to interfere, but in the stronger sense that she has claims upon Alan that require him to refrain from blocking her interference, or refrain from the use of his liberty to which she objects. The basic liberal principle, then, supposes a relationship among morally autonomous agents. Both are capable of setting aside their instrumental reasons and acting on duty.

IV Public Reason, The General Will, and Autonomous Legislation

IVa Post-Enlightenment Public Reasoning
Kant conceives of moral autonomy as both a property of the will that is presupposed by morality and as a substantive moral principle.[54] Thus far, I have been concerned with autonomy in the former sense; I shall now argue that the fundamental liberal principle also leads to a substantive morality of autonomy.

The fundamental liberal principle requires that interference be justified. We have arrived at the following conclusion: such justifications are possible (Section IIIg, 1); they present reasons that do not simply appeal to the goals of the person being interfered with (Section IIIg, 2); they are not typically merely permissions (Section IIIg, 3), and so typically constitute claims on the person being interfered with (Section IIIg, 4). It is on this last category of reasons for interference that I shall now focus. I have also argued that for R to be a reason justifying Betty's claim on Alan, it must be the case that a rational Alan would act on R (Section IIIe). So interpreted, the fundamental liberal principle implies that the justification for interfering with Alan must be recognized by a rational Alan *as a reason*. When advancing a moral claim on Alan – that he has a duty not to use his liberty in some way, and so Betty's interference with him is justified – she is appealing to Alan as a morally autonomous agent, one who can act on moral reasons even if that requires putting aside his instrumental reasons. In the second stage of the argument, in which Betty is seeking to meet the onus of justification by showing that her interference is justified, she now occupies the role of claimant trying to show that Alan has a duty to her (recall that on Hohfeld's analysis, Betty's claim right on Alan implies a duty of Alan toward Betty). Thus, all our conclusions about how Alan must conceive of Betty as an autonomous agent now apply to how Betty must see Alan: both assume that the other as well as himself or herself possess moral autonomy.

Betty's assertion that Alan does wrong by ignoring her claim on him presupposes that he has a reason to act on this claim. Betty's justification, then, must be a justification addressed to Alan as a rational moral agent. She is barred from presenting a consideration C as a justification of her interference if C would not be acknowledged by a rational Alan as providing him with a reason to act. It is not sufficient that C is a reason for Betty – that would not in itself show that Alan has a reason, and only if Betty can claim that Alan has a reason to act can she intelligibly claim that he does wrong by ignoring her claim (Section IIIc).

To be sure, if, as some assert, R is a reason for Betty if and only if it is a reason for all rational agents, this is a distinction without importance.[55] Any consideration that is a reason for Betty necessarily would be a reason for any rational agent, and so for Alan. If Betty knows her own reasons, then she would know his too. Justifying to herself would be equivalent to justifying to him. (Indeed, there would be no "justification *to*," only "justification *that*"). Some recent philosophers have sought to uphold this position, or one that approximates it, by appealing to Wittgenstein. Adopting his argument against private language, they seek to show that reasons must be inherently public, and shared.[56] I cannot examine this Wittgensteinian-inspired argument here[57] (or the allied arguments of some pragmatists). Suffice it to say for our present purposes that even if in some sense all reasons are social, and so there are no entirely private reasons, this would not show that all reasons are shared among all members of society. Languages are public and shared, but within a society, people speak different languages and numerous dialects. So even if reasons must be shared with some others, it would still be entirely possible, and indeed, likely, that some fully rational people will not share my reasons. If so, then the distinction between justifying *to Alan* and justifying *to Betty* becomes real and important.

This distinction is brought to the fore by what might be appropriately deemed "the post-Enlightenment insight." On one plausible view, the European Enlightenment of the seventeenth and eighteenth centuries was based on the supposition that the use of human reason produces, over the long term, convergence on truth in morals as well science.[58] The free inquiry of scientists was thought to produce agreement because (1) the truth is the same for everyone, (2) reason is a shared capacity of all human beings, and (3) the norms of good reasoning are universal. Thus, people reasoning correctly about the world will arrive at the same answer. Any premise p that is true for one person is necessarily true for all others; if the inferential rule $(p\ \&\ [p \to q]) \to q$ is valid for one person, it is necessarily valid for all. The true and valid results of one person's reasoning are thus necessarily true and valid for all. Now, as Rawls puts it, the post-Enlightenment insight is that it is a "permanent feature of the public culture of a democracy" that the free exercise of human reason leads us to embrace a diversity of reasonable moral and religious views.[59] The fundamental feature of the political culture of such societies is that not even rational citizens would share all the same reasons.

To be sure, Enlightenment figures such as Kant recognized the ubiquity of disagreement. Despite his belief that the free exercise of human reason could reveal universal moral principles, Kant also believed that on many questions concerning the good and justice, actual people come to divergent conclusions. For Kant, relying on one's individual judgment about justice characterizes "the state of nature" – "even if men were to be ever so good natured and righteous before a public lawful state of society is established, individual men, nations and states can never be certain they are secure against violence from one another because each will have the right to do what *seems just and good to him*, entirely independently of the opinion of others."[60] For Kant, reason tells us that if we are to avoid such conflict, we must submit to a lawful public authority to adjudicate disputes about justice. It is plausible, though, to understand Kant as insisting merely that politics must come to grips with our failure to be rational; our errors in understanding what reasons we actually have lead to conflicts of private judgment that government must adjudicate.

At least on one interpretation of Kant, it would seem, (fully) rational agents would recognize the same reasons for action. Recall, however, the distinction advanced in Section IIIe between a mere definition of a rational agent as one who is moved by the best reasons, and the conceptual claim that, given our understanding of rational agents, they will be moved by their recognition of the best reasons. On this latter view, the idea of a rational agent is not simply derived from a notion of best reasons, but relies on a substantive model of good deliberation, evidence gathering, and so on. If the former, defintional, idea is employed, then certainly if (1) R is a reason for anyone it is a reason for everyone, and (2) fully rational agents (by definition) recognize and act upon the best reasons, then (3) if Alan and Betty disagree whether R is a reason, at least one of them is not fully rational (though they both might still qualify as "reasonable"). But the idea of being fully rational really does no work here; it follows entirely from the notion of best reasons. We do, though, possess a notion of the rational that is not simply derivative of our understanding of what is the best reason. A rational person takes into account all the relevant available evidence, makes no errors when evaluating it, makes all the correct inferences, and so is not subject to various distortions of deliberation or action (for example, he is not under the influence of drugs or compulsions), and so on. It is still a demanding ideal, much more demanding than being simply a reasonable person (although it does not require omniscience; rational people do not know all there is to be known). Nevertheless, we can apply it even when we do not know what is the best reason. If a person displays the virtues of rational deliberation and action and none of the vices, then, given our understanding of a rational agent, we should conclude that he qualifies as such.

On this understanding of rational agency, even if we accept premise (1) in the previous paragraph, it does not follow that if Alan and Betty disagree on whether R is a reason, at least one of them must have experienced a failure of rationality – that is, not be fully rational. Even if there is a truth to the matter, fully rational people can arrive at differing conclusions. If so, then even if there is a truth to the matter, Betty cannot advance her conclusion C as a justification to Alan on the grounds that if it is a justifying reason for her, it must, *ipso facto*, be a reason any fully rational Alan would be moved by. Given this, Betty must present justifications that are addressed *to others* – that is, she must seek to show that her interference is justified by reasons that rational others would recognize (Section IIIe).

Insofar as liberalism is to function as a public morality regulating life among diverse strangers, justifications of interferences must be addressed to all members of the relevant public, as morally autonomous agents: all have moral reasons to accept this limitation on the pursuit of their goals. And that, we have seen, implies the claim that if they were fully rational – displaying the excellences of evidence gathering, deliberation, and action that constitute our concept of practical rationality – they would all recognize such reasons and act on them. The liberal principle, together with what I have called the post-Enlightenment insight, thus implies a non-trivial commitment to principles of social morality that are justified through reasons we share as rational agents – public reasons.[61]

IVb   Universal Laws and Moral Autonomy
In explaining a morality based on autonomy Kant writes:

If we now look back upon all previous attempts which have ever been undertaken to discover the principle of morality, it is not to be wondered that they all had to fail. Man is seen to be bound to laws by his duty, but it was not seen that he is subject only to his own, yet universal, legislation, and that he is only bound to act in accordance with his own will.... For if one thought of him as a subject only to a law (whatever it may be), this necessarily implied some interest as a stimulus or compulsion to obedience because the law did not arise from his will.[62]

Kant goes on to insist that all moralities moved by "some interest as a stimulus or compulsion to obedience" are heteronomous. An autonomous morality, in contrast, conceives "each rational being as a being that must regard itself as giving universal law through the maxims of its will."[63]

As I have depicted it, under a social morality justified through public reason, each rational autonomous individual has (an internal) reason to act on that morality. And not because of "some interest as a stimulus or compulsion to obedience because the law did not arise from his will," as in a heteronomous morality, but because the reason to accept and act on the moral principle is one to which the agent qua rational is committed (and this in the non-trivial sense). As rational, then, the agent wills the moral principle and the acts it requires, even though it requires a limitation on the pursuit of his goals. Thus it is the case that under public reason, moral principles are willed by all rational agents in the relevant public, and only moral principles so willed are justified under public reason. We can see, then, how an autonomous morality both limits freedom and is itself an expression of freedom. Insofar as it limits the ways in which we can pursue our ends and goals and opens us to moral claims by others that we must do as they insist, it is a restraint on freedom (and that is why moral regulation must be justified under the fundamental liberal principle); but because these demands do not confront us simply as external requirements but are confirmed by our own reasons to act, they are freely willed by all. No conception of morality that does not account for this Janus-headed nature of morality – as both a restriction and expression of our freedom – can be adequate.

We can now interpret the link between Kantian autonomy, contractualism, and the idea of the general will. Recall that for Kant, the "test of the rightfulness of every public law" is the "idea of reason," that there is "an *original contract* by means of which a civil and thus a completely lawful constitution and commonwealth alone can be established."[64] An original contract, Kant tells us, is "based on a coalition of all the private wills in a nation to form a common, public will, for the purposes of rightful legislation."[65] Contractualism, understood as a justificatory device, requires that justified principles be those that all rational individuals would accept. The hypothetical or counterfactual nature of this claim has led some critics to object that such contracts cannot bind.[66] This, though, misses the justificatory role of the contractual device given a commitment to a (non-trivial) concept of public reasoning. Only principles that could be accepted by all rational, morally autonomous persons can identify the reasons we share. If *R* could not be accepted by each and every rational, morally autonomous agent, it could not be a moral reason that each wills, and so could not qualify as part of an autonomous public morality.

Kant believed that the very idea of an original contract has the "practical reality" of obliging "every legislator to frame his laws in such a way that they could have been produced by the united will of a whole nation, and to regard each subject, in so far as he can claim citizenship, as if he had consented within the general will."[67] Thus conceived, *the idea of the general will is not only fully consistent with liberalism, but is implied by the fundamental liberal principle.* Although in the hands of Hegelians such as Bernard Bosanquet, the notion of the general will implies a collectivistic, and at least arguably, an illiberal understanding of the state, interpreted as an ideal according to which all just laws are rationally willed by all citizens, it expresses the fundamental liberal principle that interferences must be justified, conjoined with the ideal of public reason – that they must be justified to all.[68]

V Personal Autonomy

Thus far, my concern has been the place of moral autonomy within liberalism. Section III argued that the fundamental liberal principle presupposes that agents are morally autonomous. Section IV then maintained that this conception of moral autonomy, relying on an internalist conception of moral reasons, leads us to an ideal of public reasoning, and together these endorse a substantively Kantian (though, again, not Kant's own) autonomous morality, according to which the justified principles of social morality must be such as to be rationally willed by all, and we saw how this gives rise to the ideal of legislation that expresses the general will.[69] I now turn to the implications of this analysis for placing personal autonomy within liberalism.

Va Ultra-Minimal Personal Autonomy

The fundamental liberal principle supposes *an ultra-minimal conception of personal autonomy*. Thus far I have not sought to justify the fundamental liberal principle. Of the justifications that have been advanced, though, the most compelling maintains that *self-directed agents* (who are *in addition* morally autonomous persons in a world of morally autonomous persons) will necessarily be led to endorse it. Consider again Benn's story of Alan on the beach. Suppose that Betty continues to frustrate his actions, in the sense that every time he seeks to act, she seeks to interfere, by handcuffing him, taking the pebbles from the beach, or whatever. Why would Alan object? Basic to any plausible answer is that Alan conceives of himself as an agent whose deliberations about what he should do normally determine his own actions. It is not morally neutral to him whether he or Betty decides what he is to do; *the moral default is that he decides what he is to do, and some special case needs to be made for letting another's deliberations determine his actions*. It seems impossible that Alan could conceive of himself as a self-directed agent (who is also morally autonomous) without claiming this basic moral default. Suppose that he renounces this default – as a utilitarian acquaintance of mine purports to do. When such an agent decides to α, he entertains no moral presumption that he should α rather than, say, β, which is what another has decided he is to do. Should he be made to β without justification, it would be inappropriate for him to experience resentment, indignation, blame – none would be called for, since he really has no claim to α rather than β.[70] They are both competing judgments about what he should do, neither having any intrinsic moral privilege. That he has decided that he should α in itself provides no more guidance about what he should than that another has decided that he should β.

The dissent of my utilitarian acquaintance notwithstanding, such a denial undermines one's sense of one's own agency as a self-directed person. Crucial to one's own self-conception is that one's practical reason is just that: one reasons about what to do because it has the practical consequence of determining what one does. This seems not to be the case with schizoid personalities, who apparently see others as controlling their activities, and so conceive of the *deliberating* self as alienated from the *acting* self.[71] If the deliberating self is not to be similarly alienated from its activities, it must suppose that, in lieu of special considerations, its deliberations guide its activity.

Underlying this argument for the fundamental liberal principle (which I have only sketched here) is the supposition that we are indeed self-directing agents in this sense. As I said, this supposes that we are not schizoid; it also supposes that we are not "role-directed" personalities, for whom all actions are required by social scripts, and the proper performance of these scripts is determined by the audience, not each of us qua actors.[72] Imagine we were such people (as Clifford Geertz suggests the traditional Balinese might be).[73] I need not advance a moral claim to act as I have decided, for as I would conceive of myself, there is nothing special about my deliberations in deciding what I should do. The script, and the audience's reaction, is what counts. The fundamental liberal principle would be as alien to such people as many philosophers would have us believe it is to us.

My claim, then, is that the fundamental liberal principle only gets its grip on those who are self-directed in the minimal sense I have been discussing. This can be understood as the ultra-minimal conception of personal autonomy on which liberalism is founded. It is not in itself a notion of moral autonomy. Although to advance liberalism's basic moral claim the agent must be morally autonomous, before he is even interested in such a claim he must possess the non-moral characteristic of conceiving of himself as self-directed or what Benn calls a "natural person":

> The use of expressions such as "decision making," "making a choice," "forming an intention," suggest a kind of creativity in personal causation, in which the relation between agent and process is initiated by his decision is more like that between a potter and his pot or an architect and his plan, than like the relation between a skidding car and the resulting accident....
> ...It is this consciousness of one's own thought as the prolegomenon to intended action that underlies a person's conviction that he *makes* decisions – that, unlike skids or lightening strikes, they do not just happen to him.[74]

In this ultra-minimal sense, liberalism supposes that people are "self-ruled" – they are in charge of themselves.

Vb The Ultra-Minimal View Contrasted with Personal Autonomy as Self-Authorship

The case I have sketched for the fundamental liberal principle is grounded on an ultra-minimal conception of personal autonomy, and is to be distinguished from accounts of liberalism that accord primacy to a thicker conception of personal autonomy.[75] Ultra-minimal personal autonomy is consistent with many of the character traits that proponents of personal autonomy deem heteronomous. A self-directed person may be guided by superstitious beliefs, be totally unreflective about his commitments, have conflicting desires and inconsistent beliefs, or live according to traditional rules simply because he has been brought up to. All these traits are consistent with being an agent who sees his actions as following from his own deliberations (based, to be sure, on unreflective, traditional, or superstitious considerations).

Steven Wall advances a "perfectionist" conception of "personal autonomy" according to which it is an "ideal of people charting their own course through life, fashioning their character by self-consciously choosing projects and taking up commitments from a wide range of eligible alternatives, and making something out of their lives according to their own understanding of what is valuable and worth doing."[76] In a similar vein, Joseph Raz maintains that "[t]he autonomous person is one who makes his own life," while Robert Young tells us that "[t]he fundamental idea in autonomy is that of authoring one's own world."[77] Although these formulations are by no means identical, all identify autonomy with being the author of one's life. An autonomous life is chosen by the agent rather than, say, dictated by tradition; most articulations of this ideal require a wide range of choices through which "one makes something" out of one's life.

Personal autonomy as self-authorship is a controversial ideal that is difficult to publicly justify. The self-authorship metaphor points to an aesthetic view of life in which one's life is a creation and the agent the artist. The metaphor is not misleading; such conceptions of autonomy are offered by "perfectionist liberals."[78] The very idea of perfection indicates a quasi-artistic attitude towards one's life, as a work to be perfected. It hardly seems that all agents have reason to adopt such a view. Consider one whose goals are entirely focused on bringing about states of affairs that do not include the perfection of human beings but, say, the protection of nature or scientific discovery. The latter may involve the perfection of human nature (the former may well call for thwarting it), but the point is that these goals are not about human nature and its excellences; they concern the production of certain states of affairs that do not make necessary reference to the flourishing of humans.[79] If these states of affairs can be brought about without perfecting human nature, or without a life of self-authorship, that in no way detracts from their value. Agents pursuing such states of affairs are not self-focused; they do not take up an attitude of creative authorship to their lives, but possess practical reasons to investigate and change the world in a variety of ways. As such, they are not committed to personal autonomy as self-authorship or perfectionism.

To be sure, the perfectionist can argue that they *should* be: he can insist that there is a reason for them to care, and they should see it. I am not seeking to refute such arguments, but to show that they are controversial, and certainly make claims that go far beyond ultra-minimal autonomy. Our enviromentalist or scientist, I have argued, is committed to seeing himself as an agent with reasons to act, so he must conceive of himself as a self-directed agent; many do not – and as far as I can see, rationally so – conceive of themselves as authors or creators of their own lives, seeking to make something out of them through their chosen modes of self-authorship.

Still, it might be thought that all self-directed agents must possess personal (or what Forst in Chapter 10 of the present volume calls "ethical") autonomy in the sense that they have and exercise the capacity to, as Waldron says, "defy desires and inclinations" that are alien to their conception of the good (Chapter 13 in the present volume). And certainly achieving some minimal degree of integration and consistency is necessary for self-direction; it must be the case that one has enough of a self for one to be able to make decisions, as opposed to merely giving in to one inclination after another. But a self-directed person may not be one who affirms a way of life, or who sees himself as following personal imperatives about what is to be done. Self-directed agents may fall well short of fully integrated personalities.[80] They may possess nothing so grand as a conception of the good life, much less an examined life: the much-derided beer-drinking[81] football fan – whose week is, unreflectively, centered around Sunday's Buffalo Bills game – possesses ultra-minimal personal autonomy.

Vc Personal and Moral Autonomy

If I am right about this, the fundamental liberal principle does not rest on a commitment to a "perfectionist" conception of "personal autonomy." It would, however, be wrong to conclude that conceptions of personal autonomy more demanding than the ultra-minimal notion have no place within liberal morality and politics. We have seen that the appeal to the fundamental liberal principle presupposes that both the person appealing to the principle, and the person to whom the appeal is directed, possess moral autonomy (Section III). That is, both are supposed to possess the ability to distinguish her own specific wants and aims from the requirements of public morality. Now this moral capacity is bound up with fairly sophisticated cognitive skills. As the work of Lawrence Kohlberg and others has shown, to be able to distinguish what you want or prefer, or your goals and aspirations, from what can be universalized and thus accepted by rational others, requires a cognitive ability to take up the perspectives of others.[82] One must be able to put oneself in their place, consider what reasons they have, and so whether they have reasons to act in certain ways. Moreover, because the fundamental liberal principle is open-ended insofar as it only requires that justifications be provided but does not provide a canonical list of those justifications, liberal citizens have an ongoing commitment to examine proposed justifications and enter into justificatory argument.

The skills required by moral autonomy overlap with those that are often identified with personal autonomy.[83] Unless a citizen is self-reflective about her own reasons to act, and so understands whether her reasons stem from personal commitments or can be shared from a public perspective, she will be unable to determine what is required by a publicly justified morality. A person who is unable to distinguish her goals and personal commitments from moral reasons will not be able to grasp the idea that moral reasons may require her to put aside her goals, for she will insist that her beliefs and values are a seamless web. It is no defense to say of such people that the basic premises of their moral thinking lie in their personal – say, religious – convictions and so they are, understandably, unable to contemplate the possibility that the demands of public secular morality can be distinguished from, much less override, their religious convictions.[84] Because they are insufficiently reflective about the nature of their reasons, and have an insufficiently developed capacity to see things from the perspectives of others, they are apt to press morally unjustified demands, and fail to recognize the requirements of public morality.

This points to the error of hyper-ecumenical versions of "political liberalism." Political liberalism seeks to identify liberal principles endorsed by public reason. Yet many versions have been especially accommodating to religious reasoning, often including versions of fundamentalism. The idea has been that, insofar as we seek truly public reasoning, these religious reasoners must be brought into public justification. To be sure, political liberals insist on limits: to qualify as "reasonable," citizens must tolerate the competing views of others, and be willing to seek, and abide by, fair terms of social cooperation with them. But toleration of others is not sufficient to exercise moral autonomy. Consider a fundamentalist religion that is internally committed – committed simply in virtue of its own tenets – to tolerating other religions and embracing a fair scheme of cooperation with others. If this is the sole source of these commitments, when contemplating objections from others that some policy was not tolerant, or not fair, members of this religion would still appeal to their religious convictions in deciding what constitutes toleration and fairness. They would not concern themselves with providing other citizens with public reasons in support of their interpretations – they would have failed to exercise moral autonomy. Only if they have developed the cognitive ability to distinguish what is a reason to them from what is a reason for others can they justify a substantively autonomous morality and laws that express the general will.

We can now understand the ambivalent stance towards religious reasoning that, I think, has characterized most modern liberal thinking. On the one hand, liberals insist that people be free to pursue religious convictions as a matter of personal liberty. Yet because they are not public reasons, and further because many religions insist on the superiority of religious to public shared reasoning (in terms of the force of their respective reasons for actions), liberals (perhaps especially outside of America) are typically wary of appeals to religion in public life. Moreover, insofar as some religious communities are totalistic, seeking to provide a pervasive religious structure for every member's personal and intellectual life, liberals object that such communities undermine citizens' moral autonomy. This is especially troubling if communities seek to raise their young in ways that undermine their children's personal autonomy by thwarting development of their skills of self-reflection and role-taking. We might say, then, that moral autonomy requires *minimal personal autonomy*: the ability to reflect on the adequacy of one's own moral reasons, and to distinguish one's own reasons from the reasons of others.

It might be objected that this analysis endorses intolerance towards religious groups such as the Protestant fundamentalists, some types of devout Catholics, or the Amish. Such objections are based on a common but nevertheless erroneous simple inference from general philosophical principles to public policies. Public policy is the realm of complex and competing considerations, including problems of abuse of power, incentives of government agents and legislators, epistemic limits of government, difficulty of framing adequate legislation and safeguards, undesirable side-effects, and so on. Nothing directly follows about what laws ought to be enacted from a general philosophical conclusion. It does follow from this analysis, though, that ways of life that seek to undermine minimal personal autonomy, and so ultimately the moral autonomy of their members, are illiberal. How a liberal state should deal with illiberal ways of life is a complex and difficult issue, but little headway can be made without recognizing that they are indeed illiberal in the sense that they are based on practices and beliefs that are hostile to the very capacities and dispositions that render liberal public morality possible.

While the capacity for, and exercise of, critical self-reflection is required for a liberal moral order, the conception of personal autonomy is still minimalist insofar as it is not part of the justified conception that citizens reflect on their own plans and projects, except insofar as they distinguish these from public morality. Thus the commitment to personal autonomy necessary for a liberal moral order does not require that all citizens be self-reflective about their goals, aims, or projects. The requisite personal autonomy can be fully achieved by those who embrace traditional, customary, or religious ways of life, not out of explicit choice, but because they have been reared in them. However, the traditionalist cannot be so immersed in traditional culture that he is unable to distinguish the reasons it provides him from the moral reasons that apply to all.

To many this seems a precarious compromise: liberal morality allows one to be an unreflective traditionalist in many aspects of one's life, but not to become so immersed in one's traditions that one confuses them with public reason. While indeed precarious, this is precisely the line that liberal political culture walks. It can admit traditionalism, and need not seek to turn all citizens into liberal-Millian individualists – up to a point. The point is that citizens must be sufficiently liberal to reflect on their traditions and observe that they do not form the basis of public reasoning, and so they must be prepared to also live in a public world that, because religious reasons are not reasons for all citizens, must be a secular world. More than that, they must understand that these public reasons will often override their important goals.

VI Conclusion: Walking the Liberal Tightrope

My aim has been to show, first, that the most plausible understanding of the fundamental liberal principle presupposes a Kantian conception of moral autonomy. Showing this required inquiry into the nature of practical reasons and morality. It is fashionable nowadays to claim that one can engage in political philosophy without such investigations, that we can have a purely political theory of liberalism. It is impossible to see how this can be done; if liberal principles are to be practical, they must provide us with practical reasons. But then we need to know what practical reasons are, and how they relate to liberal principles. Whether or not we need a metaphysics of liberalism, we certainly require a metaethics of it. When we do develop such a metaethics, I argued in Section III, we are led to a Kantian conception of moral autonomy.

Section IV linked this conception of moral autonomy to public laws, freedom, public reason, and the general will. Kant's basic intuition, that our capacity for moral autonomy leads to a substantive universalistic morality was, in its essence, vindicated, though not, of course, simply reiterated.

Having argued in favor of a Kantian understanding of moral autonomy, I then turned in Section V to consider the relationship of liberalism to conceptions of personal autonomy. The results were not quite so neat. Although an ultra-minimal conception of personal autonomy underlies the basic liberal principle, autonomy understood as self-authorship does not; indeed it seems a controversial and rationally rejectable view. However, I have just argued that the very commitment of liberalism to moral autonomy itself leads to a public commitment to minimal personal autonomy as a capacity the exercise of which is necessary to a moral order based on the fundamental liberal principle. A liberal moral and political order, I have claimed, walks a tightrope. On one side is immersion into traditional cultures and religions, which insist that their reason is the reason of all; on the other is the public proclamation of the liberal ideal of individuality as part of the public morality, and so the illegitimacy of most traditional and religious ways of life. Only societies composed of citizens who are sufficiently self-reflective to recognize the distinction between their personal (or subcultural) and public reasons, and who embrace diverse communities while recognizing their non-public character, can walk the liberal tightrope.[85] Happily, our modern liberal societies seem reasonably adept at this particular balancing act.

Notes

1. On the idea of a liberal public morality, see my *Value and Justification: The Foundations of Liberal Theory* (Cambridge: Cambridge University Press, 1990),

pp. 323ff; *Justificatory Liberalism* (New York: Oxford University Press, 1996), pp. 120ff; *Social Philosophy* (Armonk, NY: M. E. Sharpe, 1999).
2. I consider these in Section V.
3. John Christman, after discussing the ideal of personal autonomy, notes that it seems an "abrupt departure from the traditional Kantian notion," though he adds that "despite.... [the] radical differences, there remain crucial aspects that our core idea of autonomy shares with its Kantian ancestor." "Introduction" to his edited collection, *The Inner Citadel: Essays on Individual Autonomy* (New York: Oxford University Press, 1989), p. 14. Kant scholars have agreed; see Roger J. Sullivan, *Immanuel Kant's Moral Theory* (Cambridge: Cambridge University Press, 1989), pp. 46–47. Gerald Dworkin, however, sees moral autonomy as a particular case of the wider notion of autonomy as critical self-reflection. *The Theory and Practice of Autonomy* (Cambridge: Cambridge University Press, 1988), p. 48. Compare my argument in Section V.
4. In the end, the difference between our positions may be modest: the closer one connects the two ideas, the more blurred the distinction becomes.
5. See Steven Wall, *Liberalism, Perfectionism and Restraint* (Cambridge: Cambridge University Press, 1998), Part II.
6. As attested to by the work of the most important contemporary liberal autonomist, Joseph Raz. See his *The Morality of Freedom* (Oxford: Clarendon Press, 1986), chapter 14.
7. Harry Brighouse, "Is there a Neutral Justification for Liberalism?" *Pacific Philosophical Quarterly*, vol. 77 (September 1996): 193–215, at p. 209. This, I shall argue, gets things almost precisely backwards.
8. See, for example, Joel Feinberg, *Harm to Self* (New York: Oxford University Press, 1986), chapter 18.
9. The importance of Kantian autonomy is clearest in Rawls' "Kantian Constructivism in Moral Theory" in Samuel Freeman (ed.), *John Rawls: Collected Papers* (Cambridge, MA: Harvard University Press, 1999), pp. 303–358. Kantian autonomy remains a basic feature of political liberalism. See Rawls' *Political Liberalism*, paperback edition (New York: Columbia University Press, 1996), Lecture II.
10. Stanley Benn, *A Theory of Freedom* (Cambridge: Cambridge University Press, 1988), p. 87.
11. Feinberg, *Harm to Self*, p. 9. Benn is talking about interference, a wider notion than Feinberg's "coercion," so these are not identical formulations.
12. Feinberg, *Harm to Self*, pp. 14ff.
13. John Locke, *Second Treatise of Government*, in Peter Laslett (ed.), *Two Treatises of Government* (Cambridge: Cambridge University Press, 1960), p. 287 (Section 4).
14. It is sometimes objected that this view requires that there be an uncontroversial, basic, negative conception of liberty, which is at the foundation of morality, and so does not itself presuppose any moral claims. If, it is charged, liberty is itself a moralized concept, or one that involves moral ideas (as, for example, some concepts of positive liberty seem to), then a basic claim to liberty cannot be the presupposition of all other moral claims. There is something to this charge: for the fundamental liberal principle to make

sense, there must be some sensible liberty claims that are claims to noninterference, and that do not themselves presuppose justified moral norms. Thus it must make sense – and it does – to say that in an amoral Hobbesian state of nature, people interfere with each other, and in that sense limit each other's liberty. What is not supposed by this account, however, is that this use of "liberty" exhausts all sensible liberty claims (positive or norm-based liberty claims still might make sense and be important) or that "interference" is an uncontroversial idea, such that we never disagree about what constitutes an interference. We do, of course, disagree, which means we disagree about the interpretation and application of the fundamental liberal principle.

15. Unless specified to the contrary, "reasons" throughout this chapter means "reasons for action."
16. Geoffrey Brennan and Loren Lomasky, *Democracy and Decision: The Pure Theory of Electoral Preference* (Cambridge: Cambridge University Press, 1993), p. 9. Footnote in original text omitted.
17. Robert Nozick, *The Nature of Rationality* (Princeton: Princeton University Press, 1993), p. 164.
18. See my essay "Why All Welfare States (Including *Laissez-Faire* Ones) Are Unreasonable," *Social Philosophy and Policy*, vol. 15 (June, 1998): 1–33; "Goals, Symbols, Principles: Nozick on Practical Rationality" in David Schmidtz (ed.), *Robert Nozick* (Cambridge: Cambridge University Press, 2002), pp. 83–130; "The Limits of *Homo Economicus*" in Gerald F. Gaus, Julian Lamont, and Christi Favor (eds.), *Values, Justice, and Economics* (Amsterdam: Rodopi, forthcoming).
19. This defines instrumental reason simply as effective action, with no regard to justified belief, a view that I argue against in "The Limits of *Homo Economicus*." This simple characterization suffices for our present purposes; a more adequate conception would push the analysis of rationality even more towards the internalist position defended in Sections IIId–e.
20. See David Gauthier, *Morals By Agreement* (Oxford: Clarendon Press, 1986).
21. The classic paper on this issue is, of course, William K. Frankena, "Obligation and Motivation in Recent Moral Philosophy" in K. E. Goodpaster (ed.), *Perspectives on Morality: Essays by William K. Frankena* (Notre Dame: University of Notre Dame Press, 1976), pp. 49–73. See also Philippa Foot, *Virtues and Vices* (Berkeley: University of California Press, 1978), pp. 157–173. For an effective criticism of Foot's externalism, see Michael Smith, *The Moral Problem* (Oxford: Balckwell, 1994), chapter 3.
22. This view is suggested by Wall, *Liberalism, Perfectionism, and Restraint*, p. 118.
23. I contrast internalism and externalism as accounts of obligation and of reasons, in *Value and Justification*, pp. 153ff, 261ff.
24. See Smith, *The Moral Problem*, pp. 7ff.
25. Judith Jarvis Thomson, "Killing, Letting Die and The Trolley Problem," *The Monist*, vol. 59 (1976): 204–217; "A Defense of Abortion," *Philosophy & Public Affairs*, vol. 1 (1971): 47–66.
26. See, for example, Michael Tooley, "An Irrelevant Consideration: Killing versus Letting Die" in B. Steinboch (ed.), *Killing and Letting Die* (Englewood Cliffs, NJ: Prentice-Hall, 1980), pp. 56–62.

27. See further my essays: "Goals, Symbols, and Principles," "Why All Welfare States (Including *Laissez-Faire* Ones) Are Unreasonable," and "The Limits of *Homo Economicus.*"
28. I analyze this rough idea of one reason "outweighing" another in "Why All Welfare States (Including *Laissez-Faire* Ones) Are Unreasonable" and in "The Limits of *Homo Economicus.*" The rough idea suffices for our present purposes.
29. See Donald Davidson, "Actions, Reason and Causes" in his *Essays on Actions and Events* (Oxford: Oxford University Press. 1980).
30. Foot, *Virtues and Vices*, p. 179. See also David Copp, *Morality, Normativity and Society* (New York: Oxford University Press, 1995).
31. See Stanley Benn and G. F. Gaus, "Practical Rationality and Commitment," *American Philosophical Quarterly*, vol. 23 (1986): 255–266.
32. See further my *Value and Justification*, pp. 266ff.
33. See Smith, *The Moral Problem.*
34. For a position along these lines, see David A. J. Richards, *A Theory of Reasons for Action* (Oxford: Oxford University Press, 1971).
35. See Henry E. Allison, *Kant's Theory of Freedom* (Cambridge: Cambridge University Press, 1990), p. 98.
36. "The idea that autonomy is responsiveness to reasons is of course not new. A version of this idea is central to Kant's ethical theory...." George Sher, *Beyond Neutrality: Perfectionism and Politics* (Cambridge: Cambridge University Press, 1997), p. 48.
37. See Allison, *Kant's Theory of Freedom*, p. 98.
38. Susan Wolf, *Freedom Within Reason* (Oxford: Oxford University Press, 1990), pp. 67ff.
39. Ibid., p. 68.
40. See Christine Korsgaard, *The Sources of Normativity* (Cambridge: Cambridge University Press, 1996).
41. See Sullivan, *Immanuel Kant's Moral Theory*, chapters 4 and 5; Allison, *Kant's Theory of Freedom*, chapter 5.
42. I have tried to explicate this distinction in detail in *Value and Justification*. See also my "What is Deontology?" Parts 1 and 2, *Journal of Value Inquiry*, vol. 35 (2001): 27–42, 179–193.
43. See, however, Jeremy Waldron's insightful chapter (13) in the present volume. I follow Charles Larmore in understanding the contrast between attractive and imperitival moralities as dividing pre-modern and modern ethics. See Larmore's *The Morals of Modernity* (Cambridge: Cambridge University Press, 1996), chapter 1.
44. Immanuel Kant, *Foundations of the Metaphysics of Morals*, Lewis White Beck (trans.) (Indianapolis: Bobbs-Merrill, 1959), pp. 60ff [pp. 442ff of the Prussian Academy edition].
45. See Rawls, *Political Liberalism*, pp. 50ff.
46. See my *Value and Justification*, pp. 292–330. Compare Rawls, *Political Liberalism*, p. 51.
47. Jan Narveson, *The Libertarian Idea* (Philadelphia: Temple University Press, 1988), p. 66.

48. I have considered this view in more depth in my "Property, Rights and Freedom," *Social Philosophy & Policy*, vol. 11 (Summer 1994): 209–40.
49. This claim is argued for by Hillel Steiner, *An Essay on Rights* (Cambridge, MA: Blackwell, 1994), chapters 2 and 3.
50. This could, I suppose, be interpreted as a sort of moral dilemma produced by imcompossible oughts. Although not unintelligible, I have argued that such conceptions of deontic logic are by no means compelling. See my essay "Dirty Hands" in R. G. Frey and Christopher Heath Wellman (eds.), *A Companion to Applied Ethics* (Oxford: Basil Blackwell, 2003), pp. 167–179.
51. "Central to understanding paternalism is the conjunction of two factors: an imposition and a particular rationale. X acts to diminish Y's freedom, to the end that Y's good is secured." John Kleinig, *Paternalism* (Totowa, NJ: Rowman and Allenheld, 1983), p. 18.
52. See my *Social Philosophy*, chapter 11.
53. For Hohfeld's classic analysis, see his "Some Fundamental Legal Conceptions As Applied in Judicial Reasoning," *Yale Law Review*, vol. 23 (1913): 16–59.
54. See Allison, *Kant's Theory of Freedom*, pp. 94–106.
55. This view was famously upheld by Thomas Nagel in his *The Possibility of Altruism* (Princeton: Princeton University Press, 1979). Cf. Christine Korsgaard, "The Reasons We Can Share" in her *Creating the Kingdom of Ends* (Cambridge: Cambridge University Press, 1996), pp. 275–310.
56. See, for example, Korsgaard, *The Sources of Normativity*, pp. 136ff; Philip Pettit, *The Common Mind* (Oxford: Oxford University Press, 1993).
57. See my *Contemporary Theories of Liberalism: Public Reason as a Post-Enlightenment Project* (London: Sage Publications, 2003), pp. 104–113.
58. See ibid., chapter 1. See also my entry on "Public Reason," *International Encyclopedia of the Social and Behavioural Sciences* (Oxford: Elsevier Scientific Publishers, 2002); John Gray, *Enlightenment's Wake: Politics and Culture at The Close of the Modern Age* (London: Routledge, 1995), pp. 122ff.
59. Rawls, *Political Liberalism*, p. 36.
60. Kant, *Metaphysical Elements of Justice*, Lewis White Beck, trans. (Indianapolis: Bobbs-Merrill, 1959), p. 76 (Section 44).
61. "Non-trivial" because even on the view according to which all must share all the same reasons, it is trivially true that only justifications that provide everyone with reasons justify moral impositions.
62. Kant, *Foundations of The Metaphysics of Morals*, p. 51 [p. 433 of the Prussian Academy edition].
63. Ibid.
64. Immanuel Kant, "On the Common Saying: 'This May be True in Theory, but it Does not Apply in Practice'," in Hans Reiss (ed.), *Kant's Political Writings* (Cambridge: Cambridge University Press, 1970), p. 79. Emphasis in original.
65. Ibid.
66. I consider this objection more fully in my *Social Philosophy*, chapter 5.
67. Kant, "Theory and Practice," p. 79.
68. See Bernard Bosanquet, *"The Philosophical Theory of the State,"* in Gerald Gaus and William Sweet (eds.), *The Philosophical Theory of the State and Related*

Essays (Indianapolis: St. Augustine Press, 2001). Cf. John W. Chapman, *Rousseau – Totalitarian or Liberal?* (New York: Columbia University Press, 1956).
69. I consider the relationship between legislation, public reason, and Rosseau's theory of the general will in "Does Democracy Reveal the Will of the People? Four Takes on Rousseau," *Australasian Journal of Philosophy*, vol. 75 (June 1997): 141–162.
70. On the appropriateness of emotions, see my *Value and Justification*, chapter II. See also Wolf, *Freedom Within Reason*, especially chapter 1.
71. See further my *Value and Justification*, p. 388.
72. Ibid, pp. 385–386.
73. See Clifford Geertz, "Person, Time, and Conduct in Bali" in his *The Interpretation of Cultures* (New York: Basic Books, 1973).
74. Benn, A *Theory of Freedom*, p. 91.
75. They are often run together. In the quote from Benn (fn 74), in which he is explicating self-direction, he likens a person's relation to his life as that between a pot and a potter, thus moving to self-authorship. Sharon Hayes argues that Benn's liberalism ultimately is based on a robust conception of (personal) autonomy. See her "Autonomy and Rights in S. I. Benn's A Theory of Freedom," Ph.D. thesis, School of Humanities, Queensland University of Technology, 2000.
76. Wall, *Liberalism, Perfectionism and Restraint*, p. 203. Cf. Dworkin: "What makes an individual the particular person he is in his life plan, his projects. In pursuing autonomy, one shapes one's life, one constructs its meaning. The autonomous person gives meaning to his life." *The Theory and Practice of Autonomy*, p. 31
77. Raz, *The Morality of Freedom*, p. 375; Robert Young, *Personal Autonomy: Beyond Negative and Positive Liberty* (New York: St. Martin's Press, 1986), p. 19
78. Raz and Wall, for example.
79. On the tension between this conception of autonomy and environmental ethics, see my "Respect for Persons and Environmental Values" in Jane Kneller and Sidney Axin (eds.), *Autonomy and Community: Readings in Contemporary Kantian Social Philosophy* (Albany, NY: SUNY Press, 1998), pp. 239–264.
80. Benn, A *Theory of Freedom*, chapter 10.
81. The implication, perhaps obvious to most academics, is that a wine-drinking fan would achieve an altogether higher level of autonomy.
82. See, for example, Lawrence Kohlberg, *The Philosophy of Moral Development* (New York: Harper & Row, 1981); Bärbel Inhelder and Jean Piaget, "The Growth of Logical Thinking from Childhood to Adolescence" in Howard E. Gruber and J. Jacques Vonéche (eds.), *The Essential Piaget* (London: Routledge & Kegan Paul, 1977), pp. 403–444, at 440–41. I discuss other literature in *Value and Justification*, p. 260.
83. Interestingly, Wall distances his perfectionist conception of autonomy from autonomy as self-reflection. See *Liberalism, Perfectionism and Restraint*, pp. 128–129.
84. See Christopher Eberle, *Religious Convictions in Liberal Politics* (Cambridge: Cambridge University Press, 2002).

85. I thus concur with Steven Macedo: "Liberal citizens should be committed to honoring the public demands of liberal justice in all departments of their lives. They should be alert to the possibility that religious imperatives, or even inherited notions of what it means to be a good parent, spouse, or lover, might in fact run afoul of equal freedom. A basic aim of liberal education should be to impart to all children the ability to reflect critically on their personal and public commitments for the sake of honoring our shared principles of liberal justice and equal rights for all." And Macedo is clear that "[t]he point is not to promote a comprehensive philosophical doctrine of autonomy or individuality." *Diversity and Distrust* (Cambridge, MA: Harvard University Press, 2000), pp. 238–239.

13

Moral Autonomy and Personal Autonomy

Jeremy Waldron

I

Modern philosophers distinguish between *personal* autonomy and *moral* autonomy.[1] Talk of personal autonomy evokes the image of a person in charge of his life, not just following his desires but choosing which of his desires to follow. It is not an immoral idea, but it has relatively little to do with morality. Those who value it do not value it as part of the moral enterprise of reconciling one person's interest with another's; instead, they see it as a particular way of understanding what each person's interest consists in. Moral autonomy, by contrast, is associated specifically with the relation between one person's pursuit of his own ends and others' pursuit of theirs. This is particularly true of its Kantian manifestations. A person is autonomous in the moral sense when he is not guided just by his own conception of happiness, but by a universalized concern for the ends of all rational persons.

Modern proponents of personal autonomy are anxious to emphasize the distance between their conception and the moral conception.[2] But I think it is worth considering some of the overlaps and affinities between them. We all know that autonomy in the moral sense is supposed to engage very specific capacities of rational deliberation and self-control. And these might seem out of place in a conception of autonomy oriented towards the pursuit of the good life at an individual level. In fact, modern theorists of personal autonomy have also tended to emphasize the engagement of specific capacities – the capacity for reflection, for example, and for what some have called "second-order" motivation – and these turn out to be similar in many respects to the capacities implicated in the Kantian account.

So a sharp distinction between moral autonomy and personal autonomy may not be available. Is it, in any case, desirable? I am not sure. Rawlsian liberals emphasize the importance of subjecting individuals' pursuit of the good to moral principles of justice: the right has priority over the good, they say. Now, the sharper the distinction between personal autonomy and moral autonomy, the more challenging it is to explain how this priority is supposed to work, for the more alien the requirements of morality will seem from the personal point of view. On the other hand, if we blur the distinction between pursuing a conception of the good and following principles of right, we open the possibility that each person has his own moral standards implicated already in his personal view about what makes life worth living. And this too seems unsatisfactory, because it undermines the idea of the right as something shared rather than as something intensely personal.

In what follows, I shall consider these issues from two angles. I shall look first at the contrast in Kant's moral philosophy between the pursuit of individual happiness and the realm of autonomy and free moral agency. That distinction looks clear enough; but as we shall see, Kant blurs it somewhat by characterizing an individual's entitlement to pursue his own happiness in his own way as a fundamental principle of *freedom*. Then, having complicated the Kantian picture, I would like to look more squarely at the positions held by modern liberals, and consider how sharp they need the distinction between the right and the good to be, and how sharp they can afford it to be, both in light of the tasks of morality and in light of the actual characteristics of people's moral and ethical convictions.

II

"No one," said Kant, "can coerce me to be happy in his way (as he thinks of the welfare of other human beings); instead each may seek his happiness in the way that seems good to him...." This, Kant said, was the first half of "the principle of freedom" for the constitution of a commonwealth. (The second half added the familiar proviso: "... provided he does not infringe upon that freedom of others to strive for a like end which can coexist with the freedom of everyone in accordance with a possible universal law.")[3]

"Each may seek his happiness in his own way." For us – I mean for us modern liberals – this sounds like a principle of *autonomy*. But on Kant's account, autonomy and happiness are supposed to operate in utterly different realms. In the *Groundwork*, Kant associated autonomy with the will's ability to determine itself in accordance with the form of universality, unconstrained by nature or inclination.[4] Autonomy is "the supreme principle of morality," and morality is "[t]he direct opposite of... the principle of one's own happiness [being] made the determining ground of the will."[5] Happiness is about needs and inclinations, and as such it must be regarded as "a powerful counterweight to all the commands of duty."[6] Kant says that I become an autonomous being only when I rise above any concern for happiness and follow the moral law for its own sake.

Yet Kant defines the principle with which we began as a principle of *freedom*, and freedom – while not exactly synonymous with autonomy in his system – is not as far from it as the dissonance between happiness and morality might suggest. He says it is "the only original right belonging to man by virtue of his humanity,"[7] and humanity is supposed to be something "holy" in us, something characteristic of us as ends in ourselves. So what is going on? If there is a place for the free pursuit of happiness in a Kantian system, does that pursuit have its own dimension of autonomy? If it does, what is the relation between *that* autonomy and the autonomy associated with the rigors and severity of the moral law?

Another way of posing this issue is to ask: why does it matter, from the perspective of autonomy, who lays down the conception of happiness that I follow. Why, on Kant's account, is it important that my pursuit of happiness be determined *by me* rather than by another person or by the state? Certainly the latter would involve heteronomy. But heteronomy is involved in the pursuit of happiness anyway, on Kant's account. Where one finds happiness is an empirical matter; it is a question of the relation between one's needs and inclinations and the circumstances in which one finds oneself. From this point of view, the influence of another person – or the coercive influence of the state – is just one empirical contingency among others. If by chance I grow up in Iowa, it is less likely that I will acquire a taste for surfing than if I grow up in San Diego. And if I grow up in a Lutheran community, I may not learn to dance. Why is the (sociological) fact that my community frowns on dancing any different from the (geographical) fact that I live a thousand miles from the ocean? Both are contingent features of the empirical world; and happiness, on Kant's account, is not supposed to be a matter of the existence or non-existence of empirical determinants but rather of how one's needs and desires are satisfied in relation to them. So, in this matter of the pursuit of happiness, what is so special – so specially bad – about coercion as an empirical determinant?

These questions invite us to reconsider the idea of a non-negotiable separation in Kant's theory between the rational capacities involved in morality and the capacities (whatever they are) that are involved in the pursuit of happiness.

One possibility is that the element of autonomy does enter the picture, but only in the second half of Kant's principle of freedom – that is, in the proviso about respecting the freedom of others: "[E]ach may seek his happiness in the way that seems good to him, *provided he does not infringe upon that freedom of others to strive for a like end which can coexist with the freedom of everyone in accordance with a possible universal law.*"[8] It is by seeing the force of, and following this part of, the principle that one reveals oneself as an autonomous being. This need not mean that the element of autonomy plays no role in the first part of the principle. Perhaps it folds back into the exercise of freedom in the following way: Kant suggests that one shouldn't (and a good person won't) regard as part of his happiness something that conflicts with morality. Happiness, he says, is not just a matter of satisfying the preferences I happen to have. "I must first be sure that I am not acting against my duty; only afterwards am I permitted to look around for happiness..."[9] Or perhaps my autonomy is revealed not by my egocentric interest in my own happiness but only by my moral interest in the happiness of all – my interest in what Paul Guyer refers to as a "*systematic distribution* of happiness, both in one's own life as a whole and in the whole community of human beings."[10] These are surely important themes in Kant's practical philosophy. But they do not actually implicate autonomy in the choices I make *among the morally acceptable options* for my happiness.[11] And so the question remains: why should the pursuit of happiness by individuals command the sort of respect that Kant's principle of freedom requires? Why exactly is *someone's pursuit of happiness* an appropriate source of moral constraint for me (or for anyone)? I can see why the exercise of a good will is something that commands respect: in that case, the autonomy that answers the command is an echo of the autonomy that elicits it. But there are all sorts of things about a person – the course of his dreams, his involuntary movements, or the rate of his heartbeat – that command no respect at all, because they are empirically determined. Why does my pursuit of happiness belong in the former rather than the latter category?

Maybe there is no answer to this question. Kant's principle of freedom is presented as a principle of external right, as a feature of his political philosophy, not his moral philosophy.[12] In that context the psychological or metaphysical nature of its exercise may be irrelevant. Freedom in Kant's external principle may be purely negative (in Berlin's sense):[13] it protects a space for choice, but it offers little in the way of a positive account of what ideally should go on in that space once the interference of others is cleared away. As "the sum of the conditions under which the choice of one can be united with the choice of another in accordance with a universal law," external right may take no interest in the content or the character of the choices it protects.[14]

About the pursuit of happiness, then, there may not be much more to be said than that I find myself making choices – pursuing my own happiness – and that the formalities of universalization require that I respect this also in all others. Kant recognizes that the pursuit of happiness is more or less unavoidable as a feature of the human condition: "To be happy is necessarily the demand of every rational but finite being..., satisfaction with one's whole existence is...a problem imposed upon him by his finite nature itself, because he is needy...."[15] It may not be a moral end,[16] but it is an end we have by natural necessity, an assertoric imperative.[17] So perhaps one could argue that any sort of respect for persons is bound to include respect for their pursuit of happiness, inasmuch as it is a necessary incident of their (human) being.

I wonder, though, whether it might be possible to go beyond this, in the interpretation of Kant's position. Granted that the principle of freedom protects only choice as such, without any reference to its content or character, and granted that the pursuit of happiness is not the main field in which we display our moral powers – still, is there not, on Kant's account, anything remotely like autonomy involved in our figuring out what our happiness consists in? I said at the outset that modern liberals distinguish between personal autonomy and moral autonomy in order to distance themselves from the latter, which they associate with Kant. But I want to know whether there is anything approximating personal autonomy in Kant's account of happiness.

One thing that Kant emphasizes is the uniqueness (or at least the idiosyncracy) of each person's happiness:

Only experience can teach us what brings joy. Only the natural drives for food, sex, rest, and movement, and (as our natural predispositions develop) for honor, for enlarging our cognition and so forth, can tell each of us, and each only in his particular way, in what he will *find* those joys; and, in the same way, only experience can teach him the means by which to *seek* them. All apparently a priori reasoning about this comes down to nothing but experience raised by induction to generality, a generality still so tenuous that everyone must be allowed countless exceptions in order to adapt his choice of a way of life to his particular inclinations and his susceptibility to satisfaction. . . . [18]

Allen Rosen invites us to take this as the basis of Kant's principle of freedom: "[B]ecause . . . no one else can decide what will make [a person] happy, his right to pursue his own happiness cannot be usurped by a self-appointed proxy (for example, a paternalistic government), but must instead be exercised by the individual concerned."[19] Letting each pursue happiness in his own way may not be respect for moral personality, but it is respect for something like identity – for each person's uniqueness and the particularity of his situation and experience.

Kant also puts weight in one or two places on a normative distinction between action and passivity in the pursuit of happiness. As he articulates the principle of freedom in "Theory and Practice," he deplores the passivity of people who are subject to an official conception of happiness: "the subjects, like minor children . . . , are constrained to behave only passively, so as to wait only upon the judgment of the head of state as to how they *should be* happy. . . ."[20] Paul Guyer has drawn attention to some remarks in Kant's *Reflexionen* that suggest that we are more content when we view ourselves actively as authors of our happiness, rather than simply having contentment wash over us.[21] In this regard, we should also not neglect the importance Kant accords to self-cultivation. Though this is presented in the *Groundwork* as a moral duty,[22] it is not just a matter of *moral* perfectibility. It is a moral duty in relation to all aspects of one's natural potential:

> He owes it to himself (as a rational being) not to leave idle and, as it were, rusting away the natural predispositions and capacities that his reason can some day use. . . . [A]s a being capable of ends . . . , he must owe the use of his powers not merely to natural instinct but rather to the freedom by which he determines their scope.[23]

This responsibility covers physical as well as mental self-improvement, though, as Kant goes on to say,

> [w]hich of these natural perfections should take precedence, and in what proportion one against the other it may be a human being's duty to himself to make these natural perfections his end, are matters left for him to choose in accordance with his rational reflection about what sort of life he would like to lead and whether he has the powers necessary for it (e.g., whether it should be a trade, commerce, or a learned profession).[24]

This remarkable passage puts Kant almost in the company of those like Humboldt and J. S. Mill who emphasize the importance of a person's taking responsibility for his own individuality and for the overall shape of his life and career.[25]

Finally, we should consider Kant's views about the role of reason in the pursuit of individual happiness. His observation that bestial contentment would be better secured by instinct than by reason is well known, though what is usually inferred from this is that the function of reason has nothing to do with happiness.[26] In fact, however, Kant suggests that reason does have a specific role in this regard:

> Certainly, our well-being and woe count for *a very great deal* in the appraisal of our practical reason.... The human being is a being with needs, insofar as he belongs to the sensible world, and to this extent his reason certainly has a commission for the side of his sensibility which it cannot refuse, to attend to its interests, and to form practical maxims with a view to happiness....[27]

It is important to see that reason's commission here is not just a matter of prudential calculation – that is, of the efficient relation of means to ends. That would be a modest and familiar function that even Humean reason could discharge, a function highlighted in Kant's talk of "hypothetical imperatives."[28] But Kant is quite skeptical about reason's ability to deliver in this regard. He suspects that the instrumentalities of happiness more or less defy rational calculation.[29] Christine Korsgaard has suggested that the familiar picture in which nature supplies the ends and reason the means may have to be given up as an interpretation of Kant.[30] She says we should take at face value a remark in the *Groundwork* where Kant suggests that reason has "the presumption..., to think out for itself a plan for happiness," and that we should attend also to some remarks in the essay *Conjectural Beginnings of Human History* that associate the Biblical story of the Fall with man's discovery in himself of "a power of choosing...a way of life, of not being bound without alternative to a single way, like the animals."[31] Certainly Korsgaard is right that it would be a mistake to see Kant as conceding the realm of happiness to Bentham. Though Kant talks in several places about happiness as comprising the systematic satisfaction of inclinations,[32] he denies that this is just a matter of scheduling satisfactions on the utilitarian model. For one thing, the set of possible desires that has to be taken into account in any calculus of one's future happiness is, if not infinite, then certainly radically indeterminate. And for another, humans can pick and choose in an non-quantitative way which desires they wish to give priority to in their pursuit of happiness. A man who suffers from gout, Kant says, may choose intelligibly to opt for the pleasures of port even at the cost of physical agony, which in quantity and extent, far outweighs those pleasures on any utilitarian calculation.[33]

This is an intriguing example, for it seems to present – in the domain of earthly pleasures – some sort of prototype or analog of the renunciation of desire that our moral powers involve. To be sure, for the gout-sufferer, desire (for relief from pain) is renounced for the sake of desire (for the pleasures of port). But the renunciation is not dictated mechanically by any calculus of inclination. It is dictated by *a choice* that controls and disciplines inclination even for the sake of other inclinations that are treated as incommensurate with the first.

Well, we should not exaggerate the significance of all this. What Kant makes of the gout-sufferer example is murky, to say the least. We are not presented here with a well worked-out conception of the role of reason in the choice of ends, and the comments we have considered do not add up to a theory of personal autonomy in the sense used by modern liberals. Still, they point a little bit in that direction; I mean by this that they point to something in the Kantian pursuit of happiness that is somewhat more rigorous and somewhat more worthy of respect than (say) the mere indulgence of appetites or the prudent satisfaction of inclinations. And most intriguingly, from our point of view, they seem to do so by implicating in the pursuit of individual happiness some of the capacities of practical reason that are more commonly associated with the exercise of moral autonomy.

III

We have spent same time considering how far something like the modern notion of personal autonomy is implicated in Kant's account of the pursuit of happiness. I now want to turn my attention in the other direction, and consider how far something approximating Kantian moral autonomy is implicated in modern liberal conceptions of personal autonomy.

In liberal philosophy, the principle that corresponds to Kant's principle of freedom is the principle that individuals are entitled to form and pursue their own conceptions of what makes life worth living. Sometimes we express this negatively as a principle of state neutrality: the state must be neutral on the question of what makes life worth living, or, as Ronald Dworkin puts it "political decisions must be, so far as possible, independent of any particular conception of the good life, or of what gives value to life."[34] But there are reasons for holding the state to a neutrality principle that are not centered on individual freedom or autonomy,[35] and there may be reasons for opposing neutrality that are not reasons for opposing the affirmative principle with which I began this section.[36] So I think it better just to state the liberal principle straightforwardly: individuals are entitled to form and pursue their own conceptions of what makes life worth living.

Now the idea referred to in this principle – a person's conception of what makes life worth living – may be understood narrowly or generously. In its most generous sense, it includes anyone's overall orientation towards life no matter how crude or inchoate. Dworkin puts it like this:

> Each person follows a more-or-less articulate conception of what gives value to life. The scholar who values a life of contemplation has such a conception; so does the television-watching, beer-drinking citizen who is fond of saying "This is the life," though he has thought less about the issue and is less able to describe or defend his conception.[37]

On the most generous account, a person's conception of the good is simply something revealed by his behavior. He drinks beer while watching television, he does it cheerfully, and he does little else: therefore we impute to him the thought that *that* is the good life. A principle that allowed people to pursue their conception of the good in this most generous sense amounts to little more than a principle of free action (subject of course to the other-regarding proviso): "Each may do what he likes (so long as that doesn't impact upon similar freedom for others)." And the notion that there is something important about conceiving what one likes *as good* seems to play little role in this.

Compare with this the much narrower account of personal autonomy in Joseph Raz's book, *The Morality of Freedom*. For Raz, autonomy is not just a matter of having values and revealing them in one's choices. It is a quite specific notion of self-authorship:

> An autonomous person is part author of his own life. His life is, in part, of his own making. The autonomous person's life is marked not only by what it is but also by what it might have been and by the way it became what it is. A person is autonomous only if he had a variety of acceptable options to choose from, and his life became as it is through his choice of some of these options. A person who has never had any significant choice, or was not aware of it, or never exercised choice in significant matters but simply drifted through life is not an autonomous person.[38]

Although he defines autonomy in a way that contrasts with "drifting through life without ever exercising one's capacity to choose,"[39] Raz concedes that many of the most important things in our lives may be projects we have grown up with, aspirations we discover we already have when we first undertake autonomous deliberation.[40] What matters for Razian autonomy is not the genesis of our projects, but, first, that we recognize the possibility now of abandoning or continuing to embrace them; second, that when we choose among these options, we do so for reasons that play a conscious role in our continuing practical deliberations; and third, that we identify in good faith with the choices we have made.[41]

That notion of *identification* is a deliberate echo of an idea developed by Harry Frankfurt and others. Frankfurt attributes great importance to the capacity to stand back from one's occurrent volitions, to consider whether one wants to be influenced by them, and to act at least some of the time on the basis of these "second-order desires."[42] Though Frankfurt does not explicitly associate this reflective self-evaluation with the idea of autonomy, others have used it in their accounts. Gerald Dworkin, for instance, identifies autonomy with the following condition:

> It is only when a person identifies with the influences that motivate him, assimilates them to himself, views himself as the kind of person who wishes to be moved in particular ways, that these influences are to be identified as "his."[43]

Dworkin's account also makes it clear that in the context of a theory of autonomy, the relevant second-order desires must refer the first-order desires to the concept of one's self. It is not enough for a second-order desire to be motivated (say) by the frisson of pleasure that one knows is characteristic of acting on a certain first-order desire. The conception of *who one is* – the sort of life one wants to lead, the sort of person one wants to be – is essential to the second-order reflection that constitutes autonomy. Raz, I think, sees this too when he associates autonomy with self-authorship. Though the autonomous person need not live a highly-scripted existence, he is nevertheless a person who can relate the choices he makes to some sense of the overall course of his life. He not only has options and can carry them out, but he also understands their course and significance on the matrix of "this life of mine," and he chooses among them on that basis. I guess it is possible that Ronald Dworkin's "television-watching, beer-drinking citizen who is fond of saying 'This is the life,'" qualifies as autonomous under this criterion, but it's also possible that he does not. To qualify, "This is the life" would have to refer – as it does not often refer in colloquial discourse – to some valued feature of the whole shape of the person's existence, not just the comfort of the moment.

Now the point here is not that Raz's narrower conception of autonomy might exclude some of those who qualify as having a conception of the good in Ronald Dworkin's sense. The normative direction of Raz's account is quite different: he is considering autonomy as a specific ideal that the state ought to foster, rather than as a principle that exhausts the state's duties in regard to the values held by its citizens.[44] What is remarkable, however, about this emphasis on second-order desire and identification in modern liberal accounts of personal autonomy is its resonance with conceptions of more strictly moral deliberation. It is characteristic of a common Kantian conception of morality that I show my credentials as a moral agent not by renouncing desire altogether but by being able to stand back from my desires and consider whether they are the sort of thing that I ought to be motivated by. It is characteristic, too, of this sort of conception that morality is associated with authenticity: the deliberation that considers whether a given desire is the sort of thing I ought to be motivated by is deliberation which accesses my true self, a core of moral authenticity that can defy desires and inclinations that are judged to be alien to me. So personal autonomy is *like* moral autonomy in the kind of deliberation and commitment that it emphasizes. In both cases, there is an achievement of critical distance, in both cases there is reflection, and in both cases this reflection involves the idea of "who I really am."

I am not saying that the liberal conception of personal autonomy is set up with this consonance in view. We have already seen that Raz, for one, wants a sharp distinction between personal autonomy and moral autonomy.[45] But the fact that the two sorts of autonomy privilege capacities of the same kind is helpful nonetheless. For it means that when the demands of morality do enter the picture, we are not calling upon individuals to engage in an utterly different kind of exercise from that involved in their autonomous self-authorship. The introduction of moral considerations is not the first moment at which desire is checked or spontaneous inclination subjected to scrutiny. As personally autonomous, liberal individuals are already familiar with the idea of disciplining their inclinations in the light of the sort of person they would like to be. All that happens in the moral phase is that the image of such a person is conceived as "one who lives on fair terms with others": it is now in the light of *this* self-image, rather than merely the self-image of "one who would like his life to have such-and-such a character," that inclination is checked and desire subjected to scrutiny. Morality already has a toehold, and there is no radical discontinuity between the modes of reflection and self-control appropriate to the pursuit of happiness and the modes of reflection and self-control required for submission to the right.

It is interesting to consider John Rawls's account of individual conceptions of the good in light of these considerations. A theory of justice, on Rawls's account, defines a framework within which each person will be able to pursue his own conception of the good; and indeed the moral equality of persons and their entitlement to justice is defined partly in terms of their capacity for a conception of the good.[46] Now, we distinguished earlier between narrower and more generous understandings of "conception of the good." In Rawls's theory, the pursuit of a conception of the good seems to be defined in a quite specific way:

> We are to suppose... that each individual has a rational plan of life drawn up subject to the conditions that confront him. This plan is designed to permit the harmonious satisfaction of his interests. It schedules activities so that various desires can be fulfilled without interference. It is arrived at by rejecting other plans that are either less likely to succeed or do not provide for such an inclusive attainment of aims.[47]

It is not at all clear that Ronald Dworkin's "television-watching, beer-drinking citizen" would have a conception of the good in this sense. However, the specificity of this part of Rawls's theory is misleading. Rawls says he is not imposing the plan-like aspects of his theory of the good as either an ideal for individuals or a condition of their entitlement to freedom. The theory is constructive and hypothetical.[48] He says that we are to *suppose* that each individual has a rational plan of life, and I think that means that something answering to Rawls's elaborate description of a plan of life *can be imputed* to each person for the purposes of a theory of justice[49] – imputed to him on the basis of facts about his abilities, circumstances, tastes, and so on. But in the end, for each individual the imputation of a substantive plan of life is always subject to brute facts about where he finds happiness:

> Thus imagine someone whose only pleasure is to count blades of grass in various geometrically shaped areas such as park squares and well-trimmed lawns.... The definition of the good forces us to admit that the good for this man is indeed counting blades of grass, or more accurately, his good is determined by a plan that gives an especially prominent place to this activity.[50]

So the entitlement of each to justice, on Rawls's account, does not depend on a their ends having any particular substantive character, nor does it depend on their attachment to those ends being distinguished by any narrowly-defined features of rational commitment. We may impute certain features of rationality to a person in order to work out, for the purposes of a theory of justice, what respecting each person's pursuit of his particular ends requires. But that is not the same as conditioning respect for his ends on the rationality of his attachment to them.

Now, in *A Theory of Justice*, Rawls does not use the term "autonomy" to characterize a person's pursuit of a conception of the good. As we have seen, the idea of personal autonomy in other theories is often associated with a particular mode of connection between a person and his ends: the pursuit of one's ends represents a form of self authorship, and the connection amounts to a person's higher-order evaluation of his ends, affirmative identification with them, and so on. But Rawls does not use this language in his theory of the good. Instead, he associates autonomy with morality or justice – that is, with a person's acceptance of something like the proviso in Kant's principle of freedom – "provided he does not infringe upon that freedom of others to strive for a like end," and so on.[51] Autonomy, for Rawls, is a way of characterizing the ability and willingness of a person to submit his pursuit of his conception of the good to the conditions necessary for the similar pursuit of conceptions of the good by others.

The fact that Rawlsian autonomy is supposed to refer to a capacity quite different from those implicated in an individual's pursuit of the good means that Rawls does face the difficulty we mentioned earlier. He has to explain why individuals are willing to subordinate their pursuit of the good to principles of right, and how that subordination is possible given the discontinuity between moral autonomy and the pursuit of an individual conception of the good.[52] I don't think Rawls ever gives an adequate account of this in *A Theory of Justice*. He just asserts that people are willing to subordinate their good to the demands of right, even though there is nothing about their good – or even about the constructive character that Rawls imputes to individual conceptions of the good – that explains this ability. At the very end of *A Theory of Justice*, Rawls says that people will regard their moral powers as the most fundamental aspect of their selves.[53] But this solves the problem (if it actually does) only by reversing it. Now it is the formation of a personal conception of the good that looks mysterious. If the true ground of one's being lies in the exercise of one's moral autonomy, why would quite different capacities be exercised in choosing a plan of life?

Intriguingly, we find a more complex – and somewhat more adequate – account of the relation between moral and personal autonomy in Rawls's later work.[54] In *Political Liberalism*, Rawls introduces the idea of "rational autonomy" to represent a person's "moral power to form, to revise, and rationally to pursue a conception of the good."[55] A person shows his rational autonomy, according to the argument in *Political Liberalism*, not just by identifying with his own particular ends, but by having and valuing the ability to stand back from any ends he happens to have – in other words, by using the same capacities that Joseph Raz, Harry Frankfurt, and Gerald Dworkin emphasized. Rawls contrasts this rational autonomy with "full autonomy," which continues to represent a person's overall ability to deliberate about, adopt, and comply with principles of justice.[56] Now, that may seem to add up to a contrast between personal autonomy and moral autonomy. But, in fact, the sort of critical reflection that Rawls's rational autonomy involves is not valued primarily for its connection with authenticity or self-authorship. Instead, it seems to be oriented mainly towards the priority of the right over the good. The capacity to distance onself from one's ends is connected to a person's ability to question his attachment to his ends in the light of their implications for justice.[57] In other words, it is calculated to have the effect that we noted in the case of conceptions of autonomy that made use of Frankfurt's idea. The difference is that in Rawls's case, this seems to be a deliberate strategy: Rawls evidently now feels the need to use the form of personal autonomy to explain the efficacy of the demands of morality and justice.

IV

So far we have considered what personal autonomy may require so far as the form of an individual's engagement with his ends is concerned. But what about the substantive idea, which we also find in modern liberal theory, that autonomy might be seen as engagement with *the good*? We talk of an individual's pursuing a conception of *the good*, and, although this phrase may be used casually, still in its literal sense it does connote a criterion of ethical if not moral judgment. Certainly it evokes the idea of the subjection of a individual's life to the discipline of objectively[58] appropriate or inappropriate responses to the presence or absence of value.

Joseph Raz's account places particular emphasis on this connotation, with his insistence that "autonomy is valuable only if exercised in pursuit of the good."[59]

No one would deny that autonomy should be used for the good. The question is, has autonomy any value qua autonomy when it is abused? Is the autonomous wrongdoer a morally better person than the non-autonomous wrongdoer? Our intuitions rebel against such a view. It is surely the other way round. The wrongdoing casts a darker shadow on its perpetrator if it is autonomously done by him.[60]

It follows, says Raz, that something can hardly be an abrogation of autonomy if it interferes only with the choice of valueless options: "a choice between good and evil is not enough" for autonomy.[61] From the subjective point of view as well, Raz thinks the exercise of autonomy represents *an individual's attempt to engage with the good.* A person P's experience of choosing between two ways of life, A and B, is P's experience of judging which of them it would be better for him to have; and Raz thinks it follows that anyone who chooses A on this basis is necessarily committed to the thought that if it turns out that A is undesirable (that is, if it turns out that A lacks the value that he thought it had when he chose it), then he no longer has a reason to pursue it. And this remains true, Raz insists, even if P is still convinced (mistakenly) that A is valuable, for no one thinks it is a good idea to pursue a course of life under a misapprehension about its value.[62]

Now, this is not the place to discuss the perfectionism that Raz establishes on these premises.[63] For our purposes, what is significant is the bridge that this seems to establish between personal autonomy and morality. Raz acknowledges that his account of personal autonomy ends up sounding like "a very rigoristic moral view,"[64] and that a person who lacks the power of moral discernment will not have what it takes to be personally autonomous. So now it's not just the form of commitment – critical self-reflection – but the substance of evaluation that links the two forms of autonomy. One may go even further. On David Johnston's interpretation, "Raz believes that a sense of justice is part of personal autonomy in the sense that a person who is personally autonomous would want to avoid doing things that are unjust."[65] I am not sure that I see this explicitly in *The Morality of Freedom.* But I'm also not sure that Raz can avoid it, given the moral dimension of personal autonomy on his account and his view that "all aspects of morality derive from common sources."[66] If the proper use of autonomy is to choose between good options, and not between good options and evil options, then it is hard to see how an unjust choice can be regarded as a genuine exercise of personal autonomy. This means that in the exercise of one's personal autonomy, one may already be making judgements about justice. And it may follow in turn from that that each individual associates his personal autonomy with the criteria of justice that he uses in making these judgments. If this is true, then – despite Raz's insistence on a distinction between personal and moral autonomy[67] – we are going to have to rethink the relation between them. The exercise of personal autonomy can no longer be conceived merely as the subject-matter of moral autonomy – in the sense that moral autonomy is *about* reconciling one individual's personal autonomy with another's. The task of reconciliation has now become more complicated and reflexive, inasmuch as my exercise of personal autonomy may now already involve a view about the appropriate way to reconcile it with yours.

Raz's theory has its peculiarities, but I think the points I have made can be generalized to any liberal view that associates personal autonomy with the pursuit of a conception of the good. After all, the good does not lose its normativity or its connection to other normative ideas by being involved in an individual conception of what makes life worth living. It would be odd for persons to inform their choices with a conception of the good without inferring some significant consequences as to what it is appropriate for them to do.[68] And then we have to ask: how far does this go? Is an individual's conception of the good capable also of generating conclusions about what he *ought* to do, what it is *right* for him to do, what he is *required* or *obligated* to do? If it is capable of generating these conclusions, then what becomes of the fabled priority of the right over the good in liberal theory?

There are several ways in which we may understand a claim that the right has priority over the good. (1) It may be understood as a claim about the deontological character of political morality – as a denial of consequentialism, for example. The idea here would be that we do not construct our political morality by figuring out, first, what is valuable and, second, how best to promote it; instead, we establish certain moral absolutes – rights, for example – deontologically, without reference to the goals that it might be worthwhile for individuals or societies to pursue.[69] Or (2) the priority of the right over the good may be understood as a claim about the relation between individual aspirations and the social demands of morality. People have their own individual conceptions of the good, but these are subject to the demands of right conceived as a system of morally reconciling individual ends:

> The principles of right, and so of justice, put limits on which satisfactions have value; they impose restrictions on what are reasonable conceptions of one's good. In drawing up plans and in deciding on aspirations men are to take these constraints into account.[70]

In principle, these two versions of the priority are distinct. One might have a teleological conception of social morality and still insist on (2) – that is, on the priority of that conception over individual ends: a utilitarian might say, for example, that an individual is not entitled to pursue his own happiness when the exigencies of the general happiness require otherwise. Or there might be deontological elements in the conceptions that individuals pursue and identify with, but these might still be subordinated to social morality (however that is configured).

This latter possibility is of particular interest. Suppose that individual conceptions of the good yield elements of deontological right or requirement. What is the relation of these personal deontological elements to the demands of morality conceived as a social enterprise of reconciling individual interests? Or suppose that personal autonomy is not conceived primarily in terms of "good" at all, but *ab initio* in terms of right or requirement? What is the relation between the moralism that personal autonomy might exhibit and the social morality of a theory of justice?

Another way of approaching the same issue is to ask about the relation between autonomy and conscience. For most of this chapter, I have presented personal autonomy as a matter of self-determination in the pursuit of value in one's life: one chooses to pursue knowledge, for example, or love or aesthetic excellence. On another account, however, personal autonomy is a matter of responding to something that presents itself in one's inner life as an imperative. "Here I stand; I can do no other" has quite a different flavor from (say) "I have chosen to find value and enjoyment in a life of literary achievement." Perhaps the two may be assimilated if we associate "I can do no other" with the ethics of authenticity: "I just have to respond to my inner urgings. I have no choice but to be a poet."[71] But if conscience is understood as a subjective representation of law-like requirements rather than the subjective representation of personal destiny, then it is a little more difficult to relate it to the modern notion of autonomy. For then it is no longer just a matter of self-determination, or of what I make of myself. Instead it is a matter of my heeding or not heeding an inner representation of "what is to be done." I am not saying it is utterly independent of the notion of the self: conscience associates itself with integrity, and there is a sense that failing to heed its moralistic demands amounts to a form of self-betrayal. Still, the relation of the self to these demands is now much more complex. The demands are not thought of as originating from the self, for all that they are bound up with integrity. Instead, the demands represent the self's participation in a moral order defined in a way that is independent of it.[72] If personal autonomy takes on this character, it is going to be much harder to keep it from usurping the role played by a social theory of right.

It is tempting to respond that this sort of autonomy – the sense of autonomy associated with conscience – is to be filed under "moral autonomy" and kept strictly apart from the modern liberal notion of "personal autonomy." And then one would say that a constructive theory of the right is supposed to model the claims of conscience, or to stand in reflective equilibrium with them, but not to accept them as inputs, in the way that it accepts individual conceptions of the good. One can concede that in the real world, the broad moral powers of actual individuals will tangle these things together – plan of life, commitment to values, views about rightness, and deliverances of conscience. But – according to the response I am now considering – that just makes it all the more important to draw the theoretical distinction, even if some quite delicate dissection is necessary to distinguish those elements that are properly analyzed under the auspices of "individual conception of the good" and those elements that are properly analyzed under the auspices of "individual views about morality and justice."

But I don't think this response works; it is no longer enough to defuse the challenge posed here by the phenomenology of conscience. For the question now is whether the distinction between personal and moral autonomy actually stands up – that is, whether the phenomenon that the liberal describes as forming and pursuing a conception of the good can be kept apart from the phenomenology of experiencing and responding to moral demands. John Rawls's theory, for example, requires there to be not only a verbal distinction here, but a real distinction in terms of modes of construction and criteria of validity. Apart from anything else, he says, we do not want the sort of proliferation in the realm of right that we have – and welcome – in the realm of individual good:

[I]t is, in general, a good thing that individuals' conceptions of their good should differ in significant ways, whereas this is not so for their conceptions of the right.... In a well-ordered society,... the plans of life of individuals are different in the sense that these plans give prominence to different aims, and persons are left free to determine their good, the views of others being counted as merely advisory.... But the situation is quite otherwise with justice: here we require not only common principles but sufficiently similar ways of applying them... so that a final ordering of conflicting claims can be defined.[73]

Rawls acknowledges that some have taken a different approach: "They have suggested that autonomy is the complete freedom to form our moral opinions and that the conscientious judgment of every moral agent ought absolutely to be respected."[74] But he says this is mistaken. When people make assertions of right based on conscience, "[h]ow do we ascertain that their conscience and not ours is mistaken...?"[75] In matters of the good, a view gets some credentials from the mere fact that it is held by an individual: individuals are, after all, self-originating sources of moral claims.[76] But in matters of the right, an individual's personal attachment to a view counts for nothing at all, on Rawls's approach. In matters of right, correctness is associated exclusively with what people would agree to in the original position, not with the conscience or intuitions of the participants. Unless Rawls can hold the line between conceptions of the right and conceptions of the good, he cannot stem this proliferation, nor can he justify holding conceptions of the right to quite the same standards as those to which conceptions of the good are held. But the normative implications of "the good" seem to threaten this distinction, all the way down the line.

V

We seem to have identified the horns of a dilemma. On the one hand, we have the position that if too sharp a distinction is drawn between personal autonomy and moral autonomy, we cannot explain how the former is subordinated to the latter. On the other hand, we have the position that if the line between them is blurred, then there is the prospect of a proliferation of standards of right – one per person – with individuals committed to them in a way that seems to command the same respect as their commitment to their conceptions of the good. Clearly what is called for is some sort of moderate or intermediate position. This chapter has not sought to identify that third way, but I hope it has helped illuminate some of the perils as well as some of the advantages of a distinction between personal and moral autonomy.

A sharp distinction between the two seems indispensable for analytic clarity. But if we erect too high a wall of separation, we conceal the common features and analogies that have prompted the use of the same term "autonomy" in both cases. We will miss the various ways in which the two ideas are interrelated – not only the fact that personal autonomy is often the subject-matter of moral autonomy, as morality attempts to reconcile one person's autonomous pursuit of his ends with others' autonomous pursuit of theirs, but also the fact that individuals' exercise of personal autonomy must be amenable to the demands of morality, and their personal autonomy must be capable of being integrated with the exercise of their moral autonomy, normally understood as equally indispensable to their individual being. And we will miss, too, the damage that personal autonomy may do to moral autonomy when, through conscience or through the normativity of its own value-conceptions, it challenges the latter's attempt to monopolize the realm of the right and the just.

Notes

1. There is a useful discussion of this distinction in David Johnston, *The Idea of a Liberal Theory* (Princeton, NJ: Princeton University Press, 1994), pp. 72–7.
2. See, for example, Joseph Raz, *The Morality of Freedom* (Oxford: Clarendon Press, 1986), p. 370 on: "Personal autonomy, which is a particular ideal of individual well-being should not be confused with the only very indirectly related notion of moral autonomy."
3. "On the Common Saying: That May Be Correct in Theory But It Is of No Use in Practice" (hereinafter "Theory and Practice"), in Immanuel Kant, *Practical Philosophy*, translated and edited by Mary Gregor (Cambridge: Cambridge University Press, 1996), 277, at p. 291. For convenience, I will add to all citations from Kant a parenthetical page-reference to the relevant volume of the standard Prussian Academy edition of Kant's works. The reference for this passage is p. 290 of volume 8, or, as I shall abbreviate it (8: 290).
4. Immanuel Kant, *Groundwork of the Metaphysics of Morals*, in Kant, *Practical Philosophy*, 41, at pp. 83 ff. (4: 433 ff).
5. Immanuel Kant, *Critique of Practical Reason*, in Kant, *Practical Philosophy*, 133, at p. 168 (5: 25).
6. Kant, *Groundwork*, p. 59 (4: 405).
7. Immanuel Kant, *The Metaphysics of Morals*, in Kant, *Practical Philosophy*, 353, at p. 393 (6: 237).
8. Kant, "Theory and Practice" p. 291 (8: 290); my emphasis.
9. Ibid., p. 285 (8: 283).
10. See Paul Guyer, *Kant on Freedom, Law and Happiness* (Cambridge: Cambridge University Press, 2000), p. 98.
11. The same is true of a number of other ways in which happiness and morality are connected in Kantian moral philosophy. In the *Groundwork*, p. 49 (4: 393), Kant suggests that one has to have a morally good will to be worthy of happiness. A little later – ibid., p. 52 (4: 396) – he defines "moral happiness" as "satisfaction with one's person and one's own moral conduct." Third, there is happiness conceived of as the reward for the blessed in the life to come; see Kant, *Metaphysics of Morals*, p. 519 (6: 387). These suggestions, however, are not what we are looking for. Though they do connect autonomy with the pursuit of happiness, they do so in a backhanded way.
12. See Alexander Kaufman, *Welfare in the Kantian State* (Oxford: Clarendon Press, 1999), p. 39, for the suggestion that Kant's principle of freedom in "Theory and Practice" is to be read as an attack on contemporary cameralism, which held that the ultimate aim of every republic is the common happiness.
13. See Isaiah Berlin, "Two Concepts of Liberty," in his collection *Four Essays on Liberty* (Oxford: Oxford University Press, 1969). For a slightly different contrast between positive and negative freedom in moral philosophy, see Kant, *Groundwork*, p. 94 (4: 446).

14. Kant, *Metaphysics of Morals*, p. 387 (6: 230).
15. Kant, *Critique of Practical Reason*, p. 159 (5:25)
16. However, as Kant points out, "[t]o assure one's own happiness is a duty (at least indirectly); for, want of satisfaction with one's condition, under pressure from many anxieties and amid unsatisfied needs, could easily become a great *temptation to transgression of duty*." [Kant, *Groundwork*, p. 54 (4: 399); emphasis in original.]
17. For "assertoric imperative," see Kant, *Groundwork*, p. 68 (4: 415–6).
18. Kant, *Metaphysics of Morals*, p. 371 (6:215–6). See also Kant, *Critique of Practical Reason*, p. 159 (5: 25).
19. Allen D. Rosen, *Kant's Theory of Justice* (Ithaca: Cornell University Press, 1993), pp. 70–1.
20. Kant, "Theory and Practice," p. 291 (8: 290–1).
21. Guyer, *Kant on Freedom, Law and Happiness*, pp. 111–2.
22. Kant, *Groundwork*, pp. 74–5 (4: 422–3).
23. Kant, *Metaphysics of Morals*, p. 565 (6: 444).
24. Ibid., p. 566 (6: 445).
25. Cf. John Stuart Mill, *On Liberty*, ed. Currin V. Shields (Indianapolis: Bobbs Merrill, 1956), pp. 69–72.
26. Kant, *Groundwork*, p. 51 (4: 395).
27. Kant, *Critique of Practical Reason*, p. 189 (5: 61). See also the discussion in John Rawls, *Lectures on the History of Moral Philosophy* (Cambridge, MA: Harvard University Press, 2000), p. 232.
28. Cf. David Hume, *A Treatise of Human Nature*, second edition, eds. L. A. Selby-Bigge and P. H. Nidditch (Oxford: Clarendon Press, 1978), pp. 413 ff. For "hypothetical imperatives," see Kant, *Groundwork*, pp. 67–8 (4: 414–5).
29. This is partly because of the indeterminacy of the ends that constitute our happiness, and partly because of the unpredictable vicissitudes of the empirical world. Kant says in *Groundwork*, pp. 70–1 (4: 418):

    > [I]t is impossible for the most insightful and at the same time most powerful but still finite being to frame for himself a determinate concept of what he really wills here. If he wills riches, how much anxiety, envy, and intrigue might he not bring upon himself in this way!... If he at least wills health, how often has not bodily discomfort kept someone from excesses into which unlimited health would have let him fall, and so forth.... One cannot therefore act on determinate principles for the sake of being happy, but only on empirical counsels...

30. Christine M. Korsgaard, *Creating the Kingdom of Ends* (Cambridge: Cambridge University Press, 1996), pp. 111–3.
31. Kant, *Groundwork*, p. 51 (4:395). The passage from *Conjectural Beginnings of Human History* is cited in Korsgaard, *Creating the Kingdom of Ends*, p. 112
32. For example, Kant, *Critique of Practical Reason*, p. 199 (5:73).
33. Kant, *Groundwork*, p. 54 (4: 399). See also the discussion in Victoria S. Wike, *Kant on Happiness in Ethics* (Albany: State University of New York Press, 1994), pp. 6–13.
34. Ronald Dworkin, "Liberalism," in *A Matter of Principle* (Cambridge, MA: Harvard University Press, 1985), 181, at p. 191.

35. The state may be incompetent to make decisions about what makes life worth living: see Bruce Ackerman, *Social Justice in the Liberal State* (New Haven: Yale University Press, 1980), p. 12.
36. There may be aspects of the state's other duties that make neutrality impossible: see the discussion in Jeremy Waldron, "Legislation and Moral Neutrality," in *Liberal Rights: Collected Papers 1981–1991* (Cambridge: Cambridge University Press, 1993), 143, at pp. 149–50.
37. Dworkin, "Liberalism," p. 191. See also Stephen Macedo, *Liberal Virtues: Citizenship, Virtue, and Community in Liberal Constitutionalism* (Oxford: Clarendon Press, 1990), p. 253: "Explicitly or not, liberal regimes endorsee and promote autonomy. But we still respect the non-autonomous: people have the right to lead lazy, narrow-minded lives..."
38. Raz, *The Morality of Freedom*, p. 204; see also ibid., p. 369.
39. Ibid., p. 371.
40. Ibid., pp. 290–1.
41. Ibid., p. 382. I have adapted part of this paragraph from Jeremy Waldron, "Autonomy and Perfectionism in Raz's *The Morality of Freedom*," *Southern California Law Review*, 62 (1989), 1097.
42. Harry G. Frankfurt, "Freedom of the Will and the Concept of a Person," *Journal of Philosophy*, 68 (1971), 5–20, at p. 7.
43. Gerald Dworkin, "The Concept of Autonomy," in John Christman (ed.) *The Inner Citadel: Essays on Individual Autonomy* (New York: Oxford University Press, 1989), 54–62, at p. 60.
44. See Raz, *The Morality of Freedom*, pp. 391–4.
45. See note 2.
46. John Rawls, *A Theory of Justice*, (Oxford: Oxford University Press, 1971), p. 505.
47. Ibid., p. 93.
48. See ibid., pp. 423–4.
49. For an account of the role played in a theory of justice by this theorizing about individuals' conceptions of the good, see ibid., pp. 396–8.
50. Ibid., p. 432.
51. Ibid., p. 515. The Kantian character of the account is explicit at ibid., pp. 252 ff.
52. Sandel, *Liberalism and the Limits of Justice*, p. 157, states the problem as follows:

> [W]e need to know in greater detail how the constraint of justice makes itself felt, how exactly it enters into the deliberation of the agent. Are the constraints of right somehow built into the activity of deliberation such that only just desires or conceptions of the good can arise in the first place, or does the agent form values and aims based on certain unjust desires only to suppress them in practice or set them aside once it becomes clear that they violate justice?

53. Rawls, *A Theory of Justice*, pp. 561–3.
54. I say "intriguingly" because in his later work, Rawls is usually at pains to minimize the distinctive or philosophically controversial aspects of the conceptions he deploys. Thus, for example, he rejects some of the distinctive features of Joseph Raz's conception of autonomy because they are part of a

comprehensive philosophical conception and thus unsuitable for a political theory of justice: see John Rawls, *Political Liberalism*, revised edition (New York: Columbia University Press, 1996), p. 135n.
55. Rawls, *Political Liberalism*, p. 72.
56. Ibid., pp. 75–81.
57. Ibid., pp. 73–4.
58. Or quasi-objectively: the argument here is presented without prejudice to the debate about moral realism. [See Jeremy Waldron, "The Irrelevance of Moral Objectivity," in Robert George (ed.) *Natural Law Theory: Contemporary Essays* (Oxford: Clarendon Press, 1992), 158, at pp. 165–7.]
59. Raz, *The Morality of Freedom*, p. 381.
60. Ibid., p. 380.
61. Ibid., p. 379.
62. Ibid., pp. 140–2.
63. Ibid., p. 417: "The autonomy principle permits and even requires governments to create morally valuable opportunities, and eliminate repugnant ones." See Waldron, "Autonomy and Perfectionism," pp. 1127 ff.
64. Ibid., p. 381. (It's an impression he mitigates only because of the plurality of goods: there are multiple valuable ways of living one's life.)
65. Johnston, *The Idea of a Liberal Theory*, p. 78.
66. Raz, *The Morality of Freedom*, pp. 161 and 213–6.
67. See note 2.
68. See R. M. Hare, *The Language of Morals* (Oxford: Clarendon Press, 1952), chapter 8.
69. See Robert Nozick, *Anarchy, State and Utopia* (New York: Basic Books, 1974), pp. 28 ff.; for an attack on this proposition, see Charles Taylor, "Atomism," in his collection *Philosophy and the Human Sciences: Philosophical Papers 2* (Cambridge: Cambridge University Press, 1985), pp. 187–210.
70. Rawls, *Theory of Justice*, p. 31.
71. Cf. Charles Taylor, *The Ethics of Authenticity* (Cambridge, MA: Harvard University Press, 1991), pp. 26 ff.
72. In this connection, we must not neglect the fact that in the real world, people associate this conscientious aspect of their autonomy with the demands of their religion – the demands of God, even – and that they see this as a consummation of their integrity, not as something that detracts from it.
73. Rawls, *Theory of Justice*, pp. 447–8
74. Ibid., p. 518.
75. Ibid., p. 515.
76. Rawls, *Political Liberalism*, pp. 32–33 .

14

Autonomy, Self-Knowledge, and Liberal Legitimacy

John Christman

In the Enlightenment tradition of the justification of political authority, institutions of state power are seen as legitimate only if such institutions can be freely supported by those living under them. Liberal legitimacy, then, assumes that autonomous citizens can endorse the principles that shape the institutions of political power. The conception of autonomy functioning in such a picture, moreover, requires that such citizens uniformly enjoy the capacity to rationally reflect upon and critically appraise their own values, moral commitments, and political convictions. In this way, political power is an outgrowth of autonomous personhood and choice.

This traditional understanding of political legitimacy has been challenged from any number of directions, most notably from those who charge that the picture of the autonomous person underlying the mechanism of authority is parochial, exclusionary, and in tension with the sought-for legitimacy it is used to support.[1] In this last vein, it can be charged that the requirements of general support for principles of justice in a modern, pluralistic society are in tension with the assumptions concerning individual autonomy underlying that concept. For the problem facing liberal conceptions of justice and legitimacy is that political power can be seen as justified only when supported by autonomous citizens, but the requirements of autonomy, in many construals of that term, are too stringent to be met by the majority of citizens bound by political institutions. Or, in other versions of this critique, the conditions set out for autonomy refer at best only to some in the population and not others, thereby valorizing certain personality types, value perspectives, and social positions over others. So modern institutions fail to achieve the desired legitimacy. It is this concern that I will deal with here.

More specifically, the difficulty I want to examine here is that for political institutions to be legitimate, citizens living under them must achieve, for example, a level of self-knowledge and reflective self-endorsement that most fail to meet and that, in fact, would run counter to other processes of value commitment and moral obligation that motivate our moral choices. Two parallel questions arise at this point: what exactly are the conditions of autonomy that best support the role that concept plays in principles of justice and legitimacy? And what reasons are there for assuming that citizens expressing endorsement of political institutions (of the sort required by liberal legitimacy) be autonomous in this way, especially when the conditions of such autonomy do not obtain universally for all in the population?

I will approach these issues by first focusing on the concept of autonomy, where I will examine the general pattern that theorists of that notion have followed, and propose a particular view on the concept's meaning, at least as it might be used in the context of liberal political theory. The problems that have been raised about seeing autonomy in this way – in particular that it would demand certain capacities and practices that are at once difficult to achieve for most of us as well as being disruptive of our most basic value commitments – will be noted. Indeed, I will add to the usual chorus of complaints on this score, pointing out the ways that some understandings of autonomy may require levels of self-understanding and reflection that few of us ever achieve (or would want to achieve). Nevertheless, I want to suggest that the process of legitimating principles of justice in the liberal tradition require seeing autonomy in this way. That is, despite the fact that people generally do not exhibit levels of self-knowledge that some conceptions of autonomy assume, it is nonetheless important to treat them as the fundamental representatives of their own values and commitments, and it is correspondingly important to ask them to reflectively appraise those commitments as part of the process of giving reasons that political legitimacy demands.

To keep track of the rather circuitous route I will be taking through these issues, let me lay out the plan: I will first discuss the concept of autonomy; in doing so, I will propose a version of that concept that takes competence and the capacity for self-reflection as central. Then I will consider problems with such requirements, in that understanding autonomy this way appears to assume a level of self-knowledge that most people cannot achieve. Moreover, acts of reflection can in some ways disturb moral commitment and manifest aspects of personhood that are not definitive of the most settled aspects of the self. With these challenges laid out, I then turn to political theory, in particular to the requirements for the legitimacy of political authority in the liberal tradition. In doing so, I will make some general claims about the nature of liberalism, in particular its commitment to pluralism, rejecting certain forms of perfectionism, and in requiring citizen endorsement for all legitimate state institutions and the principles that guide them (the so-called "endorsement constraint"). I then distinguish two importantly different strains in liberal thinking – one in which legitimacy is established as a result of self-interested bargaining for the purposes of establishing stable social environments (within which citizens can pursue valued projects), and the other in which legitimacy is seen as grounded in a *moral* commitment to political institutions resting on mutual respect and reciprocity. And I support the latter view of political justification over the former. I then return to the question of the nature of autonomy, where I will claim that the mechanisms for establishing legitimacy in the strand of liberalism worth defending need not attribute levels of self-knowledge to citizens that they are unable systematically to meet (or if they are, they must be treated as meeting them nonetheless). And reflective self-appraisal of the sort demanded by liberal legitimacy is not problematic in the ways that our earlier concerns pointed to.

In the end, then, the kind of autonomy assumed in the mechanisms of liberal legitimacy does not assume levels of self-knowledge or capacities of reflection that citizens either cannot or would not want generally to exercise.

I The Conditions of Autonomy

Various conceptualizations of autonomy have been put forward, and the contrasts among these highlight differences in the way that this concept operates in different theoretical terrains.[2] In certain contexts, stress has been placed on the way that autonomy has traditionally rested on a single and parochial conception of the self – one, for example, that assumed a "true" or "core" self residing inside of us like an "inner citadel."[3] But as many have pointed out, there are several reasons to avoid reference to a singly conceived notion of a self in models of autonomy. For there are far too many contrasting conceptualizations of our selves relevant in various settings and relative to various needs for any one of them to unproblematically count as our authentic core. Our embodiment, for instance, is sometimes the most prominent aspect of our person (in medical settings, for example), whereas in others our identification as a member of a particular group, religion, culture, or ethnicity is salient. Moreover, as communitarian critics of liberalism have repeatedly stressed, our identities are often constituted by our deepest value commitments.[4] But these foci of selfhood vary from context to context and hence cannot, singly, play the role of the "true self" of which autonomy is meant to be an expression. So insofar as a conception of autonomy assumes a model of selfhood that features one of these aspects to the exclusion of the others, it can rightly be labeled as overly narrow and hence problematic.

Some theorists have therefore approached autonomy, not as the operation of a core set of identity-creating characteristics, but rather as a range of capacities, competences, and functions. This "functional" account of autonomy may be in a better position to avoid charges of narrowness that have plagued more traditional notions.[5] Such accounts focus on a number of conditions that manifest the "self-government" of the person, while at the same time acknowledging the deeply embedded, interpersonally constructed, and historically situated nature of the self. The first set picks out those characteristics by which a person effectively makes competent decisions: rationality, self-control, freedom from psychosis and other pathologies, access to minimally accurate information, motivational effectiveness, and the like. The second set refers to requirements that the person's values and decisions are truly her own; these most often include the condition that persons reflect on their personal characteristics[6] and identify with (or at least not feel deeply alienated from) them. Whereas the first family of requirements ensures that the autonomous person effectively acts (rules), the second guarantees that the ruling is truly her own. Thereby the self-rule promised by the etymology of the word "autonomy" is established.

So on the view offered here, autonomy requires that the person be able to submit the factors of her personality to critical self-reflection.[7] This requires that factors relevant to identity, decision, and choice be such that, hypothetically, the person could reflect upon them without repudiation in light of how they came about. In this way, the autonomous person is competent (in the ways described) as well as authentic in the sense of being moved by values that would withstand self-scrutiny.

Note also the reference to the *history* of the agent relative to the trait in question. I have argued in earlier work that the processes by which a person develops a trait are relevant to her autonomy vis-à-vis that trait.[8]

The way that attention to personal history should be captured is that a person cannot be labeled autonomous if some aspect of the manner in which a characteristic is developed would, if known, cause her to disavow that trait, to become deeply alienated from it. Let us say that a person discovered that the only reason she remains so devoted to her revolutionary activities is that she was kidnaped and tortured at an earlier time (a memory she had suppressed until now). Her autonomy is clearly in question if, were she to realize how these attitudes came about, she would disavow them. However, what matters is the person's relation to the attitude or characteristic *given* its etiology rather than her attitude *toward* that etiology *simpliciter*: I might think that the way I was raised was too restrictive, but I accept the way I turned out nonetheless, because it wasn't *so* restrictive that I want to reject or disavow the character traits that developed from it.

The requirement of self-reflection demands that the person is autonomous (relative to some factor) if, were piecemeal reflection in light of the history of the factor's development to take place, she would not feel deeply *alienated* from the characteristic in question. To be alienated from some aspect of oneself is to experience negative affect relative to it, and to experience diluted or conflicted motivation stemming from it, and to feel constricted by it, as though by an external force. It is, moreover, to feel a need to *repudiate* that desire or trait, to reject it and alter it as much as possible, and to resist its effects. If I reflect on some addiction I have, for example – one that I did not bring upon myself voluntarily – I view it as distanced from me, as something about which I feel regret or dismay and that is less than fully motivating (relative to non-alienated desires).[9] Moreover, the reflection required of autonomous agents is considered to be piecemeal, requiring that agents reflect on *particular* aspects of their character without ever presupposing the ability to look at the whole of themselves from a completely disembodied perspective.

Further, a mere *capacity* to reflect is too weak: if a person has a capacity to reflect on herself but never does, and some of her first-order traits would be unacceptable to her if she did, we would not call her autonomous as she continues blithely to act on the basis of those traits.[10] It is not merely that the person can reflect but that, were she to do so, she would not feel alienated in the manner described. Moreover, the capacity to reflect alone, even if exercised, seems insufficient to pick out a meaningful conception of autonomy. An unwilling addict, who may be unable to resist the debilitating grip of his destructive cravings, but nevertheless retains a tragically robust ability to reflect on his life and take in all of its deficiencies, is not autonomous despite this tragic self-knowledge. So an autonomous person must be able to alter those characteristics toward which she feels resistance, alienation, and repugnance.[11]

Non-alienation is also a different condition from the familiar requirement of identification, which one typically finds in discussions of autonomy. On the one hand, I can feel no alienation toward a characteristic but not fully identify with it, in the sense of wholehearted endorsement without regret.[12] We all contain some measure of internal conflict and complexity, and an attitude of ironic acceptance of the tensions of our own psyches is inevitable, and perhaps healthy, in a multi-dimensional and perplexing world. But to be alienated in the sense I mean here is to be actively derisive of some aspect of the self, to want to reject and resist it. An alienated person feels no affinity with such traits, wants to change or, if that is not feasible, distance herself from them; she is a divided and conflicted person, and is unable to present a minimally settled sense of herself to others in practical discourse. On the other hand, non-alienation is stronger than identification when the latter is considered as mere acknowledgment: I can admit that a trait is, alas, part of my identity (especially in my motivational structure), but still not want to repudiate and distance myself from it. Therefore, on the present view, a person is not autonomous relative to those aspects of herself that would produce such feelings of self-repudiation were she to reflect on them in light of how they came about. (Notice also how non-alienation adds an *affective* element to autonomy, in contrast to the picture of the disengaged cognizer described in our earlier discussion of reasons-responsiveness.)[13]

One final point: for a person to be autonomous on this model, the hypothetical reflection being considered cannot itself operate under the influence of factors that effectively prevent normal self-awareness. This prevents the possibility of a regress when considering the ways in which manipulative factors constrain both choice *and* reflection.[14] So self-reflection – even the hypothetical reflection being considered here – cannot be the result of distorting factors that guarantee that the self-appraisal in question has a particular result. Such factors include the influence of drugs or substances that prevent settled concentration, torture or intimidation that prevents the person from considering alternative ideas, educational backgrounds that severely limit opportunities to raise questions and come to minimally independent conclusions, and the like. As we will notice later, this condition will need to be refined in light of the ways that we all engage in "distorted" self-reflection in systematic ways.[15]

Interesting challenges, however, have been raised about the conceptualization (and related valorization) of autonomy, challenges that concern both the "competence" conditions and the "authenticity" conditions. For example, critics have claimed that autonomy problematically assumes herculean powers of self-knowledge, that the competence assumed in such accounts demands that agents have understandings of their motives and inner selves that few, if any, tend to realize. Moreover, such competency requirements have tended to emphasize the intellectual capacities over the emotional and affective.[16] This is shown in the characterization of competence as "rationality" and reflective self-endorsement in terms akin to the justification of belief. Concerning reflection, critics have charged that second-order appraisals of first-order motives and habits often reveal less authentic aspects of the self and, worse, cause dangerous disruption in people's deepest commitments, disrupting settled and authentic agency rather than securing it. Such emphasis on reflective re-evaluation and revision of the self both causes and reflects an unmerited valuation of change, instability, and hyper-mobility.[17]

I want to investigate these charges in greater detail, and indeed I will emphasize and support versions of these claims. For the sake of brevity, we can examine these concerns as focused on the general requirement of "competent self-reflection" assumed in models of autonomy. We will further discuss the specific conceptual conditions of autonomy later; for now, we can assume that the conditions of autonomy at issue involve the competent self-reflection and inner endorsement just described. The idea is that autonomy requires that the agent in question be competent in the sense that she suffers from none of the disabilities that would systematically hamper reflective decision-making and that she exhibit minimal abilities to reflect, choose, and act. As a result of such reflection, the agent must not repudiate the characteristic in question to be autonomous. Let us survey, then, problems raised about such a model.

II Difficulties With Self-Reflection

There are many initially compelling reasons to resist taking the reflective functions of the person as centrally indicative of her autonomy. Two families of reasons can be given on this score: one is that reflection itself is often costly, and carries with it effects on commitment and devotion that raise questions about its role in self-determination; a second is that the reflective voice in all of us often does not speak for our most settled and authentic personae in that such voices can cover over or mis-diagnose the inner workings of our psyches. Let us look at these concerns more closely.

The first set of problems involve the way in which reflectively questioning our commitments and motivations can often disrupt and undercut those very commitments. This problem of first-order motivational distortion can best be brought out in a two-person case: consider longtime spouses or romantic partners. One day, one of them enters the breakfast room to announce that she has lately been reflecting on the value of the relationship for her and on her commitment to it. Now, even if the result of such re-thinking is to redouble the strength of her commitment, the partner hearing this may well be disappointed and shocked, and the ties between the two deeply shaken. Now if we collapse this dynamic into a single mental life, we have cases where self-evaluation leads to self-doubt and diminished motivation.[18] The paradox is that if a person reflects, she loses the autonomy she seemed to enjoy before the moment of re-appraisal.

Second, critics have charged that in many ways, our introspective judgments fail to reflect our settled, authentic selves. Such reflections merely give voice to a rationalizing super-ego attempting to quash the more central elements of our motivational system, elements that, if allowed to move us, would issue in action that is more truly our own. For an illustration of such a phenomenon, consider the character Jude in Thomas Hardy's *Jude the Obscure*. For a good part of the novel, Jude is clearly in love with his cousin Sue, though he is still married to his estranged wife Arabella, to whom he still feels a strong obligation of fidelity (backed by all the force of his North Wessex Christian upbringing). But Jude's most basic motivational drive is clearly his love for Sue, evidenced by the cold sweats he experiences at the thought of her leaving, and his fits of jealousy at the sight of her with another man. Reflecting on these emotions, driven by the thought that he is still officially married and that Sue is, after all, his cousin, Jude mis-characterizes these emotions as merely those of a platonic concern of a friend toward a family member. As the events in the novel soon bear out, Jude's true nature is not revealed by his reflective voices but by those first-order affective drives.

Now, in addition to revealing the important place that emotions have in the specification of our authentic selves, this case indicates how the voice of reflection may distort rather than clarify our self-conceptions. Reflection, for Jude, produces profound alienation from his emotions and destroys whatever authentic motivation he might experience were he, as he eventually does, to allow his feelings of love to move him to act. Only without the self-reflection that autonomy demands (under self-reflection views) can Jude, and those like him, act authentically.[19]

The other set of problems for requiring reflection of this sort concerns the inaccuracies (so to speak) of the judgments made from the higher-order perspective of our reflective selves. For it is clear that only a marginal proportion of the self implicated in behavior and social interaction can ever be said to be available to conscious reflection, both generally and at any particular time. Factors connected with embodiment, demeanor, habit, and the emersion of the self in the ongoing flow of events operate outside of the purview of reflection, and often completely beyond its scope. Hence, a person's inner picture of her motivational matrix can be highly incomplete and, in many other ways, innaccurate.

Psychoanalysis provides one of the starkest models of the self's misunderstanding of itself.[20] The fundamental theoretical commitment of psychoanalytic theory is the postulate that mental contents that are not integrated into the dominant – that is, consciously available – schema of self-organization exert influences on thought and behavior. The picture that emerges is, of course, of a conflicted and non-rational psychic mechanism whose operations are accessible to conscious reflections only in distorted form or through the mediation of therapeutic intervention or other complex self-interpretive techniques.

Of course, psychoanalysis is controversial, and many rightly raise questions about the reliability of (at least the details of) the postulates it produces concerning sub-conscious mechanisms. But evidence of systematic self-misunderstanding can be gleaned from several other traditions in individual and social psychology.[21] Cognitive dissonance theory, for example, trades on the postulate that a fundamental operation of mental reflection is to embrace propositions that accord with established self-conceptions and resist those that destabilize them, independent of the epistemological ground of such information. Internal coherence trumps probable truth. In addition, any number of (often self-serving) biases shape judgements about internal states, capabilities, and traits. A general tendency has been observed toward attributing responsibility for positive outcomes to the self while explaining failures in terms of environmental factors (the "self-serving attribution bias"). Also, people will find flaws in evidence that portrays them in an unflattering light, and they are selective in sorting through memory when considering evidence for desirable traits.[22]

More generally, what psychologists call the "fundamental attribution error" refers to the systematic tendency to mis-estimate the role of either personal characteristics or environmental factors in explaining one's own or others' behaviors.[23] People routinely and predictably attribute behavior to character traits or dispositions when overwhelming evidence (available to them) indicates otherwise. And agents' perceptions of themselves and their own motives follow the same pattern as observation of others: the tendency to misidentify motives and the causes of our behavior is psychologically ubiquitous.[24] And our appraisals of our own emotions and attitudes tends to be equally prone to "error," indicating little, if any, advantage we have in having direct (introspective) access to such feelings.[25]

Material of this sort, admittedly presented here only selectively, does much to bolster skepticism concerning the possibilities of self-transparency. What emerges from these several angles is a picture of systematic self-delusion or, at best, a fundamental disconnect between introspective understanding and actual structures of motivation, thought, and behavior. In these ways, to the extent that autonomy demands that we reflect accurately on our motivations, desires, and reasons, most of us are systematically heteronomous in identifiable ways.

Indeed, this is a more empirically-minded way of expressing what commentators writing in a post-modern mode have been saying about the liberal conception of the self for some time – namely, that such a conception wrongly assumes a transparent, unified, fully rationalized self-conception of a sort no one realistically can realize.[26] Even when avoiding the psychoanalytic models mentioned earlier, such critics decry the fiction of a fully self-transparent consciousness as a basic presupposition of the model of the (autonomous) person at the heart of liberal theories of justice.

With all these reasons for questioning the reliability of our reflective functions in capturing and representing ourselves, why should we continue to require reflective endorsement of any kind for autonomy? Answering such a question involves two complicated steps. The first is to examine the role the concept of autonomy plays in various theoretical and practical contexts, here the context of liberal political theory, thereby locating the manner in which self-reflection figures in that dynamic. The second is returning to the concept of autonomy and refining the conditions of self-knowledge that (1) capture what is required by the concept's role in those political/theoretical settings, and (2) squares with the information just outlined concerning the systematic limits of the typical person's self-understanding. What I will suggest is that autonomy, when viewed a certain way, plays a role in the legitimation of political principles in such a manner that reflective self-appraisal will be a crucial requirement, despite (and in come cases because of) the complex effects that such reflection has on motivation, self-understanding, and social interaction.

III Autonomy and Varieties of Liberalism

The context in which the conception of autonomy at issue here will be tested is that of modernist liberal theories of justice, ones in which political authority is generated by way of citizen endorsement of collective social values. Liberal views reject a metaphysically ordered hierarchy of values, and thereby embrace a degree of value pluralism. No single overriding value and no fixed ordering of values can be determined to be objectively valid for all agents, on this view.[27] Liberalism rests on the idea, then, that political power is legitimate only if it is endorsed or accepted by citizens living under it "in light of their common human reason" (as Rawls puts it).[28] This implies that the principles expressive of this power rest on respect for citizens' abilities to rationally endorse the content of those principles. Therefore, liberalism rests on respect for individual autonomy as conceived generally as the "moral power" of judging both principles of justice and conceptions of value.[29] This respect is afforded equally to all and is reflected in the manner in which both basic principles and more specific social policies are derived (that is, democratically).

Justice, then, is formulated in a way that expresses this respect, where people are considered ultimately able to reflect upon and embrace (or reject or revise) conceptions of value for themselves.[30] Liberalism can be seen to rest on the fundamental valuation of persons as having a basic interest in pursuing their own conceptions of what is valuable, and doing so "from the inside." This conception of justice as the set of principles claimed as legitimate by those living under them utilizes what some have labeled the "endorsement constraint" on value assumed in liberal theory.[31]

It is important to note how liberalism, in this general sketch, is fundamentally opposed to certain kinds of perfectionism (in both moral and political theory). Although there are varieties of perfectionist liberals, most of those views take it that the fundamental (perfectionist) value that just institutions must respect is autonomy itself.[32] What liberalism of all these sorts opposes is the view that there are values or moral imperatives that are valid (for a person) independent of that person's subjective appraisal, and hence first-person endorsement, of that value. Not only the (European) medieval worldview concerning a metaphysically structured value scheme in which humans played only a part, but contemporary views of the objectivity of value must be put to one side here, at least as a means to provide foundations for political principles.[33] The tradition of political thought in which autonomy plays a crucial role and is the subject of examination here is one that contrasts deeply with that perfectionist standpoint.

But we must recognize a sharp distinction in liberal views of the authority of the state. In one, which we can call the Hobbesean variant, collective choice (via either the original social contract or ongoing democratic mechanisms) is seen as an aggregation of individual rational desires. The purpose of political institutions, on this view, is to provide stability and peace in order that citizens may pursue their own rational life plans, separately and for their own reasons. The ground of political authority, in this tradition, is self-interested rationality manifested in strategic interaction with others.[34] In the second tradition, emanating from Locke, Rousseau, and Kant, citizens are understood to have a *moral* connection to the authority of the state, insofar as such authority is a collective manifestation of their own autonomy. Collective choice, on this model, is simply the social version of the independent self-government that grounds all morality and obligation. Political authority, then, is grounded in a moral obligation (rather than simply rational bargaining).[35]

Indeed, we can generalize this distinction to apply to any social interaction whose purpose is to generate norms that will, in turn, constrict, guide, or constitute the resultant activities of the participants. In the Hobbesean case, agents view each other in a purely strategic manner, where knowledge and empathic understanding of the other's experiences or perspective are, at best, of instrumental importance to the interacting parties. There is no constitutive relation between recognition of the thoughts, preferences, and experiences of others and the binding nature of the outcome of such an interaction. Whatever one's social compatriots think or feel, on this model, one relates to them as instrumental to the achievement of the outcome of the exchange. Call this the purely strategic relation.

In the other case, the interpersonal exchange involves at least a respectful understanding of the other's perspective (at some level of abstraction or description), an understanding that is a crucial component of the reciprocity involved in this kind of social dynamic. And this attempt at understanding forms an ineliminable part of the normative grounding of the outcome. That is, participants view both the process of collective deliberation and confrontation, as well as the result, as normatively significant in part because of their shared understanding and projected moral judgment. Such an interaction must involve mutual respect and a sense of reciprocity in the familiar Kantian sense, where one attributes basic moral weight to the capacities of one's co-citizens to deliberate and decide. But it also includes an attempt at empathic comprehension of the subjectivity and motivations of others. This need not involve a flawless or even accurate understanding of another's deliberative processes, but it does require an attempt to see the point of view (together with affective and subjective elements of it when relevant) of those with whom one shares a common relation to a collectively formulated outcome, incomplete though this process will inevitably be. Again, this can take place at virtually any level of abstraction, rising, say to the point of merely saying, "I think I can understand what it is like being a motivated human who is passionate about a cause such as that." We will call this empathic respect.[36]

The normative hold that the outcomes of this type of interaction has on participants will be constitutively related to this emphatic respect. Such a theory will be grounded much more firmly in one's own perceived value-commitments. In the case of strategic interaction – the Hobbesean model – one's commitment to outcomes of interchange extends only as deep as one's occurrent self-interest, and that outcome and commitment remain stable only as a function of the initial power relations that made the compromise with the objectified other possible. We will return to this point later.

Liberal political theory, then, presupposes a conception of the (autonomous) person that is both the object of respect (upon which those principles are built) and the model for basic interests that those principles protect. (Rawls's use of the index of social primary goods as a measure of just distributive shares is an example of this, based as it is on the projection of persons as capable of forming and embracing conceptions of both justice and the good.) Parallel to this commitment, though, is the liberal presupposition of value pluralism noted earlier. Liberal theory developed (historically) by rejecting various medieval and Scholastic metaphysical conceptions that postulated a teleologically structured order of the universe. These rejected pictures of the world served to specify completely the virtues and values for both individuals and societies. Liberalism, in both its Hobbesean and Kantian varieties, replaced this metaphysical framework with (what would later galvanize into) a conception of moral commitment with the human *will* at its center. Political principles, then, and the sense of obligation binding citizens to them, are seen as grounded in the individual and collective judgments of the people involved, expressed by their rational wills.[37]

Value pluralism is the understanding that various individuals will embrace irreducibly divergent, but equally valid, moral conceptions. And political principles must take into account what Rawls calls the "fact of reasonable pluralism" – citizens pursue divergent comprehensive moral conceptions but recognize this divergence itself and accept it as a permanent fact of modern life.[38] Social values and the political principles reflective of them are generated (in part, at least) by way of collective choice and deliberation, and not given fully formed from above.

Such public endorsement of dominant political values must also occur against the backdrop of the inevitabilities of social existence. That is, contrary to the traditional assumption of a state of nature by which to measure the benefits of a specific political arrangement (a pre-social arena to which disgruntled citizens can retreat), political principles are judged by citizens who take the ongoing, historically embedded dynamics of social existence as an unavoidable fact (along with the pluralism of value-conceptions this brings with it).[39]

Therefore, interaction and collective deliberation among divergent viewpoints is fundamental to the process of legitimation and justification of social power. This view has been the dominant theme in the recent work of both Rawls and Habermas. The latter has developed the most complex picture of the centrality of discursive communicative action in the justification of both moral and political principles (indeed all of the claims to validity that underlie the use of language itself).[40] Indeed, on Habermas's view of the development of individualized *identity* (individuation), the person (child) internalizes the social meanings and normative structures of the surrounding, usually parental, voices.[41] The dialogic interaction with a "generalized other" takes the place of the assumption of a disembodied and objective viewpoint of Enlightenment (that is, purely Kantian) thinking. Intersubjective validity replaces depersonalized objectivity, and such intersubjectivity is established by ongoing, linguistically mediated social interaction with surrounding others. Normative (moral) validity is fixed in reference to a principle whereby all affected by a decision could freely accept the consequences of its general observance given their needs and interests.[42] Individuation occurs with the development of capacities of questioning, reflection, and critique as a component of the participation in dialogue and internalization of social meanings that such a test of validity requires.[43] Hence, as a view of *personal* development, this model mirrors the requirements of legitimacy that liberal theories require of *social* principles. That is, the ability to reflectively negotiate collectively generated norms and to present critical points of view in the dynamic of such deliberations is central to the legitimacy of the political principles expressive of those norms. The relevance of this comparison will arise presently when we discuss the requirements of self-understanding in the social negotiations so described.

While the social contract tradition has expressed the establishment of the collective endorsement of political principles as a *hypothetical* agreement among rational parties, recent developments in liberal theory have underscored the need for *actual* social interaction and ongoing negotiation to be seen as constitutive of political legitimacy.[44] The traditional view of a hypothetical and philosophically determined ground for agreement has been rightly challenged by those who insist that these abstract conceptions of social and individual life utilized in such hypothetical models very likely betray actual biases and exclusionary tendencies inherent in the contemporary social milieu out of which they arise (valorizing certain middle-class, white, male value-conceptions to the relative denigration of other, marginalized groups).[45] Even standard liberal theorists have claimed the centrality of democratic deliberation in the determination of the principles of justice, at least in their final form.[46]

Therefore, insofar as actual public deliberation and communication must occur for the principles of liberal justice to be settled upon and political legitimacy to be established, *self*-expression will be crucial in the functions of the citizen acting in this process. The ability to settle upon and give, publically, *reasons* for claims will function as an ineluctable element in the determination of just principles. Final determination for the order of values that will be represented in the principles of a just society must be given to citizens themselves, and such values must be defined by way of ongoing, open, discussion among autonomous citizens (and/or their representatives) in a diachronic process of refining justice and maintaining legitimacy. Thus, persons themselves must be in a position to reflect upon, and report in public settings, the value commitments that they wish to receive weight in such political deliberations.

But there are importantly different positions one can occupy with regard to the expression to others of one's own experiences, ideas, and preferences. In cases where the person speaks for herself in expressing her beliefs, desires, values, and experiences, there are two ways that this first-person representational "authority" can be understood. In the first way, we view the person as the *epistemic* authority on what she is representing:

she speaks for herself because she knows herself (perhaps more than others or perhaps absolutely). In the second way, she has *personal* authority where she is designated as the expressive voice of those value commitments, independent of her actual ongoing hold on the content of those expressions. The point of this distinction is that one can enjoy the second type of self-representational authority without claiming the first. I might be assigned a role of expressing some material for reasons independent of my epistemic position in regards to it.

Epistemic authority over self-expressions is grounded in the assumption of a "truth of the matter" regarding the content of what is to be represented. That is, granting someone expressive authority on epistemic grounds makes sense only if (1) there is a settled truth concerning which representation is appointed or accepted, and (2) the representing agent is in the best epistemic position to know that content.[47] However, in cases where these two provisions fail to hold, the case for granting representative authority on epistemic grounds becomes weaker. And as we will see later, the assumptions about the kind of social deliberation involved in processes of liberal legitimacy cannot presuppose that there is a "fact of the matter" concerning value-statements independent of the person's own internal grasp and endorsement of that value; being in the best position to know what is "true" is less important than being in a position to adopt *for oneself* that to which one is committed.

Now let us return to the conception of the *autonomous* person to which liberal theory relies so that we can connect our endorsement of self-reflection as a component of autonomy while acknowledging the difficulties in its operation outlined earlier.

IV Autonomy and Self-Reflection Revisited

In contexts where interaction with others brings about collective decisions, the normative anchor that such outcomes provide for the participants depends heavily on the acknowledgment of the autonomy of one's co-deliberators. But autonomy in what sense? The model I have suggested here requires that the autonomous person exhibit minimal cognitive competence and hypothetical self-endorsement (interpreted as non-alienation) via self-reflection. That is, the authenticity that autonomy requires obtains when, were one to turn a reflective eye toward the motives, values, and concepts that structure one's judgments (and do so in a piecemeal manner), one would not feel deep self-alienation, self-repudiation, and unresolvable conflict.

An important point to note here is that the hypothetical self-reflection involved in this test for authenticity does not imply accurate self-knowledge or self-transparency. The test is purely subjective in that it takes as its perspectival orientation the agent's own point of view, independent of any external account of the motives, values, and beliefs to which she might turn her attention. Moreover, the non-alienation characteristic of the autonomous person has both phenomenological and affective elements: the agent would not feel a sense of self-repudiation in the internal grasping of her sense of the motives and impulses that move her to action.[48]

But in what way can this model of the liberal (autonomous) person square with the accepted levels of self-*mis*understanding that we outlined above? To see if it does, we need first to recall the distinction between two kinds of self-expressive authority – epistemic and personal authority: the lack of self-understanding we accepted only touches the assumption of (some kind of) epistemic authority on the part of self-representing agents. Insofar as the reasons for granting self-representational authority in collective decisions are personal rather than epistemic, then failures of epistemic access to the content of one's expressions – one's self-knowledge in this case – will be less serious. (Though they will by no means be irrelevant: see later discussion.)

Second, we need to focus on the distinction between the two kinds of liberalism noted earlier: In the Hobbesean variant, the point of granting individual rights of self-expression and participation in the process of legitimating state power is that such expression functions as a conduit for the promotion of the rational interests of the parties. State power, remember, is justified as a coordination device for the maximal satisfaction of such interests. Therefore, the authority granted to citizens to express their own judgments is clearly *epistemic* authority: it is the authority to judge and express their own interests, interests that are well defined independently of the process of subjective grasping and endorsement. That is, according to Hobbesean contract theory, state power is designed to protect the *idealized* desires of the participants. Their own judgments of what those desires are may well, for the reasons outlined in our examination of self-knowledge, be systematically distorted.

So for Hobbesean liberalism, full self-knowledge (as a condition of the autonomy assumed in citizens) is a necessary condition for the validity of outcomes of collective choice. Only when actual interests are expressed in deliberation will the process of aggregating such interests – which, on the Hobbesean model, is the fundamental role of the state – operate correctly. And the interests in question are determinable independent (in principle) of the person's judgment about them: a person can be mistaken about her interests (as well as her motives, psychological states, and the like, as we saw earlier).

However, one need not accept the Hobbesean account of political authority. While I cannot argue for this here, there is good reason to avoid seeing the legitimacy of political institutions as fundamentally the coordination of individually determined interests of the citizens living under it.[49] The assumption of individualized self-interest, to take one example of a core assumption of the Hobbesean view, is highly problematic; moreover, it is not at all clear that even if citizens were self-interested and motivated by individualized desires, social stability of the sort promised by Hobbesean political theory would materialize or be maintained.[50]

On the other hand, the Kantian variant of liberalism grants individuals powers of self-government for a different reason – only when political principles are embraced authentically by those governed by them are they valid for those people. Collective deliberation in order to legitimate state power and to generate new legislation functions by way of mutual respect and what I called "empathic respect" for others' differences. For the later Rawls, for example (who departs from the literal Kantianism of his earlier view but remains in the category I am here labeling "Kantian"), the overlapping consensus that legitimates principles of justice must be "affirmed" from within each citizen's comprehensive moral view, and hence must involve a moral commitment to cooperative interaction with others whose views differ. For Habermas, valid (political) claims presuppose sincere and free interchange among participants, all of whom implicitly accept the normative presuppositions of discourse itself. Sincerity involves not simply reporting what is in fact true but expressing what one deeply believes. One can be sincere but incorrect, and it is sincerity that is presupposed in discursive interchange. Therefore, *personal* (self-representational) authority (in my sense) is what is granted in communicative action.

Thus, no presumption of epistemic authority over a person's motives and desires must be granted in this matrix; representational authority is all that is needed to ground the mutual respect (and empathic understanding) that, I have argued, functions to legitimate state power. It is as if we say to each other: you may be often mistaken about what truly moves you and what is in your best interest, but nevertheless you always get to speak for yourself on such matters. The reason for this position is moral/political, not epistemic: in order to ensure the personal endorsement necessary for the validity of value commitments one must embrace and express for oneself such commitments; externally determined validity (a "fact of the matter" fixed independent of such endorsement) of values is not recognized.

Democratic institutions that arise as part of (and, some would argue, a *constitutive* part of) principles of justice require that citizens (perhaps through their representatives) be in a position to advance *reasons* for the interests they wish to see promoted collectively in their society. Democratic deliberation, then, also requires participants' abilities to reflectively endorse, indeed publically defend, the points of view, values, interests, and opinions that are the inputs to such deliberative processes (the "outputs" of which are social principles and policies). This provides further reason for the presupposition that the autonomous person is able to reflectively grasp and present her values and perspective. This accords her the kind of representational authority over those points of view but also necessitates their capacity to reflect on their values as part of the dynamic of social interchange that produces collectively justified principles. So autonomy as competent, self-reflective endorsement (non-alienation) is central to this understanding of justice and politics.

Therefore, for reasons of social legitimation, interpreted as the liberal principle of legitimacy for political institutions and principles, self-reflection is a crucial mark of the autonomous citizen whose status is respected and whose interests are protected in just political arrangements. Only if a person is put in a position to *speak for herself*, can the collectively generated principles of justice claim the legitimacy required by liberal theory. Advancing her interests in a way that thoroughly bypasses reflective endorsement of them threatens to violate the requirement that values promoted in a society obtain validity only by being subject to the citizens' endorsement of them. So liberal legitimacy presupposes a model of the (autonomous) person able to reflectively endorse her interests, respect for which is reflected in the structure of the principles themselves.[51]

What, then, should be the standards of self-understanding and cognitive competence that autonomy, used in this context, requires? To answer this question, we must say a bit more about the epistemic standards of public reason, within which autonomous self-expression plays such a crucial role. This is a complex subject, but, beyond what has already been said, we will have to be brief.[52] First, in order for public justification to proceed in a way consistent with the endorsement constraint, we must assume at least a modest internalism as our epistemic standard of justification at the individual level. That is to say, no value claim can be said to be valid for a person (or no belief about such a claim or its components) unless there is an inferential relation between such a claim and other elements of that person's belief/value corpus. Pure externalism would deny this and claim that some beliefs are justified for a person wholly independent (in principle) of that person's belief set. But the endorsement constraint implies that, ideally at least, a person could come to embrace (or at least not be deeply alienated from) the value in question. This is not possible unless there is a hermeneutic or otherwise inferential relation between that value and things the person already holds.[53]

Second, a person must have a level of understanding of her own psyche so that she is a relatively *consistent* representative of a viewpoint. If manifest inconsistencies arise from or are involved already in her corpus of desires and values, then the process of deliberation and negotiation cannot fruitfully proceed. So absence of manifest inconsistencies – where fully contradictory beliefs or values are held in ways that could bring them easily to mind – is a necessary part of autonomy competence. But this is compatible, it must be stressed, with sincere ambivalence and measured changes of mind. I meet this requirement even if I am torn in two directions on an issue or if I alter my view in light of new information and deliberation itself. But a person who is notably pulled by inconsistent desires in ways she does not admit – acting on or expressing one at one moment and doing the opposite the next – is not a competent deliberator and hence not autonomous in the requisite sense.

Third, mis-identification of motives as specific as those described in the various attribution errors described earlier need not disturb the self-expressive authority assumed in autonomy-based liberalism. One need not correctly identify the motivating reasons for action or decisions, as long as one takes responsibility for such decisions once they are made. As for the mis-labeling of either the character or the source of our emotions and attitudes, public deliberation need not be seen as a process of *discovery* of stable and independently existing attitudes that such deliberation serves merely to coordinate or (as appropriate) aggregate. At least under what I am calling the Kantian rubric, public discourse is itself a process of moral importance not reducible to its revelatory role in uncovering nascent internal states of the agent. We are not merely counting votes. So when people's interaction in public debate functions in ways that "distort" their reporting of their own attitudes, their public stance in that debate thereby becomes the position they are committed to, independent of its representational accuracy concerning the internal states of the person.

A matter of some importance here is the manner in which commitments to beliefs or value claims can be made valid upon the decision to commit oneself to them. This is akin to the existentialist point that our existence (and our choices) precedes our essence, and our commitments follow in part from our choices themselves, thereby constituting our being. However, we should add (hence deviating from Sartrean doctrine) that the validity of a norm for a person need not be understood as wholly subjective. As Charles Taylor has argued, a fundamental aspect of human agency is a commitment to "strong evaluations" – value judgments whose validity lies, in part at least, beyond the merely subjective choice to accept them. Moreover, the process of public reason itself demands the giving of reasons to others that are (1) sincere (so held as valid by the person making the claim), and (2) grounded in considerations that could appeal to those others, hence not wholly grounded in subjective choice.

But the endorsement constraint continues to operate here. For it implies that subjective embrace of a value is a necessary component of its validity (for a person). So a person's *act* of embracing a view, or embracing a view as part of a process of publically expressing it in the dynamics of public deliberation, makes it her *own* in this crucial sense. Even if I am somewhat out of touch with my motives, or systematically mistaken about the psychological sources of my opinions and values, I commit myself to them as I advance them to others in public discourse. I, therefore, *construct* myself (in part) by committing myself to this or that belief. At least I construct and commit myself provisionally in that I am open to reasons from others and, as a sincere and non-strategic communicator, I listen to others in ways that may lead me to reconsider my own views. But as a participant in this process, I commit myself to views I judge to be right by expressing them, not (or not always) by simply discovering them as a settled aspect of my nexus of other beliefs, desires, and values.

In this way, the fact that reflective self-appraisal tends to undercut the person's own commitments (or merely serve as a rationalization of some of them) becomes less troubling: the public stand one takes in discourse and deliberation becomes the position to which one is held responsible in the process of generating valid social norms and the legitimacy they enjoy. It is hoped (not entirely without reason) that the *process* of public interchange itself can induce dynamic reconsideration of one's own position on various matters that will reduce whatever disconnect there might exist between a public report and a private drive.

Hence, psychoanalytic, and indeed post-modern, pictures of the fragmented and decentered self do not conflict with this picture of liberal autonomy insofar as the requirements of self-understanding in the model of autonomy at work make no demands of strict internal unity, stable emotional or attitudinal matrices, opaque psychological mechanisms, and the like. What it demands is that the person's characteristics (values, desires, and the like) be subject to her own reflective appraisal and, if not found to be deeply repugnant, presented publicly as a position for which she is held responsible. If the very act of discursive interchange in effect constructs the value position that is the focus of this responsibility, that is consistent with the anti-perfectionism implicit in the version of liberalism alluded to here: under this view, there is no pre-determined value scheme that lies outside of human embrace and construction waiting to be found.

V Summing Up

Several objectives were pursued in this chapter. One was to claim that conceptions of autonomy should not rest on a single conception of the "self," since conceptualization of selves are (validly) understood to be multiple and variable. Second, a model of autonomy was put forward and (in part) defended, though problems with a central element of that model (the requirement of self-reflection) were aired and expanded. But we came back to the view that autonomy requires self-reflection because of the role that the concept of autonomy plays in certain political principles prominent in current theoretical constructions.

These constructions found no independent defense here, of course, and those who reject them in whole or in part will not be particularly satisfied with the chapter's conclusions. But these constructions were sketched in broad enough form (breadth that carried with it that degree of vagueness and imprecision) that they should seem compelling to many, if only because they are intended to represent a large current in modern(ist) approaches to political legitimacy and justice. To show that autonomy in something like the form defended here is necessary for the acceptability of those broadly construed theoretical constructions is no mean accomplishment, fragile though it is.

Notes

1. See, for example, Michael Sandel *Liberalism and the Limits of Justice*, 2nd ed. (Cambridge: Cambridge University Press, 1999); Iris Young, *Justice and the Politics of Difference* (Princeton, NJ: Princeton University Press, 1990); and Daniel Bell, *Communitarianism and its Critics*. Oxford: Clarendon, 1993.

2. For a survey of literature on autonomy, see John Christman, "Constructing the Inner Citadel: Recent Work on the Concept of Autonomy" in *Ethics* vol. 99, no. 1 (Fall, 1988), 109–24. See also Catriona Mackenzie and Natalie Stoljar, "Introduction: Autonomy Reconfigured" in Mackenzie and Stoljar, eds., *Relational Autonomy: Feminist Perspectives on Autonomy, Agency, and the Social Self* (New York: Oxford University Press, 2000), 3–31; and the essays in *The Inner Citadel: Essays on Individual Autonomy* (New York: Oxford University Press, 1989). Other discussions of note of the concept include Lawrence Haworth, *Autonomy: An Essay in Philosophical Psychology and Ethics* (New Haven: Yale University Press, 1986); Gerald Dworkin, *The Theory and Practice of Autonomy* (Cambridge: Cambridge University Press, 1990); Alfred Mele, *Autonomous Agents* (New York: Oxford University Press, 1995); Diana T. Meyers, *Self, Society and Personal Choice* (New York: Columbia University Press, 1989); and Bernard Berofsky, *Liberation from Self* (Cambridge: Cambridge University Press, 1995).
3. Isaiah Berlin, "Two Concepts of Liberty" in *Four Essays On Liberty* (Oxford: Oxford University Press, 1969), 118–72.
4. See, for example, Charles Taylor, *The Ethics of Authenticity* (Cambridge, MA: Harvard University Press, 1991), 33ff.
5. Some, however, continue to insist on a close connection between autonomy and the self: see Marina Oshana (Chapter 4 in the present volume). For a focused argument for the separation between self and autonomy, see Bernard Berofsky, *Liberation from Self*.
6. Typically, the focus of models of autonomy are specifically the agent's desires. However, there is good reason to broaden this to include any aspects of the person relevant to identity, action, and choice. One can lack autonomy relative to emotions, skills, physical factors, knowledge, and general states of being as well as to desires *per se*. For discussion, see my "Liberalism, Autonomy, and Self-Transformation," *Social Theory and Practice* 27, 2 (2001). See also Richard Double, "Two Types of Autonomy Accounts," *Canadian Journal of Philosophy* 22, no. 1 (March, 1992), 66.
7. I defend this view also in "Liberalism, Autonomy, and Self-Transformation."
8. In my original formulation of this idea, I claimed that the person must reflect upon and accept the processes of self development himself. I now see the limitations of this formulation, and have amended this requirement as indicated in the text. See "Autonomy and Personal History," *Canadian Journal of Philosophy* 21, no. 1 (March, 1991), 1–24. For criticism of this version of the view, see Alfred Mele, "History and Personal Autonomy," *Canadian Journal of Philosophy* 23 (1991), 271–80; and for a reply, see "Defending Personal Autonomy: A Reply to Professor Mele," *Canadian Journal of Philosophy* 23 (1993), 281–90. For a discussion of historical views of autonomy, see Alfred Mele, *Autonomous Agents: From Self-Control to Autonomy* (New York: Oxford University Press, 1995). For a historical account of moral responsibility, see John Martin Fisher and Mark Ravizza, *Moral Responsibility and Control* (Cambridge: Cambridge University Press, 1998).
9. The concept of self-alienation is analyzed in different form in certain areas of psychoanalytic theory: see, for example, Karen Horney, *Our Inner Conflicts: A Constructive Theory of Neurosis* (New York: Norton, 1945). For a discussion of

autonomy and personal integrity, see Diana T. Meyers, *Self, Society, and Personal Choice*, 59–75. A parallel idea plays a role in Ronald Dworkin's distinction between those aspects of a person's personality for which she should be held responsible (for the purposes of distributive justice) and those that are part of her "circumstances" and hence subject to egalitarian redistribution. See *Sovereign Virtue: The Theory and Practice of Equality* (Cambridge, MA: Harvard University Press, 2000), 286–91, 322–23.

10. Gerald Dworkin's account of autonomy suffers from this (relatively minor) weakness, I think, in that all his model requires is the "capacity to raise the question of whether I will identify or reject the reasons for which I now act" (*The Theory and Practice of Autonomy*, p. 15).

11. This does not imply, as some liberal theorists have been (rightly in some cases) accused of claiming, that a person must be able to alter all aspects of her values and convictions upon reflection. The requirement is that she must be able to shed only those traits or commitments from which she feels deeply alienated. For discussion, see my "Liberalism, Autonomy, and Self-Transformation."

12. See, for example, Harry Frankfurt "Identity and Wholeheartedness" in *The Importance of What We Care About* (Cambridge: Cambridge University Press), 159–76.

13. Cf. Meyers, *Self, Society, and Personal Choice*, 72.

14. For further discussion, see my "Autonomy and Personal History".

15. For further discussion and elaboration of this condition, see my "Relational Autonomy, Liberal Individualism, and the Social Constitution of Selves," *Philosophical Studies* 117 (2004): 143–64.

16. Discussion of this issue can be found in Diana T. Meyers, *Subjection and Subjectivity: Psychoanalytic Feminism and Moral Philosophy* (New York: Routledge, 1994) as well as *Self, Society, and Personal Choice*, pp. 28ff.

17. See, for example, Bernard Williams, "Persons, Character, and Morality" in *Moral Luck* (Cambridge: Cambridge University Press, 1983), 1–19, and Robert Bellah, et. al., *Habits of the Heart* (Berkeley, CA: University of California Press, 1985). See also my "Liberalism, Autonomy, and Self-Transformation."

18. A similar argument is made by Bernard Williams concerning moral principles; see "Styles of Ethical Theory" in *Ethics and the Limits of Philosophy* (Cambridge: Cambridge University Press, 1985), 71–92.

19. These kinds of distortions are merely more specific instances of the kind of disconnect that critics have noted about the requirement of second-order reflection on first-order aspects of the self for autonomy. See Marilyn Friedman, "Autonomy and the Split-Level Self," *Southern Journal of Philosophy*, vol. 24 no. 1 (1986): 19–35, and Irving Thalberg, "Hierarchical Analyses of Unfree Action," reprinted in *The Inner Citadel*, 123–136.

20. For an overview, see Morris Eagle, "Psychoanalytic Conceptions of the Self" in Jane Strauss and George Goethals, eds., *The Self: Interdisciplinary Approaches* (New York: Springer-Verlag, 1991), 49–65.

21. For discussion of recent social psychological work on the self that reflects this tradition, see Roy Baumeister, "The Self," in *Handbook of Social Psychology*, Daniel T. Gilbert, Susan T. Fiske, and Gardner Lindzey, eds., vol. I (Boston,

MA: McGraw-Hill, 1991), 680–740. For discussion of the historical development of theories of the self, see Susan Harter, "Historical Roots of Contemporary Issues Involving Self-Concept," in Bruce A. Bracken, ed., *Handbook of Self-Concept: Developmental, Social, and Clinical Considerations* (New York: John Wiley & Sons, Inc., 1996), 1–38, and Kenneth J. Gergen *The Concept of Self* (New York: Holt, Rinehart, and Winston, 1971), 1–12.

22. See Baumeister, 690ff for overview and discussion of these observations.
23. See Richard Nisbett and Lee Ross, *Human Inference: Strategies and Shortcomings of Social Judgment* (Englewood Cliffs, NJ: Prentice Hall, 1980), 120ff. For a discussion of the relation between such errors and moral philosophy, see Gilbert Harman, "Moral Philosophy Meets Social Psychology: Virtue Ethics and the Fundamental Attribution Error," *Proceedings of the Aristotelian Society* 1998–99 (1999), 315–31.
24. See Daryl J. Bem, "Self-Perception Theory" in L. Berkowitz, ed., *Advances in Experimental Social Psychology*, vol. 6 (New York: Academic Press, 1972). For discussion, see Ross and Nisbett, *Human Inference*, 195–227.
25. This is shown in experiments in which subjects are given artificial stimuli inducing certain emotions but will mis-identify both the source and the nature of that emotion (ignoring, for example, the readily apparent artificial source): See Ross and Nisbett, *Human Inference*, 199–210, for an overview.
26. See, for example, Judith Butler, *The Psychic Life of Power* (Stanford, CA: Stanford University Press, 1997. For discussion, see Diana Meyers, *Subjection and Subjectivity*.
27. This is not to say that liberalism, by definition, is anti-perfectionist. There are plenty of perfectionist liberal views around: see, for example, Joseph Raz, *The Morality of Freedom* (Oxford: Clarendon Press, 1986); Will Kymlicka, *Liberalism, Community, and Culture*, (Oxford: Clarendon, 1989); and William Galston *Liberal Purposes* (Cambridge: Cambridge University Press, 1991). For further discussion of the contours of liberalism, see my *Social and Political Philosophy: A Contemporary Introduction* (New York: Routledge, 2002), chapter 4.
28. This is meant to express the principle of liberal legitimacy: see Rawls, *Justice as Fairness: A Restatement* (Cambridge, MA: Harvard University Press, 2001), 41.
29. See Rawls, *Political Liberalism*, 25–35, for discussion.
30. This formulation is meant to be neutral about the fundamental *grounds* for this respect, leaving open the possibility that such ground is ultimately "political" rather than metaphysical. For discussion, see Rawls, *Justice as Fairness: A Restatement*; Charles Larmore, *Patterns of Moral Complexity.* (Cambridge: Cambridge University Press, 1987); and John Gray, *Post-Liberalism: Studies in Political Thought.* New York: Routledge, 1993).
31. Kymlicka, *Liberalism, Community and Culture*, 10–12. Kymlicka sees this constraint on the view of *value* that is assumed in liberal theory, since he claims that liberalism rests on this unique conception of value rather than the assumption of the "priority of the right over the good" claimed here. For discussion of this difference, see Christman, *Social and Political Philosophy*, 97. Also, Gerald Gaus (Chapter 12 in the present volume) claims that liberalism

should be defined as the tradition of political philosophy that puts ultimate value on individual liberty (conceived as a presumptive right to noninterference). I will only mention in passing here the reason that moves me in another direction – that "liberty" cannot function in this way as a basic value since it is an essentially contested and, more importantly, derivative, political value (derivative from the conception of the "right," or justice, operative in the society). For discussion of the concept of liberty, see my *The Myth of Property*, chapter 4, and Ronald Dworkin, *Sovereign Virtue* (Cambridge, MA: Harvard University Press, 2000), chapter 3.

32. See Joseph Raz, *The Morality of Freedom*; Will Kymlicka, *Liberalism, Community, and Culture*; and Ronald Dworkin, *Sovereign Virtue*.

33. See, for example, Steven Wall, *Liberalism, Perfectionism and Restraint* (New York: Cambridge University Press, 1998); Thomas Hurka, *Perfectionism* (New York: Oxford University Press, 1993); and George Sher, *Beyond Neutrality: Perfectionism and Politics* (Cambridge: Cambridge University Press, 1997).

34. A paradigm case of this approach can be found in David Gauthier, *Morals By Agreement* (Oxford: Oxford University Press, 1986), but see also Jan Narveson *The Libertarian Idea* (Philadelphia, PA: Temple University Press, 1988), chapter 14.

35. This variant is seen most clearly in Rawls, *A Theory of Justice* (Cambridge, MA: Harvard University Press, 1971), but it survives in the view developed in *Political Liberalism* – that is, according to "political" liberalism – where principles of justice are established via an overlapping consensus among reasonable comprehensive moral views – citizens are able to "affirm" the principles from "within their own comprehensive views" (*Political Liberalism*, Lecture IV) – that is *morally*. To do otherwise is to adopt the view that justice is a mere *modus vivendi*. Also making much use of the kind of distinction described in the text (or at least one parallel to it) is Habermas, especially in the distinction he makes between "strategic" and "communicative" social interaction. See *Moral Consciousness and Communicative Action* (Cambridge, MA: MIT Press, 1991), 58. For a similar distinction in approaches to political justification, see Gerald Gaus, "Liberalism," *Stanford Encyclopedia of Philosophy* (http://plato.stanford.edu), p. 5. See also Michael Sandel, *Liberalism and the Limits of Justice*, 1–7.

36. This is an explication of a Kantian conception of the grounds of justice, utilizing the views of several writers in this tradition, most notably Rawls and Habermas (about whom more will be said later). But the call for including a sense of *empathic* respect is motivated by the arguments of Susan Moller Okin in *Justice, Gender and the Family* (New York: Basic Books, 1989), 187.

37. This is compatible, it should be repeated, with perfectionist brands of liberal thought, as long as such perfectionism retains this "endorsement constraint" and admits of a pluralism of (allegedly objective) values.

38. Rawls, *Political Liberalism*, 35ff.

39. This point is stressed in Kant (influenced, no doubt, by Rousseau): see "On the Common Saying that It May Be True in Theory but Not in Practice," in *Practical Philosophy*, Mary Gregor, trans. (Cambridge: Cambridge University

Press, 1996), 273–310. See also Jeremy Waldron, *The Dignity of Legislation* (Cambridge: Cambridge University Press, 1999), 47–52 (see especially p. 52, n. 43). This point, and its importance, is overlooked in much recent liberal theory: see, for example, Gerald Gaus, "Liberalism."

40. *The Theory of Communicative Action*, vols. I and II, Thomas McCarthy trans. (Boston, MA: Beacon Press, 1984, 1987). See also *Moral Consciousness and Communicative Action*, 43–194.

41. Habermas, "Moral Development and Ego Identity," in *Communication and the Evolution of Society*, Thomas McCarthy, trans. (Boston, MA: Beacon Press, 1979), 69–94.

42. See "Moral Consciousness and Communicative Action," 120–22, and *Between Facts and Norms*, 107. In the truncated version here, I combine what Habermas calls a rule of "argumentation" (principle "D") with the principle of universalization he labels "U." Habermas, *Between Facts and Norms*, trans. William Rehg (Cambridge, MA: MIT Press, 1996), p. 107.

43. This view of normativity and personal individuation is controversial, and certainly much more complex than this. For critical discussion, see for example, Seyla Benhabib, "The General and Concrete Other," in Eva Feder Kittay and Diana T. Meyers, eds., *Women and Moral Theory* (Totowah, NJ: Rowman and Littlefield, 1987) 154–77; and Allison Weir, "Toward A Model of Self-Identity: Habermas and Kristeva," in *Feminists Read Habermas* (New York: Routledge, 1995), 263–82.

44. To say that political principles will be "fleshed out" is to align oneself with Rawlsian political liberalism, understood a certain way, where the justification of principles is hypothetical (even via the use of public reason): these principles are justified if an overlapping consensus involving them could be established. For other theorists, actual social deliberation and democratic communication *constitutes* the justification of principles. See, for example, Habermas, *Between Facts and Norms*.

45. For arguments along these lines, see Iris Marion Young, *Justice and the Politics of Difference* (Princeton, NJ: Princeton University Press, 1990); Nancy Fraser, *Justice Interruptus* (New York: Routledge, 1997); and Jürgen Habermas, *The Inclusion of the Other* (Cambridge, MA: MIT Press, 1998). Even Rawls eventually claimed that the dynamics of public reason – real world, ongoing, interaction among persons and groups provides the ultimate anchor for the overlapping consensus on which justice is grounded: see "The Idea of Public Reason Revisited," in *The Law of Peoples* (Cambridge, MA: Harvard University Press, 1999), 129–180.

46. See, for example, Jeremy Waldron, *The Dignity of Legislation*.

47. For discussion of epistemic authority over one's own desires and motives, see Gerald Gaus, *Justificatory Liberalism* (New York: Oxford University Press, 1996), Part I.

48. It is in this way that autonomy can be seen to involve a level of self-*trust*, as has been pointed out by several writers. See, for example, Paul Benson, "Free Agency and Self-Worth," *Journal of Philosophy* 91 (1994), 650–68; Trudy Govier, "Self-Trust, Autonomy, and Self-Esteem," *Hypatia* 8 (Winter, 1993), 99–120; Carolyn McLeod and Susan Sherwin, "Relational Autonomy,

Self-Trust, and Health Care for Patients Who are Oppressed," in Mackenzie and Stoljar, eds., *Relational Autonomy*, 259-79; and Anderson and Honneth's Chapter (6) in this volume.

49. For a defense of the Hobbesean approach, as I am using that label, see Gauthier, *Morals By Agreement.* For an argument that purely instrumental rationality (on which the Hobbesean model is predicated) cannot adequately account for social stability and political authority, see Jon Elster, *The Cement of Society* (Cambridge: Cambridge University Press, 1989), chapter 3, and *Solomonic Judgments* (New York: Cambridge University Press, 1989), chapters 1 and 4. For criticism of a different type, which strikes at the heart of the Hobbesean framework, see Donald Green and Ian Shapiro, *The Pathologies of Rational Choice Theory* (New Haven, CT: Yale University Press, 1994). For general discussion of this issue, see Habermas, *The Theory of Communicative Action, Vol. II*, 119-52.

50. For a specific argument of this sort, see Thomas Christiano, "The Incoherence of Hobbesian Justifications of the State," *American Philosophical Quarterly* 31 (1994), 23-38. For a general discussion, see my *Social and Political Philosophy: A Contemporary Introduction*, chapter 2.

51. Though arrived at from a different direction, the claims being defended here involving the relation between autonomy and a persons being designated as speaking for herself resemble closely Paul Benson's views: see his Chapter 5 in the prevent volume.

52. And I rely greatly on the detailed and powerful analysis of "public justification" and its role in political legitimacy developed by Gerald Gaus in *Justificatory Liberalism.*

53. Assuming some qualified internalism for the purposes of political philosophy is not the same as claiming this as the best epistemic account, period. However, for an argument against strict externalism as an epistemic standard, see John Pollock, *Contemporary Theories of Knowledge* (London: Hutchinson, 1987), 133-49. Also, what is meant by "hermeneutic" here is that a coherent interpretation could be applied to the belief (or value set) that includes the contested element.

Bibliography

This bibliography contains works cited in the chapters of this book and so should serves as a useful reference guide for those interested in work on autonomy and liberalism (and related topics).

Ackerman, Bruce. (1980) *Social Justice in the Liberal State*. New Haven: Yale University Press.
Addelson, Kathryn. (1994) *Moral Passages: Toward a Collectivist Moral Theory*. New York: Routledge.
Allison, Henry E. (1990) *Kant's Theory of Freedom*. Cambridge: Cambridge University Press.
Anderson, Joel. (1966) "A Social Conception of Personal Volatility: Volitional Identity, Strong Evaluation, and Intersubjective Accountability." Ph.D dissertation, Northwestern University.
—— (1994) "Wünsche zweiter Ordnung, starke Wertungen und intersubjektive Kritik: Zum Begriff ethische Autonomie." *Deutsche Zeitschrift für Philosophie* 42: 97–119.
—— (2001). "Competent Need-Interpretation and Discourse Ethics," in James Bohman and William Rehg, eds., *Pluralism and the Pragmatic Turn: The Transformation of Critical Theory*. Cambridge, MA: MIT Press: 193–224.
—— (2003). "Autonomy and the Authority of Personal Commitments: From Internal Coherence to Social Normativity," *Philosophical Explorations: An International Journal for the Philosophy of Mind and Action* 6, 90–108.
—— with Warren Lux (2004). "Knowing Your Own Strength: Accurate Self-Assessment as a Requirement for Personal Autonomy" (with Warren Lux), *Philosophy, Psychiatry, and Psychology* 11 (June).
Appiah, Anthony K., and Amy Gutmann. (1996) *Color Conscious: The Political Morality of Race*. Princeton: Princeton University Press.
Arendt, Hannah. (1985) "What is Freedom?" in Arendt, *Between Past and Future*. Harmondsworth: Penguin.

Arendt, Hannah. (1985) *Between Past and Future*. Harmondsworth: Penguin Books.
Aristotle. (1996) *The Politics and the Constitution of Athens*. 2nd edition, Stephen Everson, ed. Cambridge: Cambridge University Press.
Arneson, Richard. (1985) "Freedom and Desire." *Canadian Journal of Philosophy* 15: 425–48.
—— (1991) "Autonomy and Preference Formation," in Jules Coleman and Allen Buchanan, eds., *In Harm's Way: Essays in Honor of Joel Feinberg* (Cambridge: Cambridge University Press), 42–73.
Arpaly, Nomi, and Timothy Schroeder. (1999) "Praise, Blame, and the Whole Self," *Philosophical Studies* 93: 161–88.
Babbitt, Susan. (1993) "Feminism and Objective Interests: The Role of Transformation Experiences in Rational Deliberation" in Linda Alcoff and Elizabeth Potter, eds., *Feminist Epistemologies*. New York: Routledge: 257–59.
Barber, Benjamin. (1984) *Strong Democracy. Participatory Politics for a New Age*. Berkeley, CA: University of California Press.
Baumeister, Roy (1998) "The Self," in Daniel T. Gilbert, Susan T. Fiske and Gardner Lindzey, eds., *Handbook of Social Psychology*, Vol. I, Boston, MA: McGraw-Hill.
de Beauvoir, Simone. (1952) *The Second Sex*, trans. and ed., H. M. Parshley. New York: Vintage Books.
Beckett, Christopher. (2003) "Autonomy, Liberalism, and Conjugal Love," *Res Publica* 9: 285–301.
Bell, Daniel. (1975) *The Cultural Contradictions of Capitalism*. New York: Basic Books.
Bell, Daniel. (1993) *Communitarianism and its Critics*. Oxford: Clarendon.
Bellah, Robert N., et al. (1985) *Habits of the Heart: Individualism and Commitment in American Life*. Berkeley, CA: University of California Press.
Bem, Daniel J. (1972) "Self-Perception Theory," in L. Berkowitz, ed., *Advances in Experimental Social Psychology* Vol. 6. New York: Academic Press.
Benhabib, Seyla. (1987) "The General and Concrete Other," in Eva Feder Kittay and Diana T. Meyers, eds., *Women and Moral Theory*. Totowah, NJ: Rowman & Littlefield: 154–77.
—— (1992) *Situating the Self: Gender, Community, and Postmodernism in Contemporary Ethics*. New York: Routledge.
—— ed. (1996) *Democracy and Difference*. Princeton: Princeton University Press.
—— (1997) "On Reconciliation and Respect, Justice and the Good Life: Response to Herta Nagl-Docekal and Rainer Forst," *Philosophy and Social Criticism* 23.
—— (1999) "Sexual Difference and Collective Identities: The New Global Constellation." *Signs* 24: 335–61.
Benn, Stanley. (1976) "Freedom, Autonomy and the Concept of a Person," *Proceedings of the Aristotelian Society* 66: 109–30.
—— (1986) with G.F. Gaus, "Practical Rationality and Commitment," *American Philosophical Quarterly*, vol. 23: 255–66.
—— (1988) *A Theory of Freedom*. Cambridge: Cambridge University Press.
Benson, Paul (1994) "Free Agency and Self-Worth," *Journal of Philosophy* 91 (12): 650–68.

—— (1990) "Feminist Second Thoughts About Free Agency," *Hypatia* 47–64.
—— (1991) "Autonomy and Oppressive Socialization," *Social Theory and Practice* 17: 385–408.
—— (1987) "Freedom and Value," *Journal of Philosophy* 84: 465–86.
—— (2000) "Feeling Crazy: Self-Worth and the Social Character of Responsibility," in Mackenzie and Stoljar, eds. (2000a): 72–80.
Bentley, Russell and David Owen. (2001) "Ethical Loyalties, Civic Virtue and the Circumstances of Politics," *Philosophical Explorations* IV/3: 223–39.
Berkowitz, L., and C. Turner (1972) "Perceived Anger Level, Instigating Agent, and Aggression," in H. London and R.E. Nisbett, eds., *Cognitive Alteration of Feeling States*. Chicago: Aldine: 174–89.
Berlin, Isaiah. (2002/1969) "Two Concepts of Liberty," in *Four Essays on Liberty*, Henry Hardy, ed. London: Oxford University Press, 118–72.
Berofsky, Bernard. (1995) *Liberation from Self*. New York: Cambridge University Press.
Bobbio, Norberto. (1974) *Politica e cultura*. Turin: Einaudi.
Bordo, Susan. (1993) "Are Mothers Persons? Reproductive Rights and the Politics of Subjectivity," in *Unbearable Weight*. Berkeley, CA: University of California Press.
Boxill, Bernard. (1976) "Self-Respect and Protest," *Philosophy and Public Affairs* 6: 58–69.
Bratman, Michael. (1996) "Identification, Decision, and Treating as a Reason," *Philosophical Topics* 24: 1–18.
—— (2000) "Reflection, Planning, and Temporally Extended Agency," *Philosophical Review* 109: 35–61.
Brenkert, George G. (1991) *Political Freedom*. London and New York: Routledge.
Brennan, Geoffrey and Loren Lomasky. (1993) *Democracy and Decision: The Pure Theory of Electoral Preference*. Cambridge: Cambridge University Press.
Brighouse, Harry. (1996) "Is there a Neutral Justification for Liberalism?" *Pacific Philosophical Quarterly*, vol. 77 (September): 193–215.
van den Brink, Bert. (2000) *The Tragedy of Liberalism: An Alternative Defense of a Political Tradition*. Albany, NY: SUNY Press.
Brison, Susan. (1996) "Outliving Oneself: Trauma, Memory, and Personal Autonomy," in Meyers (1996): 12–39.
—— (2003) *Aftermath: Violence and the Remaking of a Self* (Princeton: Princeton University Press.
Brodt, S.E., and P. Zimbardo. (1981) "Modifying Shyness-Related Social Behavior Through Symptom Misattribution," *Journal of Personality and Social Psychology* 41: 437–49.
Brothers, Dorothy. (1995) *Falling Backwards: An Exploration of Trust and Self-Experience*. New York: Norton.
Brown, Wendy. (1995) *States of Injury: Power and Freedom in Late Modernity*. Princeton: Princeton University Press.
Brugger, Bill. (1999) *Republican Theory in Political Thought: Virtuous or Virtual?* London: Macmillan.
Buchanan, Allan. (1989) "Assessing the Communitarian Critique of Liberalism," *Ethics* 99: 852–82.

Burtt, Shelley. (1990) "The Good Citizen's Psyche: On the Psychology of Civic Virtue," *Polity*, 23 (Fall).
—— (1993) "The Politics of Virtue Today: A Critique and a Proposal," *American Political Science Review*, 87 (June): 360–8.
Bushnell, Dana, ed. (1995) *Nagging Questions*. Lanham, MD: Rowman & Littlefield.
Buss, Sarah. (1994) "Autonomy Reconsidered," in Peter A. French, et al. eds. *Midwest Studies in Philosophy*, vol. 19. South Bend, IN: University of Notre Dame Press: 95–121.
Butler, Judith. (1990) *Gender Trouble: Feminism and the Subversion of Identity*. New York: Routledge.
—— (1997) *The Psychic Life of Power*. Stanford, CA: Stanford University Press.
Calhoun, Chesire. (1995) "Standing for Something," *Journal of Philosophy* 92: 235–60.
Chapman, John. (1956) *Rousseau–Totalitarian or Liberal?* New York: Columbia University Press.
Chodorow, Nancy. (1989) "Toward a Relational Individualism: The Mediation of Self through Psychoanalysis," in *Feminism and Psychoanalytic Theory*. New Haven: Yale University Press.
Christiano, Thomas. (1994) "The Incoherence of Hobbesian Justifications of the State," *American Philosophical Quarterly* 31: 23–38.
Christman, John. (1988) "Constructing the Inner Citadel: Recent Work on the Concept of Autonomy," *Ethics* 99, 1: 109–24.
—— ed. (1989) *The Inner Citadel: Essays on Individual Autonomy*. New York: Oxford University Press.
—— (1991a) "Autonomy and Personal History," *Canadian Journal of Philosophy* 21: 1–24.
—— (1991b) "Liberalism and Individual Positive Freedom," *Ethics* vol. 101 no. 2: 343–59.
—— (1995) "Feminism and Autonomy," in Bushnell (1995): 17–39.
—— (1995) *The Myth of Property: Toward an Egalitarian Theory of Ownership*, chapter 4. Oxford: Oxford University Press.
—— (1998) "Autonomy, Independence, and Poverty-Related Welfare Policies," *Public Affairs Quarterly* 12, 4: 383–406.
—— (2001) "Liberalism, Autonomy, and Self-Transformation," in *Social Theory and Practice* 27: 185–206.
—— (2002) *Social and Political Philosophy: A Contemporary Introduction*. London: Routledge.
—— (2002) "Autonomy in Moral and Political Philosophy," *Stanford Encyclopedia of Philosophy* (http://plato.stanford.edu/contents.html).
Cochran, David. (1999) *The Color of Freedom*. Albany, NY: SUNY Press.
Code, Lorraine. (1991) "Second Persons," in *What Can She Know? Feminist Theory and the Construction of Knowledge*. Lanham, MD: Rowman & Littlefield.
Cohen, Joshua. (1997) "The Arc of the Moral Universe," *Philosophy and Public Affairs* 26: 91–134.
Connolly, William. (1991) *Identity/Difference*. Ithaca, NY: Cornell University Press.
Constant, Benjamin. (1988) *Political Writings*, trans. and ed. Biancamaria Fontana. Cambridge: Cambridge University Press.

Copp, David. (1995) *Morality, Normativity and Society.* New York: Oxford University Press.
Cowen, Tyler. (1998) *In Praise of Commercial Culture.* Cambridge, MA: Harvard University Press.
—— (2002) *Creative Destruction.* Princeton, NJ: Princeton University Press.
Crittenden, Jack. (1992) *Beyond Individualism: Reconstituting the Liberal Self.* New York: Oxford University Press.
Dagger, Richard. (1997) *Civic Virtues: Rights, Citizenship, and Republican Liberalism.* New York: Oxford University Press.
—— (2002) "Republicanism Refashioned: Comments on Pettit's Theory of Freedom and Government," *The Good Society,* 9, 3: 50–3.
—— (1999) "The Sandelian Republic and the Encumbered Self," *The Review of Politics,* 61 (Spring): 181–208.
Davidson, Donald. (1980) *Essays on Actions and Events.* Oxford: Oxford University Press.
Dennet, Daniel. (1989) "The Origins of Selves," *Cogito* 3: 163.
—— (1991) "The Reality of Selves," in *Consciousness Explained.* Boston: Little, Brown, chapter 13.
—— (1992) "The Self as a Center of Narrative Gravity," in Frank S. Kessel, Pamela M. Cole, and Dale L. Johnson, eds., *Self and Consciousness: Multiple Perspectives.* Hillsdale, NJ: Erlbaum Associates: 103–15.
—— (1998) with Nicholas Humphrey, "Speaking for Ourselves," reprinted in *Brainchildren: Essays on Designing Minds.* Cambridge, MA: MIT Press: 31–58.
Dillon, Robin. (1997) "Self-Respect: Moral, Emotional, Political," *Ethics* 107: 226–49.
Double, Richard (1992) "Two Types of Autonomy Accounts" *Canadian Journal of Philosophy* 22: 65–80.
Dutton, D. and S. L. Painter, (1981) "Traumatic Bonding: The Development of Emotional Attachments in Battered Women and Other Relationships of Intermittent Abuse." *Victimology* 6: 139–55.
Dworkin, Gerald. (1989) "The Concept of Autonomy," in Christman, ed. (1989): 54–62.
—— (1988) *The Theory and Practice of Autonomy.* Cambridge: Cambridge University Press.
Dworkin, Ronald. (1978) "Liberalism." *Public and Private Morality,* S. Hampshire, ed. Cambridge: Cambridge University Press.
—— (1985) *A Matter of Principle.* Cambridge, MA: Harvard University Press.
—— (2000) *Sovereign Virtue: The Theory and Practice of Equality.* Cambridge, MA: Harvard University Press.
Eagle, Morris. (1991) "Psychoanalytic Conceptions of the Self," in Jane Strauss and George Goethals, eds., *The Self: Interdisciplinary Approaches.* New York: Springer-Verlag.
Eberle, Christopher. (2002) *Religious Convictions in Liberal Politics.* Cambridge: Cambridge University Press.
Ellison, Ralph. (1952) *Invisible Man.* New York: Random House.
Elster, Jon. (1989a) *The Cement of Society.* New York: Cambridge University Press.
—— (1989b) *Solomonic Judgments.* New York: Cambridge University Press.

Feinberg, Joel. (1980) "The Nature and Value of Rights," in *Rights, Justice, and the Bounds of Liberty*. Princeton: Princeton University Press.
—— (1986) *Harm to Self*. New York: Oxford University Press.
—— (1989) "Autonomy" in Christman, ed. (1989): 27–53.
Fink, Zera. (1945) *The Classical Republicans: An Essay in the Recovery of a Pattern of Thought in Seventeenth Century England*. Evanston, IL: Northwestern University Press.
Fischer, John Martin, ed. (1986) *Moral Responsibility*. Ithaca, NY: Cornell University Press.
Fischer, John Martin, and Mark Ravizza (1998) *Moral Responsibility and Control: A Theory of Moral Responsibility*. Cambridge: Cambridge University Press.
Foot, Phillippa. (1978) *Virtues and Vices*. Berkeley: University of California Press.
Forst, Rainer. (1999) "The Basic Right to Justification: Toward a Constructivist Conception of Human Rights," *Constellations* 6, 1: 35–60.
—— (1999) "Die Rechtfertigung der Gerichtigkeit. Rawls' Politischer Liberalismus und Habermas' Diskurstheorie," in *Das Recht der Republik*, section 4, Hauke Brunkhorst and Peter Niesen, eds. Frankfurt am Main: Suhrkamp.
—— (2001a) "Tolerance as a Virtue of Justice," *Philosophical Explorations* 2.
—— (2001b) "The Rule of Reasons: Three Models of Deliberative Democracy," *Ratio Juris* 14.
—— (2001c) "Towards a Critical Theory of Transnational Justice," in T. Pogge, ed., *Global Justice*. Oxford: Blackwell.
—— (2002) *Contexts of Justice: Political Philosophy Beyond Liberalism and Communitarianism*, trans. John M. Farrell. Berkeley, CA: University of California Press. German original 1994.
—— (2003a) *Toleranz im Konflikt. Geschichte, Gehalt und Gegenwart eines umstrittenen Begriffs*. Frankfurt am Main: Suhrkamp.
—— (2003b) "A Tolerant Republic?" in Jan-Werner Müller, ed., *German Ideologies Since 1945*. New York: Palgrave.
Foucault, Michel. (1970) *The Order of Things: An Archaeology of the Human Sciences*, trans. A. M. Sheridan Smith. New York: Pantheon Books.
—— (1980) "Truth and Power," in Foucault, *Power/Knowledge: Selected Interviews and Other Writings, 1972-1977*, Colin Gordon, ed. New York: Pantheon Books.
—— (1995) *Discipline and Punish: The Birth of the Prison*, trans. Alan Sheridan. New York: Vintage Books.
Frank, Robert H. (1999) *Luxury Fever*. New York: The Free Press.
Frankena, William K. (1976) "Obligation and Motivation in Recent Moral Philosophy," in K. E. Goodpaster, ed., *Perspectives on Morality: Essays by William K. Frankena*. Notre Dame: University of Notre Dame Press: 49–73.
Frankfurt, Harry G. (1987) "Freedom of the Will and the Concept of a Person," in *The Importance of What We Care About*. Cambridge: Cambridge University Press.
—— (1992) "The Faintest Passion" *Proceedings and Addresses of the Aristotelian Society* vol. 49: 113–45.
—— (1999) *Necessity, Volition, and Love*. Cambridge: Cambridge University Press.

Fraser, Nancy. (1989) *Unruly Practices: Power, Discourse, and Gender in Contemporary Social Theory.* Minneapolis: University of Minnesota Press.
—— (1997) *Justice Interruptus.* New York: Routledge.
Friedman, Marilyn. (1986) "Autonomy and the Split-Level Self," *Southern Journal of Philosophy.* vol. 24 no. 1: 19–35.
—— (1989) "Autonomy in Social Context," in Creighton Peden and James P. Sterba, eds., *Freedom, Equality, and Social Change.* Lewiston, N.Y.: Edwin Mellen, 158–69.
—— (1993) *What Are Friends For? Feminist Perspectives on Personal Relationships and Moral Theory.* Ithaca, NY: Cornell University Press.
—— (1997) "Autonomy and Social Relationships: Rethinking the Feminist Critique," in Meyers, ed.: 40–61.
—— (1998) "Feminism, Autonomy, and Emotion," in Joram Graf Haber, ed., *Norms and Values: Essays on the Work of Virginia Held.* Lanham, MD: Rowman & Littlefield.
—— (2000a) "Autonomy, Social Disruption, and Women," in Mackenzie and Stoljar, eds. (2000a): 35–51.
—— (2000b) "Feminism in Ethics: Conceptions of Autonomy," in *The Cambridge Companion to Feminism in Philosophy*, Miranda Fricker and Jennifer Hornsby, eds., Cambridge: Cambridge University Press.
—— (2000c) "John Rawls and the Political Coercion of Unreasonable People," in Victoria Davion & Clark Wolf, eds., *The Idea of a Political Liberalism: Essays on Rawls.* New York: Rowman & Littlefield: 16–33.
—— (2003) *Autonomy, Gender, and Politics.* New York: Oxford University Press.
Galbraith, John Kenneth. (1976) *The Affluent Society.* Boston: Houghton Mifflin.
Galston, William A. (1991) *Liberal Purposes: Goods, Virtues, and Diversity in the Liberal State.* Cambridge: Cambridge University Press.
Gaus, Gerald F. (1990) *Value and Justification: The Foundations of Liberal Theory.* Cambridge: Cambridge University Press.
—— (1994) "Property, Rights and Freedom," *Social Philosophy & Policy*, vol. 11 (Summer): 209–40.
—— (1996) *Justificatory Liberalism.* New York: Oxford University Press.
—— (1997) in "Does Democracy Reveal the Will of the People? Four Takes on Rousseau," *Australasian Journal of Philosophy*, vol. 75 (June): 141–62.
—— (1998) "Why All Welfare States (Including *Laissez-Faire* Ones) Are Unreasonable," *Social Philosophy and Policy*, vol. 15 (June): 1–33.
—— (1999) *Social Philosophy.* Armonk, NY: M. E. Sharpe.
—— (2001) "What is Deontology?" Parts 1 and 2, *Journal of Value Inquiry*, vol. 35: 27–42, 179–93.
—— (2002) "Goals, Symbols, Principles: Nozick on Practical Rationality," in David Schmidtz, ed., *Robert Nozick.* Cambridge: Cambridge University Press: 83–130.
—— (2003a) "Backwards into the Future: Neorepublicanism as a Postsocialist Critique of Market Society," *Social Philosophy and Policy*, 20 (Winter): 59–91.
—— (2003b) "Dirty Hands," in R. G. Frey and Christopher Heath Wellman, eds., *A Companion to Applied Ethics.* Oxford: Basil Blackwell: 167–79.

—— (2003c) *Contemporary Theories of Liberalism: Public Reason as a Post-Enlightenment Project.* London: Sage Publications.
—— (forthcoming) "The Limits of *Homo Economicus,*" in Gerald F. Gaus, Julian Lamont, and Christi Favor, eds., *Values, Justice, and Economics* (Amsterdam: Rodopi.
Gauthier, David. (1986) *Morals By Agreement.* Oxford: Clarendon Press.
Geertz, Clifford. (1973) *The Interpretation of Cultures.* New York: Basic Books.
Gergen, Kenneth J. (1971) *The Concept of Self.* New York: Holt, Rinehart, and Winston.
Geuss, Raymond. (1995) "Freedom as an Ideal," in *Proceedings of the Aristotelian Society,* suppl. vol. LXIX.
—— (2001) "Liberalism and Its Discontents," *Political Theory* vol. 30 no. 3: 320–39.
Gey, Stephen G. (1993) "The Unfortunate Revival of Civic Republicanism," *University of Pennsylvania Law Review,* 141: 801–98.
Gilligan, Carol. (1982) *In a Different Voice: Psychological Theory and Women's Development.* Cambridge, MA: Harvard University Press.
Goldsmith, M. M. (2000) "Republican Liberty Considered," *History of Political Thought,* 21 (Autumn).
Gosepath, Stephan. (1999) *Motive, Gründe, Zwecke. Theorien praktischer Rationalität.* Frankfurt am Main: Fischer.
Govier, Trudy, (1993) "Self-Trust, Autonomy, and Self-Esteem," *Hypatia* 8: 99–120.
Gray, John. (1993) *Post-Liberalism: Studies in Political Thought.* New York: Routledge.
—— (1995) *Enlightenment's Wake. Politics and Culture at the Close of the Modern Age.* London: Routledge.
Gray, Tim (1990) *Freedom.* London: Macmillan.
Green, Donald, and Ian Shapiro (1994) *The Pathologies of Rational Choice Theory.* New Haven: Yale University Press.
Grovier, Trudy. (1993) "Self-Trust, Autonomy, and Self-Esteem." *Hypatia* 8: 99–120.
Günther, Klaus. (1992) "Die Freiheit der Stellungnahme als politisches Grundrecht," *Archiv für Rechts- und Sozialphilosophie,* No. 54.
Guyer, Paul. (2000) *Kant on Freedom, Law and Happiness.* Cambridge: Cambridge University Press.
Habermas, Jürgen. (1966) *Between Facts and Norms,* trans. William Rehg. Cambridge, MA: MIT Press.
—— (1979) "Moral Development and Ego Identity," in *Communication and the Evolution of Society,* trans. Thomas McCarthy. Boston, MA: Beacon Press.
—— (1984/87) *The Theory of Communicative Action,* Vols. I and II. trans. Thomas McCarthy, Boston, MA: Beacon Press.
—— (1990) *Moral Consciousness and Communicative Action,* trans. Christian Lenhardt and Shierry Weber Nicholsen. Cambridge, MA: MIT Press.
—— (1991) *The Structural Transformation of the Public Sphere.* Cambridge, MA: MIT Press.
—— (1992) "Individuation through Socialization: On George Herbert Mead's Theory of Subjectivity," in Habermas, *Postmetaphysical Thinking,* 149–204, trans. William Hohengarten. Cambridge, MA: MIT Press, 1992.

—— (1996) *Between Facts and Norms*, trans. William Rehg. Cambridge, MA: MIT Press.

—— (1998) *The Inclusion of the Other: Stories in Political Theory*. Ciaran Cronin and Pablo De Greiff, eds., Cambridge, MA: MIT Press.

Hardcastle, Valerie Gray, and Owen Flanagan. (1999) "Mupltiplex vs. Multiple Selves: Distinguishing Dissociative Disorders," *The Monist* 82: 645–57.

Hare, R. M. (1952) *The Language of Morals*. Oxford: Clarendon Press.

Harman, Gilbert. (1999) "Moral Philosophy Meets Social Psychology: Virtue Ethics and the Fundamental Attribution Error," *Proceedings of the Aristotelian Society* 1998–99: 315–31.

Harter, Susan. (1996) "Historical Roots of Contemporary Issues Involving Self-Concept" in Bruce A. Bracken, ed., *Handbook of Self-Concept: Developmental, Social, and Clinical Considerations*. New York: Wiley.

Harvey, David. (1989) *The Condition of Postmodernity*. Oxford: Basil Blackwell.

Haworth, Lawrence. (1986) *Autonomy: An Essay in Philosophical Psychology and Ethics*. New Haven: Yale University Press.

Harvey, J. (1999) *Civilized Oppression*. Lanham, MD: Rowman & Littlefield.

Haslanger, Sally. (2000) "Gender and Race: (What) Are They? (What) Do We Want Them To Be?" *Noûs* 34: 31–55.

Hegel, G. W. F. (1805–06/1983) "Jena Lectures on the Philosophy of Spirit," in Leo Rauch, ed. and trans., *Hegel and the Human Spirit: A Translation of the Jena Lectures on the Philosophy of Spirit with Commentary*. Detroit: Wayne State University Press.

Herman, Judith. (1997/1992) *Trauma and Recovery*. New York: Basic Books.

Hill, Thomas. (1987) "The Importance of Autonomy" in Kittay and Meyers, ed. (1987): 129–38.

—— (1989) "The Kantian Conception of Autonomy," in Christman, ed. (1989): 91–105.

—— (1991) *Autonomy and Self Respect*. New York: Cambridge University Press.

Hobbes, Thomas. (1651) *Leviathan*. Richard Tuck, ed. Cambridge: Cambridge University Press, 1996.

Holmes, Stephen. (1985) *Passions and Constraint: On the Theory of Liberal Democracy*. Chicago: University of Chicago Press.

Honneth, Axel. (1995a) *The Struggle for Recognition: The Moral Grammar of Social Conflict*, trans. Joel Anderson. Cambridge, MA: Polity Press.

—— (1995b) "Decentered Autonomy: The Subject After the Fall," in Charles Wright, ed., *The Fragmented World of the Social: Essays in Social and Political Philosophy*. Albany, NY: SUNY Press: 261–72.

—— (1999) "Postmodern Identity and Object-Relations Theory: On the Supposed Obsolescence of Psychoanalysis," *Philosophical Explorations* 3: 225–42.

—— (2000) *Suffering from Indeterminacy: An Attempt at a Reactualization of Hegel's Philosophy of Right*. Assen: Van Gorcum.

—— (2001) "Invisibility: The Moral Epistemology of 'Recognition'," *The Aristotelian Society*, supp. vol. LXXV: 111–26

—— (2002) "Grounding Recognition: A Rejoinder to Critical Questions," trans. Joel Anderson, *Inquiry* 45: 499–519.

—— (2003a) "Gerechtigkeit und kommunikative Freiheit. Überlegungen im Anschluss an Hegel," in B. Merker, G. Mohr, and M. Quante, eds., *Subjektivität und Anerkennung: Festschrift Ludwig Siep*. Paderborn: Mentis Verlag.

—— with Nancy Fraser (2003b) *Redistribution or Recognition? A Political-Philosophical Exchange*, trans. J. Golb, J. Ingram, and C. Wilke. New York: Verso.

Honohan, Iseault. (2002) *Civic Republicanism*. London and New York: Routledge.

Horney, Karen. (1945) *Our Inner Conflicts: A Constructive Theory of Neurosis*. New York: Norton.

Hurka, Thomas. (1993) *Perfectionism*. New York: Oxford University Press.

Hutt, William Harold. (1936) *Economists and the Public: A Study of Competition and Opinion*. London: Jonathan Cape.

Isaac, Jeffrey. (1988) "Republicanism vs. Liberalism? A Reconsideration," *History of Political Thought*, 9 (Summer): 349–77.

Jaggar, Alison. (1983) *Feminist Politics and Human Nature*. Totowa, NJ: Rowman & Allanheld.

James, Susan. (2000) "Feminism in Philosophy of Mind: The Question of Personal Identity," in Miranda Fricker and Jennifer Hornsby, eds., *The Cambridge Companion to Feminism in Philosophy*. Cambridge: Cambridge University Press.

Johnston, David. (1994) *The Idea of a Liberal Theory*. Princeton: Princeton University Press.

Kant, Immanuel. (1959) *Foundations of the Metaphysics of Morals*, trans. Lewis White Beck. Indianapolis: Bobbs-Merrill, pp. 6off [pp. 442ff of the Prussian Academy edition].

—— (1970) "On the Common Saying: This May be True in Theory, But it Does Not Apply in Practice," in Hans Reiss, ed., *Kant's Political Writings*. Cambridge: Cambridge University Press.

—— (1996) *Practical Philosophy*, trans. and ed. Mary J. Gregor. Cambridge: Cambridge University, Press.

Kaufman, Alexander. (1999) *Welfare in the Kantian State*. Oxford: Clarendon Press.

Kittay, Eva Feder, and Diana T. Meyers. (1987) *Women and Moral Theory*. Lanham, MD: Rowman & Littlefield.

—— (1999) *Love's Labor: Essays on Women, Equality, and Dependency*. New York: Routledge.

Kleinig, John. (1983) *Paternalism*. Totowa, NJ: Rowman & Littlefield.

Kneller, Jane, and Sidney Axin, eds. (1998) *Autonomy and Community: Readings in Contemporary Kantian Social Philosophy*. Albany, NY: SUNY Press.

Kohlberg, Lawrence. (1981) *The Philosophy of Moral Development*. New York: Harper & Row.

Korsgaard, Christine M. (1989) "Personal Identity and the Unity of Agency: A Kantian Response to Parfit," *Philosophy and Public Affairs* 18: 101–32.

—— (1996) *The Sources of Normativity*. Cambridge: Cambridge University Press.

—— (1996a) *The Sources of Normativity*. Cambridge: Cambridge University Press.

—— (1996b) *Creating the Kingdom of Ends*. Cambridge: Cambridge University Press.

—— (1999) "Self-Constitution in the Ethics of Plato and Kant," *Journal of Ethics* 3: 1–29.

Krakauer, Jon. (1997) *Into Thin Air.* New York: Villard, pp. 69–72.
Kristinsson, Sigurður. (2000) "The Limits of Neutrality: Toward a Weakly Substantive Account of Autonomy," *Canadian Journal of Philosophy* 30, 2: 257–86.
Kymlicka, Will. (1989) *Liberalism, Community and Culture.* Oxford: Clarendon.
—— (1995) *Multicultural Citizenship: A Liberal Theory of Minority Rights.* Oxford: Oxford University Press.
—— (2001) *Politics in the Vernacular.* Oxford: Oxford University Press.
Larmore, Charles. (1987) *Patterns of Moral Complexity.* Cambridge: Cambridge University Press.
—— (1994) *The Morals of Modernity.* Cambridge: Cambridge University Press.
Lindley, Richard. (1986) *Autonomy.* Atlantic Highlands, NJ: Humanities Press International.
Locke, John. (1960) *Second Treatise of Government,* in *Two Treatises of Government,* section 4, p. 287, Peter Laslett, ed. Cambridge: Cambridge University Press.
Lugones, María. (1987) "Playfulness, 'World'-travelling, and Loving Perception," *Hypatia* 2: 3–19.
—— (1990) "Hispaneando y Lesbiando: On Sarah Hoagland's *Lesbian Ethics,*" *Hypatia* 5, 138–46.
—— (1991) "On the Logic of Pluralist Feminism," in Claudia Card, ed., *Feminist Ethics.* Lawrence, KS: University Press of Kansas: 35–44.
Luther, Martin. *Speech at the Diet of Worms,* April 18, 1521.
Macedo, Stephen (1990). *Liberal Virtues: Citizenship, Virtue, and Community in Liberal Constitutionalism.* Oxford: Clarendon Press.
—— (2000) *Diversity and Distrust.* Cambridge, MA: Harvard University Press.
Machiavelli, Niccolo. (1513) In *Modern Moral and Political Philosophy,* Robert C. Cummins and Thomas D. Christiano, eds. London: Mayfield, 1999.
MacIntyre, Alasdair. (1984) *After Virtue.* Notre Dame, IN: University of Notre Dame Press.
—— (1987) *Whose Justice? Which Rationality?* Notre Dame, IN: University of Notre Dame Press.
—— (1995) "Is Patriotism a Virtue?" in Ronald Beiner, ed., *Theorizing Citizenship.* Albany, NY: State University of New York Press.
—— (1999) *Dependent Rational Animals: Why Human Beings Need the Virtues.* Chicago: Open Court.
Mackenzie, Catriona, and Natalie Stoljar, eds. (2000a) *Relational Autonomy: Feminist Perspectives on Autonomy, Agency, and the Social Self.* New York: Oxford University Press.
—— (2000b) "Introduction: Autonomy Refigured," in Mackenzie and Stoljar eds. (2000a): 3–31.
Macleod, Christine. (1995) "The Politics of Gender, Language and Hierarchy in Mamet's 'Oleanna'," *Journal of American Studies* 29: 199–213.
Mamet, David. (1994) *A Whore's Profession: Notes and Essays.* London and Boston: Faber.
Margalit, Avishai. (1996) *The Decent Society,* trans. Naomi Goldblum. Cambridge, MA: Harvard University Press.
May, Thomas. (1994) "The Concept of Autonomy," *American Philosophical Quarterly* 31: 133–44.

McDowell, John. (1994) *Mind and World*. Cambridge, MA: Harvard University Press.
McKinnon, Catriona, and Dario Castiglione, eds. (2003) *The Culture of Toleration in Diverse Societies: Reasonable Tolerance*. Manchester: Manchester University Press.
Mead, George Herbert. (1955) *Mind, Self, and Society*. Chicago: University of Chicago Press.
Mele, Alfred R. (1993) "History and Personal Autonomy," *Canadian Journal of Philosophy* 23: 271–80.
—— (1995) *Autonomous Agents: From Self-Control to Autonomy*. New York: Oxford University Press.
Meyers, Diana T. (1987a) "The Socialized Individual and Individual Autonomy," in *Women and Moral Theory*, E. Kittay and D. Meyers, eds. Lanham, MD: Rowman and Littlefield: 239–54.
—— (1987b) "Personal Autonomy and the Paradox of Feminine Socialization," *Journal of Philosophy* 84: 619–28.
—— (1989) *Self, Society, and Personal Choice*. New York: Columbia University Press.
—— (1994) *Subjectivity and Subjection: Psychoanalytic Feminism and Moral Philosophy*. New York: Routledge.
—— ed. (1997) *Feminists Rethink the Self*. Boulder, CO: Westview Press.
—— (2000a) "Feminism and Women's Autonomy: The Challenge of Female Genital Cutting," *Metaphilosophy* vol. 31 no. 5 (October): 469–91.
—— (2000b) "Intersectional Identity and the Authentic Self: Opposites Attract," in MacKenzie and Stoljar (2000a): 151–80.
—— (2002) *Gender in the Mirror: Cultural Imagery and Women's Agency*. New York: Oxford University Press.
—— (2003) "Narrative and Moral Life," in Cheshire Calhoun, ed., *Setting the Moral Compass*. New York: Oxford University Press: 288–308.
Mill, John Stuart. (1956) *On Liberty*, ed. Currin V. Shields. Indianapolis: Bobbs-Merrill.
Mill, John Stuart. (1859/1989) *On Liberty and Other Writings*, Stefan Collini, ed. Cambridge: Cambridge University Press.
Miller, David, ed. (1983) "Constraints on Freedom," *Ethics* 94: 66–86.
—— (1993) *Liberty*. Oxford: Oxford University Press.
Mills, Charles. (1997) *The Racial Contract*. Ithaca, NY: Cornell University Press.
Moon, J. Donald. (1993) *Constructing Community: Moral Pluralism and Tragic Conflicts*. Princeton: Princeton University Press.
Moran, Richard. (2001) *Authority and Estrangement: An Essay on Self-Knowledge*. Princeton: Princeton University Press.
Mullin, Amy. (1995) "Selves, Diverse and Divided: Can Feminists Have Diversity without Multiplicity?" *Hypatia* 10: 1–31.
Nagel, Thomas. (1979) *The Possibility of Altruism*. Oxford: Clarendon Press.
Narveson, Jan. (1988) *The Libertarian Idea*. Philadelphia: Temple University Press.
Nedelsky, Jennifer. (1989) "Reconceiving Autonomy: Sources, Thoughts, and Possibilities," *Yale Journal of Law and Feminism*, vol. 1 no. 7: 7–36.
Nelson, Hilde. (2001) *Damaged Identities, Narrative Repair*. Ithaca, NY: Cornell University Press.

Nisbett, Richard, and Lee Ross. (1980) *Human Inference: Strategies and Shortcomings of Social Judgment.* Englewood Cliffs, NJ: Prentice Hall.

Noddings, Nel. (1984) *Caring: A Feminist Approach to Ethics and Moral Education.* Berkeley, CA: University of California Press.

Noggle, Robert. (1999) "Kantian Respect and Particular Persons," *Canadian Journal of Philosophy* 29: 449–77.

Nozick, Robert. (1974) *Anarchy, State and Utopia.* New York: Basic Books.

——— (1993) *The Nature of Rationality.* Princeton: Princeton University Press.

Nussbaum, Martha. (2000) *Women and Human Development: A Capabilities Approach* New York: Cambridge University Press.

Okin, Susan Moller. (1989) *Justice, Gender and the Family.* New York: Basic Books.

O'Neill, Onora. (1989) *Constructions of Reason: Explorations in Kant's Practical Philosophy.* New York: Cambridge University Press.

Oshana, Marina A. L. (1998) "Personal Autonomy and Society," *The Journal of Social Philosophy* 29: 81–102.

Owen, David. (1995) *Nietzsche, Politics and Modernity.* London/Thousand Oaks, CA: Sage.

Packard, Vance. (1957) *The Hidden Persuaders.* New York: David McKay.

Pateman, Carole. (1988) *The Sexual Contract.* Stanford: Stanford University Press.

Patten, Alan. (1996) "The Republican Critique of Liberalism," *British Journal of Political Science*, 26: 25–44.

Patterson, Orlando. (1982) *Slavery and Social Death.* Cambridge, MA: Harvard University Press.

Pelczynski, Zbigniew, and John Gray, eds. (1984) *Conceptions of Liberty in Political Philosophy.* London: Athlone Press.

Pettit, Philip. (1997) *Republicanism: A Theory of Freedom and Government.* Oxford: Clarendon Press.

——— (1993) *The Common Mind.* Oxford: Oxford University Press.

——— (2001) *A Theory of Freedom: From the Psychology to the Politics of Agency.* Oxford: Oxford University Press.

——— (2002) "Keeping Republican Freedom Simple: On a Difference with Quentin Skinner," *Political Theory*, 30 (June): 339–356.

Pogge, Thomas. (1989) *Realizing Rawls.* Ithaca: Cornell University Press.

Pollock, John. (1987) *Contemporary Theories of Knowledge.* London: Hutchinson.

Pratto, Felicia. (1996) "Sexual Politics: The Gender Gap in the Bedroom, the Cupboard, and the Cabinet," in David Buss and Neil M. Malamuth, eds., *Sex, Power, Conflict.* New York: Oxford University Press: 179–230.

Rawls, John. (1971) *A Theory of Justice.* Revised edition (1999) Cambridge, MA: Harvard University Press.

——— (1993a) *Political Liberalism.* New York: Columbia University Press.

——— (1993b) "The Domain of the Political and Overlapping Consensus," in D. Copp, J. Hampton, and J. Roemer, eds., *The Idea of Democracy.* Cambridge: Cambridge University Press: 245–69.

——— (1999a) *Collected Papers*, Samuel Freeman, ed. Cambridge, MA: Harvard University Press.

—— (1999b) *The Law of Peoples*. Cambridge, MA: Harvard University Press.
—— (2000) *Lectures on the History of Moral Philosophy*. Cambridge, MA: Harvard University Press.
—— (2001) *Justice as Fairness: A Restatement*. Cambridge, MA: Harvard University Press.
Raz, Joseph. (1986) *The Morality of Freedom*. Oxford: Clarendon.
—— (1994) *Ethics in the Public Domain: Essay in the Morality of Law and Politics*. Oxford: Clarendon: 339–53.
—— (2001) *Value, Respect, and Attachment*. Cambridge: Cambridge University Press.
Richards, David, A. J. (1971) *A Theory of Reasons for Action*. Oxford: Oxford University Press.
Richardson, Henry. (2001) "Autonomy's Many Normative Presuppositions," *American Philosophical Quarterly* 38: 287–303.
Robbins, Caroline. (1959/1985) *The Eighteenth-Century Commonwealthman*. Cambridge, MA: Harvard University Press.
Rorty, Amalie O., and David Wong. (1990) "Aspects of Identity and Agency," in *Identity, Character, and Morality: Essays in Moral Psychology*. Cambridge, MA: MIT Press.
Rorty, Richard. (1986) "Freud and Moral Reflection," in Joseph Smith and William Kerrigan, eds., *Pragmatism's Freud*. Baltimore: Johns Hopkins University Press.
Rosen, Alan D. (1993) *Kant's Theory of Justice*. Ithaca: Cornell University Press.
Rössler, Beate. (2001) *Der Wert des Privaten*. Frankfurt: Suhrkamp.
Rousseau, Jean-Jacques. (1966) *Du Contract Social*. Paris: Garnier-Flammarion.
Sandel, Michael J. (1982) *Liberalism and the Limits of Justice*. Cambridge: Cambridge University Press, 2nd edition 1999.
—— (1996) *Democracy's Discontent: America in Search of a Public Philosophy*. Cambridge, MA: Harvard University Press.
Sartre, Jean-Paul. (1956) *Being and Nothingness*, trans. Hazel Barnes. New York: Philosophical Library.
Scanlon, Thomas. (1998) *What We Owe to Each Other*. Cambridge, MA: Harvard University Press.
Scarry, Elaine. (1985) *The Body in Pain: The Making and Unmaking of the World*. Oxford: Oxford University Press.
Schachter, S., and Singer, J. E. (1962) "Cognitive, Social and Physiological Determinants of Emotional States," *Psychological Review* 69: 379–99.
Schechtman, Marya. (1996) *The Constitution of Selves*. Ithaca NY: Cornell University Press.
Scheffler, Samuel. (1992) *Human Morality*. New York: Oxford University Press.
Scheman, Naomi. (1993) *Engenderings*. New York: Routledge.
Schneewind, J. B. (1998) *The Invention of Autonomy. A History of Modern Moral Philosophy*. Cambridge: Cambridge University Press.
Schudson, Michael. (1986) *Advertising, The Uneasy Persuasion*. New York: Basic Books.
Scitovsky, Tibor. (1962) "On the Principle of Consumer Sovereignty," *American Economic Review*, 52: 262–68.

Sellers, M. N. S. (1998) *The Sacred Fire of Liberty: Republicanism, Liberalism, and the Law*. London: Macmillan.
Selznick, Philip. (1993) *The Moral Commonwealth: Social Theory and the Promise of Community*. Berkeley: University of California Press.
—— (2001) "Civilizing Civil Society," in Anton van Harskamp and Albert W. Musschenga, eds., *The Many Faces of Individualism*. Leuven: Peeters, 171–85.
Sen, Amartya. (1987) *The Standard of Living*, ed. G. Hawthorne. Cambridge: Cambridge University Press.
—— (1992) *Inequality Reexamined*. Cambridge, MA: Harvard University Press.
—— (1999) *Development as Freedom*. New York: Knopf.
Sen, Amartya, and Bernard Williams, eds. (1982) *Utilitarianism and Beyond*. Cambridge: Cambridge University Press.
Shapiro, Ian, and Casiano Hacker-Cordón, eds. (1999) *Democracy's Value*. Cambridge: Cambridge University Press.
Shapiro, Tamar. (1999) "What is a Child?," *Ethics* 109: 715–38.
Sher, George. (1995) "Liberal Neutrality and the Value of Autonomy," *Social Philosophy and Policy* 12: 136–59.
—— (1997) *Beyond Neutrality: Perfectionism and Politics*. Cambridge: Cambridge University Press.
Sie, Maureen, Marc Slors, and Bert van den Brink, eds. (2004) *Reasons of One's Own*. Aldershot: Ashgate.
Skinner, Quentin. (1998) *Liberty Before Liberalism*. Cambridge: Cambridge University Press.
Smith, Michael. (1994) *The Moral Problem*. Oxford: Blackwell.
Spinner-Halev, Jeff. (2000) *Surviving Diversity: Religion and Democratic Citizenship*. Baltimore: Johns Hopkins University Press.
Spragens, Thomas. (1999) *Civic Liberalism: Reflections on Our Democratic Ideals*. Lanham, MD: Rowman & Littlefield.
Steiner, Hillel. (1994) *An Essay on Rights*. Cambridge, MA: Blackwell.
Stoljar, Natalie. (2000) "Autonomy and the Feminist Intuition," in Mackenzie and Stoljar, eds. (2000a): 94–111.
Sullivan, Roger J. (1989) *Immanuel Kant's Moral Theory*. Cambridge: Cambridge University Press.
Sunstein, Cass. (1988) "Beyond the Republican Revival," *Yale Law Journal*, 97 (July): 1539–91.
—— (1990) *After the Rights Revolution*. Cambridge, MA: Harvard University Press.
Taylor, Charles. (1985) "What is Human Agency?" in Taylor, *Human Agency and Language. Philosophical Papers I*. Cambridge: Cambridge University Press.
—— (1985) "What's Wrong with Negative Liberty," in *Philosophy and the Human Sciences*, vol. 2 of *Philosophical Papers*. Cambridge: Cambridge University Press, 211–29.
—— (1989) *Sources of the Self: The Making of Modern Identity*. Cambridge, MA: Harvard University Press.
—— (1991a) *The Ethics of Authenticity*. Cambridge, MA: Harvard University Press.
—— (1991b) "The Dialogical Self," in *The Interpretive Turn: Philosophy, Science, Culture*, David R. Hiley, James F. Bohmann, and Richard Shusterman, eds. Ithaca: Cornell University Press, 1991, 304–14.

Terchek, Ronald. (1997) *Republican Paradoxes and Liberal Anxieties.* Lanham, MD: Rowman & Littlefield.
Thalberg, Irving. (1989) "Hierarchical Analyses of Unfree Action," reprinted in Christman (1989): 123–36.
Thomas, Laurence. (1993) *Vessels of Evil: American Slavery and the Holocaust.* Philadelphia: Temple University Press.
Thomson, Judith Jarvis. (1976) "Killing, Letting Die and The Trolley Problem," *The Monist* 59: 204–17
—— (1971) "A Defense of Abortion," *Philosophy & Public Affairs* 1: 47–66.
Tomasi, John. (2001) *Liberalism Beyond Justice.* Princeton: Princeton University Press.
Tooley, Michael. (1980) "An Irrelevant Consideration: Killing versus Letting Die," in B. Steinboch, ed., *Killing and Letting Die.* Englewood Cliffs, NJ: Prentice-Hall: 56–62.
Tully, James. (1995) *Strange Multiplicity.* Cambridge: Cambridge University Press.
—— (1999) "The Agonic Freedom of Citizens," *Economy and Society,* 28/2: 161–82.
Tushnet, Mark. (1983) "Following the Rules Laid Down: A Critique of Interpretivism and Neutral Principles," *Harvard Law Review* 96 (February): 781–827.
Twitchell, James. (1999) *Lead Us into Temptation.* New York: Columbia University Press.
Veblen, Thorstein. (1979) *The Theory of the Leisure Class.* New York: Penguin.
Velleman, J. David. (1989) *Practical Reflection.* Princeton: Princeton University Press.
—— (2000a) *The Possibility of Practical Reason.* New York: Oxford University Press.
—— (2000b) "From Self-Psychology to Moral Philosophy," in *Action Theory and Freedom, Philosophical Perspectives* 14: 349–77.
—— (2002) "Identification and Identity," in Sarah Buss and Lee Overton, eds., *Contours of Agency: Essays on Themes from Harry Frankfurt.* Cambridge, MA: MIT Press, 91–123.
—— (2003) "Narrative Explanation." *The Philosophical Review* 112: 1–25.
Viroli, Maurizio. (2002) *Republicanism,* trans. Antony Shugaar. New York: Hill & Wang.
Walker, Margaret. (1998) *Moral Understandings.* New York: Routledge.
—— (1999) "Getting Out of Line: Alternatives to Life as a Career," in *Mother Time.* New York: Rowman & Littlefield, 97–106.
Waldron, Jeremy, ed. (1984) *Theories of Rights.* Oxford: Oxford University Press.
—— (1989) "Autonomy and Perfectionism in Raz, "The Morality of Freedom," *Southern California Law Review,* 62 (1989), 1097.
—— (1992) "The Irrelevance of Moral Objectivity," in Robert George, ed., *Natural Law Theory: Contemporary Essays.* Oxford: Clarendon Press, 158–78.
—— (1993) *Liberal Rights: Collected Papers 1981–1991.* New York: Cambridge University Press.
—— (1997) *The Dignity of Legislation.* Cambridge: Cambridge University Press.
—— (1999) *Law and Disagreement.* Oxford: Oxford University Press.
Wall, Steven. (1998) *Liberalism, Perfectionism and Restraint.* New York: Cambridge University Press.

Waller, Bruce. (1993) "Natural Autonomy and Alternative Possibilities," *American Philosophical Quarterly* vol. 30, no. 1 (January), 73–81.
Watson, Gary. (1975) "Free Agency," *Journal of Philosophy* 72: 205–20.
―――― (1987) "Free Action and Free Will," *Mind* 96: 145–72.
―――― (1996) "Two Faces of Responsibility," *Philosophical Topics* 24: 227–48.
Weir, Allison. (1995) "Toward A Model of Self-Identity: Habermas and Kristeva," in Johanna Meehan, ed., *Feminists Read Habermas*. New York: Routledge, 263–82.
Wellmer, Albrecht. (1990) "Models of Freedom in the Modern World," in Michael Kelly ed., *Hermeneutics and Critical Theory in Ethics and Politics*. Cambridge, MA: MIT Press.
Wike, Victoria. (1994) *Kant on Happiness in Ethics*. Albany: State University of New York Press.
Wildt, Andreas. (1992) "Recht und Selbstachtung im Anschluss an der Anerkennungslehren von Fichte und Hegel," in Michael Kahlo, Enst A. Wolf, and Rainer Zaczyk, eds., *Fichtes Lehre von Rechtsverhältnis*. Frankfurt: Klosterman.
Williams, Bernard. (1983) *Moral Luck*. Cambridge: Cambridge University Press.
―――― (1985) *Ethics and the Limits of Philosophy*. Cambridge: Cambridge University Press.
―――― (1993) *Shame and Necessity*, Berkeley: University of California Press.
Winnicott, Donald. (1965) *The Maturational Processes and the Facilitating Environment*. London: Hogarth Press.
Wolf, Susan. (1990) *Freedom within Reason*. New York: Oxford University Press.
Wolff, Robert Paul. (1970) *In Defense of Anarchism*. 3rd ed. Berkeley, CA: University of California Press.
Wood, Gordon. (1969) *The Creation of the American Republic, 1776–1787*. Chapel Hill, NC: University of North Carolina Press.
Young, Iris Marion. (1990) *Justice and the Politics of Difference*. Princeton: Princeton University Press.
Young, Robert. (1986) *Personal Autonomy: Beyond Negative and Positive Liberty*. New York: St. Martin's Press.
Zillman, D. (1978) "Attribution and Misattribution of Excitatory Reactions," in John H. Harvey, William Ickes, and Robert F. Kidd, eds., *New Directions in Attribution Research*, Vol. 2, Hillsdale, NJ: Erlbaum: 335–68.
Zillman, E., R. C. Johnson, and K. D. Day (1974) "Attribution of Apparent Arousal and Proficiency of Recovery for Sympathetic Activation Affecting Excitation Transfer to Aggressive Behavior," *Journal of Experimental Social Psychology* 10: 503–15.

Index

Ackerman, Bruce, 328
adaptive preferences, 159–61
Addelson, Kathryn, 53
advertising, 212–4
agency
  agential authority, 112
  agential unity, 60, 71
  agential ownership, 101–10, 113
  and authority, 106–17
  discursive dimension of, 109
  identification theories of, 103, 104, 107 (*see also* identification)
  agentic power, 35
  agentic skills 9, 10, 28, 36–40, 47, 48, 130 (*see also* competency)
agonistic politics, 255, 257
agreement, 4, 7, 246–66
alienation, 54, 83–90, 93, 94, 112, 334–5
Allen, Anita A., 95–6
Anderson, Joel, 172, 240
Anderson, Joel, and Axel Honneth, 7–8, 12–13, 270
Appiah, K. Anthony, 4, 89, 91, 97, 123
Aristotle, 179
Arendt, Hannah, 255
Arpaly, Nomi, 103, 106
attribution effect, 66
authenticity, 3, 5–6, 9, 11, 12, 27, 32–6, 77, 84, 86–90, 93–4, 105

autobiography, 58, 62, 65, 70, 72
autonomy
  agonistic, 16
  capacities, 127, 132
  competency (conditions), 3, 12, 49, 55, 168
  conception vs. concept of, 230
  conceptual conditions of, 332–6
  democratic, 195
  and denigration, 131
  dialogical model of, 13
  ethical, 15, 232–4
  global, 120, 198
  historical account of, 41–2, 103–4, 333
  identity-based accounts of, 112
  individualistic conception of, 128, 130
  legal, 15, 224, 234–6
  liberal conceptions of, 10–11, 272–300, 251–4
  local, 2, 94, 120
  moral, 2, 15, 17, 18, 163, 167, 196, 230–1, 256, 276–88, 296–9, 307–26
  personal, 2, 17, 18, 163, 164, 166, 167, 196, 198, 228, 229, 293–9, 307–26
  personal style theories of, 43–5
  political, 15, 236–7, 251–7

377

autonomy (*cont.*)
    and polyvocality, 134
    recognitional, 129–32, 137, 142–4
    relational, 8, 14, 130, 145
    retrospective, 41–2
    and self-conception, 90–4
    and self-respect, 132, 133
    and semantic resources, 136
    and semantic-symbolic environment, 137
    social, 12, 15, 130, 237–8
    social conditions for, 129–30, 156
    social dimensions of, 118, 151
    value of, 17, 167–9

Babbitt, Susan, 53
Baumeister, Roy, 353
Beckett, Christopher, 148
Bell, Daniel, 210
Bellah, Robert, 353
Benhabib, Seyla, 22, 55, 94, 146, 239, 356
Benn, Stanley, 274, 275, 293, 294
Benson, Paul, 5, 6, 8, 11–14, 51
Bentham, Jeremy, 313–14
Berkowitz, L., 75
Bentley, Russell, 263, 270
Berlin, Isaiah, 23, 35, 183, 185, 188, 227–9, 311
Berofsky, Bernard, 20, 352
body, as locus of control, 52 (*see also* embodiment)
Bordo, Susan, 51
Bosanquet, Bernard, 292
Boxill, Bernard, 125
Bratman, Michael, 73, 103, 121, 125
Brighouse, Harry, 301
Brink, Bert van den, 7, 16–17, 147
Brison, Susan J., 51, 53, 148
Brodt, S. E., 75
Brothers, Dorothy, 148
Brown, Wendy, 22
Burtt, Shelley, 201
Buss, David M., 169
Buss, Sarah, 121, 146

Calhoun, Cheshire, 105
Chodorow, Nancy, 53, 54
Christiano, Thomas, 357
Christman, John, 6, 18–19, 41–2, 54, 104, 106, 123, 155–6, 259, 301
civic endurance, 16, 262–3
civic responsiveness, 16, 262–5
civic virtue, 178–81, 260–6
    and corruption, 178–9
Code, Lorraine, 23
coercion, 9, 17
commodity fetishism, 211
communitarianism, 4, 5, 8
community, 237
competencies, 260, 336
compulsion, 35
Connolly, William, 22
conscience, 18, 323–5
consciousness, 60
    false, 211–14
    self-transparent, 7, 133–5
consent, 250
Constant, Benjamin, 181–2
constraint, 229, 242
consumer sovereignty, 15–16, 204–24
consumerism, 205, 218, 220
contractualism, 4, 292
critical reflection, 317, 333–40, 345–51
Crittenden, Jack, 22
cultural homogenization, 215–17

Dagger, Richard, 8, 14, 122, 149
de Beauvoir, Simone, 160–3
de Tocqueville, Alexis, 182
deliberation, 16, 29, 344
democracy, 7, 257, 348
Dennett, Daniel, 10–11, 56–73
desire, 20–1, 148
    -formation, 42
Dewey, John, 186
Dillon, Robin, 123
domination, 13, 51, 153, 157
Double, Richard, 5, 43–5, 352
Dutton, Donald G., 154

Dworkin, Gerald, 3, 20, 81, 119–20, 172, 301, 305, 316, 353
Dworkin, Ronald, 240, 313–14, 316, 318, 353

Ellison, Ralph, 111–13, 116, 119–20
Elster, John, 159
embodiment, 156
enculturation, 51
endorsement, 5, 6, 9, 11, 16, 18, 84, 87, 103
endorsement constraint, 340, 350
epistemic authority, 344, 347
evaluations, strong, 232
externalism, 277, 278
externalities, 219

Feinberg, Joel, 120, 132, 147, 274
feminism, 4, 8, 12, 31, 37, 40, 128
Fischer, John Martin, 125
Flanagan, Owen, 74, 75
Forst, Rainer, 2, 8, 14–15, 202–24, 275, 296
Foot, Philippa, 281
Foucault, Michel, 22, 39–40, 136, 255
Frank, Robert, 221, 222
Frankena, William, 302
Frankfurt, Harry, 3, 10–11, 20–22, 51, 73, 80–2, 87–9, 95, 101, 103, 106, 113, 146, 316, 320
Fraser, Nancy, 136, 147, 149
free-rider problem, 218
freedom, 13–15, 17, 128, 138, 181, 291, 309
  as non-domination, 23, 183, 184, 188–93
  as non-interference, 183
  Kant's principle of, 310, 319
  of religion, 241
  of the will, 20
  republican, 192
  (*see also* liberty)
Friedman, Marilyn, 12–14, 245, 268
fundamental attribution error, 338
fundamental liberal principles, 272, 274, 277, 279, 280, 284, 287

Galbraith, John Kenneth, 207–8, 218–20
Gaus, Gerald, 2, 16–17, 196, 240, 354
Gauthier, David, 277, 279
Geertz, Clifford, 294
Geuss, Raymond, 23, 239
Gey, Steven G., 200
Gilligan, Carol, 22
good, conception of, 18, 320–5
Govier, Trudy, 54, 148
Gray, John, 22
Green T.H., 183
Guyer, Paul, 310, 312

Habermas, Jürgen, 21, 23, 145, 146, 241, 343, 355–6
happiness, 78
  Kantian account of, 311
  pursuit of, 309–14
Hardcastle, Valerie Gray, 74
Hardy, Thomas, 337
Harman, Gilbert, 354
Harrington, James, 179
Harter, Susan, 354
Harvey, David, 22
Harvey, J., 154
Haslanger, Sally, 123
Hawkins, Jennifer, 87
Haworth, Lawrence, 20, 120
Hayes, Sharon, 305
Heath, Joseph, 8, 15–16
Hegel, G. W. F., 131, 138, 140, 146
Herman, Judith, 153–4, 171
heteronomy, 36, 155 (*see also nonautonomy*)
  and male dominance, 155–9
Hobbes, Thomas, 19, 159, 206, 218, 279
Hohfeld, Wesley, 286, 288
Honneth, Axel, 7, 8, 12–13
Horney, Karen, 352
Humboldt, Willhelm von, 312
Humphrey, Nicholas, 61–2
Hurka, Thomas, 21
Hutt, William Harold, 207–8
hypothetical agreement, 344

identification, 3, 20, 96, 316, 335
identity, 11, 15, 28, 30, 35, 77
  traits, 78, 79
  politics, 4, 8, 138
  practical, 102–6
  racial, 11, 88–92
  scripted, 91
impartiality, 139, 140
individualism, 2, 8–9, 128–30
  hyper-, 4, 8
  rights-based, 132
individuality, 54
instrumental reason, 276, 279
integration, 9, 10
internalism, 278, 281–2
intersubjectivism, 140

James, Susan, 55
John Paul II, 209
Johnston, David, 321
justice, 4, 5, 11, 13, 14, 16, 18, 97, 128, 129, 133, 137, 138, 242, 247, 252, 340
  as fairness, 141
  justification of principle of, 16
  proceduralist, 127, 139–44
  republican, 14
justification,
  justificatory regress, 2, 5–6
  public, 236

Kant, Immanuel, 2, 17–18, 20, 27, 128, 145, 160–3, 261, 282–3, 287, 289, 291–2, 308–14
Kaufman, Alexander, 326
Kittay, Eva F., 23, 146, 172
Kohlberg, Lawrence, 295–7
Korsgaard, Christine, 73, 122, 283, 313
Kristinsson, Sigurður, 21, 165
Kymlicka, Will, 21, 22, 149, 240, 354

Larmore, Charles, 303
legitimacy, 247–66, 330–51
legitimation, 5–7, 16–19, 21–2
  hierarchical conceptions of, 5–6
  political, 5, 6

liberalism
  agreement-based, 251, 254, 256, 259
  Hobbesean, 341–6
  and individualism, 118, 120
  Kantian, 341–5, 347
  without agreement, 16, 245–71
liberty, 14, 16, 20, 129, 178–9, 240, 274, 301
  intersubjective conception of, 14, 226
  of the ancients and the moderns, 181–3
  of the moderns, 14
  negative and positive conception of, 182, 188, 227–9, 238, 254
  political, 229, 236
Lindley, Richard, 20
Locke, John, 186, 275
locus of control, 71
Lugones, Maria, 105–6, 122

MacCallum, Gerald, 229
Macedo, Stephen, 306
Machiavelli, Niccolo, 150, 183
MacIntyre, Alasdair, 22, 149
Mackenzie, Catriona, 20, 22, 145
Macleod, Christine, 171
majoritarianism, 199
Mamet, David, 154
Margalit, Avishai, 147
market failure, 217–20
market neutrality, 215
Marx, Karl, 211
McDowell, John, 133–6, 148
Mead, George Herbert, 131, 146
Mele, Alfred, 20, 148, 352
Meyers, Diana Tietjens, 6–10, 94, 121, 148, 171
Mill, John Stuart, 200, 206, 312
Miller, David, 202
Mills, Charles, 21
Moon, Donald, 22, 267
moral power, 141, 143
Moran, Richard, 148
multiple personality disorder, 61–3

Nagel, Thomas, 83, 95–6
narrative, 10, 64
　coherence, 69, 70
　module, 67–9
narrativity, 21–2
Narveson, Jan, 284
Nedelsky, Jennifer, 54, 145
Nelson, Hilde, 55
Nisbett, Richard, 354
Noddings, Nell, 22
Noggle, Robert, 121
nonautonomy, 27 (see also *heteronomy*)
Nozick, Robert, 276, 329

object-relations theory, 135
original position, 141–3
Oshana, Marina, 5, 8–11, 20, 171
Owen, David, 263, 270
overlapping consensus, 18, 248

Packard, Vance, 212
Painter, Susan, 154
Pateman, Carol, 20
paternalism, 15, 206, 285, 304
Patterson, Orlando, 124
perfectionism, 5, 15, 147, 149, 208–11, 295
person(hood), 4, 18, 22, 140, 143
Pettit, Philip, 14, 23, 177, 181, 183–93, 198, 241
pluralism, 7, 16, 18, 142, 143, 249, 289, 343
Pogge, Thomas W., 145
political authority, 9
Political Liberalism, 252–3, 355
political liberalism, 245
Pollack, John, 357
postmodernism, 4
power, 7
practical intelligence, 40
practical reason, 282
Pratto, Filicia, 151
priority of right, 322
private language, 288
procedural independence, 3
procedural republic, 180

priority of the right, 16
property rights, 285
psychoanalysis, 31, 134, 135, 338
public reason, 257–60, 287–91, 298, 348

rape, 170
rationality, 53, 141, 290
Ravizza, Mark, 125
Rawls, John, 2, 8, 14–16, 18–19, 22, 51, 132–6, 138–45, 147, 186, 245, 247–9, 251–3, 257, 269, 289, 317–20, 324, 325, 342, 343, 347
Raz, Jospeh, 4, 21, 90, 97, 145, 147, 149, 164, 171, 240, 295, 301, 315, 316, 320–22
reason
　critical, 47
　instrumental, 40
reciprocity, 230, 235
recognition, 11–14, 112, 130, 131, 133, 137–9, 142, 147
reflection, 6, 9, 10, 18, 29, 135, 136
reflexivity, 110
representational authority, 347, 348
republicanism, 14, 15, 23, 177–200
　and autonomy, 193–6
　and dependence, 179–81
　and freedom, 181–7
respect, 342, 347
Richardson, Henry, 159–61, 163–4
rights, 129, 133, 137–9
　human, 231
　individualistic, 139
　socio-economic, 129
Rorty, Amelie, 78, 88
Rorty, Richard, 55
Rosen, Allen, 312
Ross, Lee, 354
Rössler, Beate, 148
Rousseau, Jean-Jacques, 179, 305

Sandel, Michael, 11–12, 21, 22, 177, 180–1, 201, 328
Santiago, John, 87, 95
Sartre, Jean-Paul, 125
Scanlon, Thomas, 239

Scarry, Elaine, 148
Schachter, S., 75
Schapiro, Tamar, 73
Schechtman, Marya, 55
Scheffler, Samuel, 122
Scheman, Naomi, 52
Schneewind, Jerome, 167
Schroeder, Timothy, 103, 106
Schudson, Michael, 225
Scitovsky, Tibor, 216–18
self, 4, 9–11, 57–73
  -alienation, 46 (see also *alienation*)
  authentic, 3, 49, 55
  -authorization, 12–13, 114–17, 119
  authorship, 295
  -concept, 79, 81–5, 89, 93, 96, 294, 337
  conceptions of, 8, 28
  -deception, 91
  -definition, 12, 28, 45–50
  -determination, 43
  -disclosure, 103
  -discovery, 9, 27, 28, 43, 45–50
  divided, 30, 105
  embodied, 31, 33, 34, 40, 44, 53
  -esteem, 131, 133, 135–8, 141, 143, 159, 160
  five-dimensional account of, 9, 50
  -government, 3, 196
  -identity, 78–80, 83–4, 86, 88, 93
  -knowledge, 338–40, 346, 348–51
  narrative, 10, 50, 55, 57–73
  -narration, 62, 64, 65, 70, 71, 73
  post-modern conception of, 339
  -reflection, 5–6, 77, 85, 96
  relational view of,. 30, 32, 34, 38, 333
  -respect, 131–3, 137, 138, 141, 143
  social, 12, 13, 29–30, 36–8
  social dimension of, 108
  and subordination, 132
  unitary, 27, 40, 47, 54, 72, 73
  -transparency, 18, 339, 346
  -transparency, 7
  true, 9, 10, 12, 332
  -trust, 22, 133–5, 137, 138, 141, 143, 356

Selznick, Philip, 270
Sen, Amartya, 132, 145, 147
Sher, George, 52, 147, 187–93, 303
Skinner, Quentin, 14–16, 181, 183, 187–96, 241
Smith, Michael, 278, 302
sovereignty, popular, 20–1
Spinner-Haley, Jeff, 172
Springer, Elise, 52
Stoljar, Natalie, 20–2, 145
subject (critique of), 134
subordination (see *domination*)
Sunstein, Cass, 177, 201, 219

taxation, 219
Taylor, Charles, 21, 73, 94, 96, 136, 146, 148, 240, 329
Thalberg, Irving, 21
Thomas, Lawrence M., 124
Thomson, Judith, 279
traumatic bonding, 158, 159
Tully, James, 248, 250, 253
Tushnet, Mark, 197

unconscious, 30, 38–9

value neutrality, 2, 4, 5, 7, 15, 145
Veblen, Thorstein, 220
veil of ignorance, 140, 141
Velleman, David, 9–10, 51, 125, 137
Viroli, Maurizio, 181, 187, 194–6, 199
virtue (see also *civic virtue*)
  social, 16
volitional character, 80
volitional necessity, 81–3, 86, 87
vulnerability, 127, 129, 130, 138, 140, 141, 143, 144, 156

Waldron, Jeremy, 2, 17–18, 20, 196, 249, 253, 296, 303
Walker, Margaret, 53, 55
Wall, Steven, 21, 147, 295–7, 305
Watson, Gary, 103, 109
Wellmer, Albrecht, 241
Wildt, Andreas, 147
Williams, Bernard, 267, 353
Winnicott, Donald, 148

Wittgenstein, Lugwig, 288
Wolf, Susan, 121, 282
Wolff, Robert Paul, 21, 195
Wong, David, 78, 88

Young, Iris Marion, 126
Young, Robert, 20, 22, 120, 145, 295

Zillman, E., 75

Printed in Great Britain
by Amazon.co.uk, Ltd.,
Marston Gate.